# Praise for *Predictive Analytics*

"The *Freakonomics* of big data."
—**Stein Kretsinger**, founding executive of Advertising.com;
former lead analyst at Capital One

"A clear and compelling explanation of the power of predictive analytics, and how it can transform companies and even industries."
—**Anthony Goldbloom**, founder and CEO, Kaggle.com

"The definitive book of this industry has arrived. Dr. Siegel has achieved what few have even attempted: an accessible, captivating tome on predictive analytics that is a must read for all interested in its potential—and peril."
—**Mark Berry**, VP, People Insights, ConAgra Foods

"A fascinating page-turner about the most important new form of information technology."
—**Emiliano Pasqualetti**, CEO, DomainBot Inc.

"As our ability to collect and analyze information improves, experts like Eric Siegel are our guides to the mysteries unlocked and the moral questions that arise."
—**Jules Polonetsky**, Co-Chair and Director, Future of Privacy Forum;
former Chief Privacy Officer, AOL and DoubleClick

"In a fascinating series of examples, Siegel shows how companies have made money predicting what customers will do. Once you start reading, you will not be able to put it down."
—**Arthur Middleton Hughes**, VP, Database Marketing Institute;
author of *Strategic Database Marketing, Fourth Edition*

"Excellent. Each chapter makes the complex comprehensible, making heavy use of graphics to give depth and clarity. It gets you thinking about what else might be done with predictive analytics."
—**Edward Nazarko**, Client Technical Advisor, IBM

"I've always been a passionate data geek, but I never thought it might be possible to convey the excitement of data mining to a lay audience. That is what Eric Siegel does in this book. The stories range from inspiring to downright scary—read them and find out what we've been up to while you weren't paying attention."
—**Michael J. A. Berry**, author of *Data Mining Techniques, Third Edition*

"Eric Siegel is the Kevin Bacon of the predictive analytics world, organizing conferences where insiders trade knowledge and share recipes. Now, he has thrown the doors open for you. Step in and explore how data scientists are rewriting the rules of business."

—**Kaiser Fung**, VP, Vimeo; author of *Numbers Rule Your World*

"Written in a lively language, full of great quotes, real-world examples, and case studies, it is a pleasure to read. The more technical audience will enjoy chapters on The Ensemble Effect and uplift modeling—both very hot trends. I highly recommend this book!"

—**Gregory Piatetsky-Shapiro**, Editor, KDnuggets; founder, KDD Conferences

"Highly recommended. As Siegel shows in his very readable new book, the results achieved by those adopting predictive analytics to improve decision making are game changing."

—**James Taylor**, CEO, Decision Management Solutions

"What is predictive analytics? This book gives a practical and up-to-date answer, adding new dimension to the topic and serving as an excellent reference."

—**Ramendra K. Sahoo**, Senior VP, Risk Management and Analytics, Citibank

"Exciting and engaging—reads like a thriller! Predictive analytics has its roots in people's daily activities, and, if successful, affects people's actions. By way of examples, Siegel describes both the opportunities and the threats predictive analytics brings to the real world."

—**Marianna Dizik**, Statistician, Google

"Competing on information is no longer a luxury—it's a matter of survival. Despite its successes, predictive analytics has penetrated only so far, relative to its potential. As a result, lessons and case studies such as those provided in Siegel's book are in great demand."

—**Boris Evelson**, VP and Principal Analyst, Forrester Research

"Fascinating and beautifully conveyed. Siegel is a leading thought leader in the space—a must-have for your bookshelf!"

—**Sameer Chopra**, VP, Advanced Analytics, Orbitz Worldwide

"A brilliant overview—strongly recommended to everyone curious about the analytics field and its impact on our modern lives."

—**Kerem Tomak**, VP of Marketing Analytics, Macys.com

"Eric explains the science behind predictive analytics, covering both the advantages and the limitations of prediction. A must read for everyone!"

—**Azhar Iqbal**, VP and Econometrician, Wells Fargo Securities, LLC

"*Predictive Analytics* delivers a ton of great examples across business sectors of how companies extract actionable, impactful insights from data. Both the novice and the expert will find interest and learn something new."

—**Chris Pouliot**, Director, Algorithms and Analytics, Netflix

"In this new world of big data, machine learning, and data scientists, Eric Siegel brings deep understanding to deep analytics."

—**Marc Parrish**, VP, Membership, Barnes & Noble

"A detailed outline for how we might tame the world's unpredictability. Eric advocates quite clearly how some choices are predictably more profitable than others—and I agree!"

—**Dennis R. Mortensen**, CEO of Visual Revenue, former Director of Data Insights at Yahoo!

"This book is an invaluable contribution to predictive analytics. Eric's explanation of how to anticipate future events is thought provoking and a great read for everyone."

—**Jean Paul Isson**, Global VP Business Intelligence and Predictive Analytics, Monster Worldwide; coauthor, *Win with Advanced Business Analytics: Creating Business Value from Your Data*

"Eric Siegel's book succeeds where others have failed—by demystifying big data and providing real-world examples of how organizations are leveraging the power of predictive analytics to drive measurable change."

—**Jon Francis**, Senior Data Scientist, Nike

"Predictive analytics is the key to unlocking new value at a previously unimaginable economic scale. In this book, Siegel explains how, doing an excellent job to bridge theory and practice."

—**Sergo Grigalashvili**, VP of Information Technology, Crawford & Company

"Predictive analytics has been steeped in fear of the unknown. Eric Siegel distinctively clarifies, removing the mystery and exposing its many benefits."

—**Jane Kuberski**, Engineering and Analytics, Nationwide Insurance

"As predictive analytics moves from fashionable to mainstream, Siegel removes the complexity and shows its power."

—**Rajeeve Kaul**, Senior VP, OfficeMax

"Dr. Siegel humanizes predictive analytics. He blends analytical rigor with real-life examples with an ease that is remarkable in his field. The book is informative, fun, and easy to understand. I finished reading it in one sitting. A must read . . . not just for data scientists!"

—**Madhu Iyer**, Marketing Statistician, Intuit

"An engaging encyclopedia filled with real-world applications that should motivate anyone still sitting on the sidelines to jump into predictive analytics with both feet."

—**Jared Waxman**, Web Marketer at LegalZoom, previously at Adobe, Amazon, and Intuit

"Siegel covers predictive analytics from start to finish, bringing it to life and leaving you wanting more."

—**Brian Seeley**, Manager, Risk Analytics, Paychex, Inc.

"A wonderful look into the world of predictive analytics from the perspective of a true practitioner."

—**Shawn Hushman**, VP, Analytic Insights, Kelley Blue Book

"An excellent exposition on the next generation of business intelligence—it's really mankind's latest quest for artificial intelligence."

—**Christopher Hornick**, President and CEO, HBSC Strategic Services

"A must—*Predictive Analytics* provides an amazing view of the analytical models that predict and influence our lives on a daily basis. Siegel makes it a breeze to understand, for all readers."

—**Zhou Yu**, Online-to-Store Analyst, Google

"[*Predictive Analytics* is] an engaging, humorous introduction to the world of the data scientist. Dr. Siegel demonstrates with many real-life examples how predictive analytics makes big data valuable."

—**David McMichael**, VP, Advanced Business Analytics

# PREDICTIVE ANALYTICS

## THE POWER TO PREDICT WHO WILL
## CLICK, BUY, LIE, OR DIE

# ERIC SIEGEL

WILEY

John Wiley & Sons, Inc.

Cover image: Zhivko Terziivanov
Cover design: Paul McCarthy
Interior image design: Matt Komhaas

Published by John Wiley & Sons, Inc., Hoboken, New Jersey.
Published simultaneously in Canada.

Jeopardy!® is a registered trademark of Jeopardy Productions, Inc.

For general information about our other products and services, please contact our Customer Care
Department within the United States at (800) 762-2974, outside the United States at (317) 572-3993
or fax (317) 572-4002.

Wiley publishes in a variety of print and electronic formats and by print-on-demand. Some material
included with standard print versions of this book may not be included in e-books or in print-on-demand.
If this book refers to media such as a CD or DVD that is not included in the version you purchased,
you may download this material at http://booksupport.wiley.com. For more information about Wiley
products, visit www.wiley.com.

*Library of Congress Cataloging-in-Publication Data:*

Siegel, Eric.
   Predictive analytics : the power to predict who will click, buy, lie, or die / Eric Siegel.
      p.   cm.
   Includes index.
   ISBN 978-1-118-35685-2 (cloth); ISBN 978-1-118-42062-1 (ebk);
   ISBN 978-1-118-41685-3 (ebk); ISBN 978-1-118-59647-0 (ebk)
      1. Social sciences—Forecasting.   2. Economic forecasting   3. Prediction (Psychology)
   4. Social prediction.   5. Human behavior.   I. Title.
   H61.4.S54   2013
   303.49—dc23
                                                                        2012047252

Printed in the United States of America
10  9  8  7  6  5  4  3  2  1

*This book is dedicated with all my heart to my mother, Lisa Schamberg, and my father, Andrew Siegel.*

# Contents

*death? An extended sidebar on fraud detection addresses the question: how does machine intelligence flip the meaning of fraud on its head?*

**Chapter 7**
Persuasion by the Numbers: How Telenor, U.S. Bank, and
the Obama Campaign Engineered Influence *(uplift)*

*What is the scientific key to persuasion? Why does some marketing fiercely backfire? Why is human behavior the wrong thing to predict? What should all businesses learn about persuasion from presidential campaigns? What voter predictions helped Obama win in 2012 more than the detection of swing voters? How could doctors kill fewer patients inadvertently? How is a person like a quantum particle? Riddle: What often happens to you that cannot be perceived, and that you can't even be sure has happened afterward—but that can be predicted in advance?*

# Foreword

This book deals with quantitative efforts to predict human behavior. One of the earliest efforts to do that was in World War II. Norbert Wiener, the father of "cybernetics," began trying to predict the behavior of German airplane pilots in 1940—with the goal of shooting them from the sky. His method was to take as input the trajectory of the plane from its observed motion, consider the pilot's most likely evasive maneuvers, and predict where the plane would be in the near future so that a fired shell could hit it. Unfortunately, Wiener could predict only one second ahead of a plane's motion, but 20 seconds of future trajectory were necessary to shoot down a plane.

In Eric Siegel's book, however, you will learn about a large number of prediction efforts that are much more successful. Computers have gotten a lot faster since Wiener's day, and we have a lot more data. As a result, banks, retailers, political campaigns, doctors and hospitals, and many more organizations have been quite successful of late at predicting the behavior of particular humans. Their efforts have been helpful at winning customers, elections, and battles with disease.

My view—and Siegel's, I would guess—is that this predictive activity has generally been good for humankind. In the context of healthcare, crime, and terrorism, it can save lives. In the context of advertising, using predictions is more efficient, and could conceivably save both trees (for direct mail and catalogs) and the time and attention of the recipient. In politics, it seems to reward those candidates who respect the scientific method (some might disagree, but I see that as a positive).

However, as Siegel points out—early in the book, which is admirable—these approaches can also be used in somewhat harmful ways. "With great power comes great responsibility," he notes in quoting *Spider-Man*. The implication is that we must be careful as a society about how we use predictive models, or we may be restricted from using and benefiting from them. Like other powerful technologies or disruptive human innovations, predictive analytics is essentially amoral, and can be used for good or evil. To avoid the evil applications, however, it is certainly important to understand what is possible with predictive analytics, and you will certainly learn that if you keep reading.

This book is focused on predictive analytics, which is not the only type of analytics, but the most interesting and important type. I don't think we need more books anyway on purely descriptive analytics, which only describe the past, and don't provide any insight as to why it happened. I also often refer in my own writing to a third type of analytics—"prescriptive"—that tells its users what to do through controlled experiments or optimization. Those quantitative methods are much less popular, however, than predictive analytics.

This book and the ideas behind it are a good counterpoint to the work of Nassim Nicholas Taleb. His books, including *The Black Swan*, suggest that many efforts at prediction are doomed to fail because of randomness and the inherent unpredictability of complex events. Taleb is no doubt correct that some events are black swans that are beyond prediction, but the fact is that most human behavior is quite regular and predictable. The many examples that Siegel provides of successful prediction remind us that most swans are white.

Siegel also resists the blandishments of the "big data" movement. Certainly some of the examples he mentions fall into this category—data that is too large or unstructured to be easily managed by conventional relational databases. But the point of predictive analytics is not the relative size or unruliness of your data, but what you do with it. I have found that "big data often equals small math," and many big data practitioners are content just to use their data to create some appealing visual analytics. That's not nearly as valuable as creating a predictive model.

Siegel has fashioned a book that is both sophisticated and fully accessible to the non-quantitative reader. It's got great stories, great illustrations, and an entertaining tone. Such non-quants should definitely read this book, because there is little doubt that their behavior will be analyzed and predicted throughout their lives. It's also quite likely that most non-quants will increasingly have to consider, evaluate, and act on predictive models at work.

In short, we live in a predictive society. The best way to prosper in it is to understand the objectives, techniques, and limits of predictive models. And the best way to do that is simply to keep reading this book.

—**Thomas H. Davenport**
Thomas H. Davenport is a Visiting Professor at
Harvard Business School, the President's
Distinguished Professor at Babson College,
cofounder of the International Institute for Analytics,
and coauthor of *Competing on Analytics* and several
other books on analytics.

# Preface

*Yesterday is history, tomorrow is a mystery, but today is a gift. That's why we call it the present.*
—Attributed to A. A. Milne, Bill Keane, and Oogway,
the wise turtle in *Kung Fu Panda*

People look at me funny when I tell them what I do. It's an occupational hazard.

The Information Age suffers from a glaring omission. This claim may surprise many, considering we are actively recording Everything That Happens in the World. Moving beyond history books that document important events, we've progressed to systems that log every click, payment, call, crash, crime, and illness. With this in place, you would expect lovers of data to be satisfied, if not spoiled rotten.

But this apparent infinity of information excludes the very events that would be most valuable to know of: *things that haven't happened yet.*

Everyone craves the power to see the future; we are collectively obsessed with prediction. We bow to prognostic deities. We empty our pockets for palm readers. We hearken to horoscopes, adore astrology, and feast upon fortune cookies.

But many people who salivate for psychics also spurn science. Their innate response says "yuck"—it's either too hard to understand or too boring. Or perhaps many believe prediction by its nature is just impossible without supernatural support.

There's a lighthearted TV show I like premised on this very theme, *Psych*, in which a sharp-eyed detective—a modern-day, data-driven Sherlock Holmesian hipster—has perfected the art of observation so masterfully, the cops believe his spot-on deductions must be an admission of guilt. The hero gets out of this pickle by conforming to the norm: he simply informs the police he is psychic, thereby managing to stay out of prison and continuing to fight crime. Comedy ensues.

I've experienced the same impulse, for example, when receiving the occasional friendly inquiry as to my astrological sign. But, instead of posing as a believer, I turn to humor: "I'm a Scorpio, and Scorpios don't believe in astrology."

The more common cocktail party interview asks what I do for a living. I brace myself for eyes glazing over as I carefully enunciate: *predictive analytics*. Most people have the luxury of describing their job in a single word: doctor, lawyer, waiter, accountant, or actor. But, for me, describing this largely unknown field hijacks the conversation every time. Any attempt to be succinct falls flat:

*I'm a business consultant in technology*. They aren't satisfied and ask, "What kind of technology?"

*I make computers predict what people will do*. Bewilderment results, accompanied by complete disbelief and a little fear.

*I make computers learn from data to predict individual human behavior*. Bewilderment, plus nobody wants to talk about data at a party.

*I analyze data to find patterns*. Eyes glaze over even more; awkward pauses sink amid a sea of abstraction.

*I help marketers target which customers will buy or cancel*. They sort of get it, but this wildly undersells and pigeonholes the field.

*I predict customer behavior, like when Target famously predicted whether you are pregnant*. Moonwalking ensues.

So I wrote this book to demonstrate for you why predictive analytics is intuitive, powerful, and awe-inspiring.

I have good news: *a little prediction goes a long way*. I call this The Prediction Effect, a theme that runs throughout the book. The potency of prediction is pronounced— as long as the predictions are better than guessing. This Effect renders predictive analytics believable. We don't have to do the impossible and attain true clairvoyance. The story is exciting yet credible: Putting odds on the future to lift the fog just a bit off our hazy view of tomorrow means pay dirt. In this way, predictive analytics combats financial risk, fortifies healthcare, conquers spam, toughens crime fighting, and boosts sales.

Do you have the heart of a scientist or a businessperson? Do you feel more excited by the very idea of prediction, or by the value it holds for the world?

I was struck by the notion of *knowing the unknowable*. Prediction seems to defy a Law of Nature: You cannot see the future because it isn't here yet. We find a work-around by building machines that learn from experience. It's the regimented discipline of using what we *do* know—in the form of data—to place increasingly accurate odds on what's coming next. We blend the best of math and technology, systematically tweaking until our scientific hearts are content to derive a system that peers right through the previously impenetrable barrier between today and tomorrow.

Talk about boldly going where no one has gone before!

Some people are in sales; others are in politics. I'm in prediction, and it's awesome.

# Introduction

## *The Prediction Effect*

I'm just like you. I succeed at times, and at others I fail. Some days good things happen
to me, some days bad. We always wonder how things could have gone differently.
I begin with six brief tales of woe:

1.  In 2009 I just about destroyed my right knee downhill skiing in Utah. The
    jump was no problem; it was landing that presented an issue. For knee **surgery**,
    I had to pick a graft source from which to reconstruct my busted ACL (the
    knee's central ligament). The choice is a tough one and can make the difference
    between living with a good knee or a bad knee. I went with my hamstring.
    *Could the hospital have selected a medically better option for my case?*
2.  Despite all my suffering, it was really my health **insurance** company that paid
    dearly—knee surgery is expensive. *Could the company have better anticipated the risk*
    *of accepting a ski jumping fool as a customer and priced my insurance premium accordingly?*
3.  Back in 1995 another incident caused me suffering, although it hurt less. I fell
    victim to **identity theft**, costing me dozens of hours of bureaucratic baloney
    and tedious paperwork to clear up my damaged credit rating. *Could the creditors*
    *have prevented the fiasco by detecting that the accounts were bogus when they were filed*
    *under my name in the first place?*
4.  With my name cleared, I recently took out a **mortgage** to buy an apartment.
    Was it a good move, or *should my financial adviser have warned me the property could*
    *soon be outvalued by my mortgage?*
5.  My professional life is susceptible, too. My **business** is faring well, but a company
    always faces the risk of changing economic conditions and growing competi-
    tion. *Could we protect the bottom line by foreseeing which marketing activities and other*
    *investments will pay off, and which will amount to burnt capital?*

1

6. Small ups and downs determine your fate and mine, every day. A precise **spam** filter has a meaningful impact on almost every working hour. We depend heavily on effective Internet **search** for work, health (e.g., exploring knee surgery options), home improvement, and most everything else. We put our faith in personalized **music and movie recommendations** from Pandora and Netflix. After all these years, my mailbox wonders why companies don't know me well enough to send less **junk mail** (and sacrifice fewer trees needlessly).

These predicaments matter. They can make or break your day, year, or life. But what do they all have in common?

These challenges—and many others like them—are best addressed with *prediction*. Will the patient's outcome from surgery be positive? Will the credit applicant turn out to be a fraudster? Will the homeowner face a bad mortgage? Will the customer respond if mailed a brochure? By predicting these things, it is possible to fortify healthcare, decrease risk, conquer spam, toughen crime fighting, and cut costs.

## PREDICTION IN BIG BUSINESS—THE DESTINY OF ASSETS

There's another angle. Beyond benefiting you and me as consumers, prediction serves the organization, empowering it with an entirely new form of competitive armament. Corporations positively pounce on prediction.

In the mid-1990s, an entrepreneurial scientist named Dan Steinberg marched into the nation's largest bank, Chase, to deliver prediction unto their management of millions of mortgages. This mammoth enterprise put its faith in Dan's predictive technology, deploying it to drive transactional decisions across a tremendous mortgage portfolio. What did this guy have on his resume?

Prediction is power. Big business secures a killer competitive stronghold by predicting the future destiny and value of individual assets. In this case, by driving mortgage decisions with predictions about the future payment behavior of homeowners, Chase curtailed risk and boosted profit—the bank witnessed a nine-digit windfall in one year.

## INTRODUCING . . . THE CLAIRVOYANT COMPUTER

Compelled to grow and propelled to the mainstream, predictive technology is commonplace and affects everyone, every day. It impacts your experiences in undetectable ways as you drive, shop, study, vote, see the doctor, communicate, watch TV, earn, borrow, or even steal.

This book is about the most influential and valuable achievements of computerized prediction, and the two things that make it possible: the people behind it, and the fascinating science that powers it.

Making such predictions poses a tough challenge. Each prediction depends on multiple factors: The various characteristics known about each patient, each home-owner, and each e-mail that may be spam. How shall we attack the intricate problem of putting all these pieces together for each prediction?

The idea is simple, although that doesn't make it easy. The challenge is tackled by a systematic, scientific means to develop and continually improve prediction—to literally *learn* to predict.

The solution is *machine learning*—computers automatically developing new knowledge and capabilities by furiously feeding on modern society's greatest and most potent *unnatural* resource: data.

## "FEED ME!"—FOOD FOR THOUGHT FOR THE MACHINE

*Data is the new oil.*
> —European Consumer Commissioner Meglena Kuneva

*The only source of knowledge is experience.*
> —Albert Einstein

*In God we trust. All others must bring data.*
> —William Edwards Deming (a business professor famous
> for work in manufacturing)

Most people couldn't be less interested in data. It can seem like such dry, boring stuff. It's a vast, endless regiment of recorded facts and figures, each alone as mundane as the most banal tweet, "I just bought some new sneakers!" It's the unsalted, flavorless residue deposited en masse as businesses churn away.

Don't be fooled! The truth is that data embodies a priceless collection of experience from which to learn. Every medical procedure, credit application, Facebook post, movie recommendation, fraudulent act, spammy e-mail, and purchase of any kind—each positive or negative outcome, each successful or failed sales call, each incident, event, and transaction—is encoded as data and ware-housed. This glut grows by an estimated 2.5 quintillion bytes per day (that's a 1 with 18 zeros after it). And so a veritable Big Bang has set off, delivering an epic sea of raw materials, a plethora of examples so great in number, only a computer could manage to learn from them. Used correctly, computers avidly soak up this ocean like a sponge.

As data piles up, we have ourselves a genuine gold rush. But data isn't the gold. I repeat, data in its raw form is boring crud. The gold is what's discovered therein.

The process of machines learning from data unleashes the power of this exploding resource. It uncovers what drives people and the actions they take—what makes us tick and how the world works. With the new knowledge gained, prediction is possible.

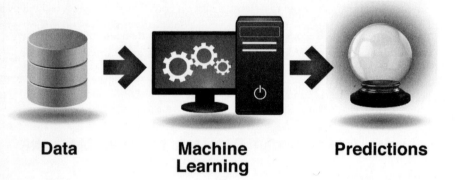

**Data**          **Machine Learning**          **Predictions**

This learning process discovers insightful gems such as:[1]

- Early retirement decreases your life expectancy.
- Online daters more consistently rated as attractive receive *less* interest.
- Rihanna fans are mostly political Democrats.
- Vegetarians miss fewer flights.
- Local crime increases after public sporting events.

Machine learning builds upon insights such as these in order to develop predictive capabilities, following a number-crunching, trial-and-error process that has its roots in statistics and computer science.

## I KNEW YOU WERE GOING TO DO THAT

With this power at hand, what do we want to predict? Every important thing a person does is valuable to predict, namely: *consume, think, work, quit, vote, love, procreate, divorce, mess up, lie, cheat, steal, kill,* and *die.* Let's explore some examples.[2]

---

[1] See Chapter 3 for more details on these examples.
[2] For more examples and further detail, see this book's Central Tables.

## PEOPLE CONSUME

- Hollywood studios predict the success of a screenplay if produced.

- Netflix awarded $1 million to a team of scientists who best improved their recommendation system's ability to predict which movies you will like.

- Australian energy company Energex predicts electricity demand in order to decide where to build out its power grid, and Con Edison predicts system failure in the face of high levels of consumption.

- Wall Street predicts stock prices by observing how demand drives them up and down. The firms AlphaGenius and Derwent Capital drive hedge fund trading by following trends across the general public's activities on Twitter.

- Companies predict which customer will buy their products in order to target their marketing, from U.S. Bank down to small companies like Harbor Sweets (candy) and Vermont Country Store ("top quality and hard-to-find classic products"). These predictions dictate the allocations of precious marketing budgets. Some companies literally predict how to best influence you to buy more (the topic of Chapter 7).

- Prediction drives the coupons you get at the grocery cash register. UK grocery giant Tesco, the world's third-largest retailer, predicts which discounts will be redeemed in order to target more than 100 million personalized coupons annually at cash registers across 13 countries. Prediction was shown to increase coupon redemption rates by a factor of 3.6 over previous methods. Similarly, Kmart, Kroger, Ralph's, Safeway, Stop & Shop, Target, and Winn-Dixie follow in kind.

- Predicting mouse clicks pays off massively. Since websites are often paid per click for the advertisements they display, they predict which ad you're mostly likely to click in order to instantly choose which one to show you. This, in effect, selects more relevant ads and drives millions in newly found revenue.

## PEOPLE LOVE, WORK, PROCREATE, AND DIVORCE

- The leading career-focused social network, LinkedIn, predicts your job skills.

- Online dating leaders Match.com, OkCupid, and eHarmony predict which hottie on your screen would be the best bet at your side.

- Target predicts customer pregnancy in order to market relevant products accordingly. Nothing foretells consumer need like predicting the birth of a new consumer.

- Clinical researchers predict infidelity and divorce. There's even a self-help website tool to put odds on your marriage's long-term success (www.divorce360.com), and public rumors have suggested credit card companies do the same.

*(continued)*

(*continued*)

## PEOPLE THINK AND DECIDE

- Obama was re-elected in 2012 with the help of voter prediction. The Obama for America Campaign predicted which voters would be positively persuaded by campaign contact (a call, door knock, flier, or TV ad), and which would actually be inadvertently influenced to vote adversely by contact. Employed to drive campaign decisions for millions of swing state voters, this method was shown to successfully convince more voters to choose Obama than traditional campaign targeting.

- "What did you mean by that?" Systems have learned to ascertain the intent behind the written word. Citibank and PayPal detect the customer sentiment about their products, and one researcher's machine can tell which Amazon.com book reviews are sarcastic.

- Student essay grade prediction has been developed for possible use to automatically grade. The system grades as accurately as human graders.

- There's a machine that can participate in the same capacity as humans in the United States' most popular broadcast celebration of human knowledge and cultural literacy. On the TV quiz show *Jeopardy!*, IBM's Watson computer triumphed. This machine learned to work proficiently enough with English to predict the answer to free-form inquiries across an open range of topics and defeat the two all-time human champs.

- Computers can literally read your mind. Researchers trained systems to decode a scan of your brain and determine which type of object you're thinking about—such as certain tools, buildings, and food—with over 80 percent accuracy for some human subjects. In 2011, IBM predicted that mind-reading technology would be mainstream within five years.

## PEOPLE QUIT

- Hewlett-Packard (HP) earmarks each and every one of its more than 330,000 worldwide employees according to "Flight Risk," the expected chance he or she will quit their job so that managers may intervene in advance where possible, and plan accordingly otherwise.

- Ever experience frustration with your cell phone service? Your service provider endeavors to know. All major wireless carriers predict how likely it is you will cancel and defect to a competitor—possibly before you have even conceived a plan to do so—based on factors such as dropped calls, your phone usage, billing information, and whether your contacts have already defected.

- FedEx stays ahead of the game by predicting—with 65 to 90 percent accuracy—which customers are at risk of defecting to a competitor.

- The American Public University System predicted student dropouts and used these predictions to intervene successfully; the University of Alabama, Arizona State University, Iowa State University, Oklahoma State University, and the Netherlands' Eindhoven University of Technology predict dropouts as well.

- Wikipedia predicts which of its editors, who work for free as a labor of love to keep this priceless online asset alive, are going to discontinue their valuable service.

- Researchers at Harvard Medical School predict that if your friends stop smoking, you're more likely to do so yourself as well. Quitting smoking is contagious.

## PEOPLE MESS UP

- Insurance companies predict who is going to crash a car or take a bad ski jump. Allstate predicts bodily injury liability from car crashes based on the characteristics of the insured vehicle, demonstrating improvements to prediction that could be worth an estimated $40 million annually. Another top insurance provider reported savings of almost $50 million per year by expanding its actuarial practices with advanced predictive techniques.

- Ford is learning from data so its cars can detect when the driver is not alert due to distraction, fatigue, or intoxication and take action such as sounding an alarm.

- Researchers have identified aviation incidents that are five times more likely than average to be fatal, using data from the National Transportation Safety Board.

- All large banks and credit card companies predict which debtors are most likely to turn delinquent, failing to pay back their loans or credit card balances. Collection agencies prioritize their efforts with predictions of which tactic has the best chance to recoup the most from each defaulting debtor.

## PEOPLE GET SICK AND DIE

*I'm not afraid of death; I just don't want to be there when it happens.*

—Woody Allen

- In 2013 the Heritage Provider Network is handing over $3 million to whichever competing team of scientists best predicts individual hospital

*(continued)*

*(continued)*

admissions. By following these predictions, proactive preventive measures can take a healthier bite out of the tens of billions of dollars spent annually on unnecessary hospitalizations. Similarly, the University of Pittsburgh Medical Center predicts short-term hospital readmissions, so doctors can be prompted to think twice before a hasty discharge.

- At Stanford University, a machine learned to diagnose breast cancer better than human doctors by discovering an innovative method that considers a greater number of factors in a tissue sample.

- Researchers at Brigham Young University and the University of Utah correctly predict about 80 percent of premature births (and about 80 percent of full-term births), based on peptide biomarkers, as found in a blood exam as early as week 24 of pregnancy.

- University researchers derived a method to detect patient schizophrenia from transcripts of their spoken words alone.

- A growing number of life insurance companies go beyond conventional actuarial tables and employ predictive technology to establish mortality risk. It's not called *death insurance*, but they calculate when you are going to die.

- Beyond life insurance, one top-five health insurance company predicts the likelihood that elderly insurance policy holders will pass away within 18 months, based on clinical markers in the insured's recent medical claims. Fear not—it's actually done for benevolent purposes.

- Researchers predict your risk of death in surgery based on aspects of you and your condition to help inform medical decisions.

- By following one common practice, doctors regularly—yet unintentionally—sacrifice some patients in order to save others, and this is done completely without controversy. But this would be lessened by predicting something besides diagnosis or outcome: healthcare *impact* (impact prediction is the topic of Chapter 7).

### PEOPLE LIE, CHEAT, STEAL, AND KILL

- Most medium-size and large banks employ predictive technology to counter the ever-blooming assault of fraudulent checks, credit card charges, and other transactions. Citizens Bank developed the capacity to decrease losses resulting from check fraud by 20 percent. Hewlett-Packard saved $66 million by detecting fraudulent warranty claims.

- Predictive computers help decide who belongs in prison. To assist with parole and sentencing decisions, officials in states such as Oregon and

Pennsylvania consult prognostic machines that assess the risk a convict will offend again.

- Murder is widely considered impossible to predict with meaningful accuracy in general, but within at-risk populations predictive methods can be effective. Maryland analytically generates predictions as to who under supervision will kill and who will be killed. University and law enforcement researchers have developed predictive systems that foretell murder among those previously convicted for homicide.

- One fraud expert at a large bank in the United Kingdom extended his work to discover a small pool of terror suspects based on their banking activities.

- Police patrol the areas predicted to spring up as crime hot spots in Chicago, Memphis, and Richmond, Virginia.

- Inspired by the TV crime drama *Lie to Me* about a microexpression reader, researchers at the University at Buffalo trained a system to detect lies with 82 percent accuracy by observing eye movements alone.

- As a professor at Columbia University in the late 1990s, I had a team of teaching assistants who employed cheating detection software to patrol hundreds of computer programming homework submissions for plagiarism.

- The IRS predicts if you are cheating on your taxes.

## THE LIMITS AND POTENTIAL OF PREDICTION

*An economist is an expert who will know tomorrow why the things he predicted yesterday didn't happen.*

—Earl Wilson

*How come you never see a headline like "Psychic Wins Lottery"?*

—Jay Leno

Each of the preceding accomplishments is powered by prediction, which is in turn a product of machine learning. A striking difference exists between these varied capabilities and science fiction: they aren't fiction. At this point, I predict that you won't be surprised to hear that those examples represent only a small sample. You can safely predict that the power of prediction is here to stay.

But are these claims too bold? As the Danish physicist Niels Bohr put it, "Prediction is very difficult, especially if it's about the future." After all, isn't prediction basically impossible? The future is unknown, and uncertainty is the only thing about which we're certain.

Let me be perfectly clear. It's fuzzy. Accurate prediction is generally not possible. The weather is predicted with only about 50 percent accuracy, and it doesn't get easier predicting the behavior of humans, be they patients, customers, or criminals.

Good news! Predictions need not be accurate to score big value. For instance, one of the most straightforward commercial applications of predictive technology is deciding whom to target when a company sends direct mail. If the learning process identifies a carefully defined group of customers who are predicted to be, say, three times more likely than average to respond positively to the mail, the company profits big time by preemptively removing likely *nonresponders* from the mailing list. And those nonresponders in turn benefit, contending with less junk mail.

**Prediction—A person who sees a sales brochure today buys a product tomorrow.**

In this way the business, already playing a sort of numbers game by conducting mass marketing in the first place, tips the balance delicately yet significantly in its favor—and does so *without* highly accurate predictions. In fact, its utility withstands quite poor accuracy. If the overall marketing response is at 1 percent, the so-called hot pocket with three times as many would-be responders is at 3 percent. So, in this case, we can't confidently predict that any one individual customer will respond. Rather, the value is derived from identifying a group of people who—in *aggregate*—will tend to behave in a certain way.

This demonstrates in a nutshell what I call The Prediction Effect. Predicting better than pure guesswork, even if not accurately, delivers real value. A hazy view of what's to come outperforms complete darkness by a landslide.

---

> **The Prediction Effect:** *A little prediction goes a long way.*

---

This is the first of five Effects introduced in this book. You may have heard of the butterfly, Doppler, and placebo effects. Stay tuned here for the *Data, Induction, Ensemble,* and *Persuasion Effects*. Each of these Effects encompasses the fun part of science and technology: an intuitive hook that reveals how it works and why it succeeds.

## THE FIELD OF DREAMS

*People . . . operate with beliefs and biases. To the extent you can eliminate both and replace them with data, you gain a clear advantage.*
> —Michael Lewis, *Moneyball: The Art of Winning an Unfair Game*

What field of study or branch of science are we talking about here? Learning how to predict from data is sometimes called *machine learning*—but, it turns out, this is mostly an academic term you find used within research labs, conference papers, and university courses (full disclosure: I taught the Machine Learning graduate course at Columbia University a couple of times in the late 1990s). These arenas are a priceless wellspring, but they aren't where the rubber hits the road. In commercial, industrial, and government applications—in the real-world usage of machine learning to predict—it's called something else, something that in fact is the very topic of this book:

**Predictive analytics (PA)**—*Technology that learns from experience (data) to predict the future behavior of individuals in order to drive better decisions.*

Built upon computer science and statistics and bolstered by devoted conferences and university degree programs, PA has emerged as its own discipline. But, beyond a field of science, PA is a movement that exerts a forceful impact. Millions of decisions a day determine whom to call, mail, approve, test, diagnose, warn, investigate, incarcerate, set up on a date, and medicate. PA is the means to drive *per-person* decisions empirically, as guided by data. By answering this mountain of smaller questions, PA may in fact answer the biggest question of all: *How can we improve the effectiveness of all these massive functions across government, healthcare, business, nonprofit, and law enforcement work?*

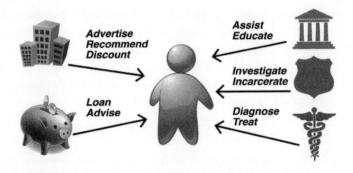

**Predictions drive how organizations treat and serve an individual, across the operations that define a functional society.**

In this way, PA is a completely different animal from *forecasting*. Forecasting makes aggregate predictions on a macroscopic level. How will the economy fare? Which presidential candidate will win more votes in Ohio? Whereas forecasting estimates the total number of ice cream cones to be purchased next month in Nebraska, predictive technology tells you which *individual* Nebraskans are most likely to be seen with cone in hand.

PA leads within the growing trend to make decisions more "data driven," relying less on one's "gut" and more on hard, empirical evidence. Enter this fact-based domain and you'll be attacked by buzzwords, including *analytics*, *big data*, *business intelligence*, and *data science*. While PA fits underneath each of these umbrellas, these evocative terms refer more to the culture and general skill sets of technologists who do an assortment of creative, innovative things with data, rather than alluding to any specific technology or method. These areas are broad; in some cases, they refer simply to standard Excel reports—that is, to things that are important and require a great deal of craft, but may not rely on science or sophisticated math. And so they are more subjectively defined. As Mike Loukides, a vice president at the innovation publisher O'Reilly, once put it, "Data science is like porn—you know it when you see it." Another term, *data mining*, is often used as a synonym for PA, but, as an evocative metaphor depicting "digging around" through data in one fashion or another, it is often used more broadly as well.

## ORGANIZATIONAL LEARNING

*The powerhouse organizations of the Internet era, which include Google and Amazon . . . have business models that hinge on predictive models based on machine learning.*
—Professor Vasant Dhar, Stern School of Business, New York University

An organization is sort of a "mega-person," so shouldn't it "mega-learn"? A group comes together for the collective benefit of its members and those it serves, be it a company, government, hospital, university, or charity. Once formed, it gains from division of labor, mutually complementary skills, and the efficiency of mass production. The result is more powerful than the sum of its parts. Collective learning is the organization's next logical step to further leverage this power. Just as a salesperson learns over time from her positive and negative interactions with sales leads, her successes and failures, PA is the process by which an organization learns from the experience it has collectively gained across its team members and computer systems. In fact, an organization that doesn't leverage its data in this way is like a person with a photographic memory who never bothers to think.

With few exceptions, we find that organizations, rather than individuals, benefit by employing PA. Organizations make the many, many operational decisions for which there's ample room for improvement; organizations are intrinsically inefficient and wasteful on a grand scale. Marketing casts a wide net—junk mail is marketing money wasted and trees felled to print unread brochures. An estimated 80 percent of all e-mail is spam. Risky debtors are given too much credit. Applications for government benefits are backlogged and delayed. And it's organizations that have the data to power the predictions that drive improvements in these operations.

In the commercial sector, profit is a driving force. You can well imagine the booming incentives intrinsic to rendering everyday routines more efficient, marketing more precisely, catching more fraud, avoiding bad debtors, and luring more online customers. Upgrading how business is done, PA rocks the enterprise's economies of scale, optimizing operations right where it makes the biggest difference.

## THE NEW SUPER GEEK: DATA SCIENTISTS

*The sexy job in the next 10 years will be statisticians.*
—Hal Varian, Chief Economist of Google and
University of California, Berkeley professor, 2009

*The alternative [to thinking ahead] would be to think backwards . . . and that's just remembering.*
—Sheldon, the theoretical physicist on *The Big Bang Theory*

Opportunities abound, but the profit incentive is not the only driving force. The source, the energy that makes it work, is Geek Power! I speak of the enthusiasm of technical practitioners. Truth be told, my passion for PA didn't originate from its value to organizations. I am in it for the fun. The idea of a machine that can actually learn seems so cool to me that I care more about what happens inside the magic box than its outer usefulness. Indeed, perhaps that's the defining motivator that qualifies one as a geek. We love the technology; we're in awe of it. Case in point: The leading free, open-source software tool for PA, called R (a one-letter, geeky name), has a rapidly expanding base of users as well as enthusiastic volunteer developers who add to and support its functionalities. Great numbers of professionals and amateurs alike flock to public PA competitions with a tremendous spirit of "coopetition." We operate within organizations, or consult across them. We're in demand, so we fly a lot. But we fly coach, at best Economy Plus.

## THE ART OF LEARNING

*What ya gonna do with your CPU to reach its potentiality?*
*Use your noggin when you login to crank it exponentially.*
*The endeavor that will render my obtuse computer clever:*
*Self-improve ingeniously by way of trial and error.*

—From "Learn This!" by the author

Once upon a time, humanity created The Ultimate General Purpose Machine and, in an inexplicable fit of understatement, decided to call it "a *computer*" (a word that until this time had simply meant a person who did computations by hand). This automaton could crank through any demanding, detailed set of endless instructions without fail or error and with nary a complaint; within just a few decades, its speed became so blazingly brisk that humanity could only exclaim, "Gosh, we really cranked that!" An obviously much better name for this device would have been the appropriately grand *La Machine*, but a few decades later this name was hyperbolically bestowed upon a food processor (I am not joking). *Quel dommage.* "What should we do with the computer? What's its true potential, and how do we achieve it?" humanity asked of itself in wonderment.

A computer and your brain have something in common that renders them both mysterious, yet at the same time easy to take for granted. If while pondering what this might be you heard a pin drop, you have your answer. They are both silent. Their mechanics make no sound. Sure, a computer may have a disk drive or cooling fan that stirs—just as one's noggin may emit wheezes, sneezes, and snores—but the mammoth grunt work that takes place therein involves no "moving parts," so these noiseless efforts go along completely unwitnessed. The smooth delivery of content on your screen—and ideas in your mind—can seem miraculous.[3]

They're both powerful as heck, your brain and your computer. So, could computers be successfully programmed to think, feel, or become truly intelligent? Who knows? At best these are stimulating philosophical questions that are difficult to answer, and at worse they are subjective benchmarks for which success could never be conclusively established. But thankfully we do have some clarity: There is one truly impressive, profound human endeavor computers *can* undertake. They can learn.

But how? It turns out that learning—generalizing from a list of examples, be it a long list or a short one—is more than just challenging. It's a philosophically deep dilemma. Machine learning's task is to find patterns that appear not only in the data at hand, but in general, so that what is learned will hold true in new situations never yet encountered. At the core, this ability to generalize is the magic bullet of PA. There is a true art in the design of these computer methods. We'll explore more later, but for now I'll give you a hint. The machine actually learns more about your next likely action by studying *others* than by studying *you*.

While I'm dispensing teasers that leave you hanging, here's one more. This book's final chapter answers the riddle: *What often happens to you that cannot be witnessed, and that you can't even be sure has happened afterward—but that can be predicted in advance?*

Learning from data to predict is only the first step. To take the next step and *act on predictions* is to fearlessly gamble. Let's kick off Chapter 1 with a suspenseful story that shows why launching PA feels like blasting off in a rocket.

---

[3] Silence is characteristic to solid state electronics, but computers didn't have to be built that way. The idea of a general-purpose, instruction-following machine is abstract, not affixed to the notion of electricity. You could construct a computer of cogs and wheels and levers, powered by steam or gasoline. I mean, I wouldn't recommend it, but you could. It would be slow, big, and loud, and nobody would buy it.

# CHAPTER 1

# Liftoff! Prediction Takes Action

*How much guts does it take to deploy a predictive model into field operation, and what do you stand to gain? What happens when a man invests his entire life savings into his own predictive stock market trading system? Launching predictive analytics means to act on its predictions, applying what's been learned, what's been discovered within data. It's a leap many take—you can't win if you don't play.*

In the mid-1990s, an ambitious postdoc researcher couldn't stand to wait any longer. After consulting with his wife, he loaded their entire life savings into a stock market prediction system of his own design—a contraption he had developed moonlighting on the side. Like Dr. Henry Jekyll imbibing his own untested potion in the moonlight, the young Dr. John Elder unflinchingly pressed "Go."

There is a scary moment every time new technology is launched. A spaceship lifting off may be the quintessential portrait of technological greatness and national prestige, but the image leaves out a small group of spouses terrified to the very point of psychological trauma. Astronauts are in essence stunt pilots, voluntarily strapping themselves in to serve as guinea pigs for a giant experiment, willing to sacrifice themselves in order to be part of history.

From grand challenges are born great achievements. We've taken strolls on our moon, and in more recent years a $10 million Grand Challenge prize was awarded to the first nongovernmental organization to develop a reusable manned spacecraft. Driverless cars have been unleashed—"Look, Ma, no hands!" Fueled as well by millions of dollars in prize money, they navigate autonomously around the campuses of Google and BMW.

Replace the roar of rockets with the crunch of data, and the ambitions are no less far-reaching, "boldly going" not to space but to a new final frontier: predicting the future. This frontier is just as exciting to explore, yet less dangerous and uncomfortable (outer space is a vacuum, and vacuums totally suck). Millions in grand challenge prize money go toward averting the unnecessary hospitalization of each patient and predicting the idiosyncratic preferences of each individual consumer.

The TV quiz show *Jeopardy!* awarded $1.5 million in prize money for a face-off between man and machine that demonstrated dramatic progress in predicting the answers to questions (IBM invested a lot more than that to achieve this win, as detailed in Chapter 6). Organizations are literally keeping kids in school, keeping the lights on, and keeping crime down with predictive analytics (PA). And success is its own reward when analytics wins a political election, a baseball championship, or . . . did I mention managing a financial portfolio?

*Black box trading*—driving financial trading decisions automatically with a machine—is the holy grail of data-driven decision making. It's a black box into which current financial environmental conditions are fed, with buy/hold/sell decisions spit out the other end. It's black (i.e., opaque) because you don't care what's on the inside, as long as it makes good decisions. When working, it trumps any other conceivable business proposal in the world: Your computer is now a box that turns electricity into money.

And so with the launch of his stock trading system, John Elder took on his own personal grand challenge. Even if stock market prediction would represent a giant leap for mankind, this was no small step for John himself. It's an occasion worthy of mixing metaphors. Going for broke by putting all his eggs into one analytical basket, John was taking a healthy dose of his own medicine.

Before continuing with the story of John's blast-off, let's establish how launching a predictive system works, not only for black box trading but across a multitude of applications.

## GOING LIVE

*Learning from data is virtually universally useful. Master it and you'll be welcomed nearly everywhere!*

—John Elder

New groundbreaking stories of PA in action are pouring in. A few key ingredients have opened these floodgates:

- Wildly increasing loads of data.
- Cultural shifts as organizations learn to appreciate, embrace, and integrate predictive technology.
- Improved software solutions to deliver PA to organizations.

But this flood built up its potential in the first place simply because predictive technology boasts an inherent generality—there are just so many conceivable ways to make use of it. Want to come up with your own new innovative use for PA? You need only two ingredients.

EACH APPLICATION OF **PA** IS DEFINED BY:

1. **What's predicted:** The kind of behavior (i.e., action, event, or happening) to predict for each individual, stock, or other kind of element.
2. **What's done about it:** The decisions driven by prediction; the action taken by the organization in response to or informed by each prediction.

Given its open-ended nature, the list of application areas is so broad and the list of example stories is so long that it presents a minor data management challenge in and of itself! So I placed this big list (147 examples total) into nine tables in the center of this book. Take a flip through to get a feel for just how much is going on. That's the sexy part—it's the "centerfold" of this book. The Central Tables divulge cases of predicting: *stock prices, risk, delinquencies, accidents, sales, donations, clicks, cancellations, health problems, hospital admissions, fraud, tax evasion, crime, malfunctions, oil flow, electricity outages, approvals for government benefits, thoughts, intention, answers, opinions, lies, grades, dropouts, friendship, romance, pregnancy, divorce, jobs, quitting, wins, votes,* and more. The application areas are growing at a breakneck pace.

Within this long list, the quintessential application for business is the one covered in the Introduction for mass marketing:

### PA APPLICATION: TARGETING DIRECT MARKETING

1. **What's predicted:** Which customers will respond to marketing contact.
2. **What's done about it:** Contact customers more likely to respond.

As we saw, this use of PA illustrates The Prediction Effect.

---

**The Prediction Effect:** *A little prediction goes a long way.*

---

Let's take a moment to see how straightforward it is to calculate the sheer value resulting from The Prediction Effect. Imagine you have a company with a mailing list of a million prospects. It costs $2 to mail to each one, and you have observed that one out of 100 of them will buy your product (i.e., 10,000 responses). You take your chances and mail to the entire list.

If you profit $220 for each rare positive response, then you pocket:

$$\text{Overall profit} = \text{Revenue} - \text{Cost}$$
$$= (\$220 \times 10,000 \text{ responses}) - (\$2 \times 1\text{million})$$

Whip out your calculator—that's $200,000 profit. Are you happy yet? I didn't think so.

If you are new to the arena of direct marketing (welcome!), you'll notice we're playing a kind of wild numbers game, amassing great waste, like one million monkeys chucking darts across a chasm in the general direction of a dartboard. As turn-of-the-century marketing pioneer John Wanamaker famously put it, "Half the money I spend on advertising is wasted; the trouble is I don't know which half." The bad news is that it's actually more than half; the good news is that PA can learn to do better.

# A FAULTY ORACLE EVERYONE LOVES

*The first step toward predicting the future is admitting you can't.*
—Stephen Dubner, Freakonomics Radio, March 30, 2011

*The "prediction paradox": The more humility we have about our ability to make predictions, the more successful we can be in planning for the future.*
—Nate Silver, *The Signal and the Noise: Why So Many Predictions Fail—but Some Don't*

*Half of what we will teach you in medical school will, by the time you are done practicing, be proved wrong.*

—Dr. Mehmet Oz

Your resident "oracle," PA, tells you which customers are most likely to respond. It earmarks a quarter of the entire list and says, "These folks are three times more likely to respond than average!" So now you have a short list of 250,000 customers of which 3 percent will respond—7,500 responses.

Oracle shmoracle! These predictions are seriously inaccurate—we still don't have strong confidence when contacting any one customer, given this measly 3 percent response rate. However, the overall IQ of your dart-throwing monkeys has taken a real boost. If you send mail to only this short list then you profit:

$$\text{Overall profit} = \text{Revenue} - \text{Cost}$$
$$= (\$220 \times 7,500 \ \text{responses}) - (\$2 \times 250,000)$$

That's $1,150,000 profit. You just improved your profit 5.75 times over by mailing to *fewer* people (and, in so doing, expending fewer trees). In particular, you predicted who wasn't worth contacting and simply left them alone. Thus you cut your costs by three-quarters, in exchange for losing only one-quarter of sales. That's a deal I'd take any day.

It's not hard to put a value on prediction. As you can see, even if predictions themselves are generated from sophisticated mathematics, it takes only simple arithmetic to roll up the plethora of predictions—some accurate, and others not so much—and reveal the aggregate bottom-line effect. This isn't just some abstract notion; The Prediction Effect means business.

## PREDICTIVE PROTECTION

Thus, value has emerged from just a little predictive insight, a small prognostic nudge in the right direction. It's easy to draw an analogy to science fiction, where just a bit of supernatural foresight can go a long way. Nicolas Cage kicks some serious bad-guy butt in the movie *Next* based on a story by Philip K. Dick. His weapon? Pure prognostication. He can see the future, but only two minutes ahead. It's enough prescience to do some damage. An unarmed civilian with a soft heart and the best of intentions, he winds up marching through something of a war zone, surrounded by a posse of heavily armed FBI agents who obey his every gesture. He sees the damage of every booby trap, sniper, and mean-faced grunt before it happens and so can command just the right moves for this Superhuman Risk-Aversion Team, avoiding one calamity after another.

In a way, deploying PA makes a Superhuman Risk-Aversion Team of the organization just the same. Every decision an organization makes, each step it takes, incurs risk. Imagine the protective benefit of foreseeing each pitfall so that it may be avoided—each criminal act, stock value decline, hospitalization, bad debt, traffic jam, high school dropout . . . and each ignored marketing brochure that was a waste to mail. *Organizational risk management*, traditionally the act of defending against singular, macro-level incidents like the crash of an aircraft or an economy, now broadens to fight a myriad of micro-level risks.

Hey, it's not all bad news. We win by foreseeing good behavior as well, since it often signals an opportunity to gain. The name of the game is "Predict 'n' Pounce" when it pops up on the radar that a customer is likely to buy, a stock value is likely to increase, a voter is likely to swing, or the apple of one's online dating eye is likely to reciprocate.

A little glimpse into the future gives you power because it gives you options. In some cases the obvious decision is to act to change what may not be inevitable, be it crime, loss, or sickness. On the positive side, in the case of foreseeing demand, you act to exploit it. Either way, prediction serves to drive decisions.

Let's turn to a real case, a $1 million example.

## A SILENT REVOLUTION WORTH A MILLION

When an organization goes live with PA, it unleashes a massive army, but it's an army of ants. These ants march out to the front lines of an organization's operations, the places where there's contact with the likes of customers, students, or patients— the people served by the organization. Within these interactions, the ant army, guided by predictions, improves millions of small decisions. The process goes largely unnoticed, under the radar . . . until someone bothers to look at how it's adding up. The improved decisions may each be ant-sized, relatively speaking, but there are so many that it comes to a powerful net effect.

In 2005, I was digging in the trenches, neck deep in data for a client who wanted more clicks on its website. To be precise, they wanted more clicks on their sponsors' ads. This was about the money—more clicks, more money. The site had gained tens of millions of users over the years, and within just several months' worth of tracking data that they handed me, there were 50 million rows of learning data—no small treasure trove from which to learn to predict . . . *clicks*.

Advertising is an inevitable part of media, be it print, television, or your online experience. Benjamin Franklin forgot to include it when he proclaimed, "Nothing can be said to be certain, except death and taxes." The flagship Internet behemoth Google credits ads as its greatest source of revenue. It's the same with Facebook.

But on this website, ads told a slightly different story than usual, which further amplified the potential win of predicting user clicks. The client was a leading student grant and scholarship search service, with one in three college-bound high school seniors using it: an arcane niche, but just the one over which certain universities and military recruiters were drooling. One ad for a university included a strong pitch, naming itself "America's leader in creative education," and culminating with a button that begged to be clicked: "Yes, please have someone from the Art Institute's Admissions Office contact me!" And you won't be surprised to hear that creditors were also placing ads, at the ready to provide these students another source of funds: loans. The sponsors would pay up to $25 per lead—for each would-be recruit. That's good compensation for one little click of the mouse. What's more, since the ads were largely relevant to the users, closely related to their purpose on the website, the response rates climbed up to an unusually high 5 percent. So this little business, owned by a well-known online job-hunting firm, was earning well. Any small improvement meant real revenue.

But improving ad selection is a serious challenge. At certain intervals, users were exposed to a full-page ad, selected from a pool of 291 options. The trick is selecting the best one for each user. The website currently selected which ad to show based simply on the revenue it generated on average, with no regard to the particular user. The universally strongest ad was always shown first. Although this tactic forsakes the possibility of matching ads to individual users, it's a formidable champion to unseat. Some sponsor ads, such as certain universities, paid such a high bounty per click, and were clicked so often, that showing any user a less powerful ad seemed like a crazy thing to consider, since doing so would risk losing currently established value.

## THE PERILS OF PERSONALIZATION

By trusting predictions in order to customize for the individual, you take on risk. A predictive system boldly proclaims, "Even though ad A is so strong overall, for this particular user it is worth the risk of going with ad B." For this reason, most online ads are not personalized for the individual user—even Google's Adwords, which allows you to place textual ads alongside search results and on other web pages at large, determines which ad to display by web page context, the ad's click rate, and the advertiser's bid (what it is willing to pay for a click). It is not determined by anything known or predicted about the particular viewer who is going to actually see the ad.

But weathering this risk carries us to a new frontier of customization. For business, it promises to "personalize!," "increase relevance!," and "engage one-to-one marketing!" The benefits reach beyond personalizing marketing treatment to customizing the individual treatment of patients and suspected criminals as well. During a speech about satisfying our widely varying preferences in choice of spaghetti sauce—chunky? sweet? spicy?—Malcolm Gladwell said, "People . . . were looking for . . . universals, they were looking for one way to treat all of us[;] . . . all of science through the 19th century and much of the 20th was obsessed with universals. Psychologists, medical scientists, economists were all interested in finding out the rules that govern the way all of us behave. But that changed, right? What is the great revolution of science in the last 10, 15 years? It is the movement from the search for universals to the understanding of variability. Now in medical science we don't want to know . . . just how cancer works; we want to know how your cancer is different from my cancer."

From medical issues to consumer preferences, individualization trumps universals. And so it goes with ads:

### PA Application: Predictive Advertisement Targeting

1. **What's predicted:** Which ad each customer is most likely to click.
2. **What's done about it:** Display the best ad (based on the likelihood of a click as well as the bounty paid by its sponsor).

I set up PA to perform ad targeting for my client, and the company launched it in a head-to-head, champion/challenger competition to the death. The loser would surely be relegated to the bin of second-class ideas that just don't make as much cash. To prepare for this battle, we armed PA with powerful weaponry. The predictions were generated from machine learning across 50 million learning cases, each depicting a micro-lesson from history of the form, "User Mary was shown ad A and she did click it" (a positive case) or "User John was shown ad B and he did not click it" (a negative case).

The learning technology employed to pick the best ad for each user was a Naïve Bayes model. Reverend Thomas Bayes was an eighteenth-century mathematician, and the "Naïve" part means that we take a very smart man's ideas and compromise them in a way that simplifies yet makes their application feasible, resulting in a practical method that's often considered good enough at prediction, and scales to the task at hand. I went with this method for its relative simplicity, since in fact I needed to generate 291 such models, one for each ad. Together, these models predict which ad a user is most likely to click on.

## DEPLOYMENT'S DETOURS AND DELAYS

As with a rocket ship, launching PA looks great on paper. You design and construct the technology, place it on the launch pad, and wait for the green light. But just when you're about to hit "Go," the launch is scrubbed. Then delayed. Then scrubbed again. The Wright brothers and others, galvanized by the awesome promise of a newly discovered wing design that generates lift, endured an uncharted rocky road, faltering, floundering, and risking life and limb until all the kinks were out.

For ad targeting and other real-time PA deployments, predictions have got to zoom in at warp speed in order to provide value. Our online world tolerates no delay when it's time to choose which ad to display, determine whether to buy a stock, decide whether to authorize a credit card charge, recommend a movie, filter an e-mail for viruses, or answer a question on *Jeopardy!* A real-time PA solution must be directly integrated into operational systems, such as websites or credit card processing facilities. If you are newly integrating PA within an organization, this can be a significant project for the software engineers, who often have their hands full with maintenance tasks just to keep the business operating normally. Thus, the *deployment* phase of a PA project takes much more than simply receiving a nod from senior management to go live: it demands major construction. By the time the programmers deployed my predictive ad selection system, the data over which I had tuned it was already about 11 months old. Were the facets of what had been learned still relevant almost one year later, or would prediction's power peter out?

## IN FLIGHT

> *This is Major Tom to Ground Control*
> *I'm stepping through the door*
> *And I'm floating in a most peculiar way . . .*
>
>                            —"Space Oddity" by David Bowie

Once launched, PA enters an eerie, silent waiting period, like you're floating in orbit and nothing is moving. But the fact is, in a low orbit around Earth you're actually screaming along at over 14,000 miles per hour. Unlike the drama of launching a rocket or erecting a skyscraper, the launch of predictive analytics is a relatively stealthy maneuver. It goes live, but daily activities exhibit no immediately apparent change. After the ad-targeting project's launch, if you checked out the website, it would show you an ad as usual, and you could wonder whether the system made any difference in this one choice. This is what computers do best. They hold the power to silently enact massive procedural changes that often go uncredited, since most aren't directly witnessed by any one person.

But, under the surface, a sea-change is in play, as if the entire ocean has been reconfigured. You actually notice the impact only when you examine an aggregated report.

In my client's deployment, predictive ad selection triumphed. The client conducted a head-to-head comparison, selecting ads for half the users with the existing champion system and the other half with the new predictive system, and reported that the new system generated at least 3.6 percent more revenue, which amounts to $1 million every 19 months, given how much moolah was already coming in. This was for the website's full-page ads only; many more (smaller) ads are embedded within functional web pages, which could potentially also be boosted with a similar PA project.

No new customers, no new sponsors, no changes to business contracts, no materials or computer hardware needed, no new full-time employees or ongoing effort—solely an improvement to decision making was needed to generate cold, hard cash. In a well-oiled, established system like the one my client had, even a small improvement of 3.6 percent amounts to something substantial. The gains of an incremental tweak can be even more dramatic: In the insurance business, one company reports that PA saves almost $50 million annually by decreasing its loss ratio by *half a percentage point*.

So how did these models predict each click?

## ELEMENTARY, MY DEAR: THE POWER OF OBSERVATION

Just like Sherlock Holmes drawing conclusions by sizing up a suspect, prediction comes of astute observation: What's known about each individual provides a set of clues about what he or she may do next. The chance a user will click on a certain ad depends on all sorts of elements, including the individual's current school year, gender, and e-mail domain (hotmail, yahoo, gmail, etc.); the ratio of the individual's SAT written to math scores (is the user more a verbal person or more a math person?), and on and on.

In fact, this website collected a wealth of information about its users. To find out which grants and scholarships they're eligible for, users answer dozens of questions about their school performance, academic interests, extracurricular activities, prospective college majors, parents' degrees, and more. So the table of learning data was long (at 50 million examples) and was also wide, with each row holding all the information known about the user at the moment the person viewed an ad.

It can sound like a tall order: *Harnessing millions of examples in order to learn how to incorporate the various factoids known about each individual so that prediction is possible.* But we can break this down into a couple of parts, and suddenly it gets much simpler. Let's start with the contraption that makes the predictions, the electronic Sherlock Holmes that knows how to consider all these factors and roll them up into a single prediction for the individual.

**Predictive model**—*A mechanism that predicts a behavior of an individual, such as click, buy, lie, or die. It takes characteristics of the individual as input, and provides a predictive score as output. The higher the score, the more likely it is that the individual will exhibit the predicted behavior.*

A predictive model (depicted throughout this book as a "golden" egg, albeit in black and white) scores an individual:

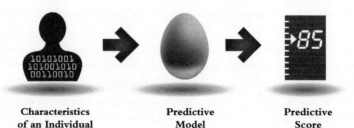

**Characteristics**          **Predictive**          **Predictive**
**of an Individual**            **Model**                **Score**

A predictive model is the means by which the attributes of an individual are factored together for prediction. There are many ways to do this. One is to weigh each characteristic and then add them up—perhaps females boost their score by 33.4, Hotmail users decrease their score by 15.7, and so on. Each element counts toward or against the final score for that individual. This is called a *linear model*, generally considered quite simple and limited, although usually much better than nothing.

Other models are composed of *rules*, like this real example:

IF the individual
   is still in high school
     AND
   expects to graduate college within three years
     AND
   indicates certain military interest
     AND
   has not been shown this ad yet
THEN the probability of clicking on the ad for the Art Institute is 13.5 percent.

This rule is a valuable find, since the overall probability of responding to the Art Institute's ad is only 2.7 percent, so we've identified a pocket of avid clickers, relatively speaking.

It is interesting that those who have indicated a military interest are more likely to show interest in the Art Institute. We can speculate, but it's important not to assume there is a *causal* relationship. For example, it may be that people who complete more of their profile are just more likely to click in general, across all kinds of ads.

Various types of models compete to make the most accurate predictions. Models that combine a bunch of rules like the one just shown are—relatively speaking—on the simpler side. Alternatively, we can go more "super-math" on the prediction problem, employing complex formulas that predict more effectively but are almost impossible to understand by human eyes.

But all predictive models share the same objective: They consider the various factors of an individual in order to derive a single predictive score for that individual. This score is then used to drive an organizational decision, guiding which action to take.

Before using a model, we've got to build it. Machine learning builds the predictive model:

| Data | Machine Learning | Predictive Model |

Machine learning crunches data to build the model, a brand-new prediction machine. The model is the product of this learning technology—it is itself the very thing that has been learned. For this reason, machine learning is also called *predictive modeling*, which is a more common term in the commercial world. If deferring to the older metaphorical term *data mining*, the predictive model is the unearthed gem.

Predictive modeling generates the entire model from scratch. All the model's math or weights or rules are created automatically by the computer. The machine learning process is designed to accomplish this task, to mechanically develop new capabilities from data. This automation is the means by which PA builds its predictive power.

The hunter returns back to the tribe, proudly displaying his kill. So, too, a data scientist posts her model on the bulletin board near the company ping-pong table. The hunter hands over the kill to the cook, and the data scientist cooks up her model, translates it to a standard computer language, and e-mails it to an engineer for integration. A well-fed tribe shows the love; a psyched executive issues a bonus. The tribe munches and the scientist crunches.

## To Act Is to Decide

*Knowing is not enough; we must act.*

—Johann Wolfgang von Goethe

*Potatoes or rice?*
*What to do with my life?*
*I can't decide.*

—From the song "I Suck at Deciding" by Muffin[1] (1996)

Once you develop a model, don't pat yourself on the back just yet. Predictions don't help unless you do something about them. They're just thoughts, just ideas. They may be astute, brilliant gems that glimmer like the most polished of crystal balls, but hanging them on the wall gains you nothing and displays nerd narcissism—they just hang there and look smart.

Unlike a report sitting dormant on the desk, PA leaps out of the lab and takes action. In this way, it stands above other forms of analysis, data science, and data mining. It desires deployment and loves to be launched—because, in what it foretells, it mandates movement.

The predictive score for each individual directly informs the decision of what action to take with that individual. Doctors take a second look at patients predicted to be readmitted, and service agents contact customers predicted to cancel. Predictive scores issue imperatives to *mail, call, offer a discount, recommend a product, show an ad, expend sales resources, audit, investigate, inspect for flaws, approve a loan, or buy a stock.* By acting on the predictions produced by machine learning, the organization is now applying what's been learned, modifying its everyday operations for the better.

To make this point, we have mangled the English language. Proponents like to say that predictive analytics is *actionable*. Its output directly informs actions, commanding the organization about what to do next. But with this use of vocabulary, industry insiders have stolen the word *actionable*, which originally has meant *worthy of legal action* (i.e., "sue-able"), and morphed it. This verbal assault comes about because people are so tired of seeing sharp-looking reports that provide only a vague, unsure sense of direction.

With this word's new meaning established, "Your fly is unzipped" is *actionable* (it is clear what to do—you can and should take action to remedy), but "You're going

---

[1] A rock band that included the author's sister, Rachel.

bald" is not (there's no cure; nothing to be done). Better yet, "I predict you will buy these button-fly jeans and this snazzy hat" is actionable, to a salesperson.

Launching PA into action delivers a critical new edge in the competitive world of business. One sees massive commoditization taking place today, as the faces of corporations appear to blend together. They all seem to sell pretty much the same thing and act in pretty much the same ways. To stand above the crowd, where can a company turn?

As Thomas Davenport and Jeanne Harris put it in *Competing on Analytics: The New Science of Winning*, "At a time when companies in many industries offer similar products and use comparable technology, high-performance business processes are among the last remaining points of differentiation." Enter predictive analytics. Survey results have in fact shown that "a tougher competitive environment" is by far the strongest reason why organizations adopt this technology.

But while the launch of PA brings real change, so too can it wreak havoc by introducing new risk. With this in mind, we now return to John's story.

## A PERILOUS LAUNCH

*Ladies and gentlemen . . . from what was once an inarticulate mass of lifeless tissues, may I present a cultured, sophisticated man about town.*
—Dr. Freddy Frankenstein (Gene Wilder) in Mel Brooks's *Young Frankenstein*

Dr. John Elder bet it all on a predictive model. He concocted it in the lab, packed it into a black box, and unleashed it on the stock market. Some people make their own bed in which they must then passively lie. But John had climbed way up high to take a leap of faith. Diving off a mountain top with newly constructed, experimental wings, he wondered how long it might take before he could be sure he was flying rather than crashing.

The risks stared John in the face like a cracked mirror reflecting his own vulnerability. His and his wife's full retirement savings were in the hands of an experimental device, launched into oblivion and destined for one of the same two outcomes achieved by every rocket: glory or mission failure. Discovering profitable market patterns that sustain is the mission of thousands of traders operating in what John points out to be a brutally competitive environment; doing so automatically with machine learning is the most challenging of ambitions, considered impossible by many. It doesn't help that a stock market scientist is completely on his own, since work in this area is shrouded in secrecy, leaving virtually no potential to learn from the successes and failures of others. Academics publish, marketers discuss, but quants hide away in their Bat Caves. What can look great on paper might be stricken with a weakness that destroys or an error that bankrupts. John puts it plainly: "Wall Street is the hardest data mining problem."

The evidence of danger was palpable, as John had recently uncovered a crippling flaw in an existing predictive trading system, personally escorting it to its grave. Opportunity had come knocking on the door of a small firm called Delta Financial in the form of a black box trading system purported to predict movements of the Standard & Poor's (S&P) 500 with 70 percent accuracy. Built by a proud scientist, the system promised to make millions, so stakeholders were flying around all dressed up in suits, actively lining up investors prepared to place a huge bet. Among potential early investors, Delta was leading the way for others, taking a central, influential role. The firm was known for investigating and championing cutting-edge approaches, weathering the risk inherent to innovation. As a necessary precaution, Delta sought to empirically validate this system. The firm turned to John, who was consulting for them on the side while pursuing his doctorate at the University of Virginia in Charlottesville. John's work for Delta often involved inspecting, and sometimes debunking, black box trading systems.

How do you prove a machine is broken if you're not allowed to look inside it? Healthy skepticism bolstered John's resolve, since the claimed 70 percent accuracy raised red flags as quite possibly too darn good to be true. But he was not granted access to the predictive model. With secrecy reigning supreme, the protocol for this type of audit dictated that John receive only the numerical results, along with a few adjectives that described its design: *new, unique, powerful!* With meager evidence, John sought to prove a crime he couldn't even be sure had been committed.

Before each launch, organizations establish confidence in PA by "predicting the past" (aka *backtesting*). The predictive model must prove itself on historical data before its deployment. Conducting a kind of simulated prediction, the model evaluates across data from last week, last month, or last year. Feeding on input that could only have been known at a given time, the model spits out its prediction, which then matches against what we now already know took place thereafter. Would the S&P 500 go down or up on March 21, 1991? If the model gets this retrospective question right, based only on data available by March 20, 1991 (the day just before), we have evidence the model works. These retrospective predictions—without the manner in which they had been derived—were all John had to work with.

## HOUSTON, WE HAVE A PROBLEM

Even the most elite of engineers commits the most mundane and costly of errors. In late 1998, NASA launched the Mars Climate Orbiter on a daunting nine-month trip to Mars, a mission that fewer than half the world's launched probes headed for that destination have completed successfully. This $327.6 million calamity crashed and burned indeed, due not to the flip of fate's coin, but rather a simple snafu. The spacecraft came too close to Mars and disintegrated in its atmosphere. The source of the navigational bungle? One system expected to receive information in metric units (newton-seconds), but a computer programmer for another system had it speak in English imperial units (pound-seconds). Oops.

John stared at a screen of numbers, wondering if anything was wrong and, if so, whether he could find it. From the long list of impressive—yet retrospective—predictions, he plainly saw the promise of huge profits that had everyone involved so excited. If he proved there was a flaw, vindication; if not, lingering uncertainty. The task at hand was to reverse engineer: Given the predictions the system generated, could he infer how it worked under the hood, essentially eking out the method in its madness? This was ironic, since all predictive modeling is a kind of reverse engineering to begin with. Machine learning starts with the data, an encoding of things that have happened, and attempts to uncover patterns that generated or explained the data in the first place. John was attempting to deduce what the other team had deduced. His guide? Informal hunches and ill-informed inferences, each of which could be pursued only by way of trial and error, testing each hypothetical mess-up he could dream up by programming it by hand and comparing it to the retrospective predictions he had been given.

His perseverance finally paid off: John uncovered a true flaw, thereby flinging back the curtain to expose a flustered Wizard of Oz. It turned out that the prediction engine committed the most sacrilegious of cheats by looking at the one thing it must not be permitted to see. It had looked at the future. The battery of impressive retrospective predictions weren't true predictions at all. Rather, they were based in part on a three-day average calculated across yesterday, today . . . and tomorrow. The scientists had probably intended to incorporate a three-day average leading up to today, but had inadvertently shifted the window by a day. Oops. This crippling bug delivered the dead-certain prognosis that this predictive model would not perform well if deployed into the field. Any prediction it would generate today could not incorporate the very thing it was designed to foresee—tomorrow's stock price—since, well, it isn't known yet. So, if foolishly deployed, its accuracy could never match the exaggerated performance falsely demonstrated across the historical data. John revealed this bug by reverse engineering it. On a hunch, he hand-crafted a method with the same type of bug, and showed that its predictions closely matched those of the trading system.

A predictive model will sink faster than the *Titanic* if you don't seal all its "time leaks" before launch. But this kind of "leak from the future" is common, if mundane. Although core to the very integrity of prediction, it's an easy mistake to make, given that each model is backtested over historical data for which prediction is not, strictly speaking, possible. The relative future is always readily available in the testing data, easy to inadvertently incorporate into the very model trying to predict it. Such temporal leaks achieve status as a commonly known gotcha among PA practitioners. If this were an episode of *Star Trek*, our beloved, hypomanic engineer Scotty would be screaming, "Captain, we're losing our temporal integrity!"

It was with no pleasure that John delivered the disappointing news to his client, Delta Financial: He had debunked the system, essentially exposing it as inadvertent fraud. High hopes were dashed as another fairy tale bit the dust, but gratitude quickly ensued as would-be investors realized they'd just dodged a bullet. The wannabe inventor of the system suffered dismay, but was better off knowing now; it would have hit the fan much harder postlaunch, possibly including prosecution for fraud, even if inadvertently committed. The project was aborted.

# THE LITTLE MODEL THAT COULD

*Every new beginning comes from some other beginning's end.*
> —From the song "Closing Time" by Semisonic

Even the young practitioner that he was, John was a go-to data man for entrepreneurs in black box trading. One such investor moved to Charlottesville, but only after John Elder, PhD, new doctorate degree in hand, had just relocated to Houston in order to continue his academic rite of passage with a postdoc research position at Rice University. He'd left quite an impression back in Charlottesville, though; people in both the academic and commercial sectors alike referred the investor to John. Despite John's distance, the investor hired him to prepare, launch, and monitor a new black box mission remotely from Houston. It seemed as good a place as any for the project's Mission Control.

And so it was time for John to move beyond the low-risk role of evaluating other people's predictive systems and dare to build one of his own. Over several months, he and a small team of colleagues he'd pulled together built upon core insights from the investor and produced a new, promising black box trading model. John was champing at the bit to launch it and put it to the test. All the stars were aligned for liftoff except one: the money people didn't trust it yet.

There was good reason to believe in John. Having recently completed his doctorate degree, he was armed with a fresh, talented mind, yet had already gained an impressively wide range of data-crunching problem-solving experience. On the academic side, his PhD thesis had broken records among researchers as the most efficient way to optimize for a certain broad class of system engineering problems (machine learning is itself a kind of optimization problem). He had also taken on predicting the species of a bat from its echolocation signals (the chirps bats make for their radar). And in the commercial world, John's pregrad positions had dropped him right into the thick of machine learning systems that steer for aerospace flight and that detect cooling pipe cracks in nuclear reactors, not to mention projects for Delta Financial looking over the shoulders of other black box quants.

And now John's latest creation absolutely itched to be deployed. Backtesting against historical data, all indications whispered confident promises for what this thing could do once set in motion. As John puts it, "A slight pattern emerged from the overwhelming noise; we had stumbled across a persistent pricing inefficiency in a corner of the market, a small edge over the average investor, which appeared repeatable." Inefficiencies are what traders live for. A perfectly efficient market can't be played, but if you can identify the right imperfection, it's payday.

### PA APPLICATION: BLACK BOX TRADING
1. **What's predicted:** Whether a stock will go up or down.
2. **What's done about it:** Buy stocks that will go up; sell those that will go down.

John could not get the green light. As he strove to convince the investor, cold feet prevailed. It appeared they were stuck in a circular stalemate. After all, this guy might not get past his jitters until seeing the system succeed, yet it couldn't succeed while stuck on the launch pad. The time was now, as each day marked lost opportunity.

After a disconcerting meeting that seemed to go nowhere, John went home and had a sit-down with his wife, Elizabeth. What supportive spouse could possibly resist the seduction of her beloved's ardent excitement and strong belief in his own abilities? She gave him the go-ahead to risk it all, a move that could threaten their very home. But he still needed buy-in from one more party.

Delivering his appeal to the client investor raised questions, concerns, and eyebrows. John wanted to launch with his own personal funds, which meant no risk whatsoever to the client, and would resolve any doubts by field-testing John's model. But this unorthodox step would be akin to the dubious choice to act as one's own defense attorney. When an individual is without great personal means, this kind of thing is often frowned upon. It conveys overconfident, foolish brashness. Even if the client wanted to truly believe, it would be another thing to expect the same from co-investors who hadn't gotten to know and trust John. But, with every launch, proponents gamble something fierce. John had set the rules for the game he'd chosen to play.

He received his answer from the investor: "Go for it!" This meant there was nothing to prevent moving forward. It could have also meant the investor was prepared to write off the project entirely, feeling there was nothing left to lose.

## HOUSTON, WE HAVE LIFTOFF

Practitioners of PA often put their own professional lives a bit on the line to push forward, but this case was extreme. Like baseball's Billy Beane of the Oakland A's, who literally risked his entire career to deploy and field-test an analytical approach to team management, John risked everything he had. It was early 1994, and John's individual retirement account (IRA) amounted to little more than $40,000. He put it all in.

"Going live with black box trading is really exciting and really scary," says John. "It's a roller coaster that never stops. The coaster takes on all these thrilling ups and downs, but with a very real chance it could go off the rails."

As with baseball, he points out, slumps aren't slumps at all—they're inevitable statistical certainties. Each one leaves you wondering, "Is this falling feeling part of a safe ride, or is something broken?" A key component to his system was a cleverly designed means to detect real quality, a measure of system integrity that revealed whether recent success had been truly deserved or had come about just due to dumb luck.

From the get-go, the predictive engine rocked. It increased John's assets at a rate of 40 percent per year, which meant that after two years his money had doubled.

The client investor was quickly impressed and soon put in a couple of million dollars himself. A year later, the predictive model was managing a $20 million fund across a group of investors, and eventually the investment pool increased to a few hundred million dollars. With this much on tap, every win of the system was multiplicatively magnified.

No question about it: All involved relished this fiesta, and the party raged on and on, continuing almost nine years, consistently outperforming the overall market all along. The system chugged, autonomously trading among a dozen market sectors such as technology, transportation, and healthcare. John says the system "beat the market each year and exhibited only two-thirds its standard deviation—a home run as measured by risk-adjusted return."

But all good things must come to an end, and, just as John had talked his client up, he later had to talk him down. After nearly a decade, the key measure of system integrity began to decline. John was adamant that they were running on fumes, so with little ceremony the entire fund was wound down. The system was halted in time, before catastrophe could strike. In the end, all the investors came out ahead.

## A PASSIONATE SCIENTIST

The early success of this streak had quickly altered John's life. Once the project was cruising, he had begun supporting his rapidly growing family with ease. The project was taking only a couple of John's hours each day to monitor, tweak, and refresh what was a fundamentally stable, unchanging method within the black box. What's a man to do? Do you put your feet up and sip wine indefinitely, with the possible interruption of family trips to Disney World? After all, John had thus far always burned the candle at both ends out of financial necessary, with summer jobs during college, part-time work during graduate school, and this black box project, which itself had begun as a moonlighting gig during his postdoc. Or, do you follow the logical business imperative: pounce on your successes, using all your free bandwidth to find ways to do more of the same?

John's passion for the craft transcended these self-serving responses to his good fortune. That is to say, he contains the spirit of the geek. He jokes about the endless insatiability of his own appetite for the stimulation of fresh scientific challenges. He's addicted to tackling something new. There is but one antidote: a growing list of diverse projects. So, two years into the stock market project, he wrapped up his postdoc, packed up his family, and moved back to Charlottesville to start his own data mining company.

And so John launched Elder Research, now the largest predictive analytics services firm (pure play) in North America. A narrow focus is key to the success of many businesses, but Elder Research's advantage is quite the opposite: its diversity. The company's portfolio reaches far beyond finance to include all major commercial sectors and many branches of government. John has also earned a top-echelon position in the industry. He chairs the major conferences, coauthors massive textbooks, takes cameos as a university professor, and served five years as a presidential appointee on a national security technology panel.

## LAUNCHING PREDICTION INTO INNER SPACE

With stories like John's coming to light, organizations are jumping on the PA bandwagon. One such firm, a mammoth international organization, focuses the power of prediction introspectively upon itself, casting PA's keen gaze on its own employees. Read on to witness the windfall and the fallout when scientists dare to ask: Do people like being predicted?

# CHAPTER 2

# With Power Comes Responsibility

## Hewlett-Packard, Target, and the Police Deduce Your Secrets

*How do we safely harness a predictive machine that can foresee job resignation, pregnancy, and crime? Are civil liberties at risk? Why does one leading health insurance company predict policy holder death? An extended sidebar on fraud detection addresses the question: How does machine intelligence flip the meaning of* fraud *on its head?*

What would happen if your boss was notified that you're allegedly going to quit—even though you had said this to no one? If you are one of the more than 330,000 who work at Hewlett-Packard (HP), your employer has tagged you—and all your colleagues—with a "Flight Risk" score. This simple number foretells whether you're likely to leave your job. As an HP employee, there's a good chance you didn't already know that. Postpone freaking out until you finish reading the full explanation in this chapter.

This story about HP arrives in the wake of media outcry against Target after learning the big-box retailer had taken to predicting customer pregnancy. This media firestorm invoked misleading accusations, fear of corporate power, postulations by television personalities, and, of course, predictive analytics (PA). To my surprise, I ended up in the thick of it.

TV news programs strike like a blunt instrument, but often in the right general direction. The media assault was reactionary and chose to misinform, yet legitimate quandaries lurk below the surface. Target's and HP's predictive power brings to focus an exceptionally challenging and pressing ethical question. Within the minefield that is the privacy debate, the stakes just rose even higher.

Why? Because prediction snoops into your private future. These cases involve the corporate deduction of previously unknown, sensitive facts: Are you considering quitting your job? Are you pregnant? This isn't a case of mishandling, leaking, or stealing data. Rather, it is *the generation of new data*, the indirect discovery of unvoluntered truths about people. Organizations predict these powerful insights from existing innocuous data, as if creating them out of thin air. Are they equipped to manage their own creation?

While we come to terms with the sheer magnitude of prediction's power, we've only begun to fathom the privacy concerns it introduces. A chain reaction triggers and surprises even the experts: Organizations exert newfound capabilities, consumers rise up, the media stir the pot, and scientists dodge bullets and then reexamine scruples.

The journey eventually takes us to a particularly uncomfortable dilemma. Beyond expectant moms and departing employees, PA also flags potential criminals, and actively helps law enforcement decide who stays in prison and who goes free.

This tale follows my journey from carefree technologist to unwitting talking head, and the journey of organizations from headstrong to humbled. The asocial domain of data and analytics is not so irrelevant after all.

# THE PREDICTION OF TARGET AND THE TARGET OF PREDICTION

In 2010, I invited an expert at Target, Andrew Pole, to keynote at Predictive Analytics World, a conference for which I serve as program chair. Pole manages dozens of analytics professionals who run various PA projects at Target. In October of that year, Pole delivered a stellar keynote on a wide range of PA deployments at Target. He took the stage and dynamically engaged the audience, revealing detailed examples, interesting stories, and meaningful business results that left the audience clearly enthused. Free to view, here it is: www.pawcon.com/Target.

Toward the end, Pole describes a project to predict customer pregnancy. Given that there's a tremendous sales opportunity when a family prepares for a newborn, you can see the marketing potential.

But this was something pointedly new, and I turned my head to scan the audience for any reactions. Nothing. Nada. Zilch. Normally, for marketing projects, PA predicts buying behavior. Here, the thing being predicted was not something marketers care about directly, but, rather, something that could itself be a strong predictor of a wide range of shopping needs. After all, the marketer's job is to discover and pounce on demand. You can think of this predictive goal as a "surrogate" (sorry) for the pertinent shopping activities a retail marketer is paid to care about.

### PA APPLICATION: PREGNANCY PREDICTION
1. **What's predicted:** Which female customers will have a baby in coming months.
2. **What's done about it:** Market relevant offers for soon-to-be parents of newborns.

From what data did Target learn to predict pregnancy, given that predictive modeling requires a number of known cases from which to learn? Remember, the predictive modeling process is a form of automated data crunching that learns from *training examples*, which must include both positive and negative examples. An organization needs to have positively identified in the past some cases of what it would like to predict in the future. To predict something like "Will buy a stereo," you can bet a retailer has plenty of positive cases. But how can you locate Target customers known to be pregnant?

You may be surprised how simple it is to answer to this puzzle. Can you guess? Let's assume no medical information or pharmaceutical data is employed for this project. Why does a customer inform Target she is pregnant? The answer is: the Target baby registry. Registrants not only disclose they're pregnant, but they also reveal their due date. In addition, Target has indicated there are other marketing programs through which more moms-to-be identify themselves, thus also serving as positive learning examples.

Target pulled together training data by merging the baby registry data with other retail customer data, and generated a "fairly accurate" predictive model. The store can now apply the model to customers who have *not* registered as pregnant. This identifies many more pregnant customers, since we can assume most such customers in fact do not register.

The model predictively evaluates a customer based on what she has purchased, which can include baby-related products, but may include combinations of other products not necessarily directly related to babies. Deriving the model is an automated act of trend spotting that explores a broad range of factors. I doubt Target's system confirmed that buying pickles and ice cream turns out to be a good indicator of pregnancy, but any and all product categories were analyzed and considered. The model identified 30 percent more customers for Target to contact with pregnancy-oriented marketing material—a significant marketing success story.

## A PREGNANT PAUSE

Strutting charismatically across the conference stage, Pole boldly lauded this unorthodox endeavor, which he led at Target. The business value was clear, the story entertaining. It's likely he was delivering what had gone over well for internal Target presentations, but now to an open forum. It made for great material and engaged the audience.

I wondered for a moment if there had been any concerns, but assumed, as one engrossed in the core technology itself may tend to do, that this project had been vetted, that concerns had been allayed and put to rest by folks at Target. Emerging from inside the PA practitioner's dark data cave, squinting at the world outside, it can be hard to imagine how unsuspecting folks walking down the street might respond to such a project. In fact, Pole reassured the audience that Target carefully adheres to all privacy and data-use laws. "Target wants to make sure that we don't end up in the newspaper or on TV because we went out and we used something that we're not supposed to be using." Little did we know where this was headed.

## MY 15 MINUTES

Because the ensuing media storm around Target's pregnancy prediction pulled me into its wake, I witnessed from a front-row seat how, if one reporter sets off just the right spark, the pundits will obediently burn and the news cycle will fan the flames.

Who spilled the beans in the first place? A few months after Pole's presentation, *New York Times* reporter Charles Duhigg interviewed me. Exploring, he asked for interesting discoveries that had come from PA. I rattled off a few and included pregnancy prediction, pointing him to the online video of Pole's talk, which had thus far been receiving little attention, and introducing him to Pole. I must admit that by now the privacy question had left my mind almost entirely.

One year later, in February 2012, Duhigg published a front-page *New York Times Magazine* article, sparking a viral outbreak that turned the Target pregnancy prediction story into a debacle. The article, "How Companies Learn Your Secrets," conveys a tone that implies wrongdoing is a foregone conclusion. It punctuates this by alleging an anonymous story of a man discovering his teenage daughter is pregnant only by seeing Target's marketing offers to her, with the unsubstantiated but tacit implication that this resulted specifically from Target's PA project. The *Times* even produced a short video to go with the article, which features dramatic, slow-motion, color-muted images of Target shoppers checking out, while creepy, suspenseful music plays and Duhigg himself states, "If they know when [your life is changing], then they can . . . manipulate you . . . so that your habits put dollars in their pockets." He refers to the practice of data-driven marketing as "spying on" customers.

This well-engineered splash triggered rote repetition by press, radio, and television, all of whom blindly took as gospel what had only been implied and ran with it. Not incidentally, it helped launch Duhigg's book, *The Power of Habit: Why We Do What We Do in Life and Business* (Random House, 2012), which hit the *New York Times* best seller list.

The tornado sucked me in because the article quoted me in addition to Pole, who, along with Target as a whole, had now unsurprisingly clammed up. As an independent consultant, I enjoyed unfettered freedom to make public appearances. I had no wise employer to hold me back.

## THRUST INTO THE LIMELIGHT

> *I can't seem to face up to the facts.*
> *I'm tense and nervous and I can't relax.*
>
>                                —The Talking Heads

This techie transmogrified into a pundit, literally overnight, as I raced to New York City on a red-eye to appear on Fox News. But placing my talking head on millions of

TVs does not magically prepare me for such a role. Thriving in an abstract pool of data, the PA professional occasionally surfaces for air, usually only by accident. For the most part, this work is an exercise in math and algorithms to discover patterns that promise to hold true tomorrow—a strange, magical game to almost defy whatever laws of physics prohibit time travel. Inside this petri dish, you're insulated, knowing nothing of the visceral angst of broken hearts or broken privacy. In asking me to shed my lab coat for a suit and tie, the powers that be declared that our previously esoteric activities buried beneath these murky depths of data are truly important after all.

The morning news program *Fox & Friends* positioned me behind a desk, and I struggled to sit still in what was clearly the hot seat. Celebrity host Gretchen Carlson looked over and raised her voice to greet me from across the studio just before we started: "Hi, Eric!" I greeted her back as if it were just another day in the studio: "Hi, Gretchen!"

Then we were live to an estimated two million viewers. Falling in line behind the *Times*, Carlson read Target the riot act for exposing a girl's pregnancy, implying this kind of collateral damage may be innate to PA's application. A third talking head, a professor of medical ethics, reinforced the theme that all applications of PA ought best be shut down, at least pending further investigation. The millions of TVs tuned to Fox at that moment displayed a Target store, overlaid with the question, "Are stores spying on you?" Later the screen proclaimed, "Target has got you in its aim."

It quickly became clear I was to serve as a foil as the news show demonized my profession. For the moment, I was the face of PA, and I had to fight back. If there is a certain carelessness to address in how organizations wield the increasing power to predict, so too is there carelessness in misleading media coverage. I took a deep breath and asserted that the *New York Times* article was misleading because it implied Target has a "supernatural" ability to accurately predict who is pregnant, and it establishes an unsubstantiated connection to the pregnant teen's alleged story. Target's predictions are not medical diagnosis and are not based on medical information. Finally, I managed to squeeze into my allotted seconds the main point: It is really important that this type of analysis not be universally stigmatized. You can watch the clip at www.pawcon.com/target-on-fox.

In another interview, I was confronted with a quote from privacy advocate Katherine Albrecht, who said, "The whole goal [of retailers] is to figure out everything you can learn about your customer. We're creating a retail zoo, where customers are the exhibits." My reply? Unlike the social sciences, PA's objective is to improve operational efficiency rather than figure people out for its own sake—and, either way, just because you're observing a person does not mean that person is being treated like an animal.

The media coverage was broad and, within a few weeks, it seemed like everyone I spoke with both inside and outside my work life had at least caught wind of the Target-pregnancy story. Even comedian Stephen Colbert covered it, suggesting Target's next move will be to predict from your spouse's shopping habits that she is having an affair, and therefore send you a coupon for a hot plate that will go perfectly with your new studio apartment (more than a joke, divorce prediction is included in this book's Central Table 1, with several corresponding citations in the Notes).

As the dust settles, we're left with a significant challenge: How can the true privacy concerns be clearly defined, even as media overblows and confuses?

## You Can't Imprison Something That Can Teleport

*Information about transactions, at some point in time, will become more important than the transaction themselves.*

—Walter Wriston, former chairman and CEO of Citicorp

Data matters. It's the very essence of what we care about.

Personal data is not equivalent to a real person—it's much better. It takes no space, costs almost nothing to maintain, lasts forever, and is far easier to replicate and transport. Data is worth more than its weight in gold—certainly so, since data weighs nothing; it has no mass.

Data about a person is not as valuable as the person, but since the data is so much cheaper to manage, it's a far better investment. Alexis Madrigal, senior editor at *The Atlantic*, points out that a user's data can be purchased for about half a cent, but the average user's value to the Internet advertising ecosystem is estimated at $1,200 per year.

Data's value—its power, its meaning—is the very thing that also makes it sensitive. The more data, the more power. The more powerful the data, the more sensitive. So the tension we're feeling is unavoidable. If nobody cared about some piece of data, nobody would try to protect it, and nobody would want to access it or even bother to retain it in the first place. John Elder reflected, "The fact that it's perceived as dangerous speaks to its power; if it were weak, it wouldn't be a threat."

Ever since the advent of paper and pen, this has been the story. A doctor scribbled a note, and the battle to establish and enforce access policies began.

But now, digital data travels so far, so fast, between people, organizations, and nations. Combine this ability of data to go anywhere at almost no cost with the intrinsic value of the stuff that's traveling, and you have the makings of a very fickle beast, a swarm of gremlins impressively tough to control. It's like trying to incarcerate the X-Men's superhero Nightcrawler, who has the ability to teleport. It's not confined to our normal three dimensions of movement, so you just can't lock it up.

Data is such a unique thing to ship, we have a special word for its telekinetic mode of transport. We call it telecommunication.

Data wants to spread like wildfire. As privacy advocate David Sobel put it, "Once information exists, it's virtually impossible to limit its use. You have all this great data lying around, and sooner or later, somebody will say, 'What else can I do with it?'"

This new, powerful currency proves tough to police. A shady deal to share consumer records is completed with no more than the press of a button—no covert physical shipment of goods required.

# LAW AND ORDER: POLICIES, POLITICS, AND POLICING

*[Privacy is] the most comprehensive of all rights and the one most cherished by a free people.*
—Supreme Court Justice Louis Brandeis, 1928

And yet, we must try our darnedest to tame this wild creature. An open free-for-all is surely not an option. The world will continue struggling to impose order on the distribution of medical facts, financial secrets, and embarrassing photos. Consternation runs deep, with an estimated one in four Facebook users posting false data due to privacy concerns.

Each organization must decide data's who, what, where, when, how long, and why:

**Retain**—What is stored and for how long.

**Access**—Which employees, types of personnel, or group members may retrieve and look at which data elements.

**Share**—What data may be disseminated to which parties within the organization, and to what external organizations.

**Merge**—What data elements may be brought together, aggregated, or connected.

**React**—How may each data element be acted upon, determining an organization's response, outreach, or other behavior.

To make it even more complicated, add to each of these items ". . . under which circumstances and for what type of intention or purpose."

Pressing conundrums ensue. Which data policies can and should be established via legislation, and which by industry best practices and rules of etiquette? For which data practices may the organization default the consumer in, in which case she must take explicit action to opt out if so desired? How are policies enforced: what security standards—encryption, password integrity, firewalls, and the like—promise to earn Fort Knox's reputation in the electronic realm?

OMG. We have our work cut out for us.

# THE BATTLE OVER DATA

*The Internet of free platforms, free services, and free content is wholly subsidized by targeted advertising, the efficacy (and thus profitability) of which relies on collecting and mining user data.*
—Alexander Furnas, writer for *The Atlantic*

The stakes increase and the opponents' resolve hardens like cooling lava.

In one corner we have privacy advocates, often loath to trust organizations, racing to squeeze shut data's ebb and flow: contain it, delete it, or prevent it from being recorded in the first place.

In the other corner we have the data hustlers, salivating: the hoarders and opportunists. This colorful group ranges from entrepreneurs to managers, techies, and board members.

Data prospectors see value, and value is exciting—from more than just a selfish or economic standpoint. We love building the brave new world: increasing productivity and efficiency, decreasing junk mail and its environmental impact, improving healthcare, and suggesting movies and music that will better entertain you. And we love taking on the scientific challenges that get us there.

And yet, even the data hustlers themselves can feel the pain. I was at Walgreens a few years ago, and upon checkout an attractive, colorful coupon spit out of the machine. The product it hawked, pictured for all my fellow shoppers to see, had the potential to mortify. It was a coupon for Beano, a medication for flatulence. I'd developed mild lactose intolerance, but, before figuring that out, had been trying anything to address my symptom. Acting blindly on data, Walgreens' recommendation system seemed to suggest that others not stand so close.

Other clinical data holds a more serious and sensitive status than digestive woes. Once, when teaching a summer program for talented teenagers, I received data I felt would have been better kept away from me. The administrator took me aside to inform me that one of my students had a diagnosis of bipolar disorder. I wasn't trained in psychology. I didn't want to prejudge the student, but there is no "delete" button in the brain's memory banks. In the end, the student was one of my best, and his supposed disorder never seemed to manifest in any perceivable way

Now we are witnessing the increasing use of location data from cell phones and cars. Some people are getting into serious trouble with their bosses, spouses, and other law enforcement agencies. Tom Mitchell, a professor at Carnegie Mellon University and a world leader in the research and development of machine learning capabilities, wrote in a *Science* article, "The potential benefits of mining such data [from cell phones that track location via GPS] are various; examples include reducing traffic congestion and pollution, limiting the spread of disease, and better using public resources such as parks, buses, and ambulance services. But risks to privacy from aggregating these data are on a scale that humans have never before faced."

These camps will battle over data for decades to come. Data hustlers must hone their radar for land mines, improving their sensitivity to sensitivity. Privacy advocates must see that data-driven technology is a tool that can serve both good and evil—like a knife. Outlawing it completely is not an option. There's no objectively correct resolution; this is a subjective, dynamic arena in which new aspects to our culture are being defined. Dialogue is critical, and a "check here to agree to our lengthy privacy policy that you are too busy to read" does not count as dialogue. Organizations and consumers are not speaking the same language. Striking a balance, together, is society's big new challenge. We have a long way to go.

# Data Mining Does Not Drill Down

Exonerate the data scientists and their darling invention. PA in and of itself does not invade privacy—its core process is the *opposite* of privacy invasion. Although it's sometimes called *data mining*, PA doesn't "drill down" to peer at any individual's data. Instead, PA actually "rolls up," learning patterns that hold true in general by way of rote number crunching across the masses of customer records. Data mining often appears to be a culprit when people misunderstand and completely reverse its meaning.

But PA palpably heightens the battle over data, escalating the warfare like a potent enzyme. Why? It ignites fire under data hustlers across the world with a greater and more urgent hunger for more data. Having more data elements per customer means better odds in number crunching's exploration for what will prove most predictive. And the more rows of customer records, the better the predictive model resulting from PA's learning process.

Don't blame the sun when a thirsty criminal steals lemonade. If data rules are fair and right, PA activities that abide by them cannot contribute to abuse or privacy invasion. In this case, PA will be deemed copacetic and be greeted with open arms, and all will be well in our happy futuristic world of prediction. Right?

Fade to black and flash forward to a dystopia. You work in a chic cubicle, sucking chicken-flavored sustenance from a tube. You're furiously maneuvering with a joystick, remotely operating a vehicle on a meteor digging for precious metals. Your boss stops by and gives you a look. "We need to talk about your loyalty to this company."

The organization you work for has deduced that you are considering quitting. It predicts your plans and intentions, possibly before you have even conceived them.

# HP Learns about Itself

*I know it hurts to say goodbye, but it's time for me to fly.*

—REO Speedwagon

In 2011, two crackerjack scientists at Hewlett-Packard broke ground by mathematically scrutinizing the loyalty of each and every one of their more than 330,000 colleagues. Gitali Halder and Anindya Dey developed predictive models to identify all "Flight Risk" employees, those with a higher expected chance of quitting their jobs.

Retaining employees is core to protecting any organization. After all, an organization's defining characteristic is that it's a collection of members. One of five ideological tenets set forth by a founder of HP is: "We achieve our common objectives through teamwork." Employees contribute complementary skills and take on complementary roles. They learn how to work together. It's bad news when a good one goes. The management of employee turnover is a significant challenge for all companies. For example, another multinational corporation looked to decrease turnover among customer service agents at a call center in Barcelona. Folks would come just to spend the summer in that beautiful city and then suddenly give notice and split. It would help to identify such job applicants in advance.

In this endeavor, the organization is aiming PA inwardly to predict its own staff's behavior, in contrast to the more common activity of predicting its patrons' behavior. As with predicting which customers are most likely to leave in order to target retention efforts, HP predicts which of its staff are likely to leave in order to do the same. In both cases, it's like identifying leaks in a boat's hull in order to patch them up and keep the ship afloat.

### PA Application: Employee Retention

1. **What's predicted:** Which employees will quit.
2. **What's done about it:** Managers take the predictions for those they supervise into consideration, at their discretion. This is an example of decision *support* rather than feeding predictions into an automatic decision process.

"I'M SURPRISED. WITH SUCH EXTENSIVE EXPERIENCE IN PREDICTIVE ANALYTICS YOU SHOULD HAVE KNOWN THAT WE WOULDN'T HIRE YOU."

## INSIGHT OR INTRUSION?

Hewlett-Packard is the iconic success story. It literally started in the proverbial garage and now leads the worldwide manufacturing of personal computers. Brace yourself: The company came in as the 27th largest employer of 2011, amassing $127 billion in revenue, which makes it one of the top few highest-earning technology companies in the world.

HP is an empire of sorts, but by no means a locked-up citadel. Some working groups report turnover rates as high as 20 percent. On a ship this big, there are bound to be some leaks, especially given the apparent short attention span of today's technology worker.

HP is a progressive analytics leader. Its analytics department houses 1,700 workers in Bangalore alone. They boast cutting-edge analytical capabilities across sales, marketing, supply chain, finance, and HR domains. Their PA projects include customer loss prediction, sales lead scoring, and supplier fraud detection.

Gitali Halder leads HP's analytics team in Bangalore focused on human resources applications. With a master's in economics from the Delhi School of Economics and several years of hands-on experience, Halder is your true PA powerhouse. Confident, well spoken, and gregarious, she compels and impresses. Having teamed with HP consultant Anindya Dey, also in Bangalore, the two shine as a well-presented dynamic duo, as evidenced by their polished presentation on this project at the Predictive Analytics World conference in November 2011 in London.

Halder and Dey compiled a massive set of training data to serve as learning material for PA. They pulled together two years of employee data such as salaries, raises, job ratings, and job rotations. Then they tacked on, for each of these employee records, whether the person had quit. Thus, HP was positioned to learn from past experience to predict a priceless gem: which combinations of factors define the type(s) of employees most likely to quit their jobs.

If this project helps HP slow its employee turnover rate, Halder and Dey may stand above the crowd as two of its most valuable employees—or become two of the most resented, at least by select colleagues. Some devoted HP workers are bound to be uncomfortable that their Flight Risk score exists. What if your score is wrong, unfairly labeling you as disloyal and blemishing your reputation?

A whole new breed of powerful human resources data emerges: speculative data. Beyond personal, financial, or otherwise private data about a person, this is an estimation of the future, and so speaks to the heart, mind, and intentions of the employee. Insight or intrusion?

It depends on what HP does with it.

## FLIGHT RISK: I QUIT!

On the other side of the world, Alex Beaux helps Halder and Dey bring the fruits of their labor to bear upon a select niche of HP employees. It's 10½ hours earlier in

Houston, where Beaux sits as a manager for HP's internal Global Business Services (GBS). With thousands of staff members, GBS provides all kinds of services across HP to departments that have something they'd like to outsource (even though "outsourcing" to GBS technically still keeps the work within HP).

Beaux, Halder, and Dey set their sights on GBS's Sales Compensation team, since its roughly 300 employees—spread across a few countries—have been exhibiting a high attrition rate of up to 20 percent. A nicely contained petri dish for a pilot field test of Flight Risk prediction, this team provides support for calculating and managing the compensation of salespeople internationally.

The message is clear: Global enterprises are complex! This is not a team of salespeople. It isn't even a regular human resources team that supports salespeople. Rather, it is a global team, mostly in Mexico, China, and Poland, that helps various human resources teams that support salespeople. And so this project is multilevel: It's the analytical HR management of a team that helps HR (that supports salespeople).

Just read that paragraph five more times and you'll be fine. I once worked on an HP project that predicted the potential demand of its corporate clients—how many computers will the company need to buy, and how much of that need is currently covered by HP's competitors? Working on that project for several months, I was on conference calls with folks from so many working groups named with so many acronyms and across so many time zones that it required a glossary just to keep up.

This organizational complexity means there's great value in retaining sales compensation staff. A lot of overhead must be expended to get each new hire ramped up. Sales compensation team members boast a very specific skill set, since they manage an intricate, large-scale operation. They work with systems that determine the nitty-gritty as to how salespeople are compensated. A global enterprise does not follow the orderly grid designed by a city planner—it takes on a patchwork quality since so much organizational growth comes of buying smaller companies, thus absorbing new sales teams with their own compensation rules. The GBS Sales Compensation team handles an estimated 50 percent of the work to manage sales compensation across the entire global organization.

## INSIGHTS: THE FACTORS BEHIND QUITTING

The data showed that Flight Risk depends on some of the things you would expect. For example, employees with higher salaries, more raises, and increased performance ratings quit less. These factors pan out as drivers that decrease Flight Risk. Having more job rotations also keeps employees on board; Beaux conjectures that for the rote, transactional nature of this work, daily activities are kept more interesting with periodic change.

One surprise is that getting a promotion is not always a good thing. Across all of HP, promotions do decrease Flight Risk, but within this Sales Compensation team, where a number of promotions had been associated with relatively low raises, the effect was reversed: Those employees who had been promoted more times were more likely to quit, unless a more significant pay hike had gone along with the promotion.

The analysis is only as good as the data (garbage in, garbage out). In a similar but unrelated project for another company, I predictively modeled how long new prospective hires for a Fortune 1000 B2B provider of credit information would stay on if hired for call center staffing. Candidates with previous outbound sales experience proved 69 percent more likely to remain on the job at least nine months. Other factors included the number of jobs in the past decade, the referring source of the applicant, and the highest degree attained. This project dodged a land mine, as preliminary results falsely showed new hires without a high school degree were 2.6 times as likely to stay on the job longer. We were only days away from presenting this result to the client— and recommending that the company hire more high school dropouts—when we discovered a perfect storm of errors in the data the client had delivered. Error-prone data usually just means fewer conclusions will be drawn, rather than strong false ones, but this case was exceptional—a close call!

As for any domain of PA, the predictive model zips up these various factors into a single score—in this case, a Flight Risk score—for each individual. Even if many of these phenomena seem obvious or intuitive, the model is where the subtle stuff comes in: how these elements weigh in relative to one another, how they combine or interact, and which other intuitive hunches that don't pan out should be eliminated. A machine learning process automates these discoveries by crunching the historical data, literally learning from it.

Halder and Dey's Flight Risk model identified $300 million in estimated potential savings with respect to staff replacement and productivity loss across all HP employees throughout all global regions. The 40 percent of HP employees with highest Flight Risk scores included 75 percent of the quitters (a predictive *lift* of 1.9).

I asked the two, who themselves are HP employees, what their own Flight Risk scores were. Had they predicted themselves likely to quit? Halder and Dey are quick to point out that they like their jobs at HP very much, but admit they are in fact members of a high-risk group. This sounds likely, since analytics skills are in high demand.

## DELIVERING DYNAMITE

When chemists synthesize a new, unstable element, they must *handle with care.*

HP's Flight Risk scores deploy with extreme caution, under lock and key. Beaux, Halder, and Dey devised a report delivery system whereby only a select few high-level managers who have been trained in interpreting Flight Risk scores and understanding their limitations, ramifications, and confidentiality may view individual employee scores—and only scores for employees under them. In fact, if unauthorized parties got their hands on the report itself, they would find there are no names or identifying elements for the employees listed there—only cryptic identifiers, which the authorized managers have the key to unscramble and match to real names. All security systems have vulnerabilities, but this one is fairly bulletproof.

For the GBS Sales Compensation team of 300 employees, only three managers see these reports. A tool displays the Flight Risk scores in a user-friendly, nontechnical view that delivers supporting contextual information about each score in order to help explain why it is high or low. The consumers of this analytical product are trained in advance to understand the Flight Risk scores in terms of their accompanying explanations—the factors about the employee that contributed to the score—so that these numbers aren't deferred to as a forceful authority or overly trusted in lieu of other considerations.

A score produced by any predictive model must be taken with a very special grain of salt. Scores speak to trends and probabilities across a large group; one individual probability by its nature oversimplifies the real-world thing it describes. If I miss a single credit card payment, the probability that I'll miss another this year may quadruple, based on that factor alone. But if you also take into account that my roof caved in that month, your view will change. In general, the complete story for an individual is in fact more than we can ever know. You can see a parallel to another scrutinized practice: diagnosing someone with a psychological disorder and thus labeling them and influencing how they're to be treated.

Over time, the Flight Risk reports sway management decisions in a productive direction. They serve as early warning signals that guide management in planning around loss of staff when it can't be avoided, and working to keep key employees where possible. The system informs what factors drive employee attrition, empowering managers to develop more robust strategies to retain their staffs in order to reduce costs and maintain business continuity.

## DON'T QUIT WHILE YOU'RE AHEAD

And the results are in. GBS's Sales Compensation staff attrition rates that were above 20 percent in some regions have decreased to 15 percent and continue to trend downward. This success is credited in large part to the impact of Flight Risk reports and their well-crafted delivery.

The project gained significant visibility within HP. Even HP's worldwide vice president of sales compensation heartily applauded the project. Flight Risk reports continue to make an impact today, and their underlying predictive models are updated quarterly over more recent data in order to remain current.

These pioneers may not realize just how big a shift this practice is from a cultural standpoint. The computer is doing more than obeying the usual mechanical orders to retain facts and figures. It's producing new information that's so powerful, it must be handled with a new kind of care. We're in a new world in which systems not only divine new, potent information, but must carefully manage it as well.

Managed well and delivered prudently, Flight Risk scores can perhaps benefit an organization without ruffling too many feathers. Given your established relationship with your boss, perhaps you'd be comfortable if he or she received a Flight Risk score for you, assuming it was considered within the right context. And perhaps it's reasonable and acceptable for an employer to crunch numbers on employee patterns and trends, even without the employees necessarily knowing about it. There's no universally approved ethical framework yet established—the jury is still out on this new case.

But, moving from employment record to criminal record, what if law enforcement officers appeared at your door to investigate you, Future Crime Risk report in hand?

## PREDICTING CRIME TO STOP IT BEFORE IT HAPPENS

*What if you could shift the intelligence paradigm from "sense, guess, and respond" to "predict, plan, and act"?*

—Sergeant Christopher Fulcher, Chief Technology Officer of the Vineland, New Jersey, Police Department

Cops have their work cut out for them. Crime rates may ebb and flow, but law enforcement by its nature will always face the impossible challenge of optimizing the deployment of limited resources such as patrolling officers and perusing auditors.

Police deploy PA to predict the location of crime and to direct cops to patrol those areas accordingly. One system, back-tested on two years of data from Santa Cruz, California, correctly predicted the locations of 25 percent of burglaries. This system directs patrols today, delivering 10 hot spots each day within this small city to send police vehicles to. The initiative was honored by *Time* magazine as one of the 50 best inventions of 2011.

### PA APPLICATION: CRIME PREDICTION
1. **What's predicted:** The location of a future crime.
2. **What's done about it:** Police patrol the area.

Another crime prediction system, revealed at a 2011 conference by Chief Information Officer Stephen Hollifield of the Richmond, Virginia, police department, serves up a crime-fighting display that marks up maps by the risk of imminent crime, and lists precincts, neighborhoods, and crime types by risk level. Since this system's deployment, Richmond crime rates have decreased. Similar systems are in development in Chicago; Los Angeles; Vineland, New Jersey; and Memphis, where prediction is credited with reducing crime by 31 percent. In 2009, the U.S. National Institute of Justice awarded planning grants to seven police departments to create crime prediction capabilities.

Lightning strikes twice. The predictive models leverage discoveries such as the trend that crimes are more—not less—likely to soon reoccur in nearby locations, as detected in Santa Cruz. In Richmond, the predictive model flags for future crime based on clues such as today's city events, whether it's a payday or a holiday, the day of the week, and the weather.

What's not to like? Law enforcement gains a new tool, and crime is defrayed. Any controversy over these deployments appears relatively tame. Even the American Civil Liberties Union gave this one a nod of the head. No harm, no foul.

In fact, there's one type of crime that elicits loud complaints when predictive models *fail* to detect it: fraud. To learn more, see the sidebar on fraud detection—or skip past the sidebar to continue on as we explore how crime-predicting computers inform how much time convicts spend in prison.

## SPECIAL SIDEBAR ON FRAUD DETECTION

Criminals can be such nice guys. I became friends with one in 1995. I was pursuing my doctorate in New York City and he was the new boyfriend of my girlfriend's sister. Extremely charismatic and supposedly a former professional athlete, the crook wooed, wowed, and otherwise ingratiated himself into our hearts and home. I'll never forget the really huge, fun dinner he treated us to at the famous Italian restaurant Carmine's. I didn't think twice about letting him use my apartment when I went on a vacation.

A year or two later I discovered he had acquired my Social Security number, stolen my identity, and soiled my sparkly clean credit rating. He had started a small water bottling business in the Los Angeles area, posing as me. Despite being a decade older than I, on the wrong coast, and not even attempting to emulate my signature, he had attained numerous credit accounts, including credit cards and leases on water bottling equipment. After building considerable debt, he abandoned the business and defaulted on the payments.

The creditors came a-knocking, and it took a couple of years of tedious paperwork to clear my name and (mostly) clean up my credit rating—although, to this day, I can't get an American Express credit card (if you work there, would you please put in a good word?). Most creditors needed to see a police report in order to clear my name. But I could not find one single officer, anywhere, who would undertake the task of filing one; they would only send me out the door, referring me to other jurisdictions. Where had the crime taken place—the place of the creditor, the place of the criminal, or the place where the Social Security number had been acquired? One day I finally resorted to putting on a huge smile and saying, "It would mean the world to me—you'd be doing me a huge favor." A cop caved, but ironically this Officer Friendly never requested my ID while we filed the report.

## SPECIAL SIDEBAR ON FRAUD DETECTION (CONTINUED)

Where's a good predictive model when you need one? Why, oh, why couldn't these credit applications have been flagged or quarantined, checking with me by way of the contact information established in my credit files? After all, once all the evidence was gathered and submitted, most auditors immediately perceived the case as obvious fraud.

If some deployments of PA give rise to concern, the absence of others does as well.[1]

### A WOLF IN SHEEP'S CLOTHING

Fraud, defined as "intentional deception made for personal gain," is the very act of a wolf dressing up in sheep's clothing. It's when someone pretends to be someone else, or to be authorized to do something the fraudster is not authorized to do. A student copies another's homework, a sumo wrestler throws a match, an online gambler cheats with illegal information as part of an inside job, fake Twitter accounts spread misinformation about a political candidate, or a death is faked in order to make a claim against a life insurance policy. All such crimes have been detected analytically.

It's a good time to be a fraudster, since they enjoy a massive, expanding stomping ground: the Internet, a transaction infrastructure for global commerce. But by connecting to everybody, we've connected to folks with malicious intent. The easier it is to conduct consumer and business transactions, the easier it is to fake them as well. And, with the buyer, seller, goods, and payment spread across four different physical locations, there is an abundance of vulnerabilities that may be exploited.

As transactions become increasingly numerous and automated, criminal opportunities abound. Fraudulent transactions such as credit card purchases, tax returns, insurance claims, warranty claims, consumer banking checks, and even intentionally excessive clicks on paid ads incur great cost. The National Insurance Crime Bureau says that insurance criminals steal over $30 billion annually, making such fraud the second most costly white-collar crime in the United States—behind tax evasion—resulting in $200 to $300 of additional insurance premiums per U.S. household; we are paying these criminals out of our pockets.

---

[1] But, thank you, Citibank! In December 2010, you caught an illegitimate charge on my credit card for $4,522 at an Apple store in New York (where I haven't lived since 2003). From what Citibank told me, my credit card number had likely been harvested from a transaction during a prior visit to New York, and the criminals had produced a physical card. Crime does pay: The transaction was flagged only after the perpetrator walked off with the Apple products.

(continued)

## SPECIAL SIDEBAR ON FRAUD DETECTION (CONTINUED)

"It is estimated that the nation's banks experience over $10 billion per year in attempted check fraud," says former Citizens Bank Vice President Jay Zhou, now a data mining consultant. Credit card fraud losses approach $5 billion annually in the United States, and Medicaid fraud is estimated to be the same amount for New York State alone. According to the most recent report published by the Federal Trade Commission, 2011 brought over 1.8 million complaints of fraud, identity theft, or other intentional deceit in business, about 40 percent more than in 2010.

Aggregate fraud loss in the United States sees estimates from $100 billion to $1 trillion.

Prediction helps. Predictively scoring and ranking transactions dramatically boosts fraud detection. A team of enforcement workers can inspect only a fixed number of suspected transactions each week. For example, Progressive Insurance employs about 200 "special investigations professionals" on this task. Delivering a more precisely identified pool of candidate transactions—fewer false alarms (false positives)—renders their time more effectively spent; more fraud is detected, and more losses are prevented or recouped.

### PA APPLICATION: FRAUD DETECTION

1. **What's predicted:** Which transactions or applications for credit, benefits, reimbursements, refunds, and so on are fraudulent.
2. **What's done about it:** Human auditors screen the transactions and applications predicted most likely to be fraudulent.

Math is fighting back. Most large—and many medium-sized—financial institutions employ fraud detection. For example, Citizens Bank developed a fraud prediction model that scores each check, predicting well enough to decrease fraud loss by 20 percent. One automobile insurance carrier showed that PA delivers 6.5 times the fraud detection capacity of that attained with no means to rank or score insurance claims. Online transaction giant PayPal suffered an almost 20 percent fraud rate soon after it was launched, a primary threat to its success. Fraud detection methods brought the rate down to a reported less than 1 percent. The people behind each of these stories have spoken at the Predictive Analytics World conference, as have those telling similar stories from 1–800-FLOWERS, the U.S. Postal Service, the Internal Revenue Service (IRS), and a leading high tech company that catches warranty claims from repair shops that didn't actually do the service at all. Even the conference, itself a small business, is periodically subjected to attempted fraud by registrants who pay with a bogus credit card and then request a paid refund.

## SPECIAL SIDEBAR ON FRAUD DETECTION (CONTINUED)

### GOVERNMENT PROTECT THYSELF

The government is working hard on fraud management—but, unlike its efforts enforcing against crimes like theft and assault, it isn't focused on protecting you, or even any business. When it comes to fraud, the U.S. government is fighting to protect its own funds. In fact, fraud detection is the number one government application of PA, as a means to decrease loss in the face of tightening budgets.

Elder Research (John Elder's company) headed a fraud modeling project for the IRS that increased the capacity to detect fraudulent returns by a factor of 25 for a certain targeted segment. A similar effort has been reported by the Mexican Tax Administration, which has its own Risk Models Office.

The U.S. Defense Finance and Accounting Service, responsible for disbursing nearly all Department of Defense funds, executes millions of payments on vendor invoices. Dean Abbott, a top PA consultant (formerly at Elder Research and now at Abbott Analytics, Inc.) who has also consulted for the IRS, led the development of a predictive model capable of detecting 97 percent of known cases of fraudulent invoices. The model scores invoices based on factors such as the time since the last invoice, the existence of other payees at the same postal address, whether the address is a P.O. Box, and whether the vendor submitted invoices out of order.

Beyond these possible signs of fraud, other innovative clues turbocharge the predictive model, helping determine which cases are flagged. 1–800-FLOWERS improved its ability to detect fraud by considering the social connections between prospective perpetrators. In fact, one fraud scheme can't be detected without this kind of social data (oxymoron, anyone?). A group of criminals open financial accounts that improve their respective credit ratings by transferring funds among themselves. Since the money transfers take place only between these accounts, the fraudsters need not spend any real money in conducting these transactions; they play their own little zero-sum game. Once each account has built up its own supposedly legitimate record, they strike, taking out loans, grabbing the money, and running. These schemes can be detected only by way of social data to reveal that the network of transactors is a closed group.

Naturally, criminals respond by growing more creative.

### THE FRAUD DETECTION ARMS RACE

> *The fraudsters were also good, and nimble, too, devising new scams as soon as old ones were compromised.*
>
> —Steven Levitt and Stephen Dubner, *SuperFreakonomics*

*(continued)*

## SPECIAL SIDEBAR ON FRAUD DETECTION (CONTINUED)

Just as competing businesses in the free market push one another to better themselves, fraud-detection capabilities drive criminals toward self-improvement by the
design of smarter techniques. The act of fraud strives to be stealthy, sneaking under
the predictive model's radar. As with the possibility of superbacteria emerging from
the overuse of antibiotics, we are inadvertently creating a stronger enemy.

But there's good news. The white hats sustain a great advantage. In addition
to exerting human creativity like our opponents, we have the data with which
to hone fraud detection models. A broad set of data containing historical
examples of both fraudulent and legitimate transactions intrinsically encodes the
inherent difference between the two. PA is the very means by which to discover this difference from data. And so, beyond storing and indexing a table of
"signatures" that betray the perpetration of known fraud schemes, the modeling
process generates detection schemes that cast a wider net. It predicts forthcoming forms of fraud by generalizing from previously observed examples. This
is the defining characteristic of a learning system.

### THIS MEANS WAR

It's a war like any other. In fact, cyber warfare itself follows the same rules. PA
bolsters information security by detecting hackers and viruses that exploit online
weaknesses, such as system bugs or other vulnerabilities. After all, the Internet's
underlying networking technology, TCP/IP, is a platform originally designed
only for interactions between mutually entrusted parties. As the broad, commercial system it evolved to be, the Internet is, underneath the hood, something of a slapped-together hack with regard to security. Like an unplanned
city, it functions, but, like a Social Security number awaiting discovery in an
unlocked drawer, it exposes outright weaknesses.

### PA APPLICATION: NETWORK INTRUSION DETECTION
1. **What's predicted:** Which low-level Internet communications originate
   from imposters.
2. **What's done about it:** Block such interactions.

PA boosts detection by taking a qualitatively new step in the escalating arms
race between white and black hats. A predictive detection system's field of
vision encompasses a broad scope of potential attacks that cannot be known by
perpetrators, simply because they don't have access to the same data used to
develop the predictive model. Hackers can't know if their techniques will be
detected. PA's deployment brings a qualitative change in the way we compete
against malicious intent.

## SPECIAL SIDEBAR ON FRAUD DETECTION (CONTINUED)

But beware! Another type of fraud attacks you and every one of us, many times a day. Are you protected?

### LIPSTICK ON A PIG

*An Internet service cannot be considered truly successful until it has attracted spammers.*
—Rafe Colburn, Internet development thought leader

Alan Turing (1912–1954), the father of computer science, proposed a thought experiment to explore the definition of what would constitute an "intelligent" computer. This so-called Turing test allows people to communicate via written language with someone or something hidden behind a closed door in order to formulate an answer to the question: Is it human or machine? The thought experiment poses this tough question: If, across experiments that randomly switch between a real person and a computer crouching behind the door, subjects can't correctly tell human from machine more often than the 50 percent correctness one could get from guessing, would you then conclude that the computer, having thereby passed the test by proving it can trick people, is intelligent? I'll give you a hint: There's no right answer to this philosophical conundrum.

In practice, computers fool people for money every day. If you don't believe me, I have some Viagra I'd like to sell you via e-mail. It's called spam. As with androids in science fiction movies like *Aliens* and *Blade Runner*, successful spam makes you believe. Spammy e-mail wants to bait you and switch. Phishing e-mail would have you divulge financial secrets. Spambots take the form of humans in social networks and dating sites in order to grab your attention. Spammy web pages trick search engines into pointing you their way.

Spam filters, powered by PA, are attempting their own kind of Turing test every day at an email in-box near you.

### PA APPLICATION: SPAM FILTERING
1. **What's predicted:** Which e-mail is spam.
2. **What's done about it:** Divert suspected e-mails to your spam e-mail folder.

Unfortunately, in the spam domain, white hats don't exclusively own the arms race advantage. The perpetrators can also access data from which to learn, by testing out a spam filter and reverse engineering it with a model of their own that predicts which messages will make it through the filter. University of California, Berkeley, researchers showed how to do this to render one spam filter useless.

*(continued)*

## SPECIAL SIDEBAR ON FRAUD DETECTION (CONTINUED)

### ARTIFICIAL ARTIFICIAL INTELLIGENCE

In contrast to these precocious computers, we sometimes witness a complete role-reversal switcheroo: a person pretends to be a machine. The Mechanical Turk, a hoax in the eighteenth century, created the illusion of a machine playing chess. The Turk was a desk-sized box that revealed mechanical gears within and sported a chessboard on top. Seated behind the desk was a mannequin whose arm would reach across the board and move the pieces. A small human chess expert who did not suffer from claustrophobia (chess is a long game) hid inside the desk, viewing the board from underneath and manipulating the mannequin's arm. Napoleon Bonaparte and Benjamin Franklin had the pleasure of losing to this wonder of innovation—I mean, this crouching, uncomfortable imposter.

In the modern-day equivalent, human workers perform low-level tasks for the Amazon Mechanical Turk, a crowdsourcing website by Amazon.com that coordinates hundreds of thousands of workers to do "things that human beings can [still] do much more effectively than computers, such as identifying objects in a photo . . . [or] transcribing audio recordings." Its slogan is "Artificial Artificial Intelligence." (This reminds me of the vegetarian restaurant with "mock mock duck" on the menu—I swear, it tastes exactly like mock duck.) As NASA put it in 1965 when defending the idea of sending humans into space, "Man is the lowest-cost, 150-pound, nonlinear, all-purpose computer system which can be mass-produced by unskilled labor."

But, for some tasks, we don't have to pretend anymore. Everything changed in 1997 when IBM's Deep Blue computer defeated then world chess champion Garry Kasparov. Predictive modeling was key. No matter how fast the computer, perfection at chess is impossible, since there are too many possible scenarios to explore. Various estimates agree there are more chess games than atoms in the universe, a result of the nature of exponential growth. So the computer can look ahead only a limited number of moves, after which it needs to stop enumerating scenarios and evaluate game states (boards with pieces in set positions), predicting whether each state will end up being more or less advantageous.

### PA APPLICATION: PLAYING A BOARD GAME

1. **What's predicted:** Which game board state will lead to a win.
2. **What's done about it:** Make a game move that will lead to a state predicted to lead to a win.

Upon losing this match and effectively demoting humankind in its standoff against machines, Kasparov was so impressed with the strategies Deep Blue

## SPECIAL SIDEBAR ON FRAUD DETECTION (CONTINUED)

exhibited that he momentarily accused IBM of cheating, as if IBM had secretly hidden another human grandmaster chess champion, squeezed in there somewhere between a circuit board and a disk drive like a really exorbitant modern-day Mechanical Turk. And so IBM had passed a "mini Turing test" (not really, but the company did inadvertently fool a pretty smart guy).

From this upset emerges a new form of chess fraud: humans who employ the assistance of chess-playing computers when competing in online chess tournaments. And yet another arms race begins, as tournament administrators look to detect such cheating players. This brings us full circle, back to computers that pose as people, as is the case with spam.

So computer "intelligence" has flipped the meaning of fraud on its head, reversing it. Rather than a chess-playing person pretending to be a machine (the Mechanical Turk), we have a machine masking as a person (cheating in human chess tournaments). It's rather like *Star Trek*'s Commander Data, an emotionally stunted android afflicted with the Pinocchio syndrome of wanting to be more human. Somebody get that Tin Man a heart, stat!

## THE DATA OF CRIME AND THE CRIME OF DATA

PA has taken on an enormous crime wave. It is central to tackling fraud, and promises to bolster street-level policing as well.

In these efforts, PA's power optimizes the assignment of resources. Its predictions dictate how enforcers spend their time—which transactions auditors search for fraud and which street corners cops search for crime.

*But how about giving PA the power to help decide who belongs in prison?*

To help make these tough decisions, judges and parole boards consult predictive models. To build these models, Philadelphia's Adult Probation and Parole Department enlisted a professor of statistics and criminology from the University of Pennsylvania. The parole department's research director, Ellen Kurtz, told *The Atlantic*, "Our vision was that every single person, when they walked through the door [of a parole hearing], would be scored by a computer" as to his or her risk of recidivism—committing crime again.

Oregon launched a crime prediction tool to be consulted by judges when sentencing convicted felons. The tool is on display for anyone to try out. If you know the convict's state ID and the crime for which he or she is being sentenced, you can enter the information on the Oregon Criminal Justice Commission's public website and see the predictive model's output: the probability the offender will be convicted again for a felony within three years of being released.

PA APPLICATION: RECIDIVISM REDICTION FOR LAW ENFORCEMENT

1. **What's predicted:** Whether a prosecuted criminal will offend again.
2. **What's done about it:** Judges and parole boards consult model predictions when making decisions about an individual's incarceration.

The predictive model behind Oregon's tool performs admirably. Machine learning generated the model by processing the records of 55,000 Oregon offenders across five years of data. The model then validated across 350,000 offender records across 30 years of history. Among the least risky tenth of criminals—those for whom the model outputs the lowest predictive scores—recidivism is just 20 percent. Yet among the top fifth receiving the highest scores, recidivism will probably occur; over half of these offenders will commit a felony again.

Law enforcement's deployment of PA to predict for individual convicts is building steam. In these deployments, PA builds upon and expands beyond a longstanding tradition of crime statistics and standard actuarial models. Virginia's and Missouri's sentencing guidelines also prescribe the consideration of quantitative risk assessment, and Maryland has models that predict murder. The machine is a respected adviser that has the attention of judges and parole boards.

Humans could use some help with these decisions, so why not introduce an objective, data-driven voice into the process? After all, studies have shown that arbitrary extraneous factors greatly affect judicial decisions. A joint study by Columbia University and Ben Gurion University (Israel) showed that hungry judges rule negatively. Judicial parole decisions immediately after a food break are about 65 percent favorable, but then drop gradually to almost zero percent before the next break. If your parole board judges are hungry, you're more likely to stay in prison.

Following this reasoning, the convict's future now rests in nonhuman hands. Given new power, the computer can commit more than just prediction errors—it can commit injustice, previously a form of misjudgment that only people were in a position to make. It's a whole new playing field for the machine, with much higher stakes. Miscalculations in this arena are more costly than for other applications of PA. After all, the price is not as high when an e-mail message is wrongly incarcerated in the spam folder or a fraud auditor's time is wasted on a transaction that turns out to be legitimate.

# MACHINE RISK WITHOUT MEASURE

In the movie *Minority Report*, Tom Cruise's science fiction cop tackles and handcuffs individuals who have committed no crime (yet), proclaiming stuff like: "By mandate of the District of Columbia Precrime Division, I'm placing you under arrest for the future murder of Sarah Marks and Donald Dubin." Rather than the punishment fitting the crime, the punishment fits the precrime.

Cruise's bravado does not go unchecked. Colin Farrell's Department of Justice agent confronts Cruise, and the two brutes stand off, mano a mano. "You ever get any false positives?" accuses Farrell.

A *false positive*, aka *false alarm*, is when a model incorrectly predicts yes, when the correct answer is no. It says you're guilty, convicting you of a crime you didn't (or in this case, won't) commit.

As self-driving cars emerge from Google and BMW and begin to hit the streets, a new cultural acceptance of machine risk will emerge as well. The world will see automobile collision casualty rates decrease overall, and eventually, among waves of ire and protest, learn to accept that on some occasions the computer is to blame for an accidental death.

But when a criminal who would not reoffend is kept in prison because of a false prediction, we will never have the luxury of knowing. There's a certain finality here, the impossibility of undoing. You can prove innocent a legitimate transaction wrongly flagged as fraudulent, but an incarcerated person has no recourse to disprove unjust assumptions about what his or her future behavior outside prison would have been. If you prevent something, how can you be certain it was ever going to happen?

This risk of injustice is nothing new, since human parole boards and judges face the same problem as they regularly make predictions about criminals' future behavior. The consequences of these decisions are dramatic, and their accuracy largely cannot be known.

What is new here, despite a general movement toward upgrading decision making with data, is entrusting a machine to contribute to these life-changing decisions for which there can be no accountability. We don't know how an incarcerated person would have fared free. We can't measure the quality of these decisions, so there's no way to determine blame. We've grown comfortable with entrusting humans, despite their cherished fallibility, to make these judgment calls. A culture shift is nigh as we broaden this sacred circle of trust. PA sometimes makes wrong predictions, but often proves to be less wrong than people. Bringing PA in to support decision making means introducing a new type of bias, a new fallibility, to balance against those of a person.

The development of computerized law enforcement presents extraordinarily tough ethical quandaries:

- Does the application of PA for law enforcement fly in the face of the very notion of judging a person as an individual? Is it unfair to predict a person's risk of bad behavior based on what other people—who share certain characteristics with that person—have done? Or, isn't the human prediction of a person's future crimes also intrinsically based only on prior observations of others, since humans learn from experience as well?

- A crime risk model dehumanizes the prior offender by paring him or her down to the extremely limited view captured by a small number of characteristics (variables input to a predictive model). But, if the integration of PA promises to lower the overall crime rate—as well as the expense of unnecessary incarceration—is this within the acceptable realm of compromises to civil liberties one endures when incarcerated in the first place?

- With these efforts underway, should not PA also be leveraged to improve the rehabilitation of offenders? Law enforcement communities could apply PA to the betterment of convicted criminals (e.g., by predicting which corrective measures could *decrease* a convict's risk of recidivism).

Security is often at odds with civil liberties. The act of balancing between the two gets even trickier with predictive technology at play.

PA threatens to attain too much authority. Like an enchanted child with a Magic 8 Ball toy (originated in 1950), which is designed to pop up a *random* answer to a yes/no question, insightful human decision makers could place a great deal of confidence in the recommendations of a system they do not deeply understand. What may render judges better informed could also sway them toward less active observation and thought, tempting them to defer to the technology as a kind of crutch and grant it undue credence. It's important for users of PA—the judges and parole board members—to keep well in mind that it bases predictions on a much more limited range of factors than are available to a person.

## THE CYCLICITY OF PREJUDICE

*Just when you thought it was safe to go back in the water.*

—*Jaws 2*

Yet another quandary lurks. Although science promises to improve the effectiveness and efficiency of law enforcement, when you formalize and quantify decision making, you inadvertently instill existing prejudices against minorities. Why? Because prejudice is cyclic, a self-fulfilling prophesy, and this cycling could be intensified by PA's deployment.

Across the United States, crime prediction systems calculate a criminal's probability of recidivism based on things like the individual's age, gender, and neighborhood, as well as prior crimes, arrests, and incarcerations. No government-sponsored predictive models explicitly incorporate ethnic class or minority status.

However, ethnicity creeps into the model indirectly. Philadelphia's recidivism prediction model incorporates the offender's ZIP code, known to highly correlate with race. For this reason, redlining, the denying of services by banks, insurance companies, and other businesses by geographical region, has been largely outlawed in the United States.

Similarly, terrorist prediction models factor in religion. Levitt and Dubner's book *SuperFreakonomics* (HarperCollins, 2009) details a search for suspects among data held by a large UK bank. Informed in part by attributes of the September 11 perpetrators, as well as other known terrorists, a fraud detection analyst at the bank pinpointed a very specific group of customers to forward to the authorities. This *micro-segment* was defined by factors such as the types of bank accounts opened, existence of wire transfers and other transactions, record of a mobile phone, status as a student who rents, and a lack of life insurance (since suicide nullifies the policy). But, to get the list of suspects down to a manageable size, the analyst filtered out people with non-Muslim names, as well as those who made ATM withdrawals on Friday afternoons—admittedly a proxy for practicing Muslims. Conceptually, this may not be a huge leap from the internment of suspected enemies of the state, although it should be noted that this was not a government-sponsored analysis. While this work has been criticized as an "egregious piece of armchair antiterrorism," the bank analyst who delivered the suspect list to the authorities may exert power by way of his perceived credibility as a bank representative.

But even if such factors are disallowed for prediction, you still can't easily get away from involving minority status.

Bernard Harcourt, a professor of both political science and law at the University of Chicago, and author of *Against Prediction: Profiling, Policing, and Punishing in an Actuarial Age*, told *The Atlantic* that minority group members discriminated against by law enforcement, such as by way of profiling, are proportionately more likely to show a prior criminal record, which artificially inflates the minority group's incidence of criminal records. Rather than race being a predictor of prior offenses, prior offenses are indicative of race. By factoring in prior offenses in order to predict future crimes, "you just inscribe the racial discrimination you have today into the future." It's a cyclic magnification of prejudice's already self-fulfilling prophecy.

Even Ellen Kurtz, who champions the adoption of the crime model in Philadelphia, admits, "If you wanted to remove everything correlated with race, you couldn't use anything. That's the reality of life in America."

Although designed for the betterment of decision making, data mining inadvertently digs up some dirty injustices. In principle, the math getting us in trouble could also remedy the problem by quantifying prejudice. But that could be done only by introducing the very data element that—so far—remains outside the analysis, albeit inside the eye of every profiling police officer: *race*. Technically, there could be an analytical means to take this on if race were input into the system, but this opens a new can of worms analogous to the debate around equal opportunity.

## GOOD PREDICTION, BAD PREDICTION

*Privacy is a compromise between the interests of the government and the citizen.*
—Eric Schmidt, Executive Chairman and former CEO, Google, 2011

*Information technology has changed just about everything in our lives. . . . But while we have new ethical problems, we don't have new ethics.*

—Michael Lotti

*When we think in terms of power, it is clear we are getting a raw deal: we grant private entities— with no interest in the public good and no public accountability—greater powers of persuasion than anyone has ever had before and in exchange we get free email.*

—Alexander Furnas, writer for *The Atlantic*

*With great power comes great responsibility.*
—Spider-Man's wise uncle (paraphrasing the Bible, Voltaire, and others)

Pregnancy prediction faces the opposite dilemma of that faced by crime prediction. Crime prediction causes damage when it predicts *wrong*, but predicting sensitive facts like pregnancy can cause damage when it's *right*. Like X-ray glasses, PA unveils new hot-button data elements, for which all the fundamental data privacy questions must be examined anew. Sherlock Holmes, as well as his modern-day doppelganger Dr. Gregory House, size you up and embarrass you: a few scuff marks on your shoe and the detective knows you're having an affair. No one wants her pregnancy unwittingly divulged; it's safe to assume organizations generally don't wish to divulge it, either.

It's tempting to write off these matters as benign in comparison to the qualms of crime prediction. KDnuggets, a leading analytics portal, took a poll: "Was Target wrong in using analytics to identify pregnant women from changes in their buying behavior?" The results were 17 percent "Yes," 74 percent "No," and 9 percent "Not sure" among the analytics community. One written comment pointed out that intent is relevant, asking, "When I yield a seat on a train to elderly people or a pregnant woman, am I 'trying to infer sensitive personal data such as pregnancy or elderliness'? Or just trying to provide the person with her needs?"

But knowledge of a pregnancy is extremely potent, and leaking it to the wrong ears can be life-changing indeed. As one online pundit proclaimed, imagine the pregnant woman's "job is shaky, and your state disability isn't set up right yet, and, although she's working on that, to have disclosure could risk the retail cost of a birth ($20,000), disability payments during time off ($10,000 to $50,000), and even her job."

Google itself appears to have sacrificed a significant boon from predictive modeling in the name of privacy by halting its work on the automatic recognition of faces within photographs. When he was Google's CEO, Eric Schmidt (currently Google's executive chairman) stated his concern that face recognition could be misused by organizations that identify people in a crowd. This could, among other things, ascertain people's locations without their consent. He acknowledges that other organizations will continue to develop such technology, but Google chooses not to be behind it.

Other organizations agree: sometimes it's better not to know. John Elder tells of the adverse reaction from one company's human resources department when the idea of predicting employee death was put on the table. Since death is one way to lose an employee, it's in the data mix. In a meeting with a large organization about predicting employee attrition, one of John's staff witnessed a shutdown when someone mentioned the idea. The project stakeholder balked immediately: "Don't show us!" Unlike healthcare organizations, this human resources group was not meant to handle and safeguard such prognostications.

Predicting death is so sensitive that it's done secretly, keeping it on the down low even when done for benevolent purposes. One top-five health insurance company predicts the likelihood an elderly insurance policy holder will pass away within 18 months, based on clinical markers in the insured's recent medical claims. On the surface, this sounds potentially dubious. With the ulterior motives of health insurance often under scrutiny, one starts to imagine the terrible implications. Might the insurance company deny or delay the coverage of treatment based in part on how likely you are to die soon anyway? Not in this case. The company's purposes are altruistic. The predictions serve to trigger end-of-life counseling (e.g., regarding living wills and palliative care). An employee of the company told me the predictive performance is strong, and the project is providing clear value for the patients. Despite this, those at the company quake in their boots that the project could go public, agreeing only to speak to me anonymously. "It's a very sensitive issue, easily misconstrued," the employee said.

The media goes too far when it sounds alarms that imply PA ought to be sweepingly indicted. To incriminate deduction would be akin to outlawing thought. It's no more than the act of figuring something out. If I glance into my friend's shopping cart and, based on certain items, draw the conclusion that she may be pregnant, have I just committed a *thoughtcrime*—the very act enforced against by Big Brother in George Orwell's *Nineteen Eighty-Four*? And so the plot twists, since perhaps critics of Target who would compare this kind of analysis to that of Big Brother are themselves calling the kettle black by judging Target for thoughtcrime. Pregnancy prediction need not be viewed as entirely self-serving—as with any marketing, this targeting does have potential to serve the customer. In the end, with all his eccentricities, Sherlock Holmes is still our hero, and his revealing deductions serve the greater good.

"Privacy and analytics are often publicly positioned as mortal enemies, but are they really?" asks Ari Schwartz of the U.S. Department of Commerce's National Institute of Standards and Technology. Indeed, some data hustlers want a free-for-all, while others want to throw the baby out with the bathwater. But Schwartz suggests, "The two worlds may have some real differences, but can probably live a peaceful coexistence if they simply understand where the other is coming from."

It's not what an organization comes to know; it's what it *does* about it. Inferring new, powerful data is not itself a crime, but it does evoke the burden of responsibility. Target does know how to benefit from pregnancy predictions without actually divulging them to anyone (the alleged story of the pregnant teen is at worst an individual yet significant gaffe). But any marketing department must realize that if it generates quasi-medical data from thin air, it must take on, with credibility, the privacy and security practices of a facility or department commonly entrusted with such data. *You made it, you manage it.*

PA is an important, blossoming science. Foretelling your future behavior and revealing your intentions, it's an extremely powerful tool—and one with significant potential for misuse. It's got to be managed with extreme care. The agreement we collectively come to for PA's position in the world is central to the massive cultural shifts we face as we fully enter and embrace the information age.

## THE SOURCE OF POWER

How does PA actually work and just how well? Let's turn to the data, starting with how all the emotional, expressive blabbing we do online relates to our economy's ups and downs.

# CHAPTER 3

# The Data Effect

## *A Glut at the End of the Rainbow*

*We are up to our ears in data, but how much can this raw material really tell us? What actually makes it predictive? Does existing data go so far as to reveal the collective mood of the human populace? If yes, how does our emotional online chatter relate to the economy's ups and downs?*

## THE DATA OF FEELINGS AND THE FEELINGS OF DATA

*The emotions aren't always immediately subject to reason, but they are always immediately subject to action.*

—William James

In 2009, two University of Illinois scientists discovered a stunning connection between our collective emotions and our collective behavior. This work addressed the question of which comes first, emotion or action. Do feelings follow behavior:

Human Behavior        Emotions

Or does action come after feelings:

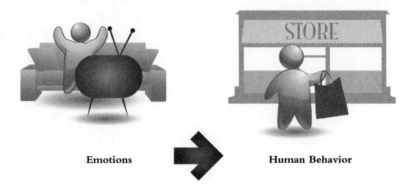

**Emotions**                    **Human Behavior**

Of course, it works both ways. Things happen in the world around you, and feelings ensue. Your client cancels an order, and you feel disappointed. Conversely, your feelings influence your behavior. You are in a terrific mood and decide to give your lazy car mechanic another chance.

Emotions don't usually fall within the domain of predictive analytics (PA). Feelings plainly are not concrete things easily tabulated in a spreadsheet as facts and figures. They're ephemeral and subjective. Sure, they may be the most important element of our human condition, but their subtleties place them outside the reach of most hard science. Some scientists have been known to experience emotions (or, at least I read that somewhere), but there's a worry that trying to explicitly measure or formally define feelings is too tall an order, or might even demote them from their sacred, ethereal status and just ruin the whole thing. There's a good number of neuroscientists out there wiring up the noggins of undergraduate students in exchange for free pizza, but many data scientists view this work as irrelevant, far removed from most applications of predictive analytics.

Dead set on bridging these two worlds, these two Illinois scientists upped the ante. Beyond measuring the feelings of an individual human, they strove to measure *collective emotions*, the moods we experience as an entire population. These ambitious researchers, then doctoral candidate Eric Gilbert and his academic adviser Karrie Karahalios, worked to establish, for the first time, a connection between emotion and behavior that operates across the masses. They were attempting a great leap, since it was unknown how to read collective emotions across a population in the first place.

What's more, Eric and Karrie strove to gauge collective emotion from spontaneous human activity taking place in the real world, outside of any lab. From where could you take such readings? Brain waves and telepathy don't qualify. One possibility, human writing, can reflect our feelings, but sources such as newspapers and magazines may be too narrow and infrequent. The two researchers turned to another public resource: blogs.

Blogs blare our emotions. The movement led by bloggers to broadcast one's thoughts transforms private, introverted "Dear Diary" writers into effusive extroverts. A mass chorus of voices expresses freely, unfettered by any preordained purpose or restriction. Through an estimated 864,000 posts per day, these authors proclaim, cry, laugh, scream, and holler. The blogosphere consists of an army of volunteers who speak on our behalf. To the degree bloggers' feelings reflect those of the population at large, we, the human race, collectively wear our emotions on our sleeves.

## PREDICTING THE MOOD OF BLOG POSTS

*If you prick me, do I not . . . leak?*
> —Data, the android on *Star Trek: The Next Generation*

In designing how to take emotional readings across the deluge of blogs, our scientists focused on fear and anxiety. Across the emotional spectrum, anxiety sustains a potent stronghold on our behavior. Surveying literature in psychology, Eric and Karrie concluded, "Fear makes people risk-averse." Calmness—a lack of anxiety—empowers you with the freedom to do as you please. But fear quashes action, causing people to conservatively pull back on the reins and play it safe.

The first step was to detect anxiety in individual blog entries, one at a time. It's no easy task for a computer to decipher the expressive jabber of a blog. To tackle the task with PA, we need example blog entries for which the presence or absence of anxiety is known. This will provide the data from which predictive modeling can learn how to distinguish entries that connote anxiety from those that convey calmness.

Eric and Karrie turned to the blogging site LiveJournal, which allows the blogger to optionally label each post with one of 132 moods, including *angry, busy, drunk, flirty, thirsty,* and *tired* (okay, they're not all moods, strictly speaking). Serving as a bit of incentive to do so, the blog entry is rewarded with a new dimension of expressiveness, stamped with a cute little mood icon depicting the emotion, such as a frightened face with eyes wide open for *anxious.*

This unusual, precious bundle of blogs connects human language to the feelings behind it. Language is an ambiguous, indirect means to express (or hide!) mood, and we don't usually have direct access to the subjective, internal experience of the writer.

### PA APPLICATION: BLOG ENTRY ANXIETY DETECTION
1. **What's predicted:** Which blog entries express anxiety.
2. **What's done about it:** Used to calculate an aggregate measure of mass mood.

The researchers held at their disposal over 600,000 blog posts from 2004, each labeled by its author with a mood. They considered those tagged as *anxious, worried, nervous,* or *fearful*—amounting to about 13,000—as *anxious* posts, and the rest to be *not anxious.* Employed as training data, these examples generated models that predict whether a blog entry is *anxious:*

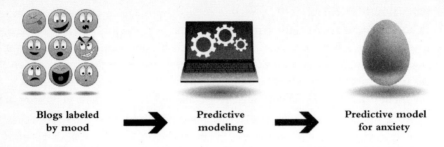

Blogs labeled by mood → Predictive modeling → Predictive model for anxiety

Most blog entries on LiveJournal (and elsewhere) do not include a mood label at all—thus, the very need for a predictive model. Blog entries in general don't discuss mood explicitly, so the bloggers' feelings must be ascertained indirectly from what they write. The predictive model serves this purpose. As always, its function is to score new individual cases for which the answer is not known:

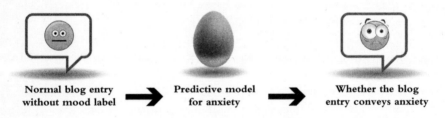

Normal blog entry without mood label → Predictive model for anxiety → Whether the blog entry conveys anxiety

When it comes to working with the complexities of human language, the anxiety-detecting models follow a relatively simple, straightforward procedure based on counting key words and applying some arithmetic. The models are not an attempt to fully "understand" the meaning of blog posts. Predictive modeling derived one model, for example, that identifies *anxious* blog posts by the presence of words such as *nervous*, *scared*, *interview*, and *hospital*, and, conversely, by the absence of words that are common within blog posts that are *not anxious*, such as *yay*, *awesome*, and *love*.

Although a rough approximation, these anxiety-predicting models promise to deliver insight about mass mood. While they manage to detect only 28 percent to 32 percent of each day's anxious blogs, this detection rate in fact serves quite well. What's important is measuring the *relative prevalence* of anxious blog entries on any given day. So, for example, if the number of anxious posts doubles from one day to the next, identifying just 30 percent of anxious posts each day will still reveal the overall increase in anxiety, even though many anxious posts are missed. Among blog entries labeled as *anxious*, the models are quite precise, mistaking *not anxious* entries as *anxious* only 3 percent to 6 percent of the time.

# THE ANXIETY INDEX

*High anxiety whenever you're near.*
*High anxiety—it's you that I fear.*

—From the Mel Brooks movie, *High Anxiety*

With this in place, Eric and Karrie could boldly ask the world, "How are you feeling today, everyone?" To answer this question, they designed the *Anxiety Index*, which is based on the prevalence of anxiety among the day's blog posts. This index is a kind of Mass Anxiety Level reported for each day. In this way, the entire population is the researchers' one and only psychometric subject, and their system tunes in to the collective psyche, taking a broad reading of population anxiety. It's a kind of "zeitgeistometer," or, in Eric and Karrie's words, "an algorithmic estimate of the mood of millions of people." On some days, we become more calm and relaxed, and on others, humanity gets up on the anxious side of the bed.

LiveJournal is a balanced source from which to take a reading of the day's Anxiety Index. Karrie and Eric say it is "known as a journaling site, a place where people record their personal thoughts and daily lives." Rather than a focused arena, it's an inclusive cross section of citizens, "from housewives to high school students."

## VISUALIZING A MOODY WORLD

Subsequent work built upon Eric and Karrie's presented views of how collective mood moves. For example, researchers at Indiana University designed a similar word-based measure for dimensions of mood such as *calm* versus *anxious* (similar to the Anxiety Index, but flipped so that positive values indicate calm and negative values indicate anxious) and *happy* versus *unhappy*. Based on Twitter rather than blogs, here's a sample of output from October 2008 to December 2008:[1]

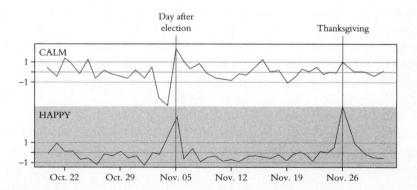

---

[1] Johan Bollen, Huina Mao, and Xiao-Jun Zeng, "Twitter Mood Predicts the Stock Market," *Journal of Computational Science* 2, no. 1 (March 2011). Figure reproduced with permission.

As we oscillate between elation and despair, the trends reveal that we are a moody bunch. The time range shown includes a U.S. presidential election, as well as Thanksgiving. Calmness rebounds once the voting of Election Day is complete. Happiness spikes on Thanksgiving.

But this kind of eyeball evaluation, focused on only a couple of particular days, isn't enough. While Eric and Karrie's Anxiety Index appears creative and innovative in design, this doesn't automatically prove its value, and doesn't get researchers published. With perish as the alternative outcome, Eric and Karrie pressed forward to validate the research, seeking proof that their measure of our subjective mood links objectively to something real and concrete. Without evidence that the system's output relates to events in the world, there's no way to argue that they have succeeded in capturing the collective mood, and the scheme's status remains "just a bunch of numbers."

## PUT YOUR MONEY WHERE YOUR MOUTH IS

*The one thing all human beings do when they're confronted with uncertainty is pull back, withdraw, disengage—and that means economic activity . . . just goes straight down.*

—Alan Greenspan

Eric and Karrie placed their hopes on one surefire winner: money. That's something we certainly get emotional about. Money is a singular measure of how people are faring, so can't we expect our emotional and financial well-being to be closely tied? A classic psychological study from 1972 even demonstrated that a dramatic increase in kindness results from discovering a single coin in a pay phone. "Free money!"—and your heart soars. One could say that everything comes down to feelings, even money. More cynically, you might ask whether it's actually the other way around. Either way, there could be a connection that would provide Eric and Karrie much needed validation for their study.

The pair drew inspiration from renowned economist and former chairman of the Federal Reserve Alan Greenspan, who had spoken prophetically on *The Daily Show with Jon Stewart* in September 2007. He said, "If I could figure out a way to determine whether or not people are more fearful or changing to euphoric . . . I [wouldn't] need any of this other stuff—I could forecast the economy better than any way I know. The trouble is that we can't figure [the public's mood] out."

They were jazzed. Karrie says Eric "was talking like mad about the Greenspan interview. He was really excited, building the belief we could do this!"

The stock market served as an ideal stomping ground within which to validate the Anxiety Index. A measure of collective mood can be validated only if there is a recorded measure of *collective action* against which to validate it. To empirically resolve the chicken-and-egg dilemma of whether emotion "hatches" action or the other way around, the economy could serve as an established standard from which to observe the optimistic and pessimistic fluctuations of society as a whole.

Beyond scientific validation, a tantalizing prospect lingered: stock market prediction. If collective emotion proved to be reflected by subsequent stock movements, the blog mood readings could serve to predict them. This kind of new predictive clue could hold the potential to make millions.

## INSPIRATION AND PERSPIRATION

*Genius is one percent inspiration, ninety-nine percent perspiration.*

—Thomas Edison

Eric and Karrie dug in to try this out. Eric pulled in the daily closing values of the Standard & Poor's (S&P) 500 (a popular index designed as a broad indicator of the U.S. stock market) for a span of several months in 2008 to see if its chaotic movement reflected the Anxiety Index values from the same time period. Could this idea possibly fall flat?

The validation of a mass mood barometer would be groundbreaking indeed, for data science, sociology, and psychology as well. But, breaking new ground is hazardous, and the forefront of research is a treacherous place to be. The territory is entirely new, so you could be an inch from greatness or nowhere at all, and you just don't know. As Karrie puts it, "We were out of our element—but if you want to do something new, you barely ever are in your element."

Demonstrating the Anxiety Index's efficacy proved tough. If you thought being the president's psychiatrist was rough, try taking on the entire world as your patient. At the outset, they thought it would take a month to show conclusive results, but numerous attempts failed. They met with expert colleagues across university departments and fields of study, including math, statistics, and economics. They spoke with Wall Street quants. But there was no established wisdom for the unmapped terrain they were traversing. Karrie says, "We were in the dark for quite a bit of time—there wasn't any existing accepted methodology."[2] After a year and a half of trials and tribulations, Eric and Karrie weren't there yet. They hadn't achieved results conclusive enough to justify publication.

There was a lot at stake, and Eric and Karrie were questioning the project's feasibility. The question of when to give up and cut their losses inevitably arose. Even if their broad theory held true, that mass mood *could* predict the stock market, did their Anxiety Index gauge the right emotional dynamic?

Then hope sprang anew. As they peered at a visual depiction of the data, a new tactic leaped out at them.

---

[2] The prior work most influential to Eric and Karrie's was a 2007 research paper by Paul Tetlock demonstrating that pessimism expressed in the *Wall Street Journal* provides novel predictive information about Dow returns. Their work moved from writings specifically about the market, which Tetlock analyzed, to blog writing in general.

# SIFTING THROUGH THE DATA DUMP

*One man's trash is another man's treasure.*

Before we delve into their discovery, let's put a broader context on Eric and Karrie's maneuver, the discovery of new value in the data avalanche.

By leveraging blogs in a new way, you could say Eric and Karrie's work makes hay of oversharing. People blog whatever the heck suits their fancy. If someone blogs, "I feel awesome today! Just wanted to share," you might assume it interests only the blogger's friends and family, and there's no value for the rest of the world. Such remarks just get thrown out there to an imaginary audience, like search for extraterrestrial intelligence (SETI) transmissions, scattered to oblivion in an attempt to reach nonhuman yet attentive ears, somewhere, someday, maybe, if they exist. Bloggers shout, unheard, into the void.

As with most applications of predictive analytics (PA), Eric and Karrie's system *repurposes data*. Whatever the intended purpose and target audience of the bloggers, they are delivering a wellspring of raw material that lies dormant, waiting to be reinterpreted by listening to it in a new way that uncovers new meaning and insight. It's as if data scientists are the intelligent aliens (personality jokes aside) we hoped for, successfully deciphering the human race's signals.

Repurposing data for PA signifies a mammoth new recycling initiative. Like millions of chicken feet the United States has realized it can sell to China rather than throw away, our phenomenal accumulation of 1's and 0's surprises us over and over with newfound applications. Calamari was originally considered junk, as was the basis for white chocolate. My mom, Lisa Schamberg, makes photographic art of compost, documenting the beauty inherent in organic waste. Mad scientists want to make use of nuclear waste. I can assure you, data scientists are just as mad.

Growing up watching *Sesame Street*, I got a kick out of the creature Oscar the Grouch, who lives in a garbage can and sings a song about how much he loves trash. It turns out Oscar isn't so crazy after all.

If blogs as a whole amount to large-scale, unregulated graffiti, so too do millions of encyclopedias' worth of organizational data scrawled onto magnetic media for miscellaneous operational functions. It's a zillion tons of human refuse that does not smell. What do ScarJo (Scarlett Johansson's unwitting nickname), Iceland, and borscht have in common with data? They're all beautiful things with unwelcoming names.

Most data is not accumulated for the purpose of prediction, but PA can learn from this massive recording of events in the same fashion that you can learn from your accumulation of life experience. As a simple example, take a company's record of your e-mail address and membership status—utilitarian yet also predictive. During one project, I found that users who signed up with an Earthlink.com e-mail address were almost five times more likely to convert from a free trial user level to the premium paid level than those with a Hotmail.com e-mail address. This could be because those who divulged their primary e-mail account were, on average, more committed to their trial membership. Whatever the reason, this kind of discovery helps a company predict who will be acquired as a paying customer.

Steve Martin put it this way, doing stand-up comedy back in the 1970s: "I've figured out a way to turn dog s—t into gold. So if you see me sniffing around down by your shoes, you'll know . . . It's. Gold. To. Me." Some so-called data dumps are more literal than you may imagine. Larry Smarr, director of a University of California–based research center, is tracking all bodily functions, including the scoop on poop, in order to form a working computational model of the body as an ecosystem. "Have you ever figured how information-rich your stool is? There are about 100 billion bacteria per gram. Each bacterium has DNA. . . . This means human stool has a data capacity of 100,000 terabytes of information stored per gram."

## THE INSTRUMENTATION OF EVERYTHING WE DO

*Count what is countable, measure what is measurable, and what is not measurable, make measurable.*
—Galileo

*Intangibles that appear to be completely intractable can be measured.*
—Douglas Hubbard, *How to Measure Anything*

Some historians assert that we are now experiencing the information revolution, following the agricultural and industrial revolutions. I buy it. Colin Shearer, a predictive analytics leader at IBM, eloquently states that the key to the information revolution is "the instrumentation of everything." More and more, each move you make, online and offline, is recorded, including transactions conducted, websites visited, movies watched, links clicked, friends called, opinions posted, dental procedures endured, sports games won (if you're a professional athlete), traffic cameras passed, flights taken, Wikipedia articles edited, and earthquakes experienced. Countless sensors deploy daily. Mobile devices, robots, and shipping containers record movement, interactions, inventory counts, and radiation levels. Personal health monitors watch your vital signs and exercise routine. The mass migration of online applications from your desktop up into the cloud (aka *software as a service*) makes even more of your computer use recordable by organizations.

Free public data is also busting out, so a wealth of knowledge sits at your fingertips. Following the *open data* movement, often embracing a not-for-profit philosophy, many data sets are available online from fields like biodiversity, business, cartography, chemistry, genomics, and medicine. Look at one central index, www.kdnuggets.com/datasets, and you'll see what amounts to lists of lists of data resources. The Federal Chief Information Officer of the United States launched Data.gov "to increase public access to high value, machine readable datasets generated by . . . the Government." Data.gov sports over 390,000 data sets, including data about marine casualties, pollution, active mines, earthquakes, and commercial flights. Its growth is prescribed: a directive in 2009 obliged all U.S. federal agencies to post at least three "high-value" data sets.

Far afield of government activities, a completely different accumulation of data answers the more forbidden question "Are you having *fun* yet?" For a dating website, I predicted occurrences of *online flirtation*. After all, as data shows, you're much more likely to be retained as a customer if you get some positive attention. When it comes to recording and predicting human behavior, what's more fundamental than our mating rituals? For this project, actions such as a virtual "wink," a message, or a request to connect as "friends" counted as "flirtatious." Working up a sort of digital tabloid magazine, I produced reports such as the average waiting times before a flirt is reciprocated, depending on the characteristics of the customer. For example:

| Sexual orientation: | Average hours before reciprocal flirt (if any): |
|---|---|
| Man seeking man | 40 |
| Woman seeking man | 33 |
| Man seeking woman | 43 |
| Woman seeking woman | 55 |

For your entertainment, here's an actual piece of code from a short 175-line computer program called "Flirtback" that I wrote (in the computer language AWK, an oldie but goodie):

```
sex = sexuality[flirt_to]; # sexual orientation
sumbysex[sex] += (delta/(60*60));
nPairsSex[sex]++
```

Come on, you have to admit that's some exciting stuff—enough to keep any computer programmer awake.

Data expresses the bare essence of human behavior. Digital encodings certainly don't capture the full dimension and innuendo of human experience—but that's okay. Organizations record the aspects of our actions important to their function, so one extraordinarily elusive, daunting task has already been completed in the production of raw materials for PA: abstracting the infinite complexity of everyday life and thereby defining which of its endless details are salient.

A new window on the world has opened. Professor Erik Brynjolfsson, an economist at Massachusetts Institute of Technology (MIT), compares this mass instrumentation of human behavior to another historic breakthrough in scientific observation. "The microscope, invented four centuries ago, allowed people to see and measure things as never before—at the cellular level," said the *New York Times*, explaining Brynjolfsson's perspective. "It was a revolution in measurement. Data measurement is the modern equivalent of the microscope." But rather than viewing things previously too small to see, now we view things previously too big.

## BATTEN DOWN THE HATCHES: T.M.I.

*You're not an iceberg, just a tip*
*So you can't rip the bottom off my ship*
> —From the song "Way Down Deep (You're Shallow)" by John Forster

*There are over 358 million trillion gallons of water on Earth.*
> —A TV advertisement for Ice Mountain Spring Water

*The world now contains more photographs than bricks.*
—John Szarkowski, Director of Photography, Museum of Modern Art (back in 1976)

All this tracking dumps upon us a data glut. The deluge of blogging that Eric and Karrie sought to leverage was just the tip of the iceberg—and what a tip it is. Six hundred blog posts are published per minute; by 2011, there were over 100 million blogs across WordPress and Tumblr alone. As for Twitter, "Every day, the world writes the equivalent of a 10-million-page book in Tweets or 8,163 copies of Leo Tolstoy's *War and Peace*," says the official Twitter blog. Stacking that many copies of the book "would reach the height of about 1,470 feet, nearly the ground-to-roof height of Taiwan's Taipei 101, the second tallest building in the world."

YouTube gains an hour of video each second. Estimates put the World Wide Web at over 8.32 billion web pages. Millions of online retail transactions take place every hour. More photos are taken daily than in the first 100 years of photography, more in two minutes than in all of the 1800s, with 200 million uploaded to Facebook every day. Femto-photography takes a trillion frames per second to capture light in motion and "see around corners." Four hundred million mobile devices capture usage statistics; by 2020 there will be 50 billion of them.

Making all this growth affordable, the cost of data storage is sinking like a rock. The cost per gigabyte on a hard drive has been exponentially decaying since the 1980s, when it approached $1 million. By 2010, it reached as low as 10 cents. We can afford to never delete.[3]

Government intelligence aims to archive vast portions of all communication. The U.S. National Security Agency's new $2 billion Utah Data Center, a facility five times the size of the U.S. Capitol, is designed to store mammoth archives of human interactions, including complete phone conversations and e-mail messages.

---

[3] When first released, Google's free e-mail service, Gmail, had no option to delete a message, only to archive it.

Scientific researchers are uncovering and capturing more and more data, and in so doing revolutionizing their own paradigms. Astronomers are building a new array of radio telescopes that will generate an exabyte of data per day (an exabyte is a quintillion bytes; a byte is a single value, an integer between 0 and 255, often representing a single letter, digit, or punctuation mark). Using satellites, wildlife conservationists track manta rays, considered vulnerable to extinction, as the creatures travel as far as 680 miles in search of food. In biology, as famed futurist Ray Kurzweil portends, given that the price to map a human genome has dropped from $1 billion to a few thousand dollars, information technology will prove to be the domain from which this field's greatest advances emerge.

Overall, data is growing at an incomprehensible speed, an estimated 2.5 quintillion bytes (exabytes) of data per day. A quintillion is a 1 with 18 zeros. In 1986, the data stored by computers, printed on double-sided paper, could have covered the Earth's land masses; by 2011, it could have done so with two layers of books.

The growth is exponential. Data more than doubles every three years. This will bring us to an estimated 8 zettabytes by 2015—that's 8,000,000,000,000,000,000,000 (21 zeros) bytes. Welcome to Big Bang 2.0.

The next logical question is: what's the most valuable thing to do with all this stuff? This book's answer: *Learn from it how to predict.*

## THE BIG BAD WOLF

*Good, better, best, bested. How do you like that for a declension, young man?*
—Edward Albee, *Who's Afraid of Virginia Woolf?*

Bow your head: the hot buzzword *big data* has ascended to royalty. It's in every news clip, every data science presentation, and every advertisement for analytics solutions. It's a crisis! It's an opportunity! It's a crisis of opportunity!

Big data does not exist. The elephant in the room is that there is no elephant in the room. What's exciting about data isn't how much of it there is, but how quickly it is growing. We're in a persistent state of awe at data's sheer quantity because of one thing that does not change: There's always so much more today than yesterday. Size is relative, not absolute. If we use the word *big* today, we'll quickly run out of adjectives: "big data," "bigger data," "even bigger data," and "biggest data." The International Conference on Very Large Databases has been running since 1975. We have a dearth of vocabulary with which to describe a wealth of data.

"Big data" is grammatically incorrect. It's like saying "big water." Rather, it should be "a lot of data" or "plenty of data."[4]

Size doesn't matter. It's the rate of expansion.

---

[4] Other buzzwords also have their issues. Calling this work *data science* is like calling a librarian a "book librarian." Calling it *data mining* is like calling gold mining "dirt mining."

# THE END OF THE RAINBOW

*The leg bone connected to the knee bone,*
*and the knee bone connected to the thigh bone,*
*and the thigh bone connected to the hip bone.*

—From the song "Dry Bones"

There's a ton of it—so what? What guarantees that all this residual rubbish, this by-product of organizational functions, holds value? It's no more than an extremely long list of observed events, an obsessive-compulsive enumeration of things that have happened.

The answer is simple. Everything is connected to everything else—if only indi-rectly—and this is reflected in data. For example:

- Your purchases relate to your shopping history, online behavior, and preferred payment method, and to the actions of your social contacts. Data reveals how to predict consumer behavior from these elements.
- Your health relates to your life choices and environment, and therefore data captures connections predictive of health based on type of neighborhood and household characteristics.
- Your job satisfaction relates to your salary, evaluations, and promotions, and data mirrors this reality.
- Financial behavior and human emotions are connected, so, as we'll reveal later in this chapter, data may reflect that relationship as well.

Data always speaks. It always has a story to tell, and there's always something to learn from it. Data scientists see this over and over again across PA projects. Pull some data together and, although you can never be certain what you'll find, you can be sure you'll discover valuable connections by decoding the language it speaks and listening. That's The Data Effect in a nutshell.

---

**The Data Effect:** *Data is always predictive.*

---

This is the assumption behind the leap of faith an organization takes when undertaking PA. Budgeting the staff and tools for a PA project requires this leap, knowing not what specifically will be discovered and yet trusting that something will be. Sitting on an expert panel at Predictive Analytics World, leading UK consultant Tom Khabaza put it this way: "Projects never fail due to lack of patterns." With The Data Effect in mind, the scientist rests easy.

Data is the new oil. It's this century's greatest possession and often considered an organization's most important strategic asset. Several thought leaders have dubbed it as such—"the new oil"—including European Consumer Commissioner Meglena Kuneva, who also calls it "the new currency of the digital world." It's not a hyperbole. In 2012,

Apple Inc. overtook Exxon Mobil Corporation, the world's largest oil company, as the most valuable publicly traded company in the world. Unlike oil, data is extremely easy to transport and cheap to store. It's a bigger geyser, and this one is never going to run out.

## PREDICTION JUICE

Prediction starts small. PA's building block is the *predictor variable*, a single value measured for each individual. For example, *recency*, the number of weeks since the last time an individual made a purchase, committed a crime, or exhibited a medical symptom, often reveals the chances he or she will do it again in the near term. In many arenas, it makes sense to begin with the most *recently* active people first, whether for marketing contact, criminal investigation, or clinical assessment.

Similarly, *frequency*—the number of times the individual has exhibited the behavior—is also a common, fruitful measure. People who have done something a lot are more likely to do it again.

In fact, it is usually what individuals *have done* that predicts what they *will do*. And so PA feeds on data that extends past dry yet essential demographics like location and gender to include *behavioral predictors* such as recency, frequency, purchases, financial activity, and product usage such as calls and web surfing. These behaviors are often the most valuable—it's always a *behavior* that we seek to predict, and indeed behavior predicts behavior. As Jean-Paul Sartre put it, "[A man's] true self is dictated by his actions."

PA builds its power by combining dozens—or even hundreds—of predictors. You give the machine everything you know about each individual, and let 'er rip. The core learning technology to combine these elements is where the real scientific magic takes place. That learning process is the topic of the next chapter; for now, let's look at some interesting individual predictors.

## FAR OUT, BIZARRE, AND SURPRISING INSIGHTS

Some predictors are more fun to talk about than others.

Are customers more profitable if they don't think? Does crime increase after a sporting event? Does hunger dramatically influence a judge's life-altering decisions? Do online daters more consistently rated as attractive receive *less* interest? Can promotions *increase* the chance you'll quit your job? Do vegetarians miss fewer flights? Does your e-mail address reveal your intentions?

Yes, yes, yes, yes, yes, yes, and yes!

Welcome to the "Ripley's Believe It or Not!" of data science. Poring over a potpourri of prospective predictors, PA's aim isn't only to assess human hunches by testing relationships that seem to make sense, but also to explore a boundless playing field of possible truths beyond the realms of intuition. And so, with The Data Effect in play, PA drops onto your desk connections that seem to defy logic. As strange, mystifying, or unexpected as they may seem, these discoveries help predict.

Here are some colorful discoveries, each pertaining to a single predictor variable:

## Bizarre and Surprising Insights—Consumer Behavior

| Insight | Organization | Suggested Explanation |
|---|---|---|
| **Guys literally drool over sports cars**. Male college student subjects produce measurably more saliva when presented with images of sports cars or money. | Northwestern University Kellogg School of Management | *Consumer impulses are physiological cousins of hunger.* |
| **If you buy diapers, you are more likely to also buy beer**. A pharmacy chain found this across 90 days of evening shopping across dozens of outlets (urban myth to some, but based on reported results). | Osco Drug | *Daddy needs a beer.* |
| **Dolls and candy bars**. Sixty percent of customers who buy a Barbie doll buy one of three types of candy bars. | Walmart | *Kids come along for errands.* |
| **Staplers reveal hires**. The purchase of a stapler often accompanies the purchase of paper, waste baskets, scissors, paper clips, folders, and so on. | A large retailer | *Stapler purchases are often a part of a complete office kit for a new employee.* |
| **Mac users book more expensive hotels**. Orbitz users on an Apple Mac spend up to 30 percent more than Windows users when booking a hotel reservation. Orbitz applies this insight, altering displayed options according to your operating system. | Orbitz | *Macs are often more expensive than Windows computers, so Mac users may on average have greater financial resources.* |
| **Your inclination to buy varies by time of day**. For retail websites, the peak is 8:00 PM; for dating, late at night; for finance, around 1:00 PM; for travel, just after 10:00 AM. This is not the amount of website traffic, but the propensity to buy of those who are already on the website. | Survey of websites | *The impetus to complete certain kinds of transactions is higher during certain times of day.* |
| **Your e-mail address reveals your level of commitment**. Customers who register for a free account with an Earthlink.com e-mail address are | An online dating website | *Disclosing permanent or primary e-mail accounts reveals a longer-term intention.* |

*(continued)*

## Bizarre and Surprising Insights—Consumer Behavior (*continued*)

| Insight | Organization | Suggested Explanation |
|---|---|---|
| almost five times more likely to convert to a paid, premium-level membership than those with a Hotmail.com e-mail address. | | |
| **Banner ads affect you more than you think**. Although you may feel you've learned to ignore them, people who see a merchant's banner ad are 61 percent more likely to subsequently perform a related search, and this drives a 249 percent increase in clicks on the merchant's paid textual ads in the search results. | Yahoo! | *Advertising exerts a subconscious effect.* |
| **Companies win by not prompting customers to think**. Contacting engaged customers can backfire— direct mailing financial service customers who have already opened several accounts *decreases* the chances they will open more accounts *(more details in Chapter 7)*. | U.S. Bank | *Customers who have already accumulated many credit accounts are susceptible to impulse buys (e.g., when they walk into a bank branch), but, when contacted at home, will respond by considering the decision and possibly researching competing products online. They would have been more likely to make the purchase if left to their own devices.* |
| **Your web browsing reveals your intentions**. Wireless customers who check online when their contract period ends are more likely to defect to a competing cell phone company. | A major North American wireless carrier | *Adverse to early termination fees, those intending to switch carriers remind themselves when they'll be free to change over.* |
| **Friends stick to the same cell phone company (a social effect)**. If you switch wireless carriers, your contacts are in turn up to seven times more likely to follow suit. | A major North American wireless carrier; Optus (Australian telecom) saw a similar effect. | *People experience social influence and/or heed financial incentives for in-network calling.* |

## Bizarre and Surprising Insights—Finance and Insurance

| Insight | Organization | Suggested Explanation |
| --- | --- | --- |
| **Low credit rating, more car accidents**. If your credit score is higher, car insurance companies will lower your premium, since you are a lower driving risk. People with poor credit ratings are charged more for car insurance. In fact, a low credit score can increase your premium more than an at-fault car accident; missing two payments can as much as double your premium. | Automobile insurers | *"Research indicates that people who manage their personal finances responsibly tend to manage other important aspects of their life with that same level of responsibility, and that would include being responsible behind the wheel of their car," Donald Hanson of the National Association of Independent Insurers theorizes.* |
| **Your shopping habits foretell your reliability as a debtor**. If you use your credit card at a drinking establishment, you're a greater risk to miss credit card payments; at the dentist, lower risk; buy cheap, generic rather than name-brand automotive oil, greater risk; buy felt pads that affix to chair legs to protect the floor, lower risk. | Canadian Tire (a major retail and financial services company) | *More cautionary activity such as seeing the dentist reflects a more conservative or well-planned lifestyle.* |
| **Small businesses' credit risk depends on the owner's behavior as a *consumer***. Unlike business loans in general, when it comes to a small business, consumer-level data about the owner is more predictive of credit risk performance than business-level data (and combining both data sources is best of all). | Creditors to the leasing industry | *A small business's behavior largely reflects the choices and habits of one individual: the owner.* |

## Bizarre and Surprising Insights—Healthcare

| Insight | Organization | Suggested Explanation |
|---|---|---|
| **Genetics foretell cheating wives**. Within a certain genetic cluster, having more genes shared by a heterosexual couple means more infidelity by the female. | University of New Mexico | *We're programmed to avoid inbreeding, since there are benefits to genetic diversity.* |
| **Retirement is bad for your health**. For a certain working category of males in Austria, each additional year of early retirement decreases life expectancy by 1.8 months. | University of Zurich | *Unhealthy habits such as smoking and drinking follow retirement. Malcolm Forbes said, "Retirement kills more people than hard work ever did."* |
| **Google search trends predict disease outbreaks**. Certain searches for flu-related information provide insight into current trends in the spread of the influenza virus. | Google Flu Trends | *People with symptoms or in the vicinity of others with symptoms seek further information.* |
| **Smokers suffer less from repetitive motion disorder**. In certain work environments, people who smoke cigarettes are less likely to develop carpal tunnel syndrome. | A major metropolitan newspaper, conducting research on its own staff's health | *Smokers take more breaks.* |
| **Positive health habits are contagious (a social effect)**. If you quit smoking, your close contacts become 36 percent less likely to smoke. Your chance of becoming obese increases by 57 percent if you have a friend who becomes obese. | Research institutions | *People are strongly influenced by their social environment.* |
| **Happiness is contagious (a social effect)**. Each additional Facebook friend who is happy increases your chances of being happy by roughly 9 percent. | Harvard University | *"Waves of happiness . . . spread throughout the network."* |
| **Knee surgery choices make a big difference**. After ACL- | Medical research institutions in Sweden | *The patellar ligament runs across your kneecap, so grafting from* |

## Bizarre and Surprising Insights—Healthcare (*continued*)

| Insight | Organization | Suggested Explanation |
|---|---|---|
| reconstruction knee surgery, knee-walking was rated "difficult or impossible" by twice as many patients who donated their own patellar tissue as a graft source rather than hamstring tissue. | | *it causes injury in that location.* |
| **Music expedites poststroke recovery and improves mood**. Stroke patients who listen to music for a couple of hours a day more greatly improve their verbal memory and attention span and improve their mood, as measured by a psychological test. | Cognitive Brain Research Unit, Department of Psychology, University of Helsinki, and Helsinki Brain Research Centre, Finland | *"Music listening activates a widespread bilateral network of brain regions related to attention, semantic processing, memory, motor functions, and emotional processing."* |
| **Yoga improves your mood**. Long-term yoga practitioners showed benefits in a psychological test for mood in comparison to non–yoga practitioners, including a higher "Vigor" score. | Research institutions in Japan | *Yoga is designed for, and practiced with the intent for, the attainment of tranquility.* |

## Bizarre and Surprising Insights—Crime and Law Enforcement

| Insight | Organization | Suggested Explanation |
|---|---|---|
| **Suicide bombers do not buy life insurance**. An analysis of bank data of suspected terrorists revealed a propensity to not hold a life insurance policy. | A large UK bank | *Suicide nullifies a life insurance policy.* |
| **Unlike lightning, crime strikes twice**. Crime is more likely to repeat nearby, spreading like earthquake aftershocks. | Departments of math, computer science, statistics, criminology, and law in California universities | *Perpetrators "repeatedly attack clusters of nearby targets because local vulnerabilities are well known to the offenders."* |

(*continued*)

## Bizarre and Surprising Insights—Crime and Law Enforcement (*continued*)

| Insight | Organization | Suggested Explanation |
|---|---|---|
| **Crime rises with public sporting events**. College football upset losses correspond to a 112 percent increase in assaults. | University of Colorado | *Psychological theories of fan aggression are offered.* |
| **Crime rises after elections**. In India, crime is lower during an election year and rises soon after elections. | Researchers in India | *Incumbent politicians crack down on crime more forcefully when running for reelection.* |
| **Phone card sales predict danger in the Congo**. Impending massacres in the Congo are presaged by spikes in the sale of prepaid phone cards. | CellTel (African telecom) | *Prepaid cards denominated in U.S. dollars serve as in-pocket security against inflation for people "sensing impending chaos."* |
| **Hungry judges rule negatively**. Judicial parole decisions immediately after a food break are about 65 percent favorable, which then drops gradually to almost zero percent before the next break. If the judges are hungry, you are more likely to stay in prison. | Columbia University and Ben Gurion University (Israel) | *Hunger and/or fatigue leave decision makers feeling less forgiving.* |

## Bizarre and Surprising Insights—Miscellaneous

| Insight | Organization | Suggested Explanation |
|---|---|---|
| **Music taste predicts political affiliation**. Kenny Chesney and George Strait fans are most likely conservative, Rihanna and Jay-Z fans liberal. Republicans can be more accurately predicted by music preferences than Democrats because they display slightly less diversity in music taste. Metal fans can go either way, spanning the political spectrum. | The Echo Nest (a music data company) | *Personality types entail certain predilections in both musical and political preferences (this is the author's hypothesis; the researchers do not offer a hypothesis).* |

## Bizarre and Surprising Insights—Miscellaneous (*continued*)

| Insight | Organization | Suggested Explanation |
| --- | --- | --- |
| **Online dating: Be cool and unreligious to succeed**. Online dating messages that initiate first contact and include the word *awesome* are more than twice as likely to elicit a response as those with *sexy*. Messages with "your pretty" get fewer responses than those with "you're pretty." "Howdy" is better than "Hey." "Band" does better than "literature" and "video games." "Atheist" far surpasses most major religions, but "Zeus" is even better. | OkCupid (online dating website) | *There is value in avoiding the overused or trite; video games are not a strong aphrodisiac.* |
| **Hot or not? People consistently considered attractive get *less* attention**. Online daters rated with a higher variance of attractiveness ratings receive more messages than others with the same average rating but less variance. A greater range of opinions—more disagreement on looks—results in receiving more contact. | OkCupid | *People often feel they don't have a chance with someone who appears universally attractive. When less competition is expected, there is more incentive to initiate contact.* |
| **A job promotion can lead to quitting**. In one division of HP, promotions increase the risk an employee will leave, unless accompanied by sufficient increases in compensation; promotions without raises hurt more than help. | Hewlett-Packard | *Increased responsibilities are perceived as burdensome if not financially rewarded.* |
| **Vegetarians miss fewer flights**. Airline customers who preorder a vegetarian meal are more likely to make their flight. | An airline | *The knowledge of a personalized or specific meal awaiting the customer provides an incentive or establishes a sense of commitment.* |
| **A photo's quality is predictable from its caption**. Even without looking at the picture itself, key words from its caption foretell whether a human | Not available | *Certain events and locations are conducive to or provide incentive for capturing more picturesque photos.* |

(*continued*)

## Bizarre and Surprising Insights—Miscellaneous (*continued*)

| Insight | Organization | Suggested Explanation |
|---|---|---|
| would subjectively rate the photo as "good." The words *Peru*, *tombs*, *trails*, and *boats* corresponded with better photos, whereas the words *graduation* and *CEO* tend to appear with lower-quality photos. | | |
| **Men on the *Titanic* faced much greater risk than women**. A woman on the *Titanic* was almost four times as likely to survive as a man. Most men died and most women lived. | Miscellaneous researchers | *Priority for access to life boats was given to women.* |
| **Solo rockers die younger than those in bands**. Although all rock stars face higher risk, solo rock stars suffer twice the risk of early death as rock band members. | Public health offices in the UK | *Band members benefit from peer support and solo artists exhibit even riskier behaviour.* |

# CORRELATION DOES NOT IMPLY CAUSATION

*Satisfaction came in the chain reaction.*

—From the song "Disco Inferno," by The Trammps

The preceding tables, packed with fun-filled facts, do not explain a single thing.

Take note, the third column is headed "*Suggested* Explanation." The left column's discoveries are real, validated by data, but the reasons behind them are unknown. Every explanation put forth, each entry in the rightmost column, is pure conjecture with absolutely no hard facts to back it up.

The dilemma is, as it is often said, *correlation does not imply causation*.[5] The discovery of a predictive relationship between A and B does not mean one causes the other, not even indirectly. No way, nohow.

Consider this: Increased ice cream sales correspond with increased shark attacks. Why do you think that is? A causal explanation could be that eating ice cream makes us taste better to sharks:

---

[5] The Latin phrase *Post hoc, ergo propter hoc* ("After this, therefore because of this") is another common expression that references the issue at hand; it refers to the unwarranted act of concluding a causal relationship.

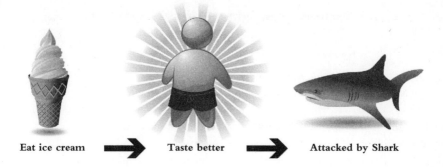

Eat ice cream → Taste better → Attacked by Shark

But another explanation is that, rather than one being caused by the other, they are both caused by the same thing. On cold days, people eat less ice cream and also swim less; on warm days, they do the opposite:

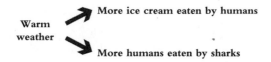

Warm weather
→ More ice cream eaten by humans
→ More humans eaten by sharks

Take the example of smokers getting less carpal tunnel syndrome, from the table of healthcare examples. One explanation is that smokers take more breaks:

Smoke → Take more breaks → Less carpal tunnel

But another could be that there's a mysterious chemical in your bloodstream that influences both things:

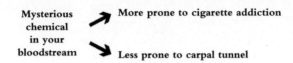

I totally made that up. But the truth is that finding the connection between smoking and carpal tunnel syndrome in and of itself provides no evidence that one explanation is more likely than the other. With this in mind, take another look through the tables. The same rule applies to each example. We know the *what*, but we don't know the *why*.[6]

When applying PA, we usually don't know about causation, and we often don't necessarily care. For many PA projects, the objective is more to predict than it is to understand the world and figure out what makes it tick.

Causality is elusive, tough to nail down. We naturally assume things do influence one another in some way, and we conceive of these effects in physical, chemical, medical, financial, or psychological terms. The noble scientists in these fields have their work cut out for them as they work to establish and characterize causal links.

In this way, data scientists have it easier with PA. It just needs to work; prediction trumps explanation. PA operates with extreme solution-oriented intent. The whole point, the "ka-ching" of value, comes in driving decisions from many individual predictions, one per patient, customer, or person of any kind. And while PA often delivers meaningful insights akin to those of various social sciences, this is usually a side effect, not the primary objective.

This makes PA a kind of "metascience" that transcends the taxonomy of natural and social sciences, abstracting across them by learning from any and all data sources that would typically serve biology, criminology, economics, education, epidemiology, medicine, political science, psychology, or sociology. PA's mission is to engineer solutions. As for the data employed and the insights gained, the tactic in play is: "Whatever works."

And yet even hard-nosed scientists fight the urge to overexplain. It's human nature, but it's dangerous. It's the difference between good science and bad science.

Stein Kretsinger, Founding Executive of Advertising.com and a director at Elder Research, tells a classic story of our overly interpretive minds. In the early 1990s, as a graduate student, Stein was leading a medical research meeting, assessing the factors that determine how long it takes to wean off a respirator. As this was before the advent

---

[6] If you add a dash of math to a diagram like those just presented and those below that have arrows indicating causal influence, you get a Bayes Network. It's a form of predictive model that can be trained over data to quantify the strength of each arrow's influence, and can also incorporate human hunches about causation on those connecting arrows where data is not available.

of PowerPoint projection, Stein displayed the factors, one at a time, via graphs on overhead transparencies. The team of healthcare experts nodded their heads, offering one explanation after another for the relationships shown in the data. After going through a few, though, Stein realized he'd been placing the transparencies with the wrong side up, thus projecting mirror images that depicted the *opposite* of the true relationships. After he flipped them to the correct side, the experts seemed just as comfortable as before, offering new explanations for what was now the very opposite effect of each factor. Our thinking is malleable—people readily find underlying theories to explain just about anything.

In another case, a published medical study discovered that women who happened to be receiving hormone replacement therapy showed a lower incidence of coronary heart disease. Could it be that a new treatment for this disease had been discovered?

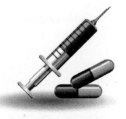 

**Receive hormone**        **Less likely to develop**
**replacement therapy**    **coronary heart disease**

Later, a proper control experiment disproved this false conclusion. Instead, the currently held explanation is that more affluent women had access to the hormone replacement therapy, and these same women had better health habits overall:

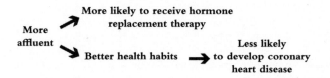

More
affluent

**More likely to receive hormone**
**replacement therapy**

**Better health habits → Less likely**
**to develop coronary**
**heart disease**

Prematurely jumping to conclusions about causality is bad science that leads to bad medical treatment. This kind of research snafu is not an isolated case. According to the *Wall Street Journal*, the number of retracted journal publications has surged in recent years.

But, in this arena, the line between apt and inept sometimes blurs. Twenty years ago while in graduate school I befriended a colleague, a chain smoker who was nevertheless brilliant with the mathematics behind probability theory. He would hang you out to dry if you attempted to criticize his bad smoking habit on the basis of clinical studies. "Smoking studies have no control group," he'd snap.[7] He was questioning the common causal conclusion:

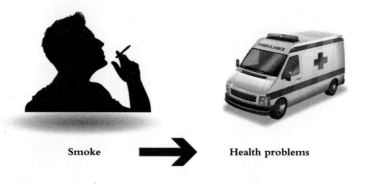

One day in front of the computer science building, as I kept my distance from his cloud of smoke, he drove this point home. New to the study of probability, I suddenly realized what he was saying and, looking at him incredulously, asked, "You mean to say that it's possible smoking studies actually reflect that stupid people smoke, and that these people also do other stupid things, and only those other things poorly affect their health?" By this logic, I had been stupid for not considering him quite possibly both stupid and healthy.

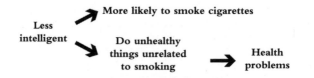

He exhaled a lungful of smoke triumphantly as if he'd won the argument and said with no irony, "Yes!" The same position had also been espoused in the 1950s by an early founder of modern statistics, Ronald Fisher. He was a pipe-smoking curmudgeon who attacked the government-supported publicity about tobacco risks, calling it egregious fearmongering.

---

[7] This is because it's not reasonable to instruct one clinical group to smoke, nor to expect another to uniformly resist smoking. To statistically prove in this way that something kills, you would need to kill some people.

In addressing the effects of tobacco, renowned healthcare statistician David Salsburg wrote that the very meaning of cause and effect is "a deep philosophical problem . . . that gnaws at the heart of scientific thought." Due in part to our understanding of how inhaled agents actively lead to genetic mutations that create cancerous cells, we as a society have defaulted to a collective belief that cigarettes are causal in their connection to cancer. I would say this is probably a reasonable position. While I implore scientists not to overinterpret results, I also implore you not to smoke.

## THE CAUSE AND EFFECT OF EMOTIONS

*Art is not a mirror with which to reflect reality, but a hammer with which to shape it.*
—Bertolt Brecht

*The heart has its reasons which reason knows nothing of . . . We know the truth not only by the reason, but by the heart.*
—Blaise Pascal

Eric Gilbert and Karrie Karahalios's efforts to validate their blog-based measure of mass emotions transcended the whole causality question. "We clearly aren't testing true causation," they wrote in a research publication. They didn't need to establish causality for vindication—they needed only to demonstrate some sort of relationship between the daily movements of their emotions barometer and the stock market's ups and downs. This would prove that their massive mood meter reflected objective reality, and rule out the possibility it was a purely arbitrary formulation.

Eric and Karrie broke protocol by searching for such an abstractly linked connection. As research normally goes, it's unusual to test for a correlation between two things without a more concrete hypothesis on how they *could* be causally related. One critic complained that their work "posited no plausible mechanism for [the correlation] to be true."

Having moved from the psychology of an individual to the emotional dynamics of an entire population, we're left with a great big mess of possible causal relationships. Does art reflect reality, or is it the other way around? Do blogs reflect phenomena in the world, or do they catalyze phenomena? How do emotions escalate within a population? Is there some kind of emotional ripple effect through the crowd? Speaking on group psychology, Freud said, "The most remarkable and also the most important result of the formation of a group is the 'exaltation or intensification of emotion' produced in every member of it." Verifying this phenomenon, research in 2008 from Harvard and other institutions has shown that happiness spreads contagiously on social networks.

Could it be that the fear expressed in blogs subsequently also affects the stock market?

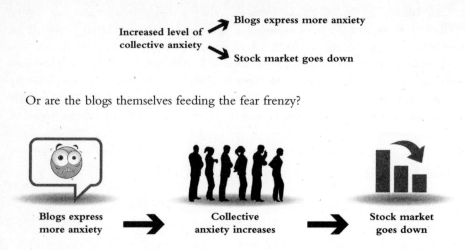

Or are the blogs themselves feeding the fear frenzy?

Eric and Karrie's research effort featured no favored hypothesis. This is in contrast, for example, to the connection between smoking and cancer. When examining the possible effects of smoking, there is a much more focused arena in which causality is hypothesized and investigated: an element is inhaled into an individual person's body, leading to events that take place within that body.

Despite the intractable complexity of group psychology and emotions, Eric and Karrie's work was guided by the broad hypothesis that, per Alan Greenspan's sage insight, anxiety is the antithesis of a booming economy. On an anxious day, an investor may be more prone to defend against chaos by cashing out; but, when more cool, confident, and calm, the investor could be more willing to take the risk of buying. More buying means higher stock prices, so the S&P 500 rises.

But, in a way, not knowing how it all really works is the charm. We live in this universe believing it embodies a complex network of causal links between emotions and actions, and between people themselves, the holders of emotion and takers of action. The Data Effect tells us these causative relationships will manifest one way or another so we'll find predictive insights in the data.

As the results of their analysis rolled in, other members of Karrie's research group joked around, playing on tempting causal relationships they knew were unlikely to hold true. "Let's blog about puppies and kittens all day long to help improve the stock market!"

## A Picture Is Worth a Thousand Diamonds

*Pressure makes diamonds.*

—General George S. Patton

*A kiss on the hand may be quite continental, but diamonds are a girl's best friend.*

—Leo Robin (from *Gentlemen Prefer Blondes*)

Eric and Karrie suffered through endless explorations. There were too many things to try. If a public anxiety barometer did indeed predict the stock market, how far ahead would it be—how many days did it take for public anxiety to make an economic impact? Should they check for an effect one day later, or one month? Should they look to predict the direction in which the market was moving, its absolute value, its trading volume, or what? Preliminary insights tantalized the researchers, but they hadn't nailed it. The results weren't strong enough to justify drawing conclusions.

The turning point came when they made a discovery by way of visualization. A picture lets you harness the power of your eyeballs to detect possibly predictive patterns. Consider this visual snapshot of the Anxiety Index against the S&P 500:

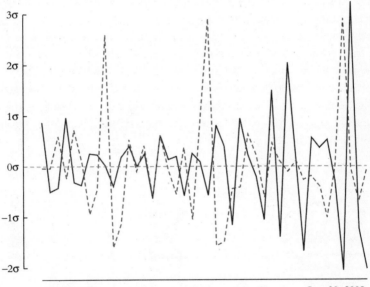

**Diamond-shaped patterns emerge in the juxtaposition of the Anxiety Index (dashed line) with a measure of S&P 500 behavior (solid line). The Anxiety Index is lagged by two days. Figure reproduced with permission.**[8]

---

[8] Eric Gilbert and Karrie Karahalios, "Widespread Worry and the Stock Market," *Proceedings of the Fourth International AAAI Conference on Weblogs and Social Media*, 2010.

The two lines are largely opposites, resulting in many *diamond-shaped patterns*. The diamond shapes appear because one line goes up while the other goes down, mirroring each other. This opposition is the hallmark of predictiveness for two reasons:

1. The Anxiety Index, which is the dashed line, goes up when the S&P 500 is showing a negative effect. "High anxiety negatively affects the market," Eric and Karrie wrote.
2. In this image, *the Anxiety Index's dashed line is shifted by two days*, so its movement is actually taking place two days before a subsequent opposite effect on the S&P 500, *foreshadowing* the market's trend. It's predictive.

By shifting the relative time frames of the overlapping plots and adjusting other settings, Eric and Karrie could visually scan many such images in search of diamond shapes that might reveal predictive patterns. As you can see, the diamond pattern is not uniformly perfect across the image, but the tendency for the two lines to oppose one another could mean prediction is possible.

Correctly interpreting emotion was a key adjustment in the formation of these diamonds. In particular, *emotional intensity is relative*. It's the *change* in intensity that tells us something. Rather than tracking the absolute level of anxiety, the Anxiety Index depicted in the figure above measures how quickly overall anxiety is *changing* from one day to the next. It's a positive value when blogger anxiety is increasing, and a negative value when blogger anxiety is decreasing. The Anxiety Index is calculated from counts of anxious and nonanxious posts:[9]

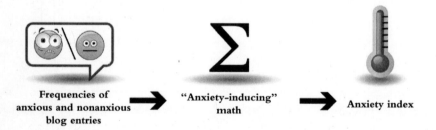

Frequencies of anxious and nonanxious blog entries → "Anxiety-inducing" math → Anxiety index

Diamonds aren't only "a girl's best friend"—data miners like digging them up, too.

---

[9] Calculating the Anxiety Index involves, to some, "anxiety-inducing" mathematics because it has logarithms in it. But the concept is simple: it reports the change in prevalence of anxious blog posts from one day to the next.

# VALIDATING FEELINGS AND FEELING VALIDATED

*The thrill of victory . . . and the agony of defeat.*

—ABC's Wide World of Sports, 1961–1998

Eyeballing helps hone the hypothesis, but it isn't proof. Eric and Karrie's next step was to "formally test the relationship between the anxiety, fear, and worry . . . and the stock market." They calculated the Anxiety Index for 174 stock market trading days in 2008, across a total of more than 20 million blog posts on LiveJournal, and pooled these alongside measurements of S&P 500 activity for the same days. They then applied a statistical test for predictive relationships developed by a winner of the Nobel Prize in economics, Clive Granger.

It worked! The study showed that the public's mood is predictive of the stock market. Eric and Karrie excitedly wrote for a conference paper, "Increases in expressions of anxiety . . . predict downward pressure on the S&P 500."

The statistical test concluded that the Anxiety Index "has novel predictive information about the stock market." This novelty tells us the Anxiety Index is wholly new, unique, and precious: it helps foretell more of future market behavior than can be ascertained by analyzing the market alone. Novelty is proven by showing that the capacity for recent market activity to predict future market activity is improved upon by also including recent Anxiety Index values to help predict.[10]

This discovery broke ground as *the first established relationship between mass mood and the economy*. The breakthrough is arguably even broader, pioneering the scientific connection between the emotional state of a vast group and a measurable behavior of that group. The work is the first to validate a measure of mass emotions from unpolled, spontaneous human behavior, outside the lab and in our real-world natural habitat.[11]

Eric, Karrie, and their colleagues celebrated their achievement, reaping the rewards of publishing and career boosting. In the weekly meeting of Karrie's research group, she says, "The energy was, like, amazing. Everyone realized this was big." The project served as part of Eric's doctoral thesis, and was integral to landing him a tenure-track professorship at Georgia Tech. "I'm deliriously excited to join their faculty," he emotionally blogged. "It's like getting picked to open for the Stones, in 1967." In this new role, he has secured prestigious government research grants and a Google faculty fellowship.

Emotion is the goose that lays the golden eggs, hatching stock market movement— but not the other way around. There's no chicken-and-egg cycle to be found. When Eric and Karrie tested for the opposite predictive effect, that the market predicts mass mood,

---

[10] Rather than predicting whether the S&P 500 will go up or down, this work predicts the change in rate of the S&P 500—that is, acceleration (or deceleration, if it is a negative number). Thus, as the researchers put it, the results "indicate that anxiety slows a market climb and accelerates a drop." This acceleration metric is depicted as the solid line in the "diamonds" figure.

[11] When it comes to the field of social computing, blogging at one's computer does indeed count as "natural habitat."

no dice. They couldn't establish anything conclusive. Perhaps the economy is only one of many factors that determine people's feelings, while, conversely, emotions constitute a major factor influencing economic activities. It appears to be a one-way street.

## SERENDIPITY AND INNOVATION

*The most exciting phrase to hear in science, the one that heralds new discoveries, is not "Eureka!" but rather "Hmm . . . that's funny . . ."*

—Isaac Asimov

If necessity is the mother of invention, serendipity is its daddy. It was only by happy accident that Alexander Fleming happened upon the potent effects of penicillin, by noticing that an old bacteria culture he was about to clean up happened to be contaminated with some mold—which was successfully killing it.

Minoxidil, the popular baldness treatment often marketed as Rogaine, was originally developed to treat blood pressure until extraneous hair growth was noticed as a surprising side effect.

By its very design, PA fosters serendipity. Predictive modeling conducts a broad, exploratory analysis, testing many predictors, and in so doing uncovers surprising findings, such as vegetarians being less likely to miss flights and other such predictive results listed in the tables earlier in this chapter.

Sometimes you stumble onto a million-dollar discovery just by preparing data for PA. Why? Unless you start to dig around, a plethora of wins and losses can remain hidden below the surface. One time, I was sifting and organizing an online service's data in preparation to predict which customers would intentionally cancel their subscriptions. Along the way I noticed a major leak in the boat. Tons of customers were involuntarily canceling due to credit card failures on their monthly or quarterly membership dues. One processing error message arose for many of these cases: "Hold—call center." This meant the merchant should keep holding the credit card and call in to see if the payment's authorization could be completed with some additional steps. Since the transactions were automatic—no merchant was physically holding a card—these customers just slipped through the cracks and were lost. As I advised the client, a process to help recover these cases could amount to an estimated $1 million in annual revenue.

Eric and Karrie's results spawned a flurry of research into the ability to predict by reading mass mood from social media such as blogs, Twitter, and Facebook. By tapping the public's mood and opinions, they're trying to predict it all:

- Product sales.
- Top music hits.
- Movie box-office revenue.
- Academy Award and Grammy winners.

- Elections.
- Unemployment statistics.
- The stock market.

Social media–based prediction quickly became a rich new fad, ripe for more investigation and very much in vogue across research labs and hedge funds alike. While research papers commonly bear rather arcane titles, this frenzy spawns many titles that read like newspaper headlines, such as "Predicting the Future with Social Media," "Can Facebook Predict Stock Market Activity?" and "Widespread Worry and the Stock Market" (the paper described in this chapter).

## INVESTMENT ADVICE FROM THE BLOGOSPHERE

When Karrie received her doctorate from MIT, around half of her graduating class had gone to Wall Street. But, when beginning this project, Karrie experienced some hesitancy to embark on research that could be seen as an attempt to play the market. The financial and academic worlds are cultural opposites. Wall Street displays a powerful entrepreneurial vibe that seems to usurp the pure scientific motives that drive an academic researcher. Karrie was, after all, advising Eric within a more erudite field of research, *social computing*, the examination of human social behavior within a computer science framework. People's behaviors are observed on computer networks, and computation serves to analyze that behavior. You can think of it as *electronic sociology*.

This shift of focus to analyzing social behavior is a sign of the times. Computer science is witnessing a twist of fate: The field has often been viewed as a particularly "unsocial science." But Karrie was struck with just the opposite revelation during her formative years as a fledgling researcher in 1993, while working on hardware in an MIT research lab. "I noticed that most of the bits passing through the network were not for sharing scientific research, the purpose for which the Internet had been built, but rather for social interactions unrelated to research."[12]

Eric and Karrie's work was well received among colleagues across university departments. But, with a lingering financial application, the mode of research threatened to change from a quest for insights to the engineering of moneymaking capabilities. Beyond an endeavor in social science, it now promised to act as applied science, serving black box trading. They perceived less enthusiasm from within the

---

[12] Computer science is actually more a "soft" science, like the social sciences, than it might have you believe. It's a catch-all for anything to do with computers, including how to try to make them "smart" (artificial intelligence), how to organize computer programs (project management topics), how to build them (a discipline of engineering), and the theory of what they can and can't do (advanced math—this part definitely counts as "hard" science). So why not also form the field "toaster science," covering how to build better toasters, as well as the culinary arts behind making the best use of them? It is said that "hard" sciences don't include *science* in their name (e.g., physics and chemistry).

social computing community than they had anticipated. It was a kind of confusion and culture clash. Most often, the first reaction they encountered was: "If this is your interest, why aren't you going off to try and make money?"

Does financial prediction have a place in the world of pure scientific research? Scientists might ask if it would be better to predict mood as an end unto itself, applying the work to try to actively improve mass mood and make the world a happier place. Does crossing into the financial realm trigger an abominable financial wanderlust that inevitably destines all scientists to chase rainbows? Chasing emotions to pursue money to make you happy—it sounds like chasing one's tail. After all, a rainbow is actually a full circle, when you can see the whole thing.

Nah, it's okay. Science and money must learn to coexist.

## MONEY MAKES THE WORLD GO 'ROUND

As it turned out, most of the inquiries Eric and Karrie received regarding this work were not from academic researchers, but from people working at—or wanting to start—hedge funds. Stock market traders hovered and salivated. Some pounced on the discovery, building and expanding upon it.

There's a growing consensus that interpreting the sentiment and intent behind the online written word—including blog entries and beyond—will become a fundamental component of trading analysis alongside standard economic gauges. Randy Saaf, the CEO of a small pioneering investment firm called AlphaGenius, presented on this very idea in early 2012 at Text Analytics World in San Francisco. "We see 'sentiment' as a diversified asset class like foreign markets, bonds, [and] gold." AlphaGenius "looks at thousands of tweets and Internet posts and decides if a security gets a buy or sell signal. If the signals point a security in a direction over a threshold, we make a trade." Another hedge fund, Derwent Capital Markets, publicizes its moves on this front, and Dutch firm SNTMNT ("sentiment") provides an API to enable any party to trade based on public sentiment as expressed on Twitter. "There are a lot of smart people (quietly) trading on textual sentiment of the news and tweets," financial trading and predictive analytics expert Ben Gimpert told me in an e-mail.

The truth is, there's not yet publicly known, conclusive proof that mass mood can predict well enough to make a killing in the stock market. The Anxiety Index's predictive power has been demonstrated across 2008—a particularly emotional year when it comes to finance, since the economy sank so dramatically. It may be that, during other years, there is proportionately much less emotional blogging connected to the market. Established success by hedge funds, if any, isn't made public in detail.[13]

---

[13] Research publications subsequent to Eric and Karrie's have made bold "gold rush" noises of predicting the market with high accuracy, but these claims have been subjected to scientific scrutiny and skepticism that question the strength of their conclusions.

Uncovered patterns do not solemnly swear to continue. Just as firms offering an investment opportunity repeatedly warn, "Past performance is no guarantee of future results," so too is there never 100 percent certainty that a historical pattern will persist. Statistics consultant Ben Bullard at Elder Research spelled it out: "In research, since we may have limited data but many ideas to try out, we often run the risk of stumbling upon a correlation only by chance—one that's not 'real' and won't continue to hold in the future."

Case in point, in the next chapter, which addresses the question "How can we trust what the computer claims to have learned?," we'll see research that searches and "re-searches" too far and wide, eventually unearthing a cockamamie relationship between dairy products in Bangladesh and the U.S. stock market!

With this risk of false discoveries in mind—although an expert in black box trading—Ben is "initially skeptical of virtually any attempt to predict the stock market." But he does find Eric and Karrie's work "particularly novel and interesting, and worthy of further investigation."

Leaving no stone unturned, the financial world aggressively hunts for any novel source of predictive information. The fact that "emotional data" is unusual speaks to its potential. Only if a new indicator is both predictive and substantially different from data sources already in play can it improve prediction. A new edge could be worth millions.[14]

## PUTTING IT ALL TOGETHER

The Anxiety Index is but one example of an unbridled trend: Exploding quantities of increasingly diverse data are springing forth, and organizations are innovating to turn all this unprocessed sap into maple syrup. As with all sources of data, to leverage its predictive potential, the mood barometer must be combined with other data sources. Predictive analytics is the mixing bowl into which raw materials must be poured so they can jointly improve decision making.

To make this work, there's one central scientific challenge: how to deftly and intricately combine the data streams to improve prediction. You can't just stir the bowl with a big spoon. You need an apparatus that learns from the data itself how best to mix and combine it. The next chapter shows you how it's done.

---

[14] On the other hand, the world's awareness of this research's discovery could hinder its potential. As Eric and Karrie wrote, "Even the publication of this very paper may nullify its impact."

# CHAPTER 4

# The Machine That Learns

## *A Look Inside Chase's Prediction of Mortgage Risk*

*What form of risk has the perfect disguise? How does prediction transform risk to opportunity? What should all businesses learn from insurance companies? Why does machine learning require art in addition to science? What kind of predictive model can be understood by everyone? How can we confidently trust a machine's predictions? Why couldn't prediction prevent the global financial crisis?*

This is a love story about a man named Dan and a bank named Chase, and how they learned to persevere against all odds—more precisely, how they deployed *machine learning* to empower prediction, which in turn mitigates risk. Exploring this story, we'll uncover how machine learning really works under the hood.[1]

## BOY MEETS BANK

Once upon a time, a scientist named Dan Steinberg received a phone call because the largest U.S. bank faced new levels of risk. To manage risk, they were prepared to place their bets on this man of machine learning.

'Twas a fortuitous engagement, as Dan had just the right means and method to assist the bank. An entrepreneurial scientist, he had built a commercial predictive analytics system that delivered leading research from the lab into corporate hands. The bank held as dowry electronic plunder: endless rows of 1's and 0's that recorded its learning experience.

The bank had the fuel, and Dan had the machine. It was a match made in heaven. Daydreaming, I often doodle in the margins:

---

[1] Further technical details for the Chase case study are available in a 2005 conference presentation referenced in this chapter's Notes.

Data + Machine Learning = ♥ ︱A

true love always

A more adult business professional might open his heart in a more formal way, depicting this as we did in a previous chapter:

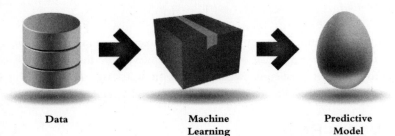

| Data | Machine Learning | Predictive Model |

**Machine learning processes training data to produce a predictive model.**

## BANK FACES RISK

For any organization, financial risk creeps up stealthily, hidden by a perfect, simple disguise: Major loss accumulates from many small losses, each of which alone seems innocuous. Minor individual misfortunes, boring and utterly undramatic, slip below the radar. They're practically invisible.

Soon after a megamerger in 1996 that rendered Chase Bank the nation's largest, the bank's home finance team recognized a new degree of risk. Their pool of mortgage holders had grown significantly. It was now composed of what had originally been six banks' worth of mortgages: millions of them. Each one represented a bit of risk—a *micro-risk*. That's when Dan received the call.

Ironically, there are two seemingly opposite ways a mortgage customer can misbehave. They can fail to pay you back, or they can pay you back in full but too quickly:

**Micro-risk A:** Customer defaults on the mortgage payments.

**Micro-risk B:** Customer *prepays* the mortgage all at once, early, due to refinancing with a competing bank or selling the house. Prepayment is a loss because the bank fails to collect the mortgage's planned future interest payments.

These losses are demoted to "micro" because, for a bank, any one mortgage customer just isn't that big a deal. But micro-losses threaten to add up. In the financial world, the word *risk* most often refers to *credit risk*, i.e., micro-risk A, wherein an outstanding debt is never recovered and is lost forever. But when your bread and butter is interest payments, micro-risk B is no picnic either. To put it plainly, your bank doesn't want you to get out of debt.[2]

## PREDICTION BATTLES RISK

*Most discussions of decision making assume that only senior executives make decisions or that only senior executives' decisions matter. This is a dangerous mistake.*
— Peter Drucker, an American educator and writer born in 1909

Chase's mortgage portfolio faced risk factors amounting to hundreds of millions of dollars. Every day is like a day at the beach—each grain of sand is one of a million micro-risks. Once a mortgage application is stamped "low-risk" and approved, the risk management process has actually only just begun. The bank's portfolio of open mortgages must be tended to like cows on a dairy farm. The reason? Risk lurks. Millions of mortgages await decisions as to which to sell to other banks, which to attempt to keep alive, and which to allow refinancing for at a lower interest rate.

Predictive analytics (PA) serves as an antidote against the poisonous accumulation of micro-risks. PA stands vigil, prospectively marking each micro-risk so the organization can do something about it.

It's nothing new. The notion is mainstream and dates back to the very origin of PA. Predicting consumer risk is well known as the classic *credit score*, provided by FICO and credit bureaus such as Experian. The credit score's origin dates back to 1941, and the term is now a part of the common vernacular. Its inception was foundational for PA,

---

[2] Similarly, credit card issuers aren't pleased if you always pay in full and never pay interest.

and its success has helped propel PA's visibility. Modern-day risk scores are often built with the same predictive modeling methods that fuel PA projects.

The benefits of fighting risk with PA can be demonstrated with ease. While prediction itself may be an involved task, it only takes basic arithmetic to calculate the value realized once prediction is working. Imagine you run a bank with thousands of outstanding loans, 10 percent of which are expected to default. With one of every 10 debtors an impending delinquent account, the future drapes its usual haze: you just don't know which will turn out to be bad.

Say you score each loan for risk with an effective predictive model. Some get high-risk scores and others low-risk scores. If these risk scores are assigned well, the top half predicted as most risky could see almost twice as many as average turn out to be defaulters—to be more realistic, let's say 70 percent more than the overall default rate. That would be music to your ears. A smidgeon of arithmetic shows you've divided your portfolio into two halves, one with a 17 percent default rate (70 percent more than the overall 10 percent rate), and the other with a 3 percent default rate (since 17 and 3 average out to 10).

**High-risk loans:** 17 percent will default.

**Low-risk loans:** 3 percent will default.

You've just divided your business into two completely different worlds, one safe and one hazardous. You now know where to focus your attention.

Following this promise, Chase took a large-scale, calculated *macro*-risk. It put its faith in prediction, entrusting it to drive hundreds of millions of dollars' worth of decisions. But Chase's story will earn its happy ending only if prediction works—if what's learned from data pans out in the great uncertainty that is the future.

Prediction presents the ultimate dilemma. Even with so much known of the past, how can we justify confidence in technology's vision of the unknowable future?

Before we get into how prediction works, here are a few words on risk.

# RISKY BUSINESS

*The revolutionary idea that defines the boundary between modern times and the past is the mastery of risk: the notion that the future is more than a whim of the gods and that men and women are not passive before nature. Until human beings discovered a way across that boundary, the future was a mirror of the past or the murky domain of oracles and soothsayers who held a monopoly over knowledge of anticipated events.*

—Peter Bernstein, *Against the Gods: The Remarkable Story of Risk*

*There's no such thing as bad risk, only bad pricing.*

—Stephen Brobst, Chief Technology Officer, Teradata

Of course, banks don't bear the entire burden of managing society's risk. Insurance companies also play a central role. In fact, their core business is the act of data crunching to quantify risk so it can be efficiently distributed. Eric Webster, a vice president at State Farm Insurance, put it brilliantly: "Insurance is nothing but management of information. It is pooling of risk, and whoever can manipulate information the best has a significant competitive advantage." Simply put, these companies are in the business of prediction.

The insurance industry has made an art of risk management. In his book *The Failure of Risk Management*, Douglas Hubbard points out what is poignant for all organizations that aren't insurance companies: "No certified, regulated profession like the actuarial practice exists outside of what is strictly considered insurance."

Despite this, any and all organizations can master risk the way insurance does. How? By applying PA to predict bad things. For any organization, a predictive model essentially achieves the same function as an insurance company's *actuarial* approach: rating individuals by the chance of a negative outcome. In fact, we can define PA in these very terms.[3]

Here's the original definition:

**Predictive analytics (PA)**—*Technology that learns from experience (data) to predict the future behavior of individuals in order to drive better decisions.*

What an organization effectively learns with PA is *how to decrease risk by way of anticipating micro-risks.* Here's an alternative, risk-oriented definition:

**Predictive analytics (PA)**—*Technology that learns from experience (data) to manage micro-risk.*

Both definitions apply, since each one implies the other.

Like the opportunistic enterprise Tom Cruise's adolescent entrepreneur launches in his breakout movie of 1983, *Risky Business*, all businesses are risky businesses. And, like insurance companies, all organizations benefit from measuring and predicting the risk of bad behavior, including defaults, cancellations, dropouts, accidents, fraud, and crime. In this way, PA transforms risk to opportunity.

For the economy at large, where could risk management be more important than in the world of mortgages? The mortgage industry, measured in the trillions of dollars, serves as the financial cornerstone of home ownership, the hallmark of family prosperity. And, as important as mortgages are, risky ones are generally considered a central catalyst to the recent financial crisis or Great Recession.

Micro-risks matter. Left unchecked, they threaten to snowball. Our best bet is to learn to predict.

---

[3] It works in the other direction as well: While standard actuarial methods involve manual steps such as tabulation and analysis, insurance companies are widely augmenting these practices with predictive modeling in order to better predict outcome. Predictive modeling methods, the topic of this chapter, are more automated and souped up.

## THE LEARNING MACHINE

To learn from data: the process isn't nearly as complex as you might think.[4]

Start with a modest question: What's the *simplest* way to begin distinguishing between high- and low-risk mortgages? What single factor about a mortgage is the most telling?

Dan's learning system made a discovery within Chase's data: *If a mortgage's interest rate is under 7.94 percent, then the risk of prepayment is 3.8 percent; otherwise, the risk is 19.2 percent.*[5]

Drawn as a picture:

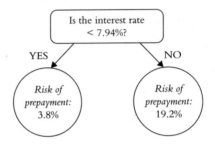

What a difference! Based only on interest rate, we divide the pool of mortgages into two groups, one five times riskier than the other, with respect to the chances of *prepayment* (a customer making an unforeseen payoff of the entire debt, thereby denying the bank future earnings from interest payments).

This discovery is valuable, even if not entirely surprising. Homeowners paying a higher interest rate are more inclined to refinance or sell than those paying a lower rate. If this was already suspected, it's now confirmed empirically, and the effect is precisely quantified.

Machine learning has taken its first step.

## BUILDING THE LEARNING MACHINE

You're already halfway there. Believe it or not, there is only one more step before you witness the full essence of machine learning—the ability to generate a predictive model from data, to learn from examples and form an electronic Sherlock Holmes that sizes up an individual and predicts.

---

[4] Hands-on familiarity with machine learning is on the rise. Stanford University's computer science department (one of the top three in the United States) first made its Machine Learning course available online for free in 2011, drawing an international enrollment of over 100,000. This success inspired its professor, Andrew Ng, to cofound Coursera, offering free online courses across subject areas.

[5] The study detailed in this chapter is across 21,816 fixed-rate mortgages with terms of at least 15 years that are relatively new, between one and four years old, and therefore face a higher prepayment risk than average, since borrowers who have been paying off their mortgages for more than four years are more likely to stick with their mortgage as is. Note that interest rates are relative to those in the late 1990s when this project took place and its data was collected.

You're inches away from the key to one of the coolest things in science, the most audacious of human ambitions: *the automation of learning.*

No sophisticated math or computer code required; in fact, I can explain the rest in two words. But first, let's take a moment to fully define the scientific challenge at hand.

The insight established so far, that interest rate predicts risk, makes for a crude predictive model. It puts each individual mortgage into one of two predictive categories: high-risk and low-risk. Since it considers only one factor, or *predictor variable*, about the individual, we call this a *univariate* model. All the examples in the previous chapter's tables of bizarre and surprising insights are univariate—they each pertain to one variable such as your salary, your e-mail address, or your credit rating.

We need to go *multivariate.* Why? An effective predictive model surely must consider multiple factors together at once, instead of just one. And therein lies the rub. As a refresher, here's the definition:

> **Predictive model**—*A mechanism that predicts a behavior of an individual, such as click, buy, lie, or die (or prepay a mortgage). It takes characteristics (variables) of the individual as input, and provides a* predictive score *as output. The higher the score, the more likely it is that the individual will exhibit the predicted behavior.*

Once created with machine learning, a predictive model predicts the outcome for one customer at a time:

| Characteristics of an Individual | Predictive Model | Predictive Score |

Consider a mortgage customer who looks like this:

**Borrower:** Sally Smithers

**Mortgage:** $174,000

**Property value:** $400,000

**Property type:** Single-family residence

**Interest rate:** 8.92 percent

**Borrower's annual income:** $86,880

**Net worth:** $102,334

**Credit score:** Strong

**Late payments:** 4

**Age:** 38

**Marital status:** Married

**Education:** College

**Years at prior address:** 4

**Line of work:** Business manager

**Self-employed:** No

**Years at job:** 3

Those are the predictor variables, the characteristics fed into the predictive model. The model's job will be to consider any and all such variables, and squeeze them into a single predictive score. Call it the calculation of a new *über-variable*. The model spits out the score, putting all the pieces together to proclaim a singular conclusion.

That's the challenge of machine learning. Your mission is to program your mindless laptop to crunch data about individuals and automatically build the multivariate predictive model. If you succeed, your computer will be learning how to predict.

## LEARNING FROM BAD EXPERIENCES

*Experience is the name everyone gives to his mistakes.*

—Oscar Wilde

*My reputation grows with every failure.*

—George Bernard Shaw

There's another requirement for machine learning. A successful method must be designed to gain knowledge from a bittersweet mix of good and bad experience, from both the positive and the negative outcomes listed in the data. Some past mortgages went smoothly, whereas others suffered the fate of prepayment. Both of these flavors of data must be leveraged.

To predict, the question we strive to answer is: "How can you distinguish between positive and negative individuals ahead of time?" Learning how to replicate past successes by examining only the positive cases won't work.[6] Negative examples are critical. Mistakes are your friend.

---

[6] Analyzing positive cases only is sometimes called *profiling* and *cloning* customers.

## HOW MACHINE LEARNING WORKS

And now, here's the intuitive, elegant answer to the big dilemma, the next step of learning that will move beyond univariate to multivariate predictive modeling, guided by both positive and negative cases: *Keep going.*

So far, we've established two risk groups. Next, in the low-risk group, find another factor that best breaks it down even further, into two subgroups that themselves vary in risk. Then do the same thing in the high-risk group. And then keep going within the subgroups. Divide and conquer and then divide some more, breaking down to smaller and smaller groups. And yet, as we'll discover, don't go too far.

This learning method, called *decision trees*, isn't the only way to create a predictive model, but it's consistently voted as the most or second most popular by practitioners, due to its balance of relative simplicity with effectiveness. It doesn't always deliver the most precise predictive models, but since the models are easier on the eyes than impenetrable mathematical formulas, it's a great place to start, not only for learning about PA, but at the outset of almost any project that's applying PA.

Let's start growing the decision tree. Here's what we had so far:

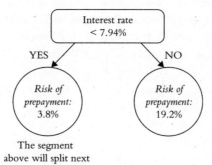

The segment
above will split next

Now let's find a predictor variable that breaks the low-risk group on the left down further. On this data set, Dan's decision tree software picks the debtor's income:[7]

---

[7] The decision tree shown, as well as the decision trees shown later that also predict mortgage prepayment, are simplified depictions in that it is not shown how unknown values are handled. For example, some mortgage holders' income levels are unknown. For such missing values, an alternative *surrogate variable* is referenced by the decision tree method in order to decide whether to go left or right at that decision point. Although built from real data, the example decision trees in this chapter are not from the deployed Chase mortgage project.

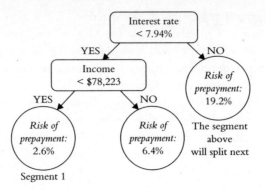

Segment 1

You can see the tree is growing downward. As any computer scientist will tell you, trees are upside down and the *root* is on the top (but if you prefer, you may turn this book upside down).

As shown, the mortgage holder's income is very telling of risk. The lower-left *leaf* (end point of the tree) labeled "Segment 1" corresponds with a subgroup of mortgage holders for whom the interest rate is under 7.94 percent and income is under $78,223. So far, this is the lowest-risk group identified, with only a 2.6 percent chance of prepayment.

Data trumps the gut. Who would have thought individuals with lower incomes would be less likely to prepay? After all, people with lower incomes usually have a higher incentive to refinance their mortgages. It's tough to interpret; perhaps those with a lower income tend to pursue less aggressive financial tactics. As always, we can only conjecture on the causality behind these insights.

Moving to the right side of the tree, to further break down the high-risk group, the learning software selects mortgage size:

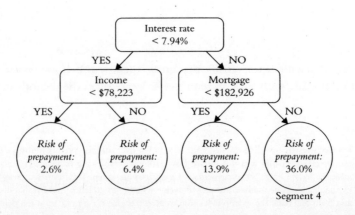

Segment 4

With only two factors taken into consideration, we've identified a particularly risky pocket: higher-interest mortgages that are larger in magnitude, which show a whopping 36 percent chance of prepayment (Segment 4).

Before this model grows even bigger and becomes more predictive, let's talk trees.

## DECISION TREES GROW ON YOU

It's simple, elegant, and precise. It's practically mathless. To use a decision tree to predict for an individual, you start at the top (the root) and answer yes/no questions to arrive at a leaf. The leaf indicates the model's predictive output for that individual. For example, beginning at the top, if your interest rate is not less than 7.94 percent, proceed to the right. Then, if your mortgage is under $182,926, take a left. You end up in a leaf that says, based on these two factors, the risk that you will prepay is 13.9 percent.

Here's an example that decides what you should do if you accidentally drop your food on the floor (excerpted from "The 30-Second Rule: A Decision Tree" by Audrey Fukuman and Andy Wright)—this one was not, to my knowledge, derived from real data:

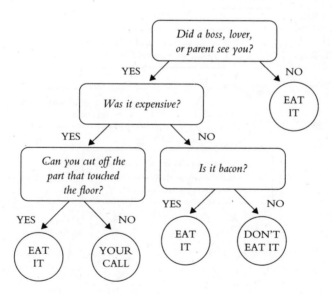

Imagine you just dropped an inexpensive BLT sandwich in front of your mom. Follow the tree from the top and you'll be instructed to eat it anyway.

A decision tree grows upon the rich soil that is data, repeatedly dividing groups of individuals into subgroups. Data is a recording of prior events, so this procedure is learning from the way things turned out in the past. The data determines which variables are used and at what splitting value (e.g., "Income < \$78,223" in the mortgage decision tree). Like other forms of predictive modeling, its derivation is completely automatic—load the data, push a button, and the decision tree grows, all on its own. It's a rich discovery process, the kind of data mining that strikes gold.

Extending far beyond the business world, decision trees are employed to decide almost anything, whether it is medical, legal, governmental, astronomical, industrial, or you name it. The learning process is intrinsically versatile, since a decision tree's area of specialty is determined solely by the data upon which it grows. Provide data from a new field of study, and the machine is learning about an entirely new domain.

One decision tree was trained to predict votes on U.S. Supreme Court rulings by former Justice Sandra Day O'Connor. This tree, built across several hundred prior rulings, is from a research project by four university professors in political science, government, and law ("Competing Approaches to Predicting Supreme Court Decision Making," by Andres D. Martin et al.):

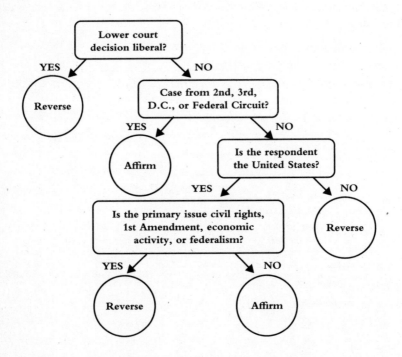

It's simple yet effective. The professors' research shows that a group of such decision trees working together outperforms human experts in predicting Supreme Court rulings. By employing a separate decision tree for each justice, plus other means to predict whether a ruling will be unanimous, the gaggle of trees succeeded in predicting subsequent rulings with 75 percent accuracy, while human legal experts, who were at liberty to use any and all knowledge about each case, predicted at only 59 percent. Once again, data trumps the gut.[8]

## COMPUTER, PROGRAM THYSELF

*Find a bug in a program, and fix it, and the program will work today. Show the program how to find and fix a bug, and the program will work forever.*

—Oliver Selfridge

The logical flow of a decision tree amounts to a simple computer program, so, in growing it, the computer is literally programming itself. The decision tree is a familiar structure you have probably already come across, if you know about any of these topics:

- **Taxonomy.** The hierarchical classification of species in the animal kingdom is in the form of a decision tree.
- **Computer programs.** A decision tree is a nested if-then–else statement. It may also be viewed as a flow chart with no loops.
- **Business rules.** A decision tree is a way to encode a series of if-then business rules; each path from the root to a leaf is one rule (aka a *pattern*, thus the data mining term *pattern discovery*).
- **Marketing segmentation.** The time-honored tradition of segmenting customers and prospects for marketing purposes can be conceived in the form of a decision tree. The difference is that marketing segments are usually designed by hand, following the marketer's intuition, whereas decision trees generated automatically with machine learning tend to drill down into a larger number of smaller, more specific subsegments. We could call it *hyper-segmentation.*
- **The game "20 Questions."** To pass time during long car rides, you think of something and your opponent tries to guess what it is, narrowing down the possibilities by asking up to 20 yes/no questions. Your knowledge for playing this game can be formed into a decision tree. In fact, you can play "Guess the Dictator or Sitcom Character" against the computer at www.smalltime.com/Dictator; if after asking yes/no questions it comes up dry, it will add the person you were thinking of to its internal decision tree by saying "I give up" and asking for a new yes/no question (a new *variable*) with which to expand the tree. My first computer in 1980 came with this game ("Animal," on the Apple ][+). It kept the decision tree saved on my $5^{1}/_{4}$" floppy disk.

---

[8] Ian Ayres provides an informative overview of the fundamental *intuition versus data* debate in the Chapter "Experts versus Equations" of *Super Crunchers: Why Thinking-by-Numbers Is the New Way to Be Smart* (Bantam, 2007).

# LEARN BABY LEARN

*Old statisticians never die; they just get broken down by age and sex.*

—Anonymous

Let's keep growing on Chase's data. This is the fun part: pushing the "go" button, which feels like pressing the gas pedal did the first time you drove a car. There's a palpable source of energy at your disposal: the data, and the power to expose discoveries from it. As the tree grows downward, defining smaller subsegments that are more specific and precise, it feels like a juice squeezer that is crushing out knowledge juice. If there are ways in which human behavior follows patterns, the patterns can't escape undetected—they'll be squeezed out into view.

Before modeling, data must be properly arranged in order to access its predictive potential. Like preparing crude oil, it takes a concerted effort to prepare this digital resource as *learning data* (aka *training data*). This involves organizing the data so two time frames are juxtaposed: (1) stuff we knew in the past, and (2) the outcome we'd like to predict, which we came to find out later. It's all in the past—history from which to learn—but pairing and relating these two distinct points in time is an essential mechanical step, a prerequisite that makes learning to predict possible. This *data preparation* phase can be quite tedious, an involved hands-on technical process often more cumbersome than anticipated, but it's a small price to pay.

Given this potent load of prepared training data, PA software is ready to pounce. "If only these walls could speak . . ." Actually, they can. Machine learning is a universal translator that gives a voice to data.

Here's the tree on Chase mortgage data after several more learning steps (this depiction has less annotation—per convention, go left for "yes" and right for "no"):

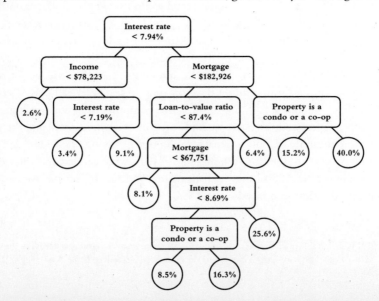

Learning has now discovered 10 distinct segments (tree leaves), with risk levels ranging from 2.6 percent all the way up to 40 percent. This wide variety means something is working. The process has successfully found groups that differ greatly from one another in the likelihood the thing being predicted, prepayment, will happen. Thus, it has learned how to rank by future probabilities.

To be predicted, an individual tumbles down the tree from top to bottom like a ball in the pinball–like game Pachinko, cascading down through an obstacle course of pins, bouncing left and right. For example, Sally Smithers, the example mortgage customer from earlier in this chapter, starts at the top (tree root) and answers yes/no questions:

> **Q:** *Interest rate < 7.94 percent?*
> **A:** No, go right.
> **Q:** *Mortgage < $182,926?*
> **A:** Yes, go left.
> **Q:** *Loan-to-value ratio < 87.4 percent?*
> **A:** Yes, go left *(the loan is less than 87.4 percent of the property value).*
> **Q:** *Mortgage < $67,751?*
> **A:** No, go right.
> **Q:** *Interest rate < 8.69 percent?*
> **A:** No, go right.

Thus, Sally comes to a landing in the segment with a 25.6 percent propensity. The average risk overall is 9.4 percent, so this tells us there is a relatively high chance she will prepay her mortgage.

*Business rules* are found along every path from root to leaf. For example, following the path Sally took, we derive a rule that applies to Sally as well as many other homeowners like her (the path has five steps, but the rule can be summarized in fewer lines because some steps revisit the same variable):

---

IF:

    *the mortgage is greater than or equal to $67,751 and less than $182,926*
      AND:

    *the interest rate is greater than or equal to 8.69 percent*
      AND:

    *the loan-to-value ratio is less than 87.4 percent*
THEN:

    *the probability of prepayment is 25.6 percent.*

---

# BIGGER IS BETTER

Continuing to grow the mortgage risk model, the learning process goes further and lands on an even bigger tree, with 39 segments (leaves), that has this shape to it:

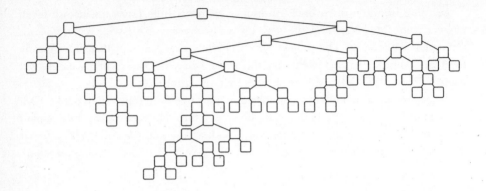

**A decision tree with 39 segments.**

As the decision tree becomes bigger and more complex, the predictive performance continues to increase, but more gradually. There are diminishing returns.

A single metric compares the performance of predictive models: *lift*. A common measure, lift is a kind of *predictive multiplier*. It tells you how many more target customers you can identify with a model than without one.

Think of the value of prediction from the perspective of the bank. Every prepayment is the loss of a profitable customer. More broadly, the departure of customers is called *customer attrition*, *churn*, or *defection*. Predicting customer attrition helps target marketing outreach designed to keep customers around. Offers designed to retain customers are expensive, so, instead of contacting every borrower, the bank must target very precisely.

### PA APPLICATION: CUSTOMER RETENTION WITH CHURN MODELING
1. **What's predicted:** Which customers will leave.
2. **What's done about it:** Retention efforts targeting at-risk customers.

Suppose the bank stands to lose 10 percent of its mortgage borrowers. Without a predictive model, the only way to be sure to reach all of them is to contact every single borrower. More realistically, if the marketing budget will allow only one in five borrowers to be contacted, then, by selecting randomly without a model, only one in five of those customers soon to be lost will be contacted (on average). Of course, with a crystal ball that predicted perfectly, we could zero in on just the right customers—wouldn't that be nice! Instead, with a less fantastical but reasonably accurate predictive model, we can target much more effectively.

Three times more effectively, to be precise. With the full-sized decision tree model shown previously, it turns out that the 20 percent scored as most high risk includes

60 percent of all the would-be defectors. That is 300 percent as many as without the model, so we say that the model has a *lift* of three at the 20 percent mark. The same marketing budget now has three times as many opportunities to save a defecting customer as before. The bank's bang for its marketing buck just tripled.

The trees we've seen achieve various lifts at the 20 percent mark:

| Decision Tree | Lift at 20 Percent |
| --- | --- |
| 4 segments | 2.5 |
| 10 segments | 2.8 |
| 39 segments | 3.0 |

As the tree gets bigger, it keeps getting better, so why stop there? Shall we keep going? Slow down, Icarus! I've got a bad feeling about this.

## OVERLEARNING: ASSUMING TOO MUCH

*If you torture the data long enough, it will confess.*
—Ronald Coase, Professor of Economics, University of Chicago

*There are three kinds of lies: lies, damned lies, and statistics.*
—British Prime Minister Benjamin Disraeli (quote popularized by Mark Twain)

*An unlimited amount of computational resources is like dynamite: If used properly, it can move mountains. Used improperly, it can blow up your garage or your portfolio.*
—David Leinweber, *Nerds on Wall Street*

A few years ago, Berkeley Professor David Leinweber made waves with his discovery that the annual closing price of the S&P 500 stock market index could have been predicted from 1983 to 1993 by the rate of butter production in Bangladesh. Bangladesh's butter production mathematically explains 75 percent of the index's variation over that time. Urgent calls were placed to the Credibility Police, since it certainly cannot be believed that Bangladesh's butter is closely tied to the U.S. stock market. If its butter production boomed or went bust in any given year, how could it be reasonable to assume that U.S. stocks would follow suit? This stirred up the greatest fears of PA skeptics, and vindicated nonbelievers. Eyebrows were raised so vigorously, they catapulted Professor Leinweber onto national television.

Crackpot or legitimate educator? It turns out Leinweber had contrived this analysis as a playful publicity stunt, within a chapter entitled "Stupid Data Miner Tricks" in his book *Nerds on Wall Street*. His analysis was designed to highlight a common misstep by exaggerating it. It's dangerously easy to find ridiculous correlations, especially when you're "predicting" only 11 data points (annual index closings for 1983 to 1993). By searching through a large number of financial indicators across many countries, something or other will show similar trends, just by chance. For example, shiver me timbers, a related study showed buried treasure discoveries in England and Wales predicted the Dow Jones Industrial Average a full year ahead from 1992 to 2002.

Predictive modeling can worsen this problem. If, instead of looking at how one factor simply shadows another, you apply the dynamics of machine learning to create models that combine factors, the match can appear even more perfect. It's a catch-phrase favored by naysayers: "Hey, throw in something irrelevant like the daily temperature as another factor, and a regression model gets *better*—what does that say about this kind of analysis?" Leinweber got as far as 99 percent accuracy predicting the S&P 500 by allowing a regression model to work with not only Bangladesh's butter production, but Bangladesh's sheep population, U.S. butter production, and U.S. cheese production. As a lactose-intolerant data scientist, I protest!

Leinweber attracted the attention he sought, but his lesson didn't seem to sink in. "I got calls for years asking me what the current butter business in Bangladesh was looking like and I kept saying, 'Ya know, it was a joke, it was a joke!' It's scary how few people actually get that." As *Black Swan* author Nassim Taleb put it in his suitably titled book, *Fooled by Randomness*, "Nowhere is the problem of induction more relevant than in the world of trading—and nowhere has it been as ignored!" Thus the occasional overzealous yet earnest public claim of economic prediction based on factors like women's hemlines, men's necktie width, Super Bowl results, and Christmas day snowfall in Boston.

The culprit that kills learning is *overlearning* (aka *overfitting*). Overlearning is the pitfall of mistaking noise for information, assuming too much about what has been shown within data. You've overlearned if you've read too much into the numbers, led astray from discovering the underlying truth.

Decision trees can overlearn like nobody's business. Just keep growing the tree deeper and deeper—a clear temptation—until each leaf narrows down to just one individual in the training data. After all, if a rule in the tree (formed by following a path from root to leaf) references many variables, it can eliminate all but one individual. But such a rule isn't general; it applies to only one case. Believing in such a rule is accepting *proof by example*. In this way, a large tree could essentially memorize the entire training data. You've only rewritten the data in a new way.

Rote memorization is the antithesis of learning. Say you're teaching a high school class and you give your students the past few years of final exams to help them study for the exam they'll take next week. If a student simply memorizes the answer to each question in the prior exams, he hasn't actually learned anything and he won't do well on a new exam with all-new questions. Our learning machine has got to be a better student than that.

Even without going to that extreme, striking a delicate balance between learning and overlearning is a profound challenge. For any predictive model a pressing question persists: Has it learned something true that holds in general, or only discovered patterns that hold within this data set? *How can we be confident a model will work tomorrow when it is called upon to predict under unique circumstances never before encountered?*

## THE CONUNDRUM OF INDUCTION

*It must be allowed that inductive investigations are of a far higher degree of difficulty and complexity than any questions of deduction.*
—William Stanley Jevons, economist and logician, 1874

*To understand God's thoughts, we must study statistics, for these are the measure of his purpose.*
—Florence Nightingale

*Though this be madness, yet there is method in it.*
—*Hamlet,* by William Shakespeare

*Life would be so much easier if we only had the source code.*
—Hacker aphorism

The objective of machine learning is *induction*:

**Induction**—*Reasoning from detailed facts to general principles.*

This is not to be confused with *deduction*, which is essentially the very opposite:

**Deduction**—*Reasoning from the general to the particular (or from cause to effect).*

Deduction is much more straightforward. It's just applying known rules. If all men are mortal and Socrates is a man, then deduction tells us Socrates is mortal.

Induction is an art form. At our disposal we have a detailed manifestation of how the world works: data's recording of what happened. From that we seek to generalize, to draw grand conclusions, to ascertain patterns that will hold true in situations not yet seen. We attempt to *reverse engineer* the world's laws and principles. It's the discovery of the method in the madness.

Although a kind of reasoning, induction always behaves unreasonably. This is because it must be based on overly simplistic assumptions. Assumptions are key to the inductive leap we strive to take. You simply cannot design a learning method without them. We don't know enough about the way the world works to design perfect learning. If we did, we wouldn't need machine learning to begin with. For example, with decision trees, the implicit assumption is that the rules within a decision tree, as simple as they may be, are an astute way to capture and express true patterns.

Carnegie Mellon professor Tom Mitchell, founding chair of the world's first Machine Learning Department and the author of the first academic textbook on the subject, *Machine Learning*, calls this kind of assumption an *inductive bias*. Establishing these foundational assumptions, part and parcel to inventing new induction methods, is the art behind machine learning. There's no one best answer, no one learning method that always wins above all others. It depends on the data.[9]

Machine induction and the induction of birth have something in common. In both cases, there's a genesis.

# THE ART AND SCIENCE OF MACHINE LEARNING

*Modeling means modifying models incrementally.*
*With a geek technique to tweak, it will reach the peak eventually.*
*Each step is taken to improve prediction on the training cases.*
*One small step for man; one giant leap—the human race is going places!*
*Although it is not logical, I hope this rap's pedagogical.*
*My true love will not toggle, but, if you kiss a prince-turned-frog, it will.*

—From "Predict This!" by the author

Modeling methods vary, but they all face the same challenge: to learn as much as possible, yet not learn too much. Among the competing approaches to machine learning, decision trees are often considered the most user friendly, since they consist of rules you can read like a long (if cumbersome) English sentence, while other methods are more mathy, taking the variables and plugging them into equations.

Most learning methods *search* for a good predictive model, starting with a trivially simple and often inept model and tweaking it repeatedly, as if applying "genetic mutations," until it evolves into a robust prediction apparatus. In the case of a decision tree, the process starts with a small tree and grows it. In the case of most mathematical equation-based methods, it starts with a random model by selecting random parameters, and then repeatedly nudges the parameters until the equation is predicting well. For all learning techniques, the training data guides each tweak as it strives to improve prediction across that data set. To put names on the mathy methods that

---

[9] This non-existence of a universal solution to machine learning is known as the "no free lunch" theorem.

compete with decision trees, they include *artificial neural networks, loglinear regression, support vector machines,* and *TreeNet.*

Machine learning's ruthless, incessant adaptation displays an eerie power. It even discovers and exploits weaknesses or loopholes inadvertently left in place by the data scientist. In one project with my close friend Alex Chaffee (a multitalented software architect), we set up the computer to "evolve" a Tetris game player, learning how to decide where to drop each piece while playing the game. In one run of the system, we accidentally reversed the objective (a single errant minus sign instead of a plus sign within thousands of lines of computer code!) so that, instead of striving to tightly pack the game pieces, it was rewarded for packing *less* densely by creating big, vacant holes. Before we realized it was chasing a bug, we were perplexed to see the resulting game player stacking pieces up diagonally from the bottom left of the game board to the top right, a creative way to play as *poorly* as possible.[10] It conjures the foreboding insight of brooding scientist Ian Malcolm in Michael Crichton's dinosaur thriller *Jurassic Park*: "Life finds a way."

Regardless of the learning technique and its mathematical sophistication, there's always the potential to overlearn. After all, commanding a computer to learn is like teaching a blindfolded monkey to design a fashion diva's gown. The computer knows nothing. It has no notion of the meaning behind the data, the concept of what a mortgage, salary, or even a house is. The numbers are just numbers. Even clues like "$" and "%" don't mean anything to the machine. It's a blind, mindless automaton stuck in a box forever enduring its first day on the job.

Every attempt to predictively model faces this central challenge to establish general principles and weed out the noise, the artifacts peculiar only to the limited data at hand. It's the nature of the problem. Even if there are millions or billions of examples in the data from which to learn, it's still a limited portion compared to how many conceivable situations could be encountered in the future. The number of possible combinations that may form a learning example is exponential. And so, architecting a learning process that strikes the balance between learning too much and too little is elusive and mysterious to even the most hard-core scientist.

In solving this conundrum, art comes before science, but the two are both critical components. Art enables it to work, and science proves it works:

1. **Artistic design:** Research scientists craft machine learning to attempt to avert overlearning, often based on creative ideas that sound just brilliant.
2. **Scientific measure:** The predictive model's performance is objectively evaluated.

---

[10] To view a non-buggy, proficient Tetris player we evolved, see www.predictionimpact.com/tetris.

But, for number 2, what method of evaluation could possibly suffice? If we can't entirely trust the design of machine learning, how can we trust a measure of its performance? Of course, all predictions can be evaluated by simply waiting to see if they come true. But, when predicting months into the future, this isn't practical—it takes too long. We need an almost instantaneous means to gauge performance so that, if overlearning takes place, it can be detected and the course of learning corrected by backtracking and trying again.

## FEELING VALIDATED: TEST DATA

*The proof is in the pudding.*

There's no fancy math required to test for true learning. Don't get me wrong; they've tried. Theoretical work abounds—these deep thinkers have even met for their 25th Annual Conference on Learning Theory. But the results to date are limited. They just can't design a learning method that's guaranteed to not overlearn. It's a seriously hard scientific problem. It might be impossible.

Instead, a clever, mind-numbingly simple trick is employed to test for overlearning: *Hold aside some data to test the model.* Randomly select a *test set* (aka *validation* or *out-of-sample set*) and quarantine it. Use only the remaining portion of data, the *training set*, to create the model. Then, evaluate the resulting model across the test set. Since the test set was not used to create the model, there's no way the model could have captured its esoteric aspects, its eccentricities. The model didn't have the opportunity to memorize it in any way. Therefore, however well the model does on the test set is a reasonable estimation of how well the model does in general, a true evaluation of its ability to predict. For evaluating the model, the test set is said to be *unbiased*.

| Training data | Testing data |
|---|---|
| Used by machine learning to generate a predictive model | Used to evaluate the predictive model |

No mathematical theory, no advanced science, just an elegant, practical solution. This is how it's done, always. It's common practice. Every predictive modeling software tool has a built-in routine to hold aside and evaluate over test data. And every research journal article reports predictive performance over test data (unless you're poking fun at the industry's more egregious errors with a humorous example about Bangladesh's butter and the stock market).

There's one downside to this approach. You sacrifice the opportunity to learn from the examples in the test set, generating the model only from the now-smaller training set. Typically this is a loss of 20 percent or 30 percent of the training data, which is held aside as test data. But the training set that remains is often plenty big, and the sacrifice is a small price to pay for a true measure of performance.

Following this practice, let's take a look at the true test performance of the decision tree models we've looked at so far. Recall that the *lift* performance of our increasingly larger trees, as evaluated over the 21,816 cases in the training set, was:

| Decision Tree | Lift at 20 Percent on the Training Set |
| --- | --- |
| 4 segments | 2.5 |
| 10 segments | 2.8 |
| 39 segments | 3.0 |

It turns out, for these trees, no overlearning took place. As evaluated on another 5,486 examples, the test set, the lifts for these three models held at 2.5, 2.8, and 3.0, respectively. Success!

| Decision Tree | Lift on the Training Set | Lift on the Test Set |
| --- | --- | --- |
| 4 segments | 2.5 | 2.5 |
| 10 segments | 2.8 | 2.8 |
| 39 segments | 3.0 | 3.0 |

Keep going, though, and you'll pass your limit. If the tree gets even bigger, branching out to a greater number of smaller segments, learning will become over-learning. Taking it to an extreme, once we get to a tree with 638 segments (i.e., end points or leaves), the lift on the training set is 3.8, the highest lift yet. But the performance on that data, which was used to form the model in the first place, is biased. Trying out this large tree on the test set reveals a lift of 2.4, lower than that of the small tree with only four segments.

| Decision Tree | Lift on the Training Set | Lift on the Test Set |
|---|---|---|
| 638 segments | 3.8 | 2.4 (*overlearning*) |

The test data guides learning, showing when it has worked and when it has gone too far.


## CARVING OUT A WORK OF ART

*In every block of marble I see a statue as plain as though it stood before me, shaped and perfect in attitude and action. I have only to hew away the rough walls that imprison the lovely apparition to reveal it to the other eyes as mine see it.*

—Michelangelo

*Everything should be made as simple as possible, but not simpler.*

—Albert Einstein (as paraphrased by Roger Sessions)

The decision tree fails unless we tame its wild growth. This presents a tough balance to strike. Like a parent, we strive to structure our progeny's growth and development so they're not out of control, and yet we cannot bear to quell creativity. Where exactly to draw the line?

When they first gained serious attention in the early 1960s, decision trees failed miserably, laughed out of court for their propensity to overlearn. "They were called 'a recipe for learning something wrong,'" says Dan Steinberg. "This was a death sentence, like a restaurant with *E. coli*. Trees were finished."

For those researchers who didn't give up on trees, formally defining the line between learning and overlearning proved tricky. It seemed as though, no matter where you drew the line, there was still a risk of learning too little or too much. Dramatic tension mounted like an unresolvable tug-of-war.

As with the theater, irony eases the tension. The most popular solution to this dilemma is ironic. Instead of holding back so as to avoid learning too much, don't hold back at all. Go all the way—learn way too much . . . and then take it all back, piece by piece, unlearning until you're back to square one and have learned too little. Set forth and make mistakes! Why? Because the mistakes are apparent only after you've made them.

In a word, grow the tree too big and bushy, and then prune it back. The trick is that pruning is guided not by the training data that determined the tree's growth, but by the testing data that now reveals where that growth went awry. It's an incredibly elegant solution that strikes the delicate balance between learning and overlearning.

To prune back a tree is to backtrack on steps taken, undoing some of machine learning's tweaks that have turned out to be faulty. By way of these undo's that hack and chop tree branches, a balanced model is unearthed, not timidly restricted and yet not overly self-confident. Like Michelangelo's statue, revealed within his block of marble by carving away the extraneous material that shrouds it, an effective predictive model is discovered within.

It's easy to take a wrong turn while building a predictive model. The important thing is to ensure that such steps are undone. In a training workshop I lead, trainees build predictive models by hand, following their own process of trial and error. When they try out a change that proves to hurt a model rather than improve it, they've been heard to exclaim, "Go back, go back—we should go back!"

To visualize the effect, consider the improvement of a decision tree during the training process:

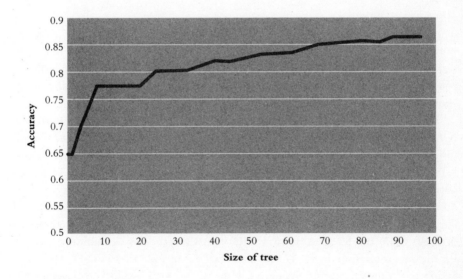

From *Machine Learning*, by Tom Mitchell

As shown, while the tree grows, the accuracy—as measured over the training data used to grow it—just keeps improving. But during the same growth process, if we test for true, unbiased accuracy over the test set, we see that it peaks early on, and then further growth makes for overlearning, only *hurting* its predictions:

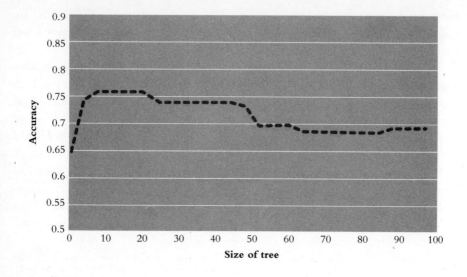

From *Machine Learning*, by Tom Mitchell

Hedging these bushes follows the principle known as *Occam's razor*. Seek the simplest explanation for the data available. The philosophy is, by seeking more parsimonious models, you discover better models. This tactic defines part of the inductive bias that intentionally underlies decision trees. It's what makes them work. If you care about your model, give it a KISS: "Keep it simple, stupid!"

The leading decision tree modeling standard, called *Classification and Regression Trees* (CART), employs this elegant form of pruning, plus numerous other bells and whistles in its routines.[11] CART was established by a 1984 book of the same name by four legendary researchers from Berkeley and Stanford: Leo Breiman, Jerome Friedman, Charles Stone, and Richard Olshen. I call them the "Fab Four." As with most major inventions such as the television and the airplane, other parties released competing decision tree–based techniques around the same time, including researchers in Australia (ID3) and South Africa (CHAID). CART is the most commonly adopted; PA software tools from the likes of IBM and StatSoft include a version of CART. Dan Steinberg's company, Salford Systems, sells the only CART product co-developed by the Fab Four, who are also investors.

An entrepreneurial scientist, Dan earned the Fab Four's trust to deliver CART from their research lab to the commercial world. Dan hails from Harvard with a PhD in econometrics. Not to put the CART before the horse, he founded his company soon after CART was invented.

---

[11] CART® is a registered trademark licensed exclusively to Salford Systems.

The validation of machine learning methods such as CART is breaking news: "Human Intuition Achieves Astounding Success." The fact that machine learning works tells us that we humans are smart enough—the hunches and intuitions that drive the design of methods to learn yet not overlearn pan out. I call this The Induction Effect:

> **The Induction Effect:** *Art drives machine learning; when followed by computer programs, strategies designed in part by informal human creativity succeed in developing predictive models that perform well on new cases.*

## PUTTING DECISION TREES TO WORK FOR CHASE

Dan agreed to help Chase with mortgage prediction (in a collaborative effort alongside a large consulting company), and the rubber hit the road. He pulled together a small team of scientists to apply CART to Chase's mortgage data.

Chase had in mind a different use of churn prediction than the norm. Most commonly, a company predicts which customers will leave (aka *churn* or *defect*—in the case of mortgage customers, *prepay*) in order to target *retention* activities meant to convince them to stay.

But Chase's plans put a new twist on the value of predicting churn. The bank intended to use the predictive scores to estimate the expected future value of individual mortgages in order to decide whether it would be a good move to sell them to other banks. Banks buy and sell mortgages at will. At any time, a mortgage could be sold based on its current market price, given the profile of the mortgage. But the market at large didn't have access to these predictive models, so Chase held a strong advantage. It could estimate the future value of a mortgage based on the predicted chance of prepayment. In a true manifestation of prediction's power, Chase could calculate whether selling a mortgage was likely to earn more than holding on to it. Each decision could be driven with prediction.

### PA APPLICATION: MORTGAGE VALUE ESTIMATION

1. **What's predicted:** Which mortgage holders will prepay within the next 90 days.
2. **What's done about it:** Mortgages are valued accordingly in order to decide whether to sell them to other banks.

Chase intended to drive decisions across many mortgages with these predictions. Managing millions of mortgages, Chase was putting its faith in prediction to drive a large-scale number of decisions.

PA promised a tremendous competitive edge for Chase in the mortgage marketplace. While the market price for a mortgage depended on only several factors, a

CART model incorporates many more variables, thus serving to more precisely predict each mortgage's future value.

With prediction, risk becomes opportunity. A mortgage destined to suffer the fate of prepayment is no longer bad news if it's predicted as such. By putting it up for sale accordingly, Chase tips the outcome in its favor.

With data covering millions of mortgages, the amount available for analysis far surpassed the training set of about 22,000 cases employed to build the example decision trees depicted in this chapter. Plus, for each mortgage, there were in fact *hundreds* of predictor variables detailing its ins and outs, including summaries of the entire history of payments, home neighborhood data, and other information about the individual consumer. As a result, the project demanded 200 gigabytes of storage. You could buy this much today for $30 and place it into your pocket, but in the late 1990s, the investment was about $250,000, and the storage unit was the size of a refrigerator.

The Chase project required numerous models, each specialized for a different category of mortgage. CART trees were grown separately for fixed-rate versus variable-rate mortgages, for mortgages of varying terms, and at different stages of tenure. After grouping the mortgages accordingly, a separate decision tree was generated for each group. Since each tree addressed a different type of situation, the trees varied considerably, employing their own particular group of variables in divergent ways. Dan's team delivered these eclectic decision trees to Chase for integration into the bank's systems.

## MONEY GROWS ON TREES

The undertaking was a stunning success. People close to the project at Chase reported that the predictive models generated an additional $600 million in profit during the first year of deployment (adjusted for inflation, this comes to over $800 million today). The models correctly identified 74 percent of mortgage prepayments before they took place, and drove the management of mortgage portfolios successfully.

As an institution, Chase was bolstered by this success. To strengthen its brand, it issued press releases touting its competency with advanced analytics.

Soon after the project launch, in 2000, Chase achieved yet another mammoth milestone to expand. It managed to buy JPMorgan, thus becoming JPMorgan Chase, now the largest U.S. bank by assets.

## THE RECESSION—WHY MICROSCOPES CAN'T DETECT ASTEROID COLLISIONS

Needless to say, PA didn't prevent the global financial crisis that began several years later. That wasn't its job. Applied to avert micro-risks, PA packs a serious punch. But tackling macroscopic risk is a completely different ballgame. PA is designed to rank individuals by their *relative* risk, but not to adjust the *absolute* measurements of risk when a broad shift in the economic environment is nigh. The predictive model operates on variables about the individual, such as age, education, payment history, and property type. These factors don't change even as the world around the individual changes, so the predictive score for the individual doesn't change, either.[12]

Predicting macroscopic risk is a tall order, with challenges surpassing those of micro-risk prediction. The pertinent factors can be intangible and human. As the *New York Times*'s Saul Hansell put it, "Financial firms chose to program their risk-management systems with overly optimistic assumptions . . . Wall Street executives had lots of incentives to make sure their risk systems didn't see much risk." Professor Bart Baesens of the University of Southampton's Centre for Risk Research adds, "There's an inherent tension between conservative instincts and profit-seeking motives." If we're not measuring and reporting on the truth, there's no analytical cure.

Efforts in economic theory attempt to forecast macroscopic events, although such work in forecasting is not usually integrated within the scope of predictive analytics. However, Baesens has suggested that, "By incorporating macroeconomic factors into a model, we can perform a range of data-driven stress tests." Such work must introduce a new set of variables in order to detect worldwide shifts, and requires a different analytical approach, since there are no sets of training data replete with an abundance of Black Swan events from which PA may learn. The rarest things in life are the hardest to predict.

## AFTER MATH

Decision trees vanquish, but do they satisfy the data scientist's soul? They're understandable to the human eye when viewed as rules, each one an interpretable (albeit clunky) English sentence. This is surely an advantage for some organizations, but on other occasions we'd gladly exchange simplicity for performance.

In the next chapter, we pursue Netflix's heated public competition to outpredict movie ratings. Fine-tuning predictive performance is the name of the game. Must souping up model precision involve overwhelming complexity, or is there an elegant way to build and scale?

---

[12] The form of micro-risk relevant to the economic crisis is that of delinquent debtors, rather than the micro-risk predicted in this chapter's case study, mortgage prepayments. But predicting delinquent accounts with PA is also subject to these same limitations.

## CHAPTER 5

# The Ensemble Effect

### *Netflix, Crowdsourcing, and Supercharging Prediction*

*To crowdsource predictive analytics—outsource it to the public at large—a company launches its strategy, data, and research discoveries into the public spotlight. How can this possibly help the company compete? What key innovation in predictive analytics has crowdsourcing helped develop? Must supercharging predictive precision involve overwhelming complexity, or is there an elegant solution? Is there wisdom in nonhuman crowds?*

## CASUAL ROCKET SCIENTISTS

A buddy and I are thinking of building a spaceship next year. The thing is, we have absolutely no training or background. But who cares? I want to go to outer space.

This may sound outlandish, but in the realm of predictive analytics (PA), it is essentially what Martin Chabbert and Martin Piotte did. In 2008, this pair of Montrealers launched a mission to win the $1 million Netflix Prize, the most high-profile analytical competition of its time. Incredibly, with no background in analytics, these casual part-timers became a central part of the story.

The movie rental company Netflix launched this competition to improve the movie recommendations it provides to customers. The company challenged the world by requiring that the winner improve upon Netflix's own established recommendation capabilities by 10 percent. Netflix is a prime example of PA in action, as a reported 70 percent of Netflix movie choices arise from its online recommendations. Product recommendations are increasingly important for the retail industry in general. More than a sales ploy, these tailored recommendations provide relevancy and personalization that customers actively seek.

PA APPLICATION: MOVIE RECOMMENDATIONS
1. **What's predicted:** What rating a customer would give to a movie.
2. **What's done about it:** Customers are recommended movies that they are predicted to rate highly.

PA contests such as the Netflix Prize leverage competitive spirit to garner scientific advancement. Like a horse race, a competition levels the playing field and unambiguously singles out the best entrant. With few limitations, almost anyone in the world—old, young, tall, or short—can participate by downloading the data, forming a predictive model, and submitting.

It's winner take all. To ensure submissions are objectively compared, prediction competitions employ a clever trick: The competitor must submit not a predictive model, but its predictive scores, as generated for an evaluation data set within which the correct answers—the target values that the model is meant to infer—are withheld. Netflix Prize models predict how a customer would rate a movie (based on how he or she has rated other movies). The true ratings are suppressed in the publicly posted evaluation data, so submitters can't know exactly which examples they're getting right and which they're getting wrong at the time of submission. All said, to launch the competition, Netflix released to the public over 100 million ratings from some 480,189 customers (anonymized for privacy considerations, with names suppressed).[1]

The model's ability to predict is all that matters, not the modeler's background, experience, or academic pedigree. Such a contest is a hard-nosed, objective bake-off—whoever can cook up the solution that best handles the predictive task at hand wins kudos and, usually, cash.

# DARK HORSES

And so it was with our two Montrealers, Martin and Martin, who took the Netflix Prize by storm despite their lack of experience—or, perhaps, *because* of it. Neither had a background in statistics or analytics, let alone recommendation systems in particular. By day, the two worked in the telecommunications industry developing software.

But by night, at home, the two-member team plugged away, for 10 to 20 hours per week apiece, racing ahead in the contest under the team name PragmaticTheory. The "pragmatic" approach proved groundbreaking. The team wavered in and out of the number one slot; during the final months of the competition, the team was often in the top echelons.

---

[1] PA contests do include the target values in the main data set provided for competitors to train their models. It is up to competitors to split that data into training and testing sets during model development, as discussed in the prior chapter.

There emerges an uncanny parallel to SpaceShipOne, the first privately funded human spaceflight, which won the $10 million Ansari X Prize. According to some, this small team, short on resources with a spend of only $25 million, put the established, gargantuan NASA to shame by doing more for so much less. PA competitions do for data science what the X Prize did for rocket science.

## MINDSOURCED: WEALTH IN DIVERSITY

*[Crowdsourcing is] a perfect meritocracy, where age, gender, race, education, and job history no longer matter; the quality of the work is all that counts.*
— Jeff Howe, *Crowdsourcing: Why the Power of the Crowd Is Driving the Future of Business*

When pursuing a grand challenge, from where will key discoveries appear? If we assume for the moment that one cannot know, there's only one place to look: everywhere. Contests tap the greatest resource, the general public. A common way to enact crowdsourcing, an open competition brings together scientists from far and wide to compete for the win and cooperate for the joy. With crowdsourcing, a company outsources to the world.

The $1 million Netflix Prize attracted a white-hot spotlight and built a new appreciation for the influence crowdsourcing has to rally an international wealth of bright minds. In total, 5,169 teams formed to compete in this contest, submitting 44,014 entries by the end of the event.

PA crowdsourcing reaps the rewards brought by a diverse *brainshare*. Chris Volinsky, a member of a leading Netflix Prize team named BellKor from AT&T Research, put it to me this way: "From the beginning, I thought it was awesome how many people in the top of the leaderboard were what could be called 'amateurs.' In fact, our group had no experience with [product recommendations] when we started, either. . . . It just goes to show that sometimes it takes a fresh perspective from outside the field to make progress."

One mysterious, highly competitive team came out of the woodwork, calling itself "Just a guy in a garage." The team was anonymous, but rose at one point to sixth place on the competition's leaderboard. Later, going public, it turned out to be a one-member team, a former management consultant who went to college for psychology and graduate school for operations research (he lists himself as unemployed, and has revealed he was working out of a second bedroom in his house rather than an actual garage).

So too did our pair of dark horse laymen, team PragmaticTheory, circumvent established practices, effortlessly thinking outside a box they knew nothing of in the first place. Unbounded, they could boldly go where no one had gone before. As Martin Chabbert told me in an interview, they "figured that a more pragmatic and less dogmatic approach might yield some good results." Ironically, their competitive edge appeared to hinge less on scientific innovation and more on their actual expertise: adept software engineering. Martin provided this striking lesson:

> *Many people came up with (often good) ideas . . . but translating those words into a mathematical formula is the complicated part . . . our background in engineering and software was key. In this contest, there was a fine line between a bad idea and a bug in the code. Often you would think that the model was simply bad because it didn't yield the expected results, but in fact the problem was a bug in the code. Having the ability to write code with few bugs and the skill to actually find the bugs before giving up on the model is something that definitely helped a lot. . . . Compared to what most people think, this was more of an engineering contest than a mathematical contest.*

Cross-discipline competitors thrive, as revealed by many PA contests beyond the Netflix Prize. One competition concerned with educational applications witnessed triumph by a particle physicist (Great Britain), a data analyst for the National Weather Service (Washington, D.C.), and a graduate student (Germany); $100,000 in prize money sponsored by the Hewlett Foundation (established by a founder of Hewlett-Packard) went to these winners, who developed the best means to automatically grade student-written essays. Their resulting system grades essays as accurately as human graders, although none of these three winners had backgrounds in education or text analytics.

And guess what kind of expert excelled at predicting the distribution of dark matter in the universe? Competing in a contest sponsored by NASA and the Royal Astronomical Society, Martin O'Leary, a British PhD student in *glaciology*, generated a method the White House announced has "outperformed the state-of-the-art algorithms most commonly used in astronomy." For this contest, O'Leary provided the first major breakthrough (although he was not the eventual winner). As he explains it, aspects of his work mapping the edges of glaciers from satellite photos could extend to mapping galaxies as well.

## CROWDSOURCING GONE WILD

> *Given the right set of conditions, the crowd will almost always outperform any number of employees.*
> —Jeff Howe, *Crowdsourcing: Why the Power of the Crowd Is Driving the Future of Business*

> *The organizations I've worked with have mostly viewed the competition in business as a race that benefits from sharing, rather than a fight, where one's gain can come only from another's loss. The openness of crowdsourcing aligns with this philosophy.*
> —Stein Kretsinger, Founding Executive of Advertising.com

One small groundbreaking firm, Kaggle, has taken charge and leads the production of PA crowdsourcing. Kaggle has launched 53 PA competitions, including the essay-grading and dark matter ones mentioned above. Over 50,000 registered competitors are incentivized by prizes that usually come to around $10,000 to $20,000, but climb as high as $3 million. These diverse minds from more than 200 universities and 100 countries, about half academics, have submitted over 144,000 attempts for the win.[2]

An enterprise turns research and development completely on its head in order to leverage PA crowdsourcing. Instead of protecting strategy, plans, data, and research discoveries as carefully guarded secrets, a company must launch them fully into the public spotlight. And, instead of maintaining careful control over its research staff, the organization gets whoever cares to take part in the contest and join in on the fun (for fully public contests, as is the norm). Crowdsourcing must be the most ironic, fantastical way for a business to compete.

Crowdsourcing forms a match made in heaven. Kaggle's founder and CEO, Anthony Goldbloom (a *Forbes* "30 Under 30: Technology" honoree), spells out the love story: "On one hand, you've got companies with piles and piles of data, but not the ability to get as much out of it as they would like. On the other hand, you've got researchers and data scientists, particularly at university, who are pining for access to real-world data" in order to test and refine their methodologies.

With strong analytics experts increasingly tough to find, seeding your talent pool by reaching out to the masses starts to sound like a pretty good idea. A McKinsey report states, "By 2018, the United States alone could face a shortage of 140,000 to 190,000 people with deep analytical skills as well as 1.5 million managers and analysts with the know-how to use the analysis of big data to make effective decisions." To leave no analytical stone unturned, innovative organizations turn by necessity to the crowd at large. As Kaggle pitches, "There are countless strategies that can be applied to any predictive modeling task and it is impossible to know at the outset which technique or analyst will be most effective."

Until a few years ago, most PA competitions were held by academic institutions or research conferences. Kaggle has changed this. With the claim that it "has never failed to outperform a pre-existing accuracy benchmark, and to do so resoundingly," Kaggle has brought commercial credibility to the practice. For example, across this book's Central Tables of 147 PA examples, 14 come from Kaggle competitions—namely:[3]

---

[2] Moving beyond PA to a broader range of science and business problems, InnoCentive is the analogue to Kaggle, with over 1,300 crowdsourcing challenges posted to date. The cover illustration of this book was developed by the winner of a "crystal ball" design contest the author hosted on 99designs. By hosting a competitive 3-D video game puzzle that anyone can learn to play, Foldit broke ground in protein folding to produce three discoveries that have been published in *Nature*. Noncompetitive crowdsourcing includes the advent of Wikipedia and open source software such as the Linux operating system and R, the most popular free software for analytics, which itself is employed by more Kaggle competitors than any other tool.

[3] Kaggle competitions have also advanced the state of the art in HIV research and chess ratings. For a list of even more PA competitions than those found on Kaggle's website, including those by India's CrowdANALYTIX, which also hosts a growing number of contests, see this chapter's Notes.

| Organization | What Is Predicted | Central Table to See for More Info |
| --- | --- | --- |
| Facebook | Friendship | 1 |
| dunnhumby | Supermarket visits | 2 |
| Allstate | Bodily harm from car crashes | 3 |
| $3 million Heritage Health Prize | Days spent in the hospital | 4 |
| Researchers | HIV progression | 4 |
| New South Wales, Australia | Travel time vis-à-vis traffic | 6 |
| University of Melbourne | Awarding of grants | 7 |
| Hewlett Foundation | Student grades | 7 |
| Grockit | Student knowledge | 7 |
| Imperium | Insults | 8 |
| Ford Motor Company | Driver inattentiveness | 8 |
| Online Privacy Foundation | Psychopathy | 8 |
| Wikipedia | Editor attrition | 9 |
| CareerBuilder | Job applications | 9 |

## YOUR ADVERSARY IS YOUR AMIGO

Competition paradoxically breeds cooperation. Kaggle's tagline is "making data science a sport." But these lab coat competitors don't seem to exhibit the same fierce, cutthroat voraciousness as sweaty athletes out on the field. Despite the cash incentive to come out on top, participants are often driven by the love of science. They display a spirited tendency to collaborate and share. It's the best of *coopetition*. Netflix Prize leader Martin Chabbert told me the Prize's public forum "was also a place where people proposed new ideas; these ideas often inspired us to come up with our own creative innovations." And *Wired* magazine wrote, "The prize hunters, even the leaders, are startlingly open about the methods they're using, acting more like academics huddled over a knotty problem than entrepreneurs jostling for a $1 million payday." When John Elder took part in the competition, he took pause. "It was astonishing how many people were openly sharing and cooperating," John says. "It comes of what people do out of camaraderie."

And so a community emerges around each contest, catalyzing a petri dish of great ideas. But John Elder recognizes that disclosure can cost a competitive edge. John and some staff at Elder Research were part of a Netflix Prize team during earlier phases of the contest when much of the major headway was still being made. At one point the team held third place, having employed a key analytical method before any other competitor. The method, you will soon see, was a key ingredient both to winning the Netflix Prize and to building IBM's Watson, the *Jeopardy!* player. In a collegial spirit, John's team went as far as displaying this choice of method as their very name, thereby revealing their secret weapon. The team was called "Ensemble Experts."

## UNITED NATIONS

As competitors rounded the final bend of the horse race known as the Netflix Prize (which launched before Kaggle all but took over the field), a handful of key leaders held a tense dead heat. Ironically, the race moved along at the speed of a snail, as if watching a sporting event's slow-motion instant replay on TV. Because there were diminishing returns on the teams' efforts and their predictive models' complexity, the closer they got to their objective—a 10 percent improvement over Netflix's established method that would qualify for the $1 million win—the more slowly they progressed.

Despite the glacial pace, it was gripping. The leaders faced dramatic upsets every week as they leapfrogged one another on the contest's public leaderboard. The teams jockeyed for position by way of minuscule improvements.

While nobody, including Netflix, knew if the 10 percent mark was even possible, there was the constant sense that, at any moment, a team could find a breakthrough and catapult into the win zone.

The breakthrough popped in September 2008, temporarily leaving our heroic lay competitors in the dust. Two other teams, BellKor (from AT&T Research) and BigChaos (a strikingly young-looking team from a small start-up in Austria), formed an alliance. They joined forces and blended predictive models to form an über-team. With all the communal cooperation already taking place informally, it was time to make it official.

It was risky to team up. By sharing technology, the teams lost their mutual competitive edge against one another. If they won, they'd need to split the winnings. But if they didn't team up quickly enough, other teams could try the same tactic for the win.

It worked. The teams' predictive models were quite different from one another, and, as hoped, the strengths of one model compensated for the weaknesses of the other. By integrating the models, they achieved a performance that enjoyed the best of both models. Only by doing so did the new über-team, BellKor in BigChaos, spring ahead far enough to qualify for—and win—the contest's annual progress prize of $50,000.

## META-LEARNING

Here's where the power to advance PA begins. Combining two or more sophisticated predictive models is simple: Just apply predictive modeling to learn how to combine them together. Since each model comes about from machine learning, this is an act of "learning on top of learning"—*meta-learning*.

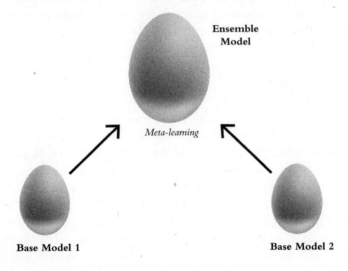

**Ensemble
Model**

*Meta-learning*

**Base Model 1**          **Base Model 2**

**An ensemble of two predictive models.**

Therefore, competitors-turned-collaborators, with two distinct, intricate models that have been developed in very different ways, don't necessarily need to work that hard to combine them. Instead of digging in and thinking intensely to compare and contrast their theories and techniques, BigChaos team member Andreas Töscher told me, they let predictive modeling do the blending. They trained a new model that sits above the two existing models like a manager. This new *ensemble model* then considers both models' predictions on a case-by-case basis. For certain cases, it can give more credence to model A rather than B, or the other way around. By so doing, the ensemble model is trained to predict which cases are weak points for each component model. There may be many cases where the two models are in agreement, but where there is disagreement, teaming the models together provides the opportunity to improve performance.

For the Netflix Prize, the rules of the game had now changed, triggering a new flurry of merging and blending as teams consolidated, rolling up into bigger and better competitors. It was like the mergers and acquisitions that take place among companies in a nascent, quickly developing industry.[4]

---

[4] We've seen such corporate roll-ups in the PA industry itself, among software companies; for example, IBM bought SPSS, which had bought Integral Solutions Limited; SAS bought Teragram (text analytics); and Pitney Bowes bought Portrait Software, which had bought Quadstone.

This merging and blending outplayed the ingenuity of our heroic lay team PragmaticTheory (the two Montrealers named Martin). But the team's success had gained the attention of its adversaries, and an invitation was extended by über-team BellKor in BigChaos to join and form an über-über-team. And so BellKor's Pragmatic Chaos came to be:

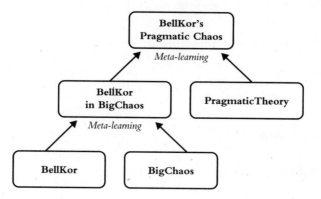

BellKor's Pragmatic Chaos made the grade. On June 26, 2009, it broke through the 10 percent barrier that qualified the super team for the $1 million Netflix Prize.

## A BIG FISH AT THE BIG FINISH

But it wasn't over yet. Per contest rules, this accomplishment triggered a 30-day countdown, during which all teams could continue to submit entries.

An arch-nemesis had emerged, called none other than The Ensemble (not to be confused with the team that included John Elder, Ensemble Experts, which employed ensemble methods internally, but did not involve combining separate teams). This rival gave BellKor's Pragmatic Chaos a serious run for the money by rolling together teams like mad. By the end, it was an amalgam of over 20 teams, one of which openly absorbed any and all teams that wished to join. By uploading its predictions, a joining team would be rewarded in proportion to the resulting improvement, the bump it contributed to the growing ensemble—but, of course, only if the overarching team won. It was like the Borg from *Star Trek*, an abominable hive-esque force that sucks up entire civilizations after declaring menacingly, "You will be assimilated!" A number of teams allowed themselves to be swallowed by this fish that ate the fish that ate the fish. After all, if you can't beat 'em, join 'em.

Although it combined the efforts of only three teams, BellKor's Pragmatic Chaos rallied to compete against this growing force. The 30 days counted down. Neck and neck, the two über-teams madly submitted new entries, tweaking, retweaking, and submitting again, even into the final hours and minutes of this multiple-year contest.

Crowdsourcing competitions cultivate a heated push for scientific innovation, engendering focus and drive sometimes compared to that attained during wartime.

Time ran out. The countdown was over and the dust was settling. The contest administrators at Netflix went silent for a few weeks as they assessed and verified. They held yet another undisclosed set of data with which to validate the submissions and determine the final verdict. Here is the top portion of the final leaderboard:

| Rank | Team Name | Best Test Score | Percentage Improvement | Best Submit Time |
|---|---|---|---|---|
| 1 | BellKor's Pragmatic Chaos | 0.8567 | 10.06 | 2009–07–26 18:18:28 |
| 2 | The Ensemble | 0.8567 | 10.06 | 2009–07–26 18:38:22 |
| 3 | Grand Prize Team | 0.8582 | 9.90 | 2009–07–10 21:24:40 |
| 4 | Opera Solutions and Vandelay United | 0.8588 | 9.84 | 2009–07–10 01:12:31 |
| 5 | Vandelay Industries ! | 0.8591 | 9.81 | 2009–07–10 00:32:20 |
| 6 | PragmaticTheory | 0.8594 | 9.77 | 2009–06–24 12:06:56 |
| 7 | BellKor in BigChaos | 0.8601 | 9.70 | 2009–05–13 08:14:09 |

BellKor's Pragmatic Chaos had won by a nose. Its final score was so close to The Ensemble's that it was considered a quantitative tie in accord with the contest's posted rules. Because of this, the determining factor was which of the tied entries had been submitted first. At the very end of a multiple-year competition, BellKor's Pragmatic Chaos had uploaded its winning entry just 20 minutes before The Ensemble. The winning team received the cash and the other team received nothing. Netflix CEO Reed Hastings reflected, "That 20 minutes was worth a million dollars."

# COLLECTIVE INTELLIGENCE

*With most things, the average is mediocrity. With decision making, it's often excellence.*
— James Surowiecki, *The Wisdom of Crowds*

Even competitions much simpler than a data mining contest can tap the wisdom held by a crowd. The magic of *collective intelligence* was lightheartedly demonstrated in 2012 at the Predictive Analytics World (PAW) conference. Charged with drawing attention

# 147 EXAMPLES OF PREDICTIVE ANALYTICS

## *A Cross-Industry Compendium*

For detailed case study documentation, see the Central Tables section in the Notes.

**Table 1**  Predictive Analytics in *Family and Personal Life*

| What's predicted: | Example organizations that use predictive analytics: |
| --- | --- |
| **Location**—*where you will be* | **Nokia:** Sponsored a competition to predict future location from cell phone tracking. Resulting methods predict location one day beforehand within 20 meters, on average, among a population based in a certain region of Switzerland, in part by incorporating the behavior of friends (i.e., the social contacts that one calls).<br><br>**Microsoft:** Helped develop technology that, based on GPS data, accurately predicts one's location up to multiple years beforehand. |
| **Friendship** | **Facebook:** Sponsored a competition to improve the precision of suggested people you may know and wish to link to.<br><br>**LinkedIn:** Considers its predictive suggestions of people you may know—"the most important data product we built." |
| **Love** | **Match.com:** For "Intelligent Matching" in online dating, predicts which prospective matches you'd be interested in communicating with.<br><br>**OkCupid:** Predicts which online dating message content is most likely to elicit a response. |
| **Pregnancy** | **Target:** Predicts customer pregnancy from shopping behavior, thus identifying 30 percent more prospects to contact with offers related to the needs of a newborn's parents *(more details in Chapter 2)*. |
| **Infidelity** | **University researchers:** Showed that cheating in a relationship is predicted more by behavioral traits than by demographic profiles, but that genetic factors are also in play. |
| **Divorce** | **Clinical researchers:** Predict divorce with 90 percent accuracy. |
| **Death** | **See tables that follow for examples in *Insurance, Healthcare, Crime Fighting* and *Safety*.** |

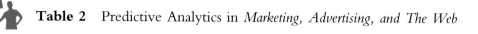

**Table 2**   Predictive Analytics in *Marketing, Advertising, and The Web*

| What's predicted: | Example organizations that use predictive analytics: |
|---|---|
| **Purchases** *in order to target marketing* | **PREMIER Bankcard:** Reduced mailing costs by $12 million.<br>**First Tennessee Bank:** Lowered mailing costs by 20 percent and increased responses by 3.1 percent for a 600 percent return on PA investment.<br>**Target:** Increased revenue 15 to 30 percent with predictive models.<br>**Harbor Sweets:** Analytically targeted lapsed customers to win them back at an impressive 40 percent response rate.<br>**Fingerhut:** Targeting reduced direct mailing 20 percent, saving almost $3 million annually, yet increasing earnings.<br>**Vermont Country Store:** More precisely targeting catalog mailings earned a return 11 times higher than the investment to do so.<br>**Harrah's Las Vegas:** This casino predicts how much a customer will spend over the long term (aka *lifetime value*).<br>**Cox Communications:** More than tripled direct mail response rate by predicting propensity to buy. Predicting demand for communications products such as home TV, Internet, and phone services achieves a 50 percent annual return.<br>**Mutual fund investment management firm:** Identified clients five times more likely than average to make additional investments.<br>**UK supermarket:** Can predict the exact date customers will return, and the amount they will spend within $10, for 19 percent of customers.<br>**Elie Tahari:** Forecasts demand for women's fashion line products. |
| **Cancellations** *in order to retain customers* | **PREMIER Bankcard:** Retained $8 million in customer value.<br>**FedEx:** Predicts which customers will defect to a competitor with 65 to 90 percent accuracy.<br>**Optus (Australia):** Identified cell phone subscribers 10 times more likely than average to cancel.<br>**Sprint:** Identified telecom customers three times more likely than average to cancel.<br>**Telenor (Norway):** Reduced cell phone subscriber turnover 36 percent; retention process return increased 11-fold *(more details in Chapter 7)*.<br>**2degrees (New Zealand):** Identified cell phone subscribers over 12 times more likely than average to cancel.<br>**Lloyds TSB:** Increased annual profit £8 million by improving the predictive modeling of customer defection.<br>**Chase:** *See entry in Table 3, Financial Risk and Insurance*<br>**Reed Elsevier:** Gained 16 percentage points in renewal rate for a magazine. |
| **Successful sales** *in order to prioritize sales leads* | **IBM:** IBM Canada predicts whether planned sales-oriented events will meet attendance goals with 83 percent confidence—*"If we host the party, will enough people show up?"* This includes IBM's sale of PA capabilities, so this effort has PA selling itself. |

| What's predicted: | Example organizations that use predictive analytics: |
| --- | --- |
| **Successful sales** *in order to prioritize sales leads (continued)* | **Hewlett-Packard:** An early warning system that alerts sales staff of business account opportunities predicts outcomes for 92 percent of sales efforts with an accuracy of 95 percent, and predicts the timing of sales closures 60 percent of the time. |
| | **Bella Pictures:** Targets brides-to-be for photography services. |
| | **Paychex:** This payroll processor decreased by 40 percent the number of phone calls needed in order to book each sales meeting, thus increasing overall sales. |
| | **Sun Microsystems:** More than doubled the number of leads per phone contact. |
| **Product choices** *for personalized recommendations* | **Amazon.com:** 35 percent of sales come from product recommendations. |
| | **Netflix:** Sponsored a $1 million competition to improve movie recommendations; a reported 70 percent of Netflix movie choices arise from its online recommendations *(more details in Chapter 5)*. |
| | **Tesco (UK):** Annually issues 100 million personalized coupons at grocery cash registers across 13 countries. Predictive modeling increased redemption rates by 3.6 times, compared to previous methods. |
| | **Target:** Increased revenue 15 to 20 percent by targeting direct mail with product choice models. |
| | **U.S. Bank:** Response doubled, cross-sell return on investment increased five-fold. |
| | **Pandora:** Recommends related songs based on 400 musical attributes. |
| **Mouse clicks** *in order to select which content to display* | **Google:** Improves search functionality by predicting which web pages will meet users' high-quality standards if shown as search results. |
| | **Education portal:** Increased ad revenue rate by $1 million every 19 months by displaying the ad you're more likely to click *(more details in Chapter 1)*. |
| **Ineffective ads** *to warn paying advertisers accordingly* | **Google:** Predicts which new ads will get many bounces (when people click on an ad, but then immediately click the back button). |
| **Viral tweets and posts** *for maximal publicity* | **MTV:** Achieved a 55 percent increase in web page views when publicizing the Video Music Awards. |
| **Spam** *to send it to your spam folder* | **Google:** Decreased Gmail's prevalence and false positive rate of spam from noticeable in 2004 down to negligible now. |
| **Hit songs and movies** | **Researchers:** Employ machine learning to predict which screenplays will be Hollywood blockbusters and which songs will hit the charts. |

**Table 3**   Predictive Analytics in *Financial Risk and Insurance*

| What's predicted: | Example organizations that use predictive analytics: |
|---|---|
| **Bodily harm from car crashes** | **Allstate:** With a predictive modeling competition in 2012, tripled the accuracy of predicting bodily injury liability based solely on the characteristics of the insured vehicle. This could be worth an estimated $40 million annually to the company. |
| **Costly workplace injuries** | **Accident Fund Insurance:** Ascertains secondary medical conditions (such as obesity and diabetes) from written workers' compensation claim notes. These conditions are predictive of which injuries will be high-cost so that, for example, insured workers may be targeted for preventive measures. |
| **Insurance claims** | **Infinity Insurance:** *See the entry in Table 7 for "Application approvals and denials."* <br><br>**Leading international commercial lines insurance provider:** Predictive models decreased the *loss ratio* by a half point, contributing to savings of almost $50 million. |
| **Death** | **Life insurance companies:** Predict age of death in order to decide upon policy application approvals and pricing. <br><br>**A top-five U.S. health insurance company:** *Death prediction is not within the usual domain for health insurance - see the* Healthcare *table below for the nature of this work.* |
| **Mortgage prepays** | **Chase:** Generated hundreds of millions of dollars with predictive models that foresee which homeowners will refinance their mortgages and thereby take all future interest payments to a competing bank *(more details in Chapter 4).* |
| **Loan defaults (risk)** | **Citigroup:** Leverages over 30 years of international loan default history to generate commercial credit risk models for individual regions (for North America and Western Europe, it breaks down further into industry-specific models), for which there are up to 3,000 internal users; models have been in existence for over 20 years. <br><br>**Canadian Tire:** Predicts late credit card bill payments in order to manage risk. <br><br>**PREMIER Bankcard:** Lowered delinquency and charge-off rates, increasing net by $10+ million. |
| **Nonpayment** | **Brasil Telecom (now Oi, which means "hi"):** Predicted bad debt to recover US$4 million. <br><br>**DTE Energy:** 700 percent increase in net savings (e.g., by preempting charge-offs and decreasing service disconnects). <br><br>**Financial institution:** Saved $2.1 million in losses by offering collection deals to those accounts that will otherwise not pay, and *not* offering to those that will. |
| **The stock market** *(black box trading)* | **London Stock Exchange:** An estimated 40 percent of London Stock Exchange trading is driven by algorithmic systems. <br><br>**John Elder:** Invested all his personal assets into a black box trading system of his own design *(more details in Chapter 1).* <br><br>**Various firms:** AlphaGenius, Cerebellum Capital, Rebellion Research, and many other firms trade algorithmically. |

## Table 4   Predictive Analytics in *Healthcare*

| What's predicted: | Example organizations that use predictive analytics: |
|---|---|
| **Death** | **A top-five U.S. health insurance company:** Predicts the likelihood an elderly insurance policy holder will pass away within 18 months in order to trigger end-of-life counseling (e.g., regarding living wills and palliative care) *(a few more details in Chapter 2)*.<br><br>**Riskprediction.org.uk:** Predicts your risk of death in surgery based on aspects of you and your condition—for minor, major, or complex operations, or for certain specialized operations such as a restorative proctocolectomy. |
| **Influenza** | **Google Flu Trends:** Shown to foresee an increase in influenza cases at one hospital 7 to 10 days earlier than the Center for Disease Control by incorporating online search trends (e.g., related to symptoms). |
| **Breast cancer (𝒟)** | **Stanford University:** Derived with predictive modeling an innovative method that diagnoses breast cancer better than human doctors in part by considering a greater number of factors in a tissue sample. |
| **Sepsis** | **Sisters of Mercy Health Systems:** Predicts severe sepsis and septic shock based on patient vital signs observed over time—detected 71 percent of cases with an acceptable false positive rate. |
| **HIV progression** | **Researchers:** Improved the accuracy of predicting disease progression from 70 to 78 percent. |
| **Effect of a drug** | **Pfizer:** Predicts the probability a patient will respond positively to pharmaceutical treatment within three weeks. |
| **Premature birth** | **Brigham Young University and University of Utah:** Correctly predict about 80 percent of premature births (and about 80 percent of full-term births), based on *peptide biomarkers*, as found in a blood exam as early as week 24 of a pregnancy. |
| **Erectile dysfunction (𝒟)** | **Pfizer:** Derived a more effective, simpler self-administered diagnostic test of five questions. |

---

𝒟 Rather than performing *prediction* in the conventional sense of the word, this application of predictive modeling performs *detection*. As with predicting the future, such applications imperfectly infer an unknown—but, in this case, the unknown could be already known by some, rather than becoming known only when witnessed in the future. This includes predicting the answer to a question, predicting a diagnosis, predicting whether a transaction is fraud, and predicting what a subject is thinking.

| What's predicted: | Example organizations that use predictive analytics: |
|---|---|
| **Hospital admissions** | **Heritage Provider Network:** $3 million competition to best predict the number of days a patient will spend in the hospital over the next year.<br><br>**University of Pittsburgh Medical Center:** Predicts a patient's risk of readmission within 30 days, in order to assist with the decision to release. |
| **Skipped drug doses** | **FICO:** Predicts patient compliance to drug prescriptions, identifying groups that will miss, on average, hundreds of days of regimen per year. Nonadherence to medication prescriptions causes an estimated 125,000 premature deaths and over $290 billion in avoidable costs annually in the United States alone. |
| **Clinical trial recruitment** | **GlaxoSmithKline (UK):** Predicts the supply of much-needed participants for the clinical trial of a new drug in order to plan and allocate expensive trial drug supplies. Clinical trials are a major bottleneck and cost in pharmaceutical research and development (R&D). |
| **Billing errors** (*D*) | **MultiCare Health System (four hospitals in Washington State):** Detected errant accounts and claims to realize $2 million in missed charges within one year. |
| **Various health risks** | **Medical centers and healthcare providers:** Proactively target marketing solicitations for preventive and early intervention healthcare to individuals with higher health risks.<br><br>**Blue Cross Blue Shield of Tennessee:** Predicts from claims data which healthcare resources individual members will need. |

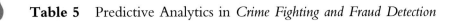

**Table 5**   Predictive Analytics in *Crime Fighting and Fraud Detection*

| What's predicted: | Example organizations that use predictive analytics |
| --- | --- |
| **Fraudulent:** *(𝒟)* | |
| *Tax returns* | **Internal Revenue Service:** Predictively ranking tax returns suspected of cheating empowered IRS analysts to find 25 times more tax evasion, without increasing the number of investigations. |
| *Government invoices* | **U.S. Department of Defense's Defense Finance and Accounting Service:** Detected 97 percent of known fraud cases in a published study. |
| *Government contracts* | **U.S. Postal Service:** Predictively ranks suspected incidents of contract fraud such as collusion or preferential treatment in order to guide investigations. |
| *Checks* | **Citizens Bank:** Predicted which checks are fraudulent well enough to decrease fraud loss by 20 percent. |
| *Automobile insurance claims* | **$40+ billion U.S. insurance company:** Predictively ranking suspected claims empowered auditors to find 6.5 times more fraud with the same number of investigations. |
| | **Aviva Insurance (UK):** Improved the detection of fraudulent auto claims that include a body injury component, amounting to a new savings of half a million pounds per month. |
| *Warranty claims* | **Hewlett-Packard:** Realized $66 million in savings over five years by detecting fraudulent warranty claims submitted by HP sales and service partners. |
| *Workers' comp claims* | **U.S. Postal Service:** Predicted which workers' compensation claims and payments are unwarranted, contributing to a savings of $9.5 million achieved by analytical approaches. |
| **Murder** | **Maryland:** Applies predictive models to detect inmates more at risk to be perpetrators or victims of murder. |
| **Street crime** | **Chicago, Los Angeles, Memphis (TN), Richmond (VA), Santa Cruz (CA), and Vineland (NJ):** Direct police to patrol areas where crime is predicted *(more details in Chapter 2)*. |
| **Terrorist attacks** | **U.S. Armed Forces:** Conduct and fund research to analytically predict terrorist attacks and armed opposition group activities based on factors such as relevant arrests, trials, financial support received, and contextual political conditions. |
| **Ducking city regulations** *(𝒟)* | **New York City:** Targeting investigations increased by five times the discovery of illegal apartments and flipped business licenses, and doubled the detection of stores selling bootlegged cigarettes. |

𝒟 Detection, not prediction, see Table 4 for more information.

| What's predicted: | Example organizations that use predictive analytics |
|---|---|
| **Recidivism (repeat offenses)** *in order to decide on prison sentencing and parole* | **Oregon and Pennsylvania:** Judges and parole boards consult predictive models in order to help decide who stays incarcerated, and for how long *(more details in Chapter 2).* |
| **Whether a murder will be solved** | **Chicago Police Department:** Found that characteristics of a homicide and its victim help predict whether the crime will be solvable. |
| **Security level** | **Amazon.com:** Predicts the appropriate security access needs of employees. |
| **Hackers and viruses** *(𝒟)* | **Researchers:** Predictively model which online activities are malicious intrusions and attacks, and which are legitimate activities. |

| What's predicted: | Example organizations that use predictive analytics: |
|---|---|
| **System failure** *to preemptively intervene*<br>*Satellites* | **Large commercial satellite company:** Discovered patterns in satellite battery failures in order to better predict which satellites will require maintenance three years out. |
| *Nuclear reactors (𝒟)* | **Argonne National Laboratory:** Predictive modeling of nuclear reactor failures (e.g., cracks in cooling pipes). |
| *City power* | **Con Edison:** In New York City, predicts failure of energy distribution cables, updating risk levels that are displayed on operators' screens three times an hour. |
| *Train tracks (𝒟)* | **BNSF Railway:** Predicts broken train tracks, the leading cause of severe train accidents, generating location-specific service failure predictions with 85 percent accuracy. |
| *Train Wheels* | **TTX:** Predicts the failure probability for each of hundreds of thousands of railcar wheels in order to forecast overall annual inventory and maintenance need within a 1.5 percent margin. |
| *Office equipment* | **Fortune 500 global technology company:** Predicts which components of electronic equipment such as printers and hard drives are most likely in need of replacement in order to preload repair dispatch trucks. |
| *Credit card payment systems (𝒟)* | **Leading payments processor:** A project to detect transaction system behavior anomalies so that problems are resolved more quickly achieved a sevenfold return on investment. |
| *Buildings* | **Universities in Iran:** Predict the strength of concrete based on how it is composed and mixed. |
| *Company networks*<br><br>*aka reliability modeling* | **Poll: 18 percent of information technology (IT) departments:** Employ predictive analytics to warn of impending IT failures in order to take corrective measures such as preparing for a spike in online activity. |
| **Defective items** *for assembly line quality control (𝒟)* | **Washing machine manufacturer:** Fault detection performance exceeding 87 percent. |
| **Oil flow rate** *in order to efficiently tap underground petroleum reserves* | **National Iranian South Oil Company:** Uses a neural network to predict the rate of oil production. |
| **Customer need** *in order to streamline service* | **Canadian Automobile Association:** New process responding to customer calls reduced dispatches 25 percent and cut labor costs when service isn't needed, yet lowered dissatisfaction 45 percent. |

𝒟 Detection, not prediction, see Table 4 for more information.

| What's predicted: | Example organizations that use predictive analytics: |
|---|---|
| **Airplane crash fatalities** (*D*) | **Analytics leaders:** Identify aviation incidents five times more likely than average to be fatal, modeling on data from the National Transportation Safety Board. |
| **Flight delays** | **Continental Airlines:** Improved aviation delays and airspace performance by predicting them with radar network data, saving tens of millions of dollars. |
| **Traffic** | **New South Wales, Australia:** Predicts travel time on Sydney, Australia's M4 freeway. Anticipated travel delays will be provided online to locals just as weather forecasts are. |
| **Dropped calls** | **Nokia Siemens Networks:** Predict customer outages on a 4G wireless network with 70 percent accuracy in order to improve service availability and continuity. |

**Table 7**  Predictive Analytics in *Government, Politics, Nonprofit, and Education*

| What's predicted: | Example organizations that use predictive analytics: |
| --- | --- |
| **Voter persuasion** | **Obama for America 2012 Campaign:** Predicted which voters would be positively influenced by campaign contact (a call, door knock, flier, or TV ad), and which would actually be caused to vote adversely by contact. Employed to drive campaign decisions for millions of swing state voters, the predictive models "showed significant lift" over traditional campaign targeting *(more details in Chapter 7)*. |
| **Donations** | **Charlotte Rescue Mission:** Increased contributions in response to fund-raising campaigns by nearly 50 percent. <br><br> **The Nature Conservancy:** Discovered how to profit $669,000 by mailing to only the 10 percent of its donor list predicted to be most likely to contribute. <br><br> **JustGiving:** Credits predictive analytics as central in an expected increase in fund-raising of hundreds of millions of British pounds. <br><br> **University of Utah's School of Business:** Increased alumni donations 73 percent by predicting respond to annual outreach. |
| **Awarding of grants** | **University of Melbourne:** Sponsored a predictive modeling competition to predict which applications for research grants will be approved. |
| **Energy consumption** | **Energex (Australia):** The country's second largest utility spatially simulates 20 years of forecasted electricity demand growth in order to direct infrastructure development and target consumers with incentives to decrease energy consumption. |
| **Microloan defaults** | **Kiva:** Detects microloan projects (to alleviate poverty) almost twice as likely as average to default on payback, in part by the absence or presence of key words such as *school* and *machine* in project descriptions. The insights could guide individual lenders, who may lend through www.kiva.org as little as $25. |
| **Application approvals and denials** | **U.S. Social Security Administration:** Sped up its response to disability claims for a significant subset of applicants, from over a month to under an hour. <br><br> **Infinity Insurance:** 1,100 percent increase in fast-tracking claims. |
| **The need for help** | **British Broadcasting Corporation:** Targeted which home TV viewers were most likely in need of technical assistance with the switch-over to digital TV, especially among the older and disabled. |
| **Dropouts** | **American Public University System, Arizona State University, Iowa State University, Netherlands' Eindhoven University, Oklahoma State University, and University of Alabama:** Predict which students are at risk of dropping out in order to intervene and assist in the hope of retaining them. |

| What's predicted: | Example organizations that use predictive analytics: |
|---|---|
| **Grades**<br><br>. . . *so the computer can grade automatically*<br><br>. . . *so academic assistance can be targeted* | **Hewlett Foundation:** Sponsored the development of automatic grading of student-written essays. The resulting system grades essays as accurately as (i.e., in agreement with) human graders.<br><br>**University of Phoenix:** Predicts which students risk failing a course in order to target intervention measures such as adviser coaching.<br><br>**Rio Salado Community College:** Predicts after eight days of class whether students will attain a C or better with 70 percent accuracy, based in part on online behavior, in order to alert professors. |
| **Knowledge** (for education) | ***Jeopardy!* winner:** Analytics expert Roger Craig predicted which practice questions he'd get wrong in order to target his many hours of studying for an appearance on this TV quiz show. He attained the highest one-day winning total ever, and won the show's 2011 Tournament of Champions *(more details in Chapter 6)*.<br><br>**Facebook, Elsevier, IBM, and Pittsburgh Science of Learning Center:** Sponsored a predictive modeling competition to predict student performance on algebra problems. Predictively tailored instruction by Intelligent Tutoring Systems promises to save a roughly estimated 250 million student hours per year.<br><br>**Grockit:** This test preparation company predicts which GMAT, SAT, and ACT questions a test taker will get wrong in order to target areas for which he or she needs more study. |

**Table 8**  Predictive Analytics in *Human Language Understanding, Thought, and Psychology*

| What's predicted: | Example organizations that use predictive analytics: |
| --- | --- |
| **Answers to questions** (𝒟) | **IBM:** Developed with predictive modeling the Watson question-answering computer, which defeated the two all-time human champions of the TV quiz show *Jeopardy!* on a televised standoff *(more details in Chapter 6).* |
| **Lies** (𝒟) | **University at Buffalo:** Researchers trained a system to detect lies with 82 percent accuracy by observing eye movements alone.<br><br>**Researchers:** Predict deception with 76 percent accuracy within written statements by persons of interest in military base criminal investigations. |
| **Insults** (𝒟) | **Imperium:** This data integrity company sponsored a competition to identify insults within online comments and blogs such as "bottom feeder" and "one sick puppy." |
| **Inappropriate comments** (𝒟) | **British Broadcasting Company:** Predicts which comments will be approved for posting on its web pages so that only one-quarter of the millions of attempted posts need be screened by human moderators. |
| **Sarcasm** (𝒟) | **Hebrew University:** Identifies 83 percent of sarcastic Amazon product reviews (e.g., "Trees died for this book?"). |
| **Dissatisfaction** (𝒟) | **PayPal:** Identifies from written feedback customers who intend to leave (aka churn or defect) with 85 percent accuracy.<br><br>**Citibank:** Categorizes incoming customer messages in order to automatically route problems to the correct support personnel. |
| **Driver inattentiveness** (𝒟) | **Ford Motor Company:** Learned from data to detect when a driver is not alert due to distraction, fatigue, or intoxication. Given an alert driver and a nonalert driver, it can identify the nonalert driver with 86 percent accuracy.<br><br>**Averitt:** This transportation company predicts truck driver fatigue, crediting this capability with a 30 percent reduction in driver accidents.<br><br>**Air Force:** Funded research to detect driver fatigue from infrared-illuminated video of the driver. |
| **Psychopathy** (𝒟) | **Online Privacy Foundation:** Sponsored a competition to predict psychopathy, as otherwise accessed via nine psychological questions, from the subject's tweets. |
| **Schizophrenia** (𝒟) | **Analytics leaders and a psychiatry professor:** Derived a method to detect patient schizophrenia from the frequent use of pronouns and the brevity of responses to questions, correctly assessing 27+ of 29 previously unseen patients from transcripts alone. |

---

𝒟 Detection, not prediction, see Table 4 for more information.

| What's predicted: | Example organizations that use predictive analytics: |
|---|---|
| **Brain activity** *in order to construct a moving image of whatever you're seeing* | **University of California, Berkeley:** Can render from your brain activities a video approximation of your visual experience. A model predicts the brain activity that will result from what you see so that fMRI readings taken from your brain while viewing a new video can be decoded—it reverse engineers what you're seeing by blending 100 selections from a large video library. |
| **Thoughts** *($\mathscr{D}$)* | **Researchers:** Computers literally read your mind. Researchers trained systems to decode from fMRI brain scans which type of object you're thinking about—such as tools, buildings, or food—with over 80 percent accuracy for some subjects. |
| | **Radica Games:** Manufactures 20Q, a yo-yo-sized toy that employs a neural network to play Twenty Questions, correctly guessing the animal/vegetable/mineral you're thinking of 98 percent of the time after asking you 25 questions; it is robust against wrong answers. |

**Table 9**   Predictive Analytics in *Staff and Employees—Human Resources*

| What's predicted: | Example organizations that use predictive analytics: |
|---|---|
| **Quitting** | **Hewlett-Packard:** Predictive models generate a "Flight Risk" score for each of its almost 350,000 worldwide employees so managers may intervene in advance where possible, and plan accordingly otherwise, thus identifying an estimated $300 million in potential savings *(more details in Chapter 2)*.<br><br>**Wikipedia:** Predicts which of its 750,000 editors, who voluntarily perform 139 million edits per year and create over 8,000 new articles a day, will discontinue their work. |
| **Job performance** | **University researchers:** Demonstrated that Facebook profiles predict job performance. Job performance evaluations correlate with personality attributes gleaned from Facebook profiles, such as curiosity, agreeability, and conscientiousness.<br><br>**U.S. Special Forces:** Predicts which candidates will be successful in this highly specialized, demanding job, worthy of investing years of training. Key predictors include grit (a better predictor than IQ) and the ability to do more than 80 pushups. |
| **Skills (*𝒟*)** | **LinkedIn:** Labels your profile with skills it predicts you have from your written contents. |
| **Job applications** | **CareerBuilder:** Predicts positions for which each job seeker will apply in order to target job recommendations. |

---

*𝒟* Detection, not prediction, see Table 4 for more information.

to his analytics company on the event's exposition floor, Gary Panchoo held a money-guessing contest. Here he is, collecting best guesses as to how many dollar bills are in the container:

The guessers as a group outsmarted every individual guess. The winner was only $10 off the actual amount, $362. But the average of the 61 guesses, $365, was off by just $3.

With no coordinated effort among the guessers, how could this phenomenon be common? One way to look at it is that all people's overestimations and under-estimations even out. If we assume that people guess too high as much as they do too low, averaging cancels out these errors in judgment. No one person can overcome his or her own limited capacity—unless you're a superhero, you can't look at the container of dollars and be superconfident about your estimation. But, across a group, the mistakes come out in the wash.

Uniting endows power. By coming together as a group, our limited capacities as individuals are overcome. Moreover, we no longer need to take on the challenging task of identifying the best person for the job. It doesn't matter which person is smartest. A diverse mix best does the trick.

The *collective intelligence* of a crowd emerges on many occasions, as explored thoroughly by James Surowiecki in his book *The Wisdom of Crowds*. Examples include:

- *Prediction markets*, wherein a group of people together estimate the prospects for a horse race, political event, or economic occurrence by way of placing bets (unfortunately, this adept forecasting method cannot usually scale to the domain of PA, in which thousands or millions of predictions are generated by a predictive model).
- The audience of the TV quiz show *Who Wants to Be a Millionaire?*, whom contestants may poll to weigh in on questions.
- Google's PageRank method, by which a web page's value and importance are informed by how many links people have created to point to the page.
- The predictive capacity of the mass mood expressed by bloggers at large to foresee stock market behavior, as covered in Chapter 3 (in fact, related work comes from MIT's aptly named Center for Collective Intelligence).

Human minds aren't the only things that can be effectively merged together. It turns out the aggregate effect emerging from a group extends also to *nonhuman* crowds—of predictive models.

## THE WISDOM OF CROWDS . . . OF MODELS

*The "wisdom of crowds" concept motivates ensembles because it illustrates a key principle of ensembling: Predictions can be improved by averaging the predictions of many.*
                                        —Dean Abbott, Abbott Analytics

Like a crowd of people, an ensemble of predictive models benefits from the same "collective intelligence" effect.[5] Each model has its strengths and weaknesses. As with guesses made by people, the predictive scores produced by models are imperfect. Some will be too high and some too low. Averaging scores from a mix of models can wipe away much of the error. Why hire the best single employee when you can afford to hire a team whose members compensate for one another's weaknesses? After all, models work for free; a computer uses practically no additional electricity to apply 100 models rather than just one.

Ensemble modeling has taken the PA industry by storm. It's often considered the most important predictive modeling advancement of this century's first decade. While its success in crowdsourcing competitions has helped bolster its credibility, the craft of

---

[5] Dean Abbott, a leading PA consultant and frequent publisher on the topic of ensemble models, brought this analogy to my attention.

ensembling pervades beyond that arena, both in commercial application and in research advancement.

But increasing complexity is paradoxical to improved learning. An ensemble of models—which can grow to include thousands—is much more involved than a single model, so it's a move away from the "keep it simple, stupid" (KISS) principle (aka Occam's razor) that's so critical to avoiding overlearning, as discussed in Chapter 4. Before ironing out this irony, let's take a closer look at how ensemble models work.

## A Bag of Models

*Modular decomposition—*
*it's the way things are . . . and ought to be.*
*If your life is hierarchical, it's really quite remarkably*
*easy to do each sub-sub-sub-sub-sub-routine.*
                        —The author, "Modular Decomposition" (musical number)

Leo Breiman, one of the Fab Four inventors of CART decision trees (detailed in Chapter 4), developed a leading method for ensemble models called *bagging* (short for *bootstrap aggregating*). The way it operates is practically self-evident. Make a bunch of models, a bagful. To predict, have each model make its prediction, and tally up the results. Each model gets to vote (voting is similar to averaging and in some cases is equivalent). The models are endowed with a key characteristic: diversity. Diversity is ensured by building each model on a different subset of the data, in which some examples are randomly duplicated so that they have a stronger influence on the model's learning process, and others are left out completely. Reflecting this random element, one variation on bagging that assembles a number of CART decision trees is dubbed *random forests*. (Doesn't this make a single tree seem *"à la CART"*?)

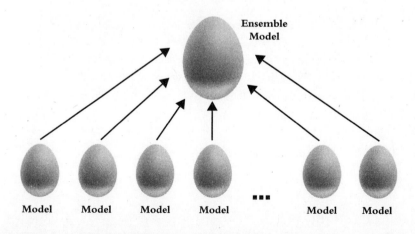

Ensemble
Model

Model    Model    Model    Model    Model    Model

**A group of models come together to form an ensemble.**

The idea of collecting models and having them vote is as simple and elegant as it sounds. In fact, other ensemble methods, all variations on the same theme, also sport friendly, self-descriptive names, including *bucket of models*, *bundling*, *committee of experts*, *meta-learning*, *stacked generalization*, and *TreeNet* (some employ voting and others meta-learn as for the Netflix Prize).

The notion of assembling components into a more complex, powerful structure is the very essence of engineering, whether constructing buildings and bridges or programming the operating system that runs your iPhone. Nobody must—indeed, nobody can—conceive of the entire massive structure at once. Tiered assembly makes architecting manageable. Each level of composition pastes together units that are themselves simple to conceive of, albeit involved and complex under the hood.

An ensemble usually kicks a single model's butt. Check out this attempt by a single decision tree to model a circle:

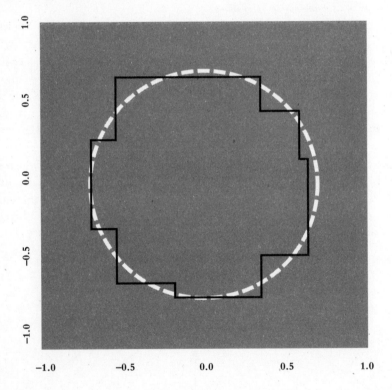

This and the following figure are reproduced with permission.[6]

[6] John Elder and Greg Ridgeway, "Combining Estimators to Improve Performance," KDD Tutorial Notes, 1999.

In this experiment, a CART decision tree was trained over a data set that was manufactured to include positive and negative examples, inside and outside the circle, respectively. Because a decision tree can only compare the predictor variables (in this case, the $x$ and $y$ coordinates) to a fixed value, and cannot perform any math on them, the tree's *decision boundary* consists only of horizontal and vertical lines. No diagonal or curvy boundaries are allowed. The resulting model does correctly label most points as to whether they're inside or outside the circle, but it's clearly a rough, primitive approximation.

Bagging a set of 100 CART trees generates a smoother, more refined model:[7]

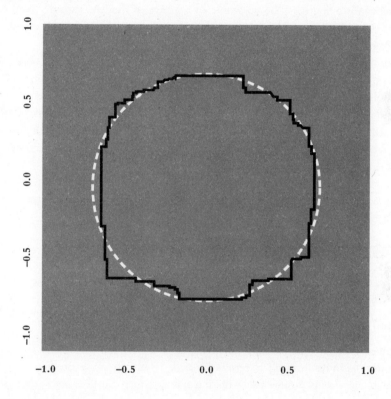

Reproduced with permission.

_____

[7] While these visuals provide an intuitive view, real PA applications are usually difficult or impossible to view in this way. These examples are two-dimensional, since each case is defined only by the $x$ and $y$ coordinates. Predictive models normally work with dozens or hundreds of variables, in which case the decision boundary cannot be viewed with a two-dimensional diagram. Further, the reality behind the data that the predictive model is attempting to ascertain—in this manufactured example, a single circle—is unknown (if it were known, there would be no need for data analysis in the first place), and is generally more complex than a circle.

# ENSEMBLE MODELS IN ACTION

*Teams often use an ensemble model to win Kaggle contests.*
—Anthony Goldbloom, founder and CEO of Kaggle

Whether assembled by the thousands or pasted together manually (as in the case when Netflix Prize teams joined forces), ensemble models triumph time after time. Research results consistently show that ensembles boost a single model's performance in the general range of 5 to 30 percent, and that integrating more models into an ensemble just keeps improving it. "The ensemble of a group of models is usually better than most of the individual models it's made up of, and often better than them all," says Dean Abbott.

Commercial deployment is expanding. Across this book's Central Tables of PA examples, at least eight employed ensemble models: IBM (*Jeopardy!*-playing Watson computer), the IRS (tax fraud), the Nature Conservancy (donations), Netflix (movie recommendations), Nokia-Siemens (dropped calls), University of California–Berkeley (brain activity, to construct a moving image of what you're seeing), U.S. Department of Defense (fraudulent government invoices), and U.S. Special Forces (job performance).[8]

It seems too good to be true. With ensembles, we are consistently rewarded with better predictive models, often without any new math or formal theory. Is there a catch?

# THE GENERALIZATION PARADOX: MORE IS LESS

*Ensembles appear to increase complexity . . . so, their ability to generalize better seems to violate the preference for simplicity summarized by Occam's Razor.*
—John Elder, "The Generalization Paradox of Ensembles"

In Chapter 4 we saw that pursuing the heady goal of machine learning, *to learn without overlearning*, requires striking a careful balance. Building up a predictive model's complexity so that it more closely fits the training data can go only so far. After a certain point, true predictive performance, as measured over a held-aside test set, begins to suffer.

Ensembles remain robust even as they become increasingly complex. They seem to be immune to this limitation, as if soaked in a magic potion against overlearning. John Elder, who humorously calls ensemble models a "secret weapon," identified this dilemma in a research paper and dubbed it "the generalization paradox of ensembles."

---

[8] Further, the Anxiety Index described in Chapter 3 employs an ensemble of two models in order to predict blog entry anxiety.

John resolves the apparent paradox by redefining *complexity*, measuring it "by function rather than form." Ensemble models look more complex—but, he asks, do they *act* more complex? Instead of considering a model's structural complexity—how big it is or how many components it includes—he measures the *complexity of the overall modeling method*. He employs a measure called *generalized degrees of freedom*, which shows how adaptable a modeling method is, how much its resulting predictions change as a result of small experimental changes to the training data. If a small change in the data makes a big difference, the learning method may be brittle, susceptible to the whims of randomness and noise found within any data set. It turns out that this measure of complexity is *lower* for an ensemble of models than for individual models. Ensembles overadapt less. In this way, ensemble models exhibit *less* complex behavior, so their success in robustly learning without overlearning isn't paradoxical after all.

Enter The Ensemble Effect. By simply joining models together, we enjoy the benefit of cranking up our model's *structural complexity* while retaining a critical ingredient: robustness against overlearning.

---

*The Ensemble Effect:* When joined in an ensemble, predictive models compensate for one another's limitations, so the ensemble as a whole is more likely to predict correctly than its component models are.

---

## THE SKY'S THE LIMIT

With the newfound power of ensemble models and the fervor to tackle increasingly grand challenges, what's next? In the following chapter, PA takes on a tremendous one: competing on the TV quiz show *Jeopardy!*

# CHAPTER 6

# Watson and the *Jeopardy!* Challenge

*How does Watson—IBM's Jeopardy!-playing computer—work? Why does it need predictive modeling in order to answer questions, and what secret sauce empowers its high performance? How does the iPhone's Siri compare? Why is human language such a challenge for computers? Is artificial intelligence possible?*

January 14, 2011. The big day had come. David Gondek struggled to sit still, battling the butterflies of performance anxiety, even though he was not the one onstage. Instead, the spotlights shone down upon a machine he had helped build at IBM Research for the past four years. Before his eyes, it was launched into a battle of intellect, competing against humans in this country's most popular televised celebration of human knowledge and cultural literacy, the quiz show *Jeopardy!*

Celebrity host Alex Trebek read off a clue, under the category "Dialing for Dialects":

> VEDIC, DATING BACK AT LEAST 4,000 YEARS, IS THE EARLIEST DIALECT OF THIS CLASSICAL LANGUAGE OF INDIA *

Watson, the electronic progeny of David and his colleagues, was competing against the two all-time champions across the game show's entire 26-year televised history.

---

*\*Jeopardy!* questions stamped with an asterisk were posed during Watson's televised match.

These two formidable opponents were of a different ilk, holding certain advantages over the machine, but also certain disadvantages. They were human.

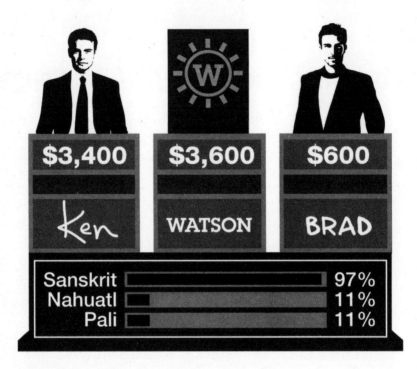

**Watson competes against two humans on *Jeopardy!***

Watson buzzed in ahead of its opponents. Deaf and unable to hear Trebek's professional, confident voice, it had received the *Jeopardy!* clue as a transmission of typed text. The audience heard Watson's synthesized voice respond, phrasing it according to the show's stylistic convention of posing each answer in the form of a question. "What is Sanskrit?"[1]

For a computer, questions like this might as well be written in Sanskrit. Human languages like English are far more complex than the casual speaker realizes, with extremely subtle nuance and a pervasive vagueness we nonmachines seem completely comfortable with. Programming a computer to work adeptly with human language is often considered the ultimate challenge of artificial intelligence (AI).

---

[1] In this chapter, I refer to each *Jeopardy!* clue as a *question* and each contestant response as an *answer*. It is a game of question answering, despite its stylistic convention of phrasing each contestant response in the form of a question beginning "What is" or "Who is."

## TEXT ANALYTICS

*It was Greek to me.*

—William Shakespeare

*I'm completely operational, and all my circuits are functioning perfectly.*
—HAL, the intelligent computer from *2001: A Space Odyssey* (1968)

Science fiction almost always endows AI with the capacity to understand human tongues. Hollywood glamorizes a future in which we chat freely with the computer like a well-informed friend. In *Star Trek IV: The Voyage Home* (1986), our heroes travel back in time to a contemporary Earth and are confounded by its primitive technology. Our brilliant space engineer Scotty, attempting to make use of a Macintosh computer, is so accustomed to computers understanding the spoken word that he assumes its mouse must be a microphone. Patiently picking up the mouse as if it were a quaint artifact, he jovially beckons, "Hello, computer!"

*2001: A Space Odyssey*'s smart and talkative computer, HAL, bears a legendary, disputed connection in nomenclature to IBM (just take each letter back one position in the alphabet); however, author Arthur C. Clarke has strenuously denied that this was intentional. Ask IBM researchers whether their question answering Watson system is anything like HAL, which goes famously rogue in the film, and they'll quickly reroute your comparison toward the obedient computers of *Star Trek*.

The field of research that develops technology to work with human language is *natural language processing* (NLP, aka *computational linguistics*). In commercial application, it's known as *text analytics*. These fields develop analytical methods especially designed to operate across the written word.

If data is all Earth's water, textual data is the part known as "the ocean." Often said to compose 80 percent of all data, it's everything we the human race know that we've bothered to write down. It's potent stuff—content-rich because it was generated with the intent to convey not just facts and figures, but human knowledge.

But text, data's biggest opportunity, presents the greatest challenge.

## OUR MOTHER TONGUE'S TRIALS AND TRIBULATIONS

*It is difficult to answer, when one does not understand the question.*
—Sarek, Spock's father, in *Star Trek IV: The Voyage Home*

Let's begin with the relatively modest goal of grammatically deconstructing the Sanskrit question, repeated here:

> VEDIC, DATING BACK AT LEAST
> 4,000 YEARS, IS THE EARLIEST
> DIALECT OF THIS CLASSICAL
> LANGUAGE OF INDIA

*

For example, consider how "of India" fits in. It's a prepositional phrase that modifies "this classical language." That may seem obvious to you, human reader, but if the final two words had been "of course," that phrase would instead modify the main verb, "is" (or the entire phrase, depending on how you look at it).

Determining how each component such as "of India" fits in relies on a real understanding of words and the things in the world that they represent. Take the classic linguistic conundrum, "Time flies like an arrow." Which is the main verb of the sentence? It is *flies* if you interpret the sentence as: "Time moves quickly, just as an arrow does." But it could be *time* if you read it as the imperative, ordering you to "Measure the speed of flies as you would measure that of an arrow."

The preferred retort to this aphorism, often attributed to Groucho Marx, is: "Fruit flies like a banana." It's funny and grammatically revealing. Suddenly *like* is now the verb, instead of a preposition.

"I had a car." If the duration of time for which this held true was one year, I would say, "I had a car *for* a year." But change one word and everything changes. "I had a baby." If the duration of labor was five hours, you would say, "I had a baby *in* five hours," not "*for* five hours." The word choice depends on whether you're describing a situation or an event, and the very meaning of the object—*car* or *baby*—makes the difference.

"I ate spaghetti with meatballs." Meatballs were part of the spaghetti dish.

"I ate spaghetti with a fork." The fork was instrumental to eating, not part of the spaghetti.

"I ate spaghetti with my friend Bill." Bill wasn't part of the spaghetti, nor was he instrumental to eating, although he was party to the eating event.

"I had a ball." Great, you had fun.

"I had a ball but I lost it." Not so much fun! But, in a certain context, the same phrase goes back to being about having a blast:

Q: *"How was your vacation and where is my video camera?"*
A: *"I had a ball but I lost it."*

In language, even the most basic grammatical structure that determines which words directly connect depends on our particularly human view of and extensive knowledge about the world. The rules are fluid, and the categorical shades of meaning are informal.[2]

## ONCE YOU UNDERSTAND THE QUESTION, ANSWER IT

*How can a slim chance and a fat chance be the same, while a wise man and wise guy are opposites?*
—Anonymous

*Why does your nose run, and your feet smell?*

—George Carlin

Beyond processing a question in the English language, a whole other universe of challenge lurks: *answering it*. Assume for a moment the language challenges have been miraculously met and the computer has gained the ability to, "understand" a *Jeopardy!* question, to grammatically break it down, and to assess the "meaning" of its main verb and how this meaning fuses with the "meanings" of the other words such as the subject, object, and prepositional phrases to form the question's overall meaning. Consider the following question, under the category "Movie Phone":

> **KEANU REEVES HAD A NOKIA PHONE, BUT IT TOOK A LAND LINE TO SLIP IN & OUT OF THIS, THE TITLE OF A 1999 SCI-FI FLICK**

A perfect language-understanding machine could invoke a routine to search a database of movies for one starring Keanu Reeves in which a plot element involves using a land-line telephone to "get out of" something—that something also being the title of the movie (*The Matrix*). Even if the reliable transformation of question to database lookup were possible, how could any database be sure to include coverage of these kinds of abstract movie plot elements, which are subjective and endless?

As another example that would challenge any database, consider this *Jeopardy!* question under the category "The Art of the Steal":

---

[2] We face yet another "Mission Impossible" trying to get the computer to write instead of read. Generating human language trips up the naïve machine. I once received a voice-synthesized call from Blockbuster reminding me of my rented movie's due date. "This is a message for Eric the Fifth Siegel," it said. My middle initial is V. Translation between languages also faces hazards. An often-cited example is that "The spirit is willing, but the flesh is weak," if translated into Russian and back, could end up as "The vodka is good, but the meat is rotten."

> THE ANCIENT "LION OF NIMRUD" WENT MISSING FROM THIS CITY'S NATIONAL MUSEUM IN 2003 (ALONG WITH A LOT OF OTHER STUFF) *

First, to succeed, the system must include the right information about each art piece, just as movie plot elements were needed for the *Matrix* question. IBM would have needed the foresight to include in a database of artworks whether, when, and where each item was stolen (for this item, the answer is Baghdad). Second, the system would also need to equate "went missing" with being stolen. That may be a reasonable interpretation regarding artwork, but if I said that my car keys went missing, we wouldn't reach the same conclusion. How endlessly involved would a mechanical incarnation of human reason need to be in order to automatically make such distinctions? Written sources such as newspaper articles did in fact use a diverse collection of words to report this art carving's *disappearance*, *looting*, *theft*, or *being stolen*.

Movies and artworks represent only the tip-top of a vast iceberg. *Jeopardy!* questions could fall within any domain, from the history of wine to philosophy to literature to biochemistry, and the answer required could be a person, place, animal, thing, year, or abstract concept. This unbounded challenge is called *open question answering*. Anything goes.

The old-school artificial intelligence researcher succumbs to temptation and fantasizes about building a Complete Database of Human Knowledge. That researcher is fun to chat with. He holds a grandiose view regarding our ability to reach for the stars by digging deep, examining our own inner cognitions, and expressing them with computer programs that mimic human reason and encode human knowledge. But someone has to break it to the poor fellow: This just isn't possible. As more pragmatic researchers concluded in the 1980s and 1990s, it's too large and too ill defined.

In reality, given these challenges, IBM concluded only 2 percent of *Jeopardy!* questions could be answered with a database lookup. The demands of open question answering reach far beyond the computer's traditional arena of storing and accessing data for flight reservations and bank records. We're going to need a smarter robot.

## THE ULTIMATE KNOWLEDGE SOURCE

*We are not scanning all those books to be read by people. We are scanning them to be read by an AI.*
—A Google employee regarding Google's book scanning, as quoted by George Dyson
in *Turing's Cathedral: The Origins of the Digital Universe*

A bit of good news: IBM didn't need to create comprehensive databases for the *Jeopardy!* challenge because the ultimate knowledge source already exists: *the written word*. I am pleased to report that people like to report; we write down what we know in books, web pages, Wikipedia entries, blogs, and newspaper articles. All this *textual data* composes an unparalleled gold mine of human knowledge.

The problem is that these things are all encoded in human language, just like those confounding *Jeopardy!* questions. So the question answering machine must overcome not only the intricacies and impossibilities of the question itself, but the same aspects of all the millions of written documents that may hold the question's answer.

Googling the question won't work. Although it's a human's primary means of seeking information from the Internet's sea of documents, Google doesn't hone down to an answer. It returns a long list of web pages, each with hundreds or thousands of possible answers within. It is not designed for the task at hand: identifying the singular answer to a question. Trying to use Google or other Internet search solutions to play *Jeopardy!*—for example, by doing a search on words from a question, and answering with the document topic of the top search result—does not cut it. If only question answering were that easy to solve! This kind of solution gets only 30 percent of the questions right.

## APPLE'S SIRI VERSUS WATSON

How does the iPhone personal assistant Siri compare with Watson? First introduced as the main selling point to distinguish the iPhone 4S from the preceding model, Siri responds to a broad, expanding range of voice commands and inquiries directed toward your iPhone.

Siri handles simpler language than Watson does: Users tailor requests for Siri knowing that they're speaking to a computer, whereas Watson fields *Jeopardy!*'s clever, wordy, information-packed questions that have been written with only humans in mind, without regard or consideration for the possibility that a machine might be answering. Because of this, Siri's underlying technology is designed to solve a different, simpler variant of the human language problem.

Although Siri responds to an impressively wide range of language usage, such that users can address the device in a casual manner with little or no prior instruction, people know that computers are rigid and will naturally constrain their inquiries. Someone might request, "Set an appointment for tomorrow at 2 o'clock for coffee with Bill," but will probably not say, "Set an appointment with that guy I ate lunch with a lot last month who has a Yahoo! e-mail address," and will definitely not say, "I want to find out when my tall,

*(continued)*

### APPLE'S SIRI VERSUS WATSON (*continued*)

handsome friend from Wyoming feels like discussing our start-up idea in the next couple weeks."

Siri flexibly handles relatively simple phrases that pertain to smartphone tasks such as placing calls, text messaging, performing Internet searches, and employing map and calendar functions (she's your *social techretary*).

Siri also fields general questions, but it does not attempt full open question answering. Invoking a system called WolframAlpha (accessible for free online), it answers simply phrased, fact-based questions via database lookup; the system can only provide answers calculated from facts that appear explicitly in the structured, uniform tables of a database, such as:

The birthdates of famous people—How old was Elton John in 1976?

Astronomical facts—How long does it take light to go to the moon?

Geography—What is the biggest city in Texas?

Healthcare—What country has the highest average life expectancy?

One must phrase questions in a simple form, since WolframAlpha is designed first to compute answers from tables of data, and only secondarily to attempt to handle complicated grammar.

Siri processes spoken inquiries, whereas Watson processes transcribed questions. Researchers generally approach processing speech (*speech recognition*) as a separate problem from processing text. There is more room for error when a system attempts to transcribe spoken language before also interpreting it, as Siri does.

Siri includes a dictionary of humorous canned responses. If you ask Siri about its origin with, "Who's your daddy?" it will respond, "I know this must mean something . . . everybody keeps asking me this question." This should not be taken to imply adept human language processing.

Siri and WolframAlpha's question answering performance is continually improved by ongoing research and development efforts, guided in part by the constant flow of incoming user queries.

# ARTIFICIAL IMPOSSIBILITY

*I'm wondering how to automate my wonderful self—*
*a wond'rous thought that presupposes my own mental health.*
*Maybe it's crazy to think thought's so tangible, or that I can sing.*
*Either way, if I succeed, my machine will attempt the very same thing.*
             —From "Knowledge Representation Rhapsody," by the author

*It is irresistible to pursue this because, as we pursue understanding natural language, we pursue the heart of what we think of when we think of human intelligence.*

—David Ferrucci, Watson Principal Investigator, IBM Research

*There's a fine line between genius and insanity.*

—Oscar Levant

Were these IBM researchers certifiably nuts to take on this grand challenge, attempting to programmatically answer any *Jeopardy!* question? They were tackling the breadth of human language that stretches beyond the phrasing of each question to include a sea of textual sources, from which the answer to each question must be extracted. With this ambition, IBM had truly doubled down.

I would have thought success impossible. After witnessing the world's best researchers attempting to tackle the task through the 1990s (during which I spent six years in natural language processing research, as well as a summer at the same IBM Research center that bore Watson), I was ready to throw up my hands. Language is so tough that it seemed virtually impossible even to program a computer to answer questions within a limited domain of knowledge such as movies or wines. Yet IBM had taken on the unconstrained, open field of questions across any domain.

Meeting this challenge would demonstrate such a great leap toward humanlike capabilities that it invokes the "I" word: intelligence. A computer pulling it off would appear as magical and mysterious as the human mind. Despite my own 20-odd years studying, teaching, and researching all things artificial intelligence (AI), I was a firm skeptic. But this task required a leap so great that seeing it succeed might leave me, for the first time, agreeing that the term *AI* is justified.

AI is a loaded term. It blithely presumes a machine could ever possibly qualify for this title. Only with great audacity does the machine-builder bestow the honor of "intelligence" upon her own creation. Invoking the term comes across as a bit self-aggrandizing, since the inventor would have to be pretty clever herself to pull this off.

The *A* isn't the problem—it's the *I*. Intelligence is an entirely subjective construct, so AI is not a well-defined field. Most of its various definitions boil down to "making computers intelligent," whatever that means! AI ordains no one particular capability as the objective to be pursued. In practice, AI is the pursuit of philosophical ideals and research grants.

What do God, Groucho Marx, and AI have in common? They'd never be a member of a club that would have them as a member. AI destroys itself with a logical paradox in much the same way God does in Douglas Adams's *Hitchhiker's Guide to the Galaxy*:[3]

---

[3] Watson's avatar, its visual depiction shown on *Jeopardy!*, consists of 42 glowing, crisscrossing threads as an inside joke and homage that references the significance this number holds in Adams's infamous *Hitchhiker's Guide*.

*"I refuse to prove that I exist," says God, "for proof denies faith, and without faith I am nothing."*

*"But," says Man, "The Babel fish [which translates between the languages of interplanetary species] is a dead giveaway isn't it? It could not have evolved by chance. It proves that you exist, and so therefore, by your own arguments, you don't. QED."*

*"Oh dear," says God, "I hadn't thought of that," and promptly disappears in a puff of logic.*

AI faces analogous self-destruction because, once you get a computer to do something, you've necessarily trivialized it. We conceive of as yet unmet "intelligent" objectives that appear big, impressive, and unwieldy, such as transcribing the spoken word (*speech recognition*) or defeating the world chess champion. They aren't easy to achieve, but once we do pass such benchmarks, they suddenly lose their charm. After all, computers can manage only mechanical tasks that are well understood and well specified. You might be impressed by its lightning-fast speed, but its electronic execution couldn't hold any transcendental or truly humanlike qualities. If it's possible, it's not intelligent.

Suffering from an intrinsic, overly grandiose objective, AI inadvertently equates to "getting computers to do things too difficult for computers to do"—artificial impossibility.

# LEARNING TO ANSWER QUESTIONS

But in fact, IBM did face a specific, well-defined task: answering *Jeopardy!* questions. And if the researchers succeeded and Watson happened to appear intelligent to some, IBM would earn extra credit on this homework assignment.

As a rule, anticipating all possible variations in language is not possible. NLP researchers derive elegant, sophisticated means to deconstruct phrases in English and other natural languages, based on deep linguistic concepts and specially designed dictionaries. But, implemented as computer programs, the methods just don't scale. It's always possible to find phrases that seem simple and common to us as humans, but trip up an NLP system. The researcher, in turn, broadens the theory and knowledge base, tweaking the system to accommodate more phrases. After years of tweaking, these hand-engineered methods still have light-years to go before we'll be chatting with our laptops just the same as with people.

There's one remaining hope: Automate the researchers' iterative tweaking so it explodes with scale as a *learning* process. After all, that is the very topic of this book:

**Predictive analytics (PA)**—*Technology that learns from experience (data) to predict the future behavior of individuals in order to drive better decisions.*

Applying PA to question answering is a bit different from most of the examples we've discussed in this book. In those cases, the predictive model foretells whether a human will take a certain action, such as *click*, *buy*, *lie*, or *die*, based on things known about that individual:

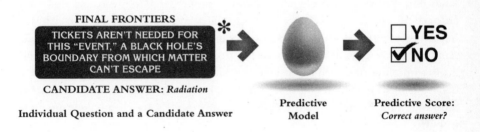

| Characteristics of an Individual | Predictive Model | Predictive Score |

IBM's Watson computer includes models that predict whether human experts would consider a *Jeopardy!* question/answer pair correct:

**FINAL FRONTIERS**

TICKETS AREN'T NEEDED FOR THIS "EVENT," A BLACK HOLE'S BOUNDARY FROM WHICH MATTER CAN'T ESCAPE

**CANDIDATE ANSWER:** *Radiation*

Individual Question and a Candidate Answer

Predictive Model

Predictive Score: *Correct answer?*

If the model is working well, it should give a low score, since *event horizon*, not *radiation*, is the correct answer (*Star Trek* fans will appreciate this question's category, "Final Frontiers"). Watson did prudently put a 97 percent score on *event horizon* and scored its second and third candidates, *mass* and *radiation*, at 11 percent and 10 percent, respectively. This approach frames question answering as a PA application:

## PA Application: Open Question Answering

1. **What's predicted:** Given a question and one candidate answer, whether the answer is correct.
2. **What's done about it:** The candidate answer with the highest predictive score is provided by the system as its final answer.

Answering questions is not *prediction* in the conventional sense—Watson does not predict the future. Rather, its models "predict" the correctness of an answer. The same core modeling methods apply—but, unlike other applications of predictive modeling, the unknown thing being "predicted" is already known by some, rather than becoming known only when witnessed in the future. Through the remainder of this chapter, I employ this alternative use of the word *predict*, meaning, "to imperfectly infer an unknown." You could even think of Watson's predictive models as answering the predictive question: "Would human experts agree with this candidate answer to the question?" This semantic issue also arises for predicting clinical diagnosis (Central Table 4), fraud (Central Table 5), human thought (Central Table 8) and other areas—all marked with $\mathscr{D}$ (for "detect") in the Central Tables.

## WALK LIKE A MAN, TALK LIKE A MAN

IBM needed data—specifically, example *Jeopardy!* questions—from which to learn. Ask and ye shall receive: Decades of televised *Jeopardy!* provide hundreds of thousands of questions, each alongside its correct answer (IBM downloaded these from fan websites, which post all the questions). This wealth of learning data delivers a huge, unprecedented boon for pushing the envelope in human language understanding. While most PA projects enjoy as data a good number of example individuals who either did or did not take the action being predicted (such as all those behaviors listed in the left columns of this book's Central Tables of PA applications), most NLP projects simply do not have many previously solved examples from which to learn.

With this abundance of *Jeopardy!* history, the computer could learn to become humanlike. The questions, along with their answer key, contribute examples of human behavior: how people answer these types of questions. Therefore, this form of data fuels machine learning to produce a model that mimics how a human would answer, "Is this the right answer to this question?"—the learning machine models the human expert's response. We may be too darn complex to program computers to mimic ourselves, but the model need not derive answers in the same manner as a person; with predictive modeling, perhaps the computer can find some innovative way to program itself for this human task, even if it's done differently than by humans.

As Alan Turing famously asked, would a computer program that exhibits humanlike behavior qualify as AI? It's anthropocentric to think so, although I've been called worse.

But having extensive *Jeopardy!* learning data did not itself guarantee successful predictive models, for two reasons:

1. Open question answering presents tremendous unconquered challenges in the realms of language analysis and human reasoning.
2. Unlike many applications of PA, success on *Jeopardy!* requires high predictive *accuracy*.

When IBM embarked upon the *Jeopardy!* challenge in 2006, the state of the art fell severely short. The most notable source of open question answering data was a government-run competition called TREC QA (Text Retrieval Conference—Question Answering). To serve as training data, the contest provided questions that were much more straightforward and simply phrased than those on *Jeopardy!*, such as, "When did James Dean die?" Competing systems would pore over news articles to find each answer. IBM had a top-five competitor that answered 33 percent of those questions correctly, and no competing system broke the 50 percent mark. Even worse, after IBM worked for about one month to extend the system to the more challenging arena of *Jeopardy!* questions, it could answer only 13 percent correctly, substantially less than the 30 percent achieved by just using Internet search.

# A BETTER MOUSETRAP

*Scientists often set their own research goals. A grand challenge takes this control out of the hands of the scientist to force them to work on a problem that is harder than one they would pick to work on themselves.*

—Edward Nazarko, Client Technical Advisor, IBM

*There ain't no Coup de Ville hiding at the bottom of a Cracker Jack box.*

—Meatloaf

Jumping on the *Jeopardy!* challenge, IBM put its name on the line. Following the 1997 chess match in which IBM's Deep Blue computer defeated then world champion Garry Kasparov, the 2011 *Jeopardy!* broadcast pitted man against machine just as publicly, and with a renewed, healthy dose of bravado. A national audience of *Jeopardy!* viewers awaited on the horizon.

As with all grand challenges, success was not a certainty. No precedent or principle had ensured it would be possible to fly across the Atlantic (Charles Lindbergh did so to win $25,000 in 1927); walk on the moon (NASA's Apollo 11 brought people there in 1969, achieving the goal John F. Kennedy's set for that decade); beat a chess grandmaster with a computer (IBM's Deep Blue in 1997); or even improve Netflix's movie recommendation system by 10 percent (2009, as detailed in the previous chapter).

*"No, I don't want to play chess. I just want you to reheat the lasagna."*

Reproduced with permission.

In great need of a breakthrough, IBM tackled the technical challenge with the force only a mega-multinational enterprise can muster. With over $100 billion in annual revenue and more than 430,000 employees worldwide, IBM is the fourth most valuable U.S. company, behind only Apple, Exxon, and Microsoft. All told, its investment to develop Watson is estimated in the tens of millions of dollars, including the dedication of a team that grew to 25 PhD's over four years at its T. J. Watson Research Center in New York State (like the *Jeopardy!*-playing computer, named after IBM's first president, Thomas J. Watson).

The power to push really hard does not necessarily mean you're pushing in the right direction. From where will scientific epiphany emerge? Recall the key innovation that the crowdsourcing approach to grand challenges helped bring to light, *ensemble models*, introduced in the prior chapter. It's just what the doctor ordered for IBM's *Jeopardy!* challenge.

## THE ANSWERING MACHINE

David Gondek and his colleagues at IBM Research could overcome the daunting *Jeopardy!* challenge only with *synthesis*. When it came to processing human language, the state of the art was fragmented and partial—a potpourri of techniques, each innovative in conception, but severely limited in application. None of them alone made the grade.

How does IBM's Watson work? It's built with ensemble models. Watson merges a massive amalgam of methodologies. It succeeds by fusing technologies. There's no secret ingredient; it's the overall recipe that does the trick. Inside Watson, ensemble models select the final answer to each question.

Before we more closely examine how Watson works, let's look at the discoveries made by a PA expert who analyzed *Jeopardy!* data in order to "program himself" to become a celebrated champion of the game show.

## MONEYBALLING *JEOPARDY!*

On September 21, 2010, a few months before Watson faced off on *Jeopardy!*, televisions across the land displayed host Alex Trebek speaking a clue tailored to the science fiction fan.

ZACHARY QUINTO SHOWED US
THE LOGIC AS THIS CHARACTER
IN 2009'S "STAR TREK"

Contestant Roger Craig avidly buzzed in. Like any technology PhD, he knew the answer was Spock.

As Spock would, Roger had taken studying to its logical extreme. *Jeopardy!* requires inordinate cultural literacy, the almost unattainable status of a Renaissance man, one who holds at least basic knowledge about pretty much every topic. To prepare for his appearance on the show, which he'd craved since age 12, Roger did for *Jeopardy!* what had never been done before. He *Moneyballed* it.

Roger optimized his study time with prediction. As a mere mortal, he faced a limited number of hours per day to study. He rigged his computer with *Jeopardy!* data. An expert in predictive modeling, he developed a system to learn from his performance practicing on *Jeopardy!* questions so that it could serve up questions he was likely to miss in order to efficiently focus his practice time on the topics where he needed it most. *He used PA to predict himself.*

**PA APPLICATION: EDUCATION—GUIDED STUDYING FOR TARGETED LEARNING**

1. **What's predicted:** Which questions a student will get right or wrong.
2. **What's done about it:** Spend more study time on the questions the student will get wrong.

This bolstered the brainiac for a breakout. On *Jeopardy!*, Roger set the all-time record for a single-game win of $77,000 and continued on, winning more than $230,000 during a seven-day run that placed him as the third-highest winning contestant (regular season) to date. He was invited back a year later for a "Tournament of Champions" and took its $250,000 first place award. He estimates his own ability to correctly answer 90 percent of *Jeopardy!* questions, placing him among a small handful of all-time best players.

Analyzing roughly 211,000 *Jeopardy!* questions (downloaded as IBM did from online archives maintained by fans of the game show), Roger gained perspective on its knowledge domain. If you learn about 10,000 to 12,000 answers, he told me, you've got most of it covered. This includes countries, states, presidents, and planets. But among many categories, you only need to go so far. Designed to entertain its audience, *Jeopardy!* doesn't get too arcane. So you only need to learn about the top cities, elements, movies, and flowers. In classical music, knowing a couple of dozen composers and the top few works of each will do the trick.

These bounds are no great relief to those pursuing the holy grail of open question answering. Predictive models often choose between only two options: *Will the person click, buy, lie, or die—yes or no?* As if that's not hard enough, for each question, Watson must choose between more than 10,000 possible answers.

The analytical improvement of human competitors was more bad news for Watson. Allowed by Roger to access his system, Watson's soon to be opponent Ken Jennings borrowed the study-guiding software while preparing for the big match, crediting it as "a huge help getting me back in game mode."

## AMASSING EVIDENCE FOR AN ANSWER

Here's how Watson works. Given a question, it takes three main steps:

1. Collect thousands of *candidate answers*.
2. For each answer, amass *evidence*.
3. Apply predictive models to *funnel down*.

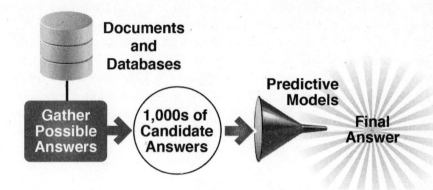

Predictive modeling has the final say. After gathering thousands of candidate answers to a question, Watson funnels them down to spit out the single answer scored most highly by a predictive model.

Watson gathers the answers and their evidence from sources that IBM selectively downloaded, a snapshot of a smart part of the Internet that forms Watson's base of knowledge. This includes 8.6 million written documents, consisting of 3.5 million Wikipedia articles (i.e., a 2010 copy of the entire English portion thereof), the Bible, other miscellaneous popular books, a history's worth of newswire articles, entire encyclopedias, and more. This is complemented by more structured knowledge sources such as dictionaries, thesauri, and databases such as the Internet Movie Database.

Watson isn't picky when collecting the candidate answers. The system follows the strategy of casting a wide, ad hoc net in order to ensure that the correct answer is in there somewhere. It rummages through its knowledge sources in various ways, including performing search in much the same way as Internet search engines like Google do (although Watson searches only within its own internal store). When it finds a relevant document, for some document types such as Wikipedia articles, it will grab the document's title as a candidate answer. In other cases, it will nab "answer-sized snippets" of text, as Watson developers call them. It also performs certain lookups and reverse lookups into databases and dictionaries to collect more candidate answers.

Like its fictional human namesake, the partner of Sherlock Holmes, Watson now faced a classic whodunit: Which of the many suspected answers is "guilty" of being the right one?[4] The mystery can only be solved with diligent detective work in order to gather as much evidence as possible for or against each candidate. Watson pounds the pavement by once again surveying its sources.

---

[4] Watson was not named after this fictional detective—it was named after IBM founder Thomas J. Watson.

With so many possible answers, uncertainty looms and threatens. It's a serious challenge for the machine to even be confident what *kind* of thing is being asked for. An actor? A movie? State capital, entertainer, fruit, planet, company, novel, president, philosophical concept? IBM showed that *Jeopardy!* calls for 2,500 different types of answers. The researchers considered tackling a more manageable task by covering only the most popular of these answer types, but it turned out that, even if they specialized Watson for the top 200, it could then answer only half the questions. The range of possibilities is too wide and evenly spread for a shortcut to work.

## ELEMENTARY, MY DEAR WATSON

Evidence counterattacks the enemy: *uncertainty*. To this end, Watson employs a diverse range of language technologies. This is where the state of the art in natural language processing comes into play, incorporating the research results from leading researchers at Carnegie Mellon University, the University of Massachusetts, the University of Southern California, the University of Texas, Massachusetts Institute of Technology, other universities, and, of course, IBM Research itself.

Sometimes, deep linguistics matters. Consider this question:

> ### IN MAY 1898 PORTUGAL CELEBRATED THE 400TH ANNIVERSARY OF THIS EXPLORER'S ARRIVAL IN INDIA

When David Gondek addressed Predictive Analytics World with a keynote, he provided an example phrase that could threaten to confuse Watson:

*In May, Gary arrived in India after he celebrated his anniversary in Portugal.*

So many words match, the system is likely to include *Gary* as a candidate answer. Search methods would love a document that includes this phrase. Likewise, Watson's evidence-seeking methods built on the comparison of words would give this phrase a high score—most of its words appear in the question at hand.

Watson needs linguistic methods that more adeptly recognize how words relate to one another so that it pays heed to, for example:

*On the 27th of May 1498, Vasco da Gama landed in Kappad Beach.*

Other than *in, of,* and, *the,* only the word *May* overlaps with the question. However, Watson recognizes meaningful correspondences. Kappad Beach is in India. *Landed in* is a way to paraphrase *arrived in.* A 400th anniversary in 1898 must correspond to a prior event in 1498.

These matches establish support for the correct answer, Vasco da Gama. Like all candidate answers, it is evaluated for compatibility with the answer type—in this case, *explorer,* as determined from *this explorer* in the question. Vasco da Gama is indeed famed as an explorer, so support would likely be strong.

These relationships pertain to the very meaning of words, their *semantics.* Watson works with databases of established semantic relationships, and seeks evidence to establish new ones. Consider this *Jeopardy!* question:

> **IN CELL DIVISION, MITOSIS SPLITS THE NUCLEUS AND CYTOKINESIS SPLITS THIS LIQUID CUSHIONING THE NUCLEUS**

Watson's candidate answers include organelle, vacuole, cytoplasm, plasma, and mitochondria. The type of answer sought being a liquid, Watson finds evidence that only one of these makes the cut. It looks up a record listing cytoplasm as a fluid, and has sufficient evidence that fluids are often liquids to award cytoplasm a higher score, lifting it above the other candidates and answering correctly.

Here, Watson performs a daredevil stunt of logic. Reasoning as humans do in the wide-open domain of *Jeopardy!* questions is an extreme sport. Fuzziness pervades—for example, most reputable sources Watson may access would state all liquids are fluids, but some are ambiguous as to whether glass is definitely solid or liquid. Similarly, all people are mortal, yet infamous people have attained immortality. Therefore, a strict hierarchy of concepts just can't apply. Because of this, as well as the vagueness of our languages' words and the difference context makes, databases of abstract semantic relationships disagree madly with one another. Like political parties, they often fail to see eye to eye, and a universal authority—an absolute, singular truth—to reconcile their differences simply does not exist.

Rather than making a vain attempt to resolve these disagreements, Watson keeps all pieces of evidence in play, even as they disagree. The resolution comes only at the end, when weighing the complete set of evidence to select its final answer to a question. In this way, Watson's solution is analogous to yours. Rather than absolutes, it adjusts according to context. Some songs are both a little bit country and a little bit rock and roll. With a James Taylor song, you could go either way, depending on the person to whom you're describing the song.

On the other hand, keeping an open mind with flexible thinking can lead to embarrassment. Avoiding absolutes means playing fast and loose with semantics, leaving an ever-present risk of gaffes—that is, mistaken answers that seem all too obvious to us humans. For example, in Watson's televised *Jeopardy!* match, it faced a question under the category "U.S. Cities":

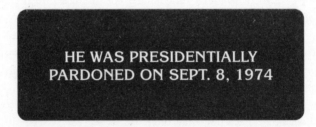

ITS LARGEST AIRPORT IS
NAMED FOR A WORLD WAR II
HERO; ITS SECOND LARGEST,
FOR A WORLD WAR II BATTLE

\*

Struggling, Watson managed to accumulate only scant evidence for its candidate answers, so it would never have buzzed in to attempt the question. However, this was the show's "Final *Jeopardy!*" round, so a response from each player was mandatory. Instead of the correct answer, Chicago, Watson answered with a city that's not in the United States at all, Toronto. Canadian game show host Alex Trebek poked a bit of fun, saying that he had learned something new.

English grammar matters. To answer some questions, phrases must be properly deconstructed. Consider this question:

HE WAS PRESIDENTIALLY
PARDONED ON SEPT. 8, 1974

In seeking evidence, Watson pulls up this phrase, which appeared in a *Los Angeles Times* article:

*Ford pardoned Nixon on Sept. 8, 1974.*

Unlike you, a computer won't easily see the answer must be Nixon rather than Ford. Based on word matching alone, this phrase provides equal support for Ford as it does for Nixon. Only by detecting that the question takes the passive voice, which means the answer sought is the receiver rather than the issuer of a pardon, and by detecting that the evidence phrase is in the active voice, is this phrase correctly interpreted as stronger support for Nixon than Ford.[5]

NLP's attempts to grammatically deconstruct don't always work. Complementary sources of evidence must be accumulated, since computers won't always grok the grammar. Language is tricky. Consider this question:

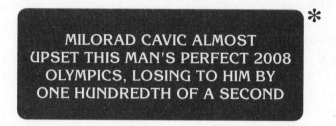

A phrase like this could be stumbled upon as evidence:

*Sam was upset before witnessing the near win by Milorad Cavic.*

If *upset* is misinterpreted as a passively voiced verb rather than an adjective, the phrase could be interpreted as evidence for Sam as the question's answer. However, it was swimmer Michael Phelps who held on to his perfect 2008 Olympics performance. Even detecting the simplest grammatical structure of a sentence depends on the deep, often intangible meaning of words.

## MOUNTING EVIDENCE

There's no silver bullet. Whether interpreting semantic relationships between words or grammatically deconstructing phrases, language processing is brittle. Even the best methods are going to get it wrong a lot of the time. This predicament is exacerbated by the clever, intricate manner in which questions are phrased on *Jeopardy!*. The show's question writers have adopted a playful, informative style in order to entertain the TV viewers at home.

The only hope is to accumulate as much evidence as possible, searching far and wide for support of, or evidence against, each candidate answer. Every little bit of evidence helps. In this quest, diversity is the name of the game. An aggregate mass of varied evidence stands the best chance, since neither the cleverest nor the simplest method may be trusted if used solo. Fortunately, diversity comes with the territory: as with scientific research in general, the natural language processing researchers who developed the methods at hand each worked to distinguish their own unique contribution, intentionally differentiating the methods they designed from those of others.

---

[5] Watson employs as its main method for grammatical parsing the *English Slot Grammar*, by IBM's own researcher Michael McCord (I had the pleasure to use this tool for my doctoral research in the mid-1990s).

Watson employs an assorted number of evidence routines that assess a candidate answer, including:

- **Passage search.** After inserting the candidate answer into the question to try it on for size (e.g., "*Nixon* was presidentially pardoned on Sept. 8, 1974") and searching, do many matches come up? How many match word for word, semantically, and after grammatical deconstruction? What's the longest similar sequence of words that each found phrase has in common with the question?
- **Popularity.** How common is the candidate answer?
- **Type match.** Does the candidate match the answer type called for by the question (e.g., entertainer, fruit, planet, company, or novel)? If it's a person, does the gender match?
- **Temporal.** Was the candidate in existence within the question's time frame?
- **Source reliability.** Does the evidence come from a source considered reliable?

For each question, you never know which of these factors (and the hundreds of variations thereof that Watson measures) may be critical to arriving at the right answer. Consider this question:

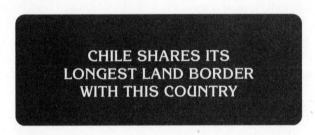

Although the correct answer is Argentina, measures of evidence based on simple search show overwhelming support for Bolivia due to a certain border dispute well covered in news articles. Fortunately, enough other supporting evidence such as from logically matched phrases and geographical knowledge sources compensates and wins out, and Watson answers correctly.

Some may view this ad hoc smorgasbord of techniques as a hack, but I do not see it that way. It is true that the most semantically and linguistically intricate approaches are brittle and often just don't work. It can also be said that the remaining methods are harebrained in their oversimplicity. But a collective capacity *emerges* from this mix of components, which blends hundreds of evidence measurements, even if each alone is crude.[6]

---

[6] Watson and PA in general are not designed to simulate how people think, predict, learn language, or answer questions. But it may be worth considering that, although as a human you experience a feeling of confidence and certainty in your answer to some questions, some components of the cognition that lead you there may be just as harebrained in isolation as Watson's components. Sometimes you have a specific recollection of the answer, as Watson does in certain cases of strong singular evidence. At other times, your confidence may only feel like a strong hunch, possibly based on a large number of weak factors.

The Ensemble Effect comes into full play: The sheer count and diversity of approaches make up for their individual weaknesses. As a whole, the system achieves operational proficiency on a previously unachievable, far-off goal: open human language question answering.

## WEIGHING EVIDENCE WITH ENSEMBLE MODELS

*There are two ways of building intelligence. You either know how to write down the recipe, or you let it grow itself. And it's pretty clear that we don't know how to write down the recipe. Machine learning is all about giving it the capability to grow itself.*
  —Tom Mitchell, Founding Chair of the world's first Machine Learning Department
(at Carnegie Mellon University)

The key to optimally joining disparate evidence is machine learning. Guided by the answer key for roughly 25,000 *Jeopardy!* questions, the learning process discovers how to weigh the various sources of evidence for each candidate answer. To this end, David Gondek led the application of machine learning in developing Watson. He had his hands on the very process that brings it all together.

Synthesizing sources of evidence to select a single, final answer propels Watson past the limits of Internet search and into the formerly unconquered domain of question answering. Here's a more detailed overview:

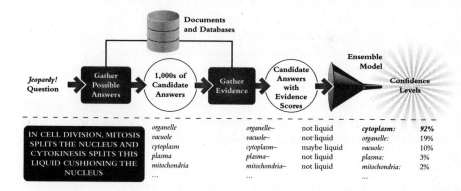

**An overview of key steps Watson takes for each question, with an example question and its candidate answers along the bottom. An ensemble model selects the final answer from thousands of candidates.**

As shown, Watson gathers candidate answers, and then evidence for each candidate. Its ensemble model then scores each candidate answer with a confidence level so that it may be ranked relative to the other candidates. Watson then goes with the answer for which it holds the highest confidence, speaking it out loud when prompted to do so on *Jeopardy!*

PA APPLICATION: OPEN QUESTION ANSWERING

1. **What's predicted:** Given a question and one candidate answer, whether the answer is correct.
2. **What's done about it:** The candidate answer with the highest predictive score is provided by the system as its final answer.

## AN ENSEMBLE OF ENSEMBLES

David led the design of Watson's innovative, intricate machine learning components, of which the ensembling of models is part and parcel. Moving from document search to open question answering demands a great leap, so the design is a bit involved. Watson incorporates ensembling in three ways:

1. **Combining evidence.** Hundreds of methods provide evidence scores for each candidate answer. Instead of tallying a simple vote across contributing evidence scores, as in some work with ensembles described in the prior chapter, the method takes it a step further by training a model to decide how best to fuse them together.[7]
2. **Specialized models by question type.** Watson has separate specialized ensemble models for specific question types, such as puzzle, multiple-choice, date, number, translation, and etymology (about the history and origin of words) questions. In this way, Watson consists of *an ensemble of ensembles*.
3. **Iterative phases of predictive models.** For each question, Watson iteratively applies several phases of predictive models, each of which can compensate for mistakes made by prior phases. Each phase filters candidates and refines the evidence. The first phase filters down the number of candidate answers from thousands to about one hundred, and subsequent phases filter out more. After each phase's filtering, the evidence scores are reassessed and refined relative to the now-smaller list of candidate answers. A separate predictive model is developed for each phase so that the ranking of the shrinking list of candidates is further honed and refined. With these phases, Watson consists of *an ensemble of ensembles of ensembles*.

## MACHINE LEARNING ACHIEVES THE POTENTIAL OF LANGUAGE PROCESSING

Despite this complexity, Watson's individual predictive models are fairly straightforward: they perform a weighted vote of the evidence measures. In this way, some forms

---

[7] *Ensemble model* commonly refers to the combination of trained predictive models. Many of Watson's evidence-scoring methods themselves were hand-designed by experts rather than developed by learning over data, so I am broadening the use of the term. The Ensemble Effect is at play; the strengths and weaknesses of competing methods even out.

of evidence count more, and others count less. Although David tested various modeling methods, such as decision trees (covered in Chapter 4), he discovered that the best results for Watson came from another modeling technique called *logistic regression*, which weighs each input variable (i.e., measure of evidence), adds them up, and then formulaically shifts the resulting sum a bit for good measure.[8]

Since the model is made up of weights, the modeling process learns to literally *weigh the evidence* for each candidate answer. The predictive model filters out weak candidate answers by assigning them a lower score. It doesn't help Watson derive better candidate answers—rather, it cleans up the bulky mass of candidates, narrowing down to one final answer.

To this end, the predictive models are trained over 5.7 million examples of a *Jeopardy!* question paired with a candidate answer. Each example includes 550 predictor variables that summarize the various measures of evidence aggregated for that answer (therefore, the model is made of 550 weights, one per variable). This large amount of training data was formed out of 25,000 *Jeopardy!* questions. Each question contributes to many training examples, since there are many incorrect candidate answers. Both the correct and incorrect answers provide experience from which the system learns how to best weigh the evidence.

Watson leverages The Ensemble Effect, propelling the state of the art in language processing to achieve its full potential and conquer open question answering. Only by learning from the guidance provided by the archive of *Jeopardy!* questions was it possible to successfully merge Watson's hundreds of language processing methods. Predictive modeling has the effect of measuring the methods' relative strengths and weaknesses. In this way, the system quantifies how much more important evidence from linguistically and semantically deep methods can be, and just how moderately simpler word-matching methods should be weighed so that they, too, may contribute to question answering.

With this framework, the IBM team empowered itself to incrementally refine and bolster Watson in anticipation of the televised *Jeopardy!* match—and moved the field of question answering forward. The system allows researchers to experiment with a continually growing range of language processing methods: Just throw in a new language processing technique that retrieves and reports on evidence for candidate answers, retrain the system's ensemble models, and check for its improved performance.

As David and his team expanded and refined the hundreds of evidence-gathering methods, returns diminished relative to efforts. Performance kept improving, but at a slower and slower pace. However, they kept at it, squeezing every drop of potential out of their brainshare and data, right up until the final weeks before the big match.

---

[8] After the weighted sum, logistic regression transforms the result with a function called an *S-curve* (aka *sigmoid squashing function*). The S-curve is designed to help the predictive model with the yes/no nature of the question it answers: *Is this answer correct, given the cumulative evidence?*

# CONFIDENCE WITHOUT OVERCONFIDENCE

*Both experts and laypeople mistake more confident predictions for more accurate ones. But over-confidence is often the reason for failure. If our appreciation of uncertainty improves, our predictions can get better too.*

—Nate Silver, *The Signal and the Noise: Why So Many Predictions Fail—but Some Don't*

*The trouble with the world is that the stupid are cocksure and the intelligent are full of doubt.*

—Bertrand Russell

*You got to know when to hold 'em, know when to fold 'em.*

—Don Schlitz, "The Gambler" (sung by Kenny Rogers)

Jeopardy! *wasn't built for players with no self-doubt.*

—Chris Jones, *Esquire* Magazine

Besides answering questions, there's a second skill each *Jeopardy!* player must hone: assessing self-confidence. Why? Because you get penalized by answering incorrectly. When a question is presented, you must decide whether to attempt to buzz in and provide an answer. If you do, you'll either gain the dollar amount assigned to the question or lose as much.

In this way, *Jeopardy!* reflects a general principle of life and business: *You need not do everything well; select the tasks at which you excel.* It's the very practice of putting your best foot forward. In fact, many commercial uses of PA optimize on this very notion. Just as Watson must predict which questions it can successfully answer, businesses predict which customers will be successfully sold to—and therefore are worth the expenditure of marketing and sales resources.

Calculating a measure of self-confidence in each answer could be a whole new can of worms for the system. Is it a tall order to require the machine to "know thyself" in this respect?

David Gondek showed that this problem could be solved "for free." The very same predictive score output by the models that serves to select the best answer also serves to estimate confidence in that answer. The scores are probabilities. For example, if a candidate answer with a score of 0.85 has a higher score than every other candidate, it will be Watson's final answer, and Watson will consider its chance of being correct at 85 percent. As the IBM team put it, "Watson knows what it knows, and it knows what it doesn't know."

Watching Watson's televised *Jeopardy!* matches, you can see these self-confidence scores in action. For each question, Watson's top three candidate answers are displayed at the bottom of your TV screen along with their confidence scores (for example, see the second figure in this chapter). Watson bases its decision to buzz in on its top candidate's score, plus its position in the game relative to its opponents. If it is behind, it will play more aggressively, buzzing in even if the confidence is lower. If ahead in the game, it will be more conservative, buzzing in to answer only when highly confident.

A player's success depends not only on how many answers are known, but on his, her, or its ability to assess self-confidence. With that in mind, here's a view that compares *Jeopardy!* players:

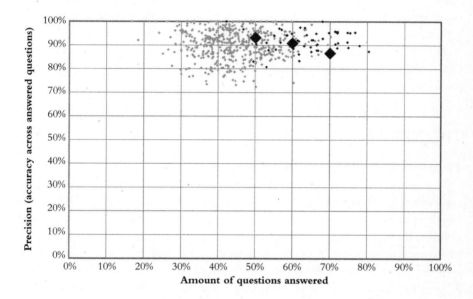

*Jeopardy!* **player performances. Each dot signifies a winner's game (the dark dots represent Ken Jennings's games). The three large diamonds represent the per-game performance Watson can achieve.**[9]

Players strive for the top-right of this graph. Most points on the graph depict the performance of an individual human player. The horizontal axis indicates what proportion of questions they successfully buzzed in for, and the vertical axis tells us, for those questions they answered, how often they were correct. Buzzing in more would put you further to the right, but would challenge you with the need to know more answers.

Human *Jeopardy!* winners tend toward the top, since they usually answer correctly, and some also reach pretty far to the right. Each light gray dot represents the performance of the winner of one game. The impressively positioned dark gray dots that stretch further to the right represent the outstanding performance of champion player Ken Jennings, whose breathtaking streak of 74 consecutive wins in 2004

---

[9] Graph adapted from D. Ferrucci et al., "Building Watson: An Overview of the DeepQA Project," *AI Magazine* 31, no. 3 (2010), 59–79.

demonstrated his prowess. He is one of the two champions against whom Watson was preparing to compete.

Watson performs at the level of human experts. Three example points (large diamonds) are shown to illustrate Watson's potential performance. When needed, Watson sets itself to buzz in more often, assuming an aggressive willingness to answer even when confidence is lower. This moves its performance to the right, and, as a result, also a bit down. Alternatively, when playing more conservatively, fewer questions are attempted, but Watson's answer is more often correct—precision is higher (unlike politics, on this graph left is more conservative).

Human sweat empowered Watson's human level of performance. The machine's proficiency is the product of four painstaking years of perseverance by the team of researchers.[10]

## THE NEED FOR SPEED

There was one more requirement. Watson had to be fast.

A *Jeopardy!* player has only a few seconds to answer a question, but on a single computer (e.g., 2.6 gigahertz), determining an answer can take a couple of hours. It's a lengthy process because Watson employs hundreds of methods to search a huge number of sources, both to accrue candidate answers and to collect evidence measurements for each one. It then predictively scores and ranks the candidates by applying the series of predictive models (I refer here only to the deployed use of Watson to play *Jeopardy!*, after the machine learning process is completed and the models are being employed without further learning).

To make it thousands of times faster, Watson employs thousands of CPUs. This supercomputer clobbers bottlenecks and zips along, thanks to a cluster of 90 servers consisting of 2,800 core processors. It handles 80 trillion operations per second. It favors 15 terabytes of RAM over slower hard-drive storage. The cost of this hardware brawn is estimated to come to $3 million, a small fraction of the cost to develop its analytical software brains.

Having thousands of CPUs means that thousands of tasks can be done simultaneously, in parallel. Watson's process lends itself so amenably to taking advantage of this hardware by way of distribution into contemporaneous subtasks that the research team considers it *embarrassingly parallel*. For example, each evidence-seeking, language-processing routine can be assigned to its own processor.

Better is bigger. To assemble Watson, IBM crated in a mammoth configuration of hardware, about 10 refrigerators' worth. Watson didn't go to *Jeopardy!*; *Jeopardy!* came

---

[10] The industry is taken with Watson. A Predictive Analytics World keynote address by Watson's machine learning leader, David Gondek, dazzled a ballroom of industry insiders, who on average rated the speech's content at an unmatched 4.7 out of 5 in a subsequent poll.

to Watson, setting up a temporary game show studio within IBM's T. J. Watson Research Center.

## DOUBLE JEOPARDY!—WOULD WATSON WIN?

Watson was not sure to win. During sparring games against human champions, Watson had tweaked its way up to a 71 percent win record. It didn't always win, and these trial runs didn't pit it against the lethal competition it was preparing to face on the televised match: all-time leading *Jeopardy!* champions Ken Jennings and Brad Rutter.

*"Once again, man beats machine!"*

The *Jeopardy!* match was to gain full-scale media publicity, exposing IBM's analytical prowess or failure. The top-rated quiz show in syndication, *Jeopardy!* attracts nearly nine million viewers every day and would draw an audience of 34.5 million for this special man–versus–machine match. If the massive popularity of *Jeopardy!* put on the pressure, so too was it the only reason this grand challenge might be doable. As the United States' greatest pop culture institution of human knowledge, *Jeopardy!*'s legacy provided the treasure trove of historical question/answer pairs from which Watson learns.

Beyond impressing or disappointing your average home viewer, Watson's impending performance held enormous professional ramifications. Within both the practical realm of information technology and the research world of artificial intelligence, IBM had loudly proclaimed that it was prepared to run a three-and-a-half-minute mile. After the immense investment, one can only imagine the seething pressure the research team must have felt from the powers at IBM to defend the corporate image and ensure against public humiliation. At this juncture, the researchers saw clear implications for their scientific careers as well as for science itself.

During its formative stages, Watson's most humorous mistakes entertained, but threatened to embarrass IBM on national TV. Under the category "The Queen's English":

GIVE A BRIT A TINKLE
WHEN YOU GET INTO TOWN AND
YOU'VE DONE THIS

**Watson said:** *urinate* **(correct answer: call on the phone).**

Under the category "*New York Times* Headlines":

AN EXCLAMATION POINT
WAS WARRANTED FOR THE
"END OF" THIS! IN 1918

**Watson said:** *a sentence* **(correct answer: World War I).**

Under the category "Boxing Terms":

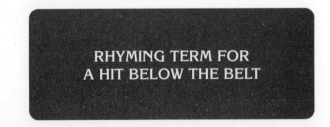

RHYMING TERM FOR
A HIT BELOW THE BELT

**Watson said:** *Wang Bang* **(correct answer: low blow).**

The team rallied for the home stretch. Watson principal investigator David Ferrucci, who managed the entire initiative, moved everyone from their offices into a common area he considered akin to a war room, cultivating a productive but crisislike level of eustress. Their lives were flipped on their heads. David Gondek moved temporarily into a nearby apartment to eliminate his commuting time. The team lived and breathed open question answering. "I think I dream about *Jeopardy!* questions now," Gondek said. "I have nightmares about *Jeopardy!* questions. I talk to people in the form of a question."

## JEOPARDY! JITTERS

*There's no such thing as human error. Only system error.*
                                        —Alexander Day Chaffee, software architect

Core Watson development team member Jennifer Chu-Carroll tried to stay calm. "We knew we probably were gonna win, but . . . what if we did the math wrong for some reason and lost by a dollar instead of won by a dollar?" Although there were provisions in their agreement with the *Jeopardy!* producers for do-overs in the case of a hardware crash (the show was taped, not broadcast live, and, like any computer, sometimes you need to turn off Watson and then start it back up again), if Watson spat out an embarrassing answer due to a software bug without crashing, nothing could be done to take it back. This was going to national television.

Groundbreaking deployments of new technology—whether destined to be in orbit or intelligent—risk life and limb, not only because they boldly go where no one has gone before, but because they launch a prototype. Moon-bound Apollo 11 didn't roll off the assembly line. It was the first of its kind. The Watson system deployed on *Jeopardy!* was beta. Rather than conducting the established, sound process of "productizing" a piece of software for mass distribution, this high-speed, real-time behemoth was constructed not by software engineers who build things, but by the same scientific researchers who designed and developed its analytical capabilities. On the software side, the deployed system and the experimental system were largely one and the same. There was no clear delineation between some of the code they used for iterative, experimental improvement with machine learning and code within the deployed system. Of course, these were world-class researchers, many with software design training, but the pressure mounted as these scientists applied virtual hammer to nail to fashion a vessel that would propel their laboratory success into an environment of high-paced, unforeseen questions.

Shedding their lab coats for engineering caps, the team dug in as best they could. As David Gondek told me, changes in Watson's code continued even until and including the very day before the big match, which many would consider a wildly unorthodox practice in preparing for a mission-critical launch of software. Nobody on the team wanted to be the programmer who confused metric and English imperial units in their code, thus crashing NASA's Mars Climate Orbiter, as took place in 1998 after a $327.6 million, nine-month trip to Mars. Recall the story of the Netflix Prize (see Chapter 5), which was won in part by two nonanalysts who found that their expertise as professional software engineers was key to their success.

The brave team nervously saw Watson off to meet its destiny. The training wheels were off. Watson operates on its own, self-contained and disconnected from the Internet or any other knowledge source. Unlike a human *Jeopardy!* player, the only connection it needs is an electrical outlet. It's scary to watch your child fly from the nest. Life has no safety net.

As a machine, Watson was artificial. The world would now witness whether it was also intelligent.


# FOR THE WIN

*You are about to witness what may prove to be an historic competition.*

—Alex Trebek


If functional discourse in human language qualifies, then the world was publicly introduced to the greatest singular leap in artificial intelligence on February 14, 2011.

As the entertainment industry would often have it, this unparalleled moment in scientific achievement was heralded first with Hollywood cheese, and only secondarily with pomp and circumstance. After all, this was a populist play. It was, in a sense, the very first conversant machine ever, and, thus, potentially easier for everyone to relate to than any other computer. Whether perceived as *Star Trek*-ian electronic buddy or HAL-esque force to be reckoned with, 34.5 million turned on the TV to watch.

The *Jeopardy!* theme song begins to play,[11] and a slick, professional voice manically declares, "From the T. J. Watson Research Center in Yorktown Heights, New York, this is *Jeopardy!*, the IBM Challenge!"

When colleagues and I watch the footage, there's a bit of culture shock: We're looking for signs of AI, and instead see glitzy show business. But this came as no surprise to the members of Team Watson seated in the studio audience, who had been preparing for *Jeopardy!* for years.

---

[11] This well-known tune is a simple exercise in major fifths composed by Merv Griffin, *Jeopardy!*'s creator. To some, it sounds suitable for repeated play as part of a brainwashing regiment in the movie *A Clockwork Orange*. Contradicting what some consider a mind-numbing quality, the song's title is the same as the IBM motto coined by the company's founder, Thomas Watson: *Think*.

Once the formalities and introductions to Watson pass, the show moves along jauntily as if it's just any other episode, as if there is nothing extraordinary about the fact that one of the players spitting out answer after answer is not an articulate scholar with his shirt buttoned up to the top, but instead a robot with a synthetic voice straight out of a science fiction movie.

But for David Gondek and his colleagues it was anything but ordinary. The team endured a very nail-biting day during the show's recording, one month before its broadcast. Watching the two-game match, which was televised over a three-day period, you see dozens of questions fly by. When the camera turns for audience reactions, it centers on the scientists, David Ferrucci, David Gondek, Jennifer Chu-Carroll, and others, who enjoy moments of elation and endure the occasional heartache.

On this day, Machine triumphed over Man. Watson answered 66 questions correctly and eight incorrectly. Of those eight, only the answer that categorized Toronto as a U.S. city was considered a gaffe by human standards. The example questions covered in this chapter marked with "★" were fielded by Watson during the match (all correctly except the one answered with Toronto). The final scores, measured in *Jeopardy!* as dollars, were Watson: $77,147, Jennings: $24,000, and Rutter: $21,600.[12]

Prompted to write down his answer to the match's final question, Ken Jennings, reciting a *Simpsons* meme originating from an H. G. Wells movie, appended an editorial: "I, for one, welcome our new computer overlords." He later ruminated, "Watson has lots in common with a top-ranked human *Jeopardy!* player: It's very smart, very fast, speaks in an uneven monotone, and has never known the touch of a woman."

## AFTER MATCH: HONOR, ACCOLADES, AND AWE

*I would have thought that technology like this was years away, but it's here now. I have the bruised ego to prove it.*

—Brad Rutter

*This was to be an away game for humanity, I realized.*

—Ken Jennings

*Maybe we should have toned it down a notch.*

—Sam Palmisano, then CEO, IBM

---

[12] This strong lead was due at least in part to the speed with which Watson could buzz in to answer questions, although that issue is involved and debated; it is complicated to truly level the playing field when human and machine compete.

One million-dollar first place award for the *Jeopardy!* match? Check (donated to charities). American Technology Awards' "Breakthrough Technology of the Year Award"? Check. *R&D* magazine "Innovator of the Year" award? Check.

Webby "Person of the Year" award? Unexpected, but check.

Riding a wave of accolades, IBM is working to reposition components of Watson and its underlying question answering architecture, which the company calls *DeepQA*, to serve industries such as healthcare and finance. Consider medical diagnosis. The wealth of written knowledge is so great, no doctor could read it all; providing for each patient a ranked list of candidate diagnoses could mean doctors miss the right one less often. Guiding the analysis of knowledge sources by learning from training data—answers in the case of *Jeopardy!* and diagnoses in the case of healthcare—is a means to "capture and institutionalize decision-making knowledge," as Robert Jewell of IBM Watson Solutions put it to me.

## IAMBIC IBM AI

Is Watson intelligent? The question presupposes that such a concept is scientific in the first place. The mistake has been made, as proselytizers have often "over-souled" AI (credit for this poignant pun goes to Eric King, of the consultancy he dubbed with the double entendre The Modeling Agency). It's easy to read a lot into the thing. Case in point: I once designed a palindrome generation system (a palindrome reads the same forward and backward) when teaching the AI course at Columbia University that spontaneously derived "Iambic IBM AI." This one is particularly self-referential in that its meter is iambic.

Some credit Watson with far too much smarts. A guard working at IBM's research facility got David Gondek's attention as he was leaving for the day. Since this was a machine that could answer questions about any topic, he suggested, why not ask it who shot JFK?

Strangely, even technology experts tend to answer this philosophical question with a strong opinion in one direction or the other. It's not about right and wrong. Waxing philosophical is a dance, a wonderful, playful pastime. I like to join in the fun as much as the next guy. Here are my thoughts:

> *Watching Watson rattle off one answer after another to diverse questions laced with abstractions, metaphors, and extraneous puns, I am dumbfounded. It is the first time I've felt compelled to anthropomorphize a machine in a meaningful way, well beyond the experience of suspending disbelief in order to feel fooled by a magic trick. To me, Watson looks and feels adept, not just with information but with knowledge. My perceptions endow it with a certain capacity to cogitate. It's a sensation I never thought I'd have cause to experience in my lifetime. To me, Watson is the first artificial intelligence.*

If you haven't done so, I encourage you to watch the *Jeopardy!* match (see the Notes for a YouTube link).

## PREDICT THE RIGHT THING

Predictive models are improving and achieving their potential, but sometimes predicting what's going to happen misses the point entirely. Often, an organization needs to decide what next action to take. One doesn't just want to predict what individuals will do—one wants to know what to do about it. To this end, *we've got to predict something other than what's going to happen*—something else entirely. Turn to the next chapter to find out what.

# CHAPTER 7

# Persuasion by the Numbers

## How Telenor, U.S. Bank, and the Obama Campaign Engineered Influence

*What is the scientific key to persuasion? Why does some marketing fiercely backfire? Why is human behavior the wrong thing to predict? What should all businesses learn about persuasion from presidential campaigns? What voter predictions helped Obama win in 2012 more than the detection of swing voters? How could doctors kill fewer patients inadvertently? How is a person like a quantum particle? Riddle: What often happens to you that cannot be perceived, and that you can't even be sure has happened afterward—but that can be predicted in advance?*

In her job in Norway, Eva Helle stood guard to protect one of the world's largest cell phone carriers from its most dire threat. Her company, Telenor, had charged her with a tough assignment because, as it happens, the mobile business was about to suddenly turn perilous.

A new consumer right exerted new corporate strain: mobile phone numbers became portable. Between 2001 and 2004, most European countries passed legislation to mandate that, if you switch to another wireless service provider, you may happily bring your phone number along with you—you need not change it (the United States did this as well; Canada, a few years later).

As customers leaped at the chance to leave, Eva faced an old truth. You just never know how fickle people are until they're untied. The consumer gains power, and the corporation pays a price.

But, as Eva and her colleagues would soon learn, the game had changed even more than they realized. Their method to woo customers and convince them to stay had stopped working. A fundamental shift in how customers respond to marketing forced Eva to reconsider how things were done.

# CHURN BABY CHURN

Before this change, Telenor had been successfully applying the industry's leading technique to hold on to its cell phone subscribers—a technique that applies predictive analytics (PA):

> **PA APPLICATION: CUSTOMER RETENTION WITH *CHURN MODELING***
> **1. What's predicted:** Which customers will leave.
> **2. What's done about it:** Retention efforts target at-risk customers.

*Churn modeling* may be the hottest marketing application of PA, and for good reason. Any seasoned executive will tell you retention is all-important because it's usually cheaper to convince a customer to stay than to acquire a new one.

Picture customer turnover as air flowing into and out of a balloon:

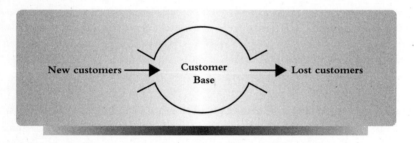

Retaining more customers is akin to clamping down on the nozzle on the right. Lessening the rate of loss just a bit, the balloon blossoms, magnifying its rate of expansion—that is, the growth rate of the company's customer base. This growth is the raison d'être of business.

Prediction and proaction are musts. Persuading someone to stay often sets a mobile carrier back a free phone or a hefty discount. A company must target this generosity to where it's needed: those customers predicted to leave. Like most major cell phone carriers, Telenor had been enjoying a clear win with churn modeling.[1]

What could possibly go wrong?

---

[1] This book's central Table 2 lists several more examples of applied churn modeling and Chapter 4 reveals how Chase applied the prediction of customer departure in a unique way.

## SLEEPING DOGS

*If I leave here tomorrow*
*Would you still remember me?*
*For I must be traveling on, now*
*'Cause there's too many places I've got to see.*

—From "Free Bird" by Lynyrd Skynyrd

Imagine you received an alluring brochure from your cell phone company that says:

Tantalized? Imagining a higher-tech toy in your pocket?

Now imagine you are newly emancipated, granted the liberty to take your phone number with you to another carrier. You've been aching to change to another carrier to join your friends who say they love it over there. In fact, your provider may have sent you this offer only because it predicted your likely departure.

Big mistake. *The company just reminded you that your contracted commitment is ending and you're free to defect.*

Contacting you backfired, increasing the chance you'll leave instead of decreasing it. If you are a sleeping dog, they just failed to let you lie.

Bad news piled on. While already struggling against rising rates of defection, Eva and her colleagues at Telenor detected this backfiring of their efforts to retain. Customer upon customer was being inadvertently turned away, triggered to leave when they otherwise, if not contacted, might have stayed. It was no longer business as usual.

## A NEW THING TO PREDICT

*You didn't have to be so nice; I would have liked you anyway.*
—The Lovin' Spoonful, 1965

*D'oh!*

—Homer Simpson

This unexpected behavior brings up the question of what PA should be used to predict in the first place. Beyond predicting departure, must a company secondarily predict how customers will respond when contacted? Must we predict the more complicated, two-part question, "Who is leaving but would stay if we contacted them?" This sounds pretty convoluted. To do so, it seems like we'd need data tracking when people change their minds!

The question of integrating a secondary prediction also pertains to another killer app of PA, the utterly fundamental targeting of marketing:

## PA APPLICATION: TARGETED MARKETING WITH RESPONSE MODELING

**1. What's predicted:** Which customers will purchase if contacted.

**2. What's done about it:** Contact those customers who are more likely to do so.

Despite *response modeling*'s esteemed status as the most established business application of PA (cf. the 11 examples listed in this book's Central Table 2), it falls severely short because it predicts only one behavior. Assume we have contacted these individuals:

If the dark gray individuals made a purchase, we may proceed with patting ourselves on the back. We must have done a great job of targeting by way of astute predictions about who would buy if contacted, since so many actually did so—relative to how direct marketing often goes, achieving response rates of a few percent, 1 percent, or even less.

One simple question jolts the most senior PA expert out of a stupor: *Which of the dark gray individuals would have purchased anyway, even if we hadn't contacted them?* In some cases, up to half of them—or even more—are so prone to purchasing, they would have either way.

Even an analytics practitioner with decades of experience tweaking predictive models can be floored and flabbergasted by this. She wonders to herself, "Have I been predicting the wrong thing the whole time?" Another bonks himself on the head, groaning, "Why didn't I ever think of that?" Analytics labs echo with the inevitable Homer Simpson exclamation, "D'oh!"

Let's step back and look logically at an organization's intentions:

- The company wants customers to stay and to buy.
- The company does not intend to *force* customers (they have free will).
- Therefore, the company needs to *convince* customers—to influence, to persuade.

If persuasion is what matters, shouldn't that be what's predicted? Let's try that on for size.

***Prediction goal:*** *Will the marketing brochure* persuade *the customer?*

Mission accomplished. This meets the company's goals with just one predictive question, integrating within it both whether the customer will do what's desired and whether it's a good idea to contact the customer.

Predicting impact impacts prediction. PA shifts substantially, from predicting a behavior to predicting *influence on behavior.*

Predicting influence promises to boost PA's value, since an organization doesn't just want to know what individuals will do—it wants to know *what it can do about it.* It makes predictive scores actionable.

I know I asked this earlier but, what could possibly go wrong?

# EYE CAN'T SEE IT

Houston, we have another problem.

How can you know something happened if you didn't see it? Take a look at this possible instance of influence:

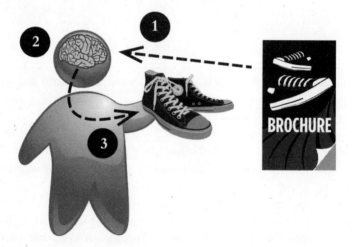

1. The individual perceives the sales brochure.
2. Something happens inside the brain.
3. The individual buys the product.

Is it safe to assume influence took place? How do we know the brochure made a difference? *Perhaps the individual would have purchased anyway.*

The brain's a black box into which we cannot peek. Even if we were conducting neuroscience, it's not clear if and when that field of science will progress far enough to detect when one changes one's mind (and, even if it could, we'd need brain readings from each consumer to employ it!).

Introspection doesn't work, either. You cannot always report on how your own decision making took place. You just can't be certain what made a difference, whether your friend, client, sister, or even you yourself would have made a purchase if circumstances had been different.

To observe influence, we'd need to detect *causality*: Did the brochure *cause* the individual to purchase? As explored in Chapter 3, our knowledge about causality is limited. To truly know causality would be to fully understand how things in the world affect one another, with all the detail involved, the chain reactions that lead one event to result in another. This is the domain of physics, chemistry, and other sciences. It's How the World Works. Ultimately, science tells us only a limited amount.

Therefore, *influence cannot be observed*. We can never witness an individual case of persuasion with complete certainty.

How then could we ever predict it?

## PERCEIVING PERSUASION

*No man ever steps in the same river twice.*

—Heraclitus

Good grief. The most valuable thing to predict can't even be detected in the first place.

The desire to influence drives every move we make. As organizations or individuals, out of self-interest or altruistically, almost everything we do is meant to produce a desired effect, such as:

- Send a brochure to a customer (or voter).
- Prescribe a medication to a patient.
- Provide social benefits intended to foster self-sufficiency.

Each action risks backfiring: The customer cancels, the patient suffers an adverse reaction, or the beneficiary becomes dependent on assistance. So we make choices not only to pursue what will work but also to avoid what won't.

In one arena in particular do we feel the pangs of misstep and failure: dating. In courtship, you are both the director of marketing and the product. You're not in the restaurant for food—rather, it is a sales call. Here are some tips and pointers to persuade. Don't be overly assertive, too frequently contacting your prospect. Yet don't remain overly passive, risking that a competitor will swoop in and steal your thunder. Try to predict what you think is the right message, and avoid communicating the wrong thing.

In the movie *Groundhog Day*, our hero Bill Murray acquires a kind of superpower: the coveted ability to perceive influence. Stuck in a magical loop, reliving the same dull day over and over, he faces a humbling sort of purgatory, apparently designed to address the character's flamboyant narcissism. He cannot escape, and he becomes despondent.

Things turn around for Bill when he recognizes that his plight in fact endows him with the ability to *test different marketing treatments on the same subject under exactly the same situation*—and then observe the outcome. Desperate to win over the apple of his eye (Andie MacDowell), and immune to the fallout and crush of failure, he endeavors in endless trial and error to eventually learn just the right way to woo her.

Only in this wonderful fantasy can we see with certainty the difference each choice makes. That's life. You never know for sure whether you made the optimal choice about anything. Should I have admitted I love reality TV shows? Should we have sent that brochure? Would the other surgical treatment have gone better? Woulda, coulda, shoulda.

In real life, there are no do-overs, so our only recourse is to predict beforehand as well as possible what will work. But, in real life, what's real? If we can't observe influence, how do we know it ever really happens at all?

## PERSUASIVE CHOICES

*Think before you speak.*

Even in dating, there's science to persuasion. Dating website OkCupid showed that messages initiating first contact that include the word *awesome* are more than twice as likely to elicit a response as those with *sexy*. "Howdy" is better than "Hey." *Band* does better than *literature* and *video games* (go figure).

Psychology professor Robert Cialdini persuaded people to commit less crime, and proved it worked. Visitors regularly steal a precious resource from Arizona's Petrified Forest National Park: chunks of petrified wood. He showed the difference it makes posting a sign saying:

PLEASE DON'T REMOVE THE PETRIFIED WOOD FROM THE PARK, IN ORDER TO PRESERVE THE NATURAL STATE OF THE PETRIFIED FOREST

. . . in comparison to posting a sign saying:

> **MANY PAST VISITORS
> HAVE REMOVED
> PETRIFIED WOOD FROM
> THE PARK, CHANGING
> THE NATURAL STATE OF
> THE PETRIFIED FOREST**

The first resulted in less than a quarter as much theft as the second, with rates of 1.67 percent and 7.92 percent, respectively. Persuasion has been proven. We can safely conclude that *relaying the first message rather than the second influences people to steal less*, possibly because the second decreases the perceived social stigma of theft by conveying that it is common behavior. Similar effects have been shown in the persuasion of hotel room towel recycling and decreasing home energy usage, as explored in Cialdini's coauthored book, *Yes! 50 Scientifically Proven Ways to Be Persuasive.*[2]

These studies prove influence takes place across a group, but ascertain nothing about any one individual, so the choice of message still cannot be individually chosen according to what's most likely to influence each person.

In the field of medicine, most clinical studies do this same thing—compare two treatments and see which tends to work better overall. For knee surgery after a ski accident, I had to select a graft source from which to reconstruct my busted anterior cruciate ligament (ACL, the knee's central ligament—previously known to me as the Association for Computational Linguists). I based my decision on a study that showed subsequent knee-walking was rated "difficult or impossible" by twice as many patients who donated their own patellar tissue rather than hamstring tissue.[3]

---

[2] Although psychological interpretations such as this destigmatizing effect are not conclusively supported by the data analysis, it is also true that persuasion "by the numbers"—the focus of this chapter—depends on the creative design of messages (more generally, treatments) to test in the first place. As always, human creativity, such as that in the field of psychology, and number crunching—the soft and the hard sciences—complement one another and are mutually interdependent.

[3] The decision was mine alone, with no personalized guidance from a physician. I found each knee surgeon to be almost entirely devoted to one graft source or another and therefore unable to provide balanced guidance for my choice. My only option was to first select a surgical procedure and then choose a doctor who focused on that procedure.

It's good but it's not personalized. I can never know if my choice for knee surgery was the best for my particular case (although my knee does seem great now). The same holds true for any treatment decision based on such studies, which provide only a one-size-fits-all result. We're left with uncertainty for each individual patient. If you take a pill and your headache goes away, you can't know for sure that the medicine worked; maybe your headache would have stopped anyway.

More generally, if you prevent something bad, how can you be sure it was ever going to happen in the first place?

## BUSINESS STIMULUS AND BUSINESS RESPONSE

Many of your everyday clicks contribute to the web's constant testing of how to improve overall persuasiveness. Google has compared 41 shades of blue to see which elicits more clicks. Websites serve the ads that get clicked the most, and run random AB tests to compare which web page design and contents lead to the most buying. Facebook conducts controlled experiments to see how changes to the rules driving which friends' posts get displayed influence your engagement and usage of the product.

I tested titles for this book, following in the footsteps of *SuperCrunchers* and *The 4-Hour Workweek*. Placed as ads on Google Adwords, *Predictive Analytics*, when displayed on tens of thousands of screens of unsuspecting experimental subjects across the country, was clicked almost twice as often as *Geek Prophecies*, and also beat out *I Knew You Were Going to Do That* and *Clairvoyant Computers*, plus the six remaining book titles that I also entered into this contest. It was convenient that the field's very name came out as the top contender, an unquestionably fitting title for this book.

In both medicine and marketing, this scheme to test *treatments* reveals the impact of selecting one outward action over another—but only as a trend across the group of subjects as a whole. The best an organization can do is run with the one most effective treatment, applying it uniformly for every individual.

In this practice, the organization is employing a blunt instrument. Looking back, we still don't know for whom the treatment was truly effective. Looking forward, we still don't know how to make personalized choices.

## THE QUANTUM HUMAN

*You are traveling through another dimension, a dimension not only of sight and sound but of mind.*
—"The Twilight Zone"

*Here's the thing about the future. Every time you look at it, it changes. Because you looked at it.*
—Nicolas Cage's clairvoyant in *Next*

*Heisenberg might have slept here.*

—Anonymous

As in quantum physics, some things are unknowable. Although you may protest being reduced to a quantum particle, there's a powerful analogy to be drawn between the uncertainty about influence on an individual and *Heisenberg's uncertainty principle*. This principle states that we can't know everything about a particle—for example, both its position and speed. It's a trade-off. The more precisely you measure one, the less precisely you can measure the other.

Likewise, we can't know everything about a human. In particular, we can't know both of the things that we'd need to know in order to conclude that a person could be influenced; for example:

1. Will Bill purchase if we send him a brochure?
2. Will Bill purchase if we *don't* send him a brochure?

If we did know the answer to both, we'd readily know this most desired fact about Bill—whether he's *influenceable*. In cases where the answers to the two questions disagree, such as:

Today                                    Tomorrow

**The answer to (1) is "Yes"—Bill receives a brochure and then purchases.**

Today                                    Tomorrow

**The answer to (2) is "No"—Bill does not receive a brochure and does not purchase.**

In this case, we would conclude that the choice of treatment has an influential effect on Bill; he is persuadable.

In cases where the answers to the questions agree, such as:

**The answer to (1) is "Yes"—Bill receives a brochure and then purchases.**

**The answer to (2) is also "Yes"—Bill does not receive a brochure but then purchases anyway.**

In this case, we conclude the choice of treatment has no influence; he would buy either way.

Other sequences exist. Sometimes a brochure backfires and adversely influences a customer who would otherwise buy not to.

But this is a fantasy—we *can't* know the answer to both questions. We can find out (1) by sending him a brochure. We can find out (2) by not sending him a brochure. But we can't both contact and not contact Bill. We can't administer medicine and not administer medicine. We can't try two different forms of surgery at once. In general, you can't test an individual with both treatments.

This uncertainty leaves us with philosophical struggles akin to those of quantum physics. Given that we could never know both, does a particle ever really have both a true position and a true speed? Similarly, do answers to both of the previous questions about a person truly exist? Answering one renders the other purely hypothetical. It's like the tree falling in the forest with no one to perceive the sound, which becomes only theoretical. This most fundamental status of a human as influenceable or not influenceable holds only as an ethereal concept. It's observable in aggregate only across a group, never established for any one person. Does influenceability exist only in the context of a group, emergently, defying true definition for any single individual? If influenceable people do walk among us, you could never be certain who they are.

**The quantum human—is he or she influenceable?**

This unknowability equates the past and the future. We don't know whether a person *was* influenced, and we don't know whether the person *could be* influenced—whether he or she is *influenceable*. It's kind of a refreshing change that prediction is no more difficult than retrospection, that tomorrow presents no greater a challenge than yesterday. Both previous and forthcoming influence can only at best be estimated.

Clearly, the future is the more valuable one to estimate. If we can know *how likely* each person is to be influenced, we can drive decisions, treating each individual accordingly.

But how can you predictively model influence? That is, how could you train a predictive model when there are no learning examples—no individual known cases—of the thing we want to predict?

## PREDICTING INFLUENCE WITH UPLIFT MODELING

A model that predicts influence will be a predictive model like any other:

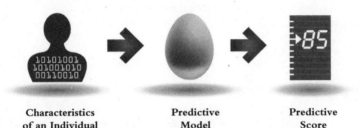

**Characteristics**          **Predictive**          **Predictive**
**of an Individual**            **Model**                  **Score**

Like all the models we've covered in this book, it takes characteristics of the individual as input, and provides a predictive score as output.

But it will be a special case of predictive models. Instead of predicting an outright behavior, we need *a model that scores according to the likelihood an individual's behavior will be influenced*. We need an *uplift model*:

> **Uplift model**—*A predictive model that predicts the influence on an individual's behavior that results from applying one treatment over another.*[4]

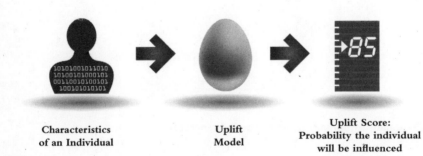

**Characteristics**          **Uplift**          **Uplift Score:**
**of an Individual**          **Model**          **Probability the individual**
                                                              **will be influenced**

---

[4] Not to be confused with the lift of a predictive model covered in Chapter 4, uplift modeling is also known as *differential response, impact, incremental impact, incremental response, net lift, net response, persuasion, true lift,* or *true response modeling.*

The uplift score answers the question, *"How much more likely is this treatment to generate the desired outcome than the alternative treatment?"* It guides an organization's choice of treatment or action, what to do or say to each individual. The secondary treatment can be the passive action of a *control set*—for example, make no marketing contact or administer a placebo instead of the trial drug—in which case an uplift model effectively decides whether or not to treat.

How do you learn about something you can't see? We never have at our disposal learning examples of the very thing we want to predict: *influenceable individuals*. We don't have the usual data from which to directly learn.

To do the seemingly impossible, *uplift modeling* needs a clever work-around. To see how it works, let's explore a detailed example from U.S. Bank.

## BANKING ON INFLUENCE

U.S. Bank assistant vice president Michael Grundhoefer isn't satisfied with good. In the mid-1990s, the bank's direct marketing efforts to sell financial products such as lines of credit fared well. Most mail campaigns turned a satisfactory profit. Michael, who headed up the analytics behind many of these campaigns, kept a keen eye on the underlying response models and how they could be improved.

Companies often misinterpret marketing campaign results. Here's where they go terribly wrong: They look at the list of customers contacted and ask, "How many responded?" That's the *response rate*. One of the original inventors of uplift modeling, Nicholas Radcliffe (now an independent consultant and sometimes visiting professor in Edinburgh), drew a cartoon about that measure's drawbacks:

Cartoon reproduced with permission.

The response rate completely overlooks how many would buy anyway, even if not contacted. Some products just fly off the shelves and sell themselves. For business, that's a good thing—but, if so, it's important not to credit the marketing. You could be wasting dollars and chopping down trees to send mail that isn't actually helping.

Just as with medicine, marketing's success—or lack thereof—is revealed by comparing to a *control set*, a group of individuals suppressed from the treatment (or administered a placebo, in the case of medicine). Therefore, we need to collect two sets of data:

If the treated customers buy more than the control customers, we know the campaign successfully persuades. This proves some individuals were influenced, but, as usual, we don't know which.

## PREDICTING THE WRONG THING

*If you come to a fork in the road, take it.*

—Yogi Berra

To target the marketing campaigns, Michael and his team at U.S. Bank were employing the industry standard: response models, which predict who will buy if contacted. That's not the same thing as predicting who will buy *because* they were contacted; it does not predict influence. Compared to a control set, Michael showed the campaigns were successful, turning a profit. But he knew the targeting would be more effective if only there were a way to predict which customers would be *persuaded* by the marketing collateral.

Standard response models predict the wrong thing and are in fact falsely named. Response models don't predict the response *caused by* contact; they predict buying *in light of* contact. But predicting for whom contact will be the cause of buying is more pertinent than predicting buying in general. Knowing who your "good" customers are—the ones who will buy more—may be nice to know, but it takes second place.[5]

For some projects, conventional response models have it backward. By aiming to increase response rate, they complacently focus on the metric that's easiest to measure.

---

[5] Driving decisions by only predicting the outcome of one treatment without predicting the result of the other is a form of *satisficing*. It's a compromise. Instead of compromising, marketing needs all the help it can get to better target. As a data miner, I actually receive e-mail inquiries from drilling supply vendors. I'm not that kind of miner. Eric King of The Modeling Agency receives job inquiries from (human) models seeking opportunity in the fashion industry.

As former U.S. Secretary of Defense Robert McNamara said, "We have to find a way of making the important measurable, instead of making the measurable important." A standard response model will gladly target customers who would buy anyway, doing nothing to dispel the sense that we as consumers receive so much junk mail. Instead, it's only a small sliver of persuadable customers who are actually worth mailing to, if we can identify them.

Standard response modeling predicts:

**1.** Will the customer buy if contacted?

Uplift modeling changes everything by adding just one word:

**2.** Will the customer buy **only** if contacted?

Although the second question may appear simple, it answers the composite of two questions: "Will the customer buy if contacted and not buy otherwise?" This two-in-one query homes in on the difference in outcome that will result from one treatment over another. It's the same as asking, "Will contacting the customer influence him or her to buy?"

## RESPONSE UPLIFT MODELING

*Weigh your options.*

Addressing a composite of two questions, uplift modeling predicts each individual's placement within four conceptual segments that distinguish along two dimensions:

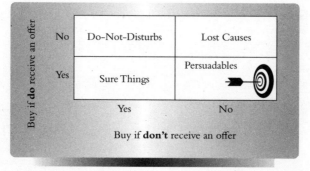

**Conceptual response segments. The lower-right segment is targeted with uplift modeling.**[6]

---

[6] Table derived from Nicholas Radcliffe, "Generating Incremental Sales: Maximizing the Incremental Impact of Cross-Selling, Up-Selling and Deep-Selling through Uplift Modeling," Stochastic Solutions Limited, February 16, 2008, and Suresh Vittal, "Optimal Targeting through Uplift Modeling: Generating Higher Demand and Increasing Customer Retention While Reducing Marketing Costs," Forrester Research white paper, 2008.

This quad first distinguishes from top to bottom which customers will buy in light of marketing contact, which is the job of conventional response modeling. But then it further distinguishes along a second dimension: Which customers will make a purchase even if not contacted?

Michael wanted to target the lower-right quadrant, those worthy of investing the cost to contact. These persuadables won't buy if not contacted, but will buy if they are. These are the individuals an uplift model aims to flag with the affirmative prediction.

### PA APPLICATION: TARGETED MARKETING WITH *RESPONSE UPLIFT* MODELING

1. **What's predicted:** Which customers will be persuaded to buy.
2. **What's done about it:** Target persuadable customers.

An uplift model provides the opportunity to reduce costs and unnecessary mail in comparison to a traditional response model. This is achieved by suppressing from the contact list those customers in the lower-left quadrant, the so-called sure things who will buy either way.

## THE MECHANICS OF UPLIFT MODELING

Uplift modeling operates simultaneously on two data sets—both the treated set and the control set—learning from them both:

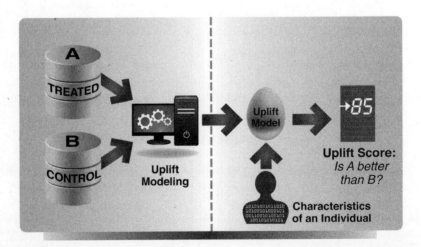

**Two training sets are used together to develop an uplift model.**

To learn to distinguish influenceables—those for whom the choice of treatment makes a difference—uplift modeling learns from both customers who were contacted and others who weren't. Processing two data sets represents a significant paradigm shift after decades of predictive modeling and machine learning research almost entirely focused on tweaking the modeling process across a single data set.

Starting first with a single-variable example, we can see that it is possible to predict the uplift by comparing behavior across the two data sets:

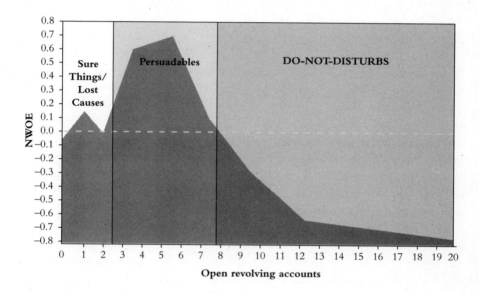

**Net weight of evidence (NWOE, a measure of uplift) varies by a customer's number of open revolving accounts. Graph courtesy of Kim Larsen.**

This fictional but typical example of a financial institution's direct marketing results illustrates that mildly engaged customers are hot, readily persuadable by direct mail. The vertical axis represents *net weight of evidence* (NWOE), a measure of uplift, and the horizontal axis represents the number of open revolving accounts the customer already holds. In this case, it turns out that customers in the middle region, who don't already hold too many or too few open revolving accounts, will be more likely to be persuaded by direct mail.

Less engaged customers on the left are unmoved—whether they were already destined to open more accounts or not, their plans don't change if contacted. They are the sure things and lost causes, respectively—either way, it isn't worth contacting them.

Avoid at all costs contacting customers on the right—they are "do-not-disturbs." Contacting these individuals, who already hold a good number of accounts, actually decreases the chance they'll buy. The curve dips down into negative numbers—a veritable *downlift*. The explanation may be that customers with many accounts are already so engaged that they are more sensitive to, aware of, and annoyed by what they consider to be unnecessary marketing contact. An alternative explanation is that customers who have already accumulated so many credit accounts are susceptible to impulse buys (e.g., when they come into a bank branch), but when contacted at home will be prone to respond by considering the decision more intently and researching competing products online.

This shows the power of one variable. How can we leverage PA's true potential by considering multiple variables, as with the predictive models of Chapter 4? Let's turn back to Michael's story at U.S. Bank for a detailed example.

## HOW UPLIFT MODELING WORKS

Despite their marketing successes, Michael at U.S. Bank had a nagging feeling things could be better. Unlike many marketers, he was aware of the difference between a campaign's response rate and the sales generated by it. Inspecting reports, he could see the response models were less than ideal. He tried out some good ideas of his own to attempt to model persuasion, which provided preliminary yet inconsistent and unstable success.

One time, Michael noted failure for certain groups within a direct mail campaign selling a home-equity line of credit to existing customers. For those groups, the campaign not only failed to cover its own printing and mailing costs, it in fact had the detrimental effect of decreasing sales, a slight *downlift* overall.

Michael was beginning to collaborate with a small company called Quadstone (now Pitney Bowes Software) that provided a new commercial approach to uplift modeling. The system could derive marketing segments that reveal persuadable customers, such as:[7]

---

**Has paid back more than 17.3% of current loan**
**-AND-**
**Is using more than 9.0% of revolving credit limit**
**-AND-**
**Is designated within a certain set of lifestyle segments**

---

**A Segment of persuadable individuals.**

This is not your usual marketing segment. It isn't customers more likely to buy. It isn't customers less likely to buy. It is customers *more likely to be influenced by marketing contact*. The difference marketing makes for this segment can be calculated only by seeing how its purchase rate differs between the treated and control sets:[8]

---

[7] Thanks to Patrick Surry at Pitney Bowes Software for this example segment derived across U.S. Bank data. The segment is simplified for this illustration.

[8] A simpler alternative to analyzing over both sets at once is to make a separate predictive model for each treatment, as was the case behind the online ad-selection case study described in Chapter 1. Michael at U.S. Bank evaluated this simpler method, concluding that the tree-based approach to uplift modeling provided stronger and more consistent results.

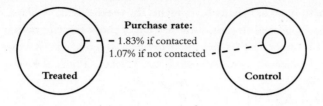

**Purchase rates of the persuadable segment described above differ, depending on whether marketing contact is received.**

Success! The direct mail elicits more responses from segment members who were contacted (the treated set) than those not contacted (the control set). By automatically deriving its defining characteristics, uplift modeling has discovered a segment of customers for which this direct mail campaign succeeds after all.

The uplift modeling method that discovers such segments is an expansion of decision trees (see Chapter 4) called *uplift trees*. Normal decision trees strive to identify segments extreme in their response rates—many responses or few responses. Uplift trees use variables to mechanically "segment down" in the same way, but seek to find segments extreme in the difference treatment makes—segments that are particularly influence-able. An uplift tree includes a number of segments such as the one shown above.[9]

For U.S. Bank, response uplift modeling delivered an unprecedented boost, increasing the marketing campaign's return on investment by a factor of five in comparison with standard response model targeting. This win resulted from decreasing both the amount of direct mail that commanded no impact and the amount that instigated an adverse response.

## CASE STUDY: U.S. BANK

Business case: Direct mail for a home-equity line of credit to existing customers.
Approach: Target campaign with an uplift model.
Resulting improvements over prior conventional analytical approach:

- Return on investment (ROI) increased over five times previous campaigns (from 75 percent to 400 percent).
- Campaign costs cut by 40 percent.
- Revenue gain increased by over 300 percent.

---

[9] Ensemble models (see Chapter 5) of decision trees are recommended when employing this analytical approach to uplift modeling to help ensure stable results. Although predicting influence rather than outright behavior, The Ensemble Effect still applies.

Uplift practitioners at Fidelity Investments also see the light: *spend less, earn more*. By avoiding sure things and do-not-disturbs, "Uplift modeling empowers your organization to capture more than 100 percent of responses by contacting less than 100 percent of the target population," says Kathleen Kane, Fidelity's Principal Decision Scientist.

## THE PERSUASION EFFECT

Uplift modeling conquers the imperceivable, influence, by newly combining two well-trodden, previously separate paradigms:

1. Comparing treated and control results.
2. Predictive modeling (machine learning, statistical regression, etc.).

Only by cleverly combining these two practices does the newfound ability to predict persuasion for each individual become possible. I call this The Persuasion Effect:

> **The Persuasion Effect:** *Although imperceivable, the persuasion of an individual can be predicted by uplift modeling, predictively modeling across two distinct training data sets that record, respectively, the outcomes of two competing treatments.*

If you haven't already figured it out, this answers the riddle posed at the beginning of this chapter. *Being influenced* is the thing that often happens to you that cannot be witnessed, and that you can't even be sure has happened afterward—but that can be predicted in advance. In this way, predictive analytics transcends human perception.

## INFLUENCE ACROSS INDUSTRIES

Uplift modeling applies everywhere: marketing, credit risk, electoral politics, sociology, and healthcare. The intent to influence is common to almost any organization, so The Persuasion Effect is put into play across industry sectors.

| Uplift Application | Decision between Treatments | Objective |
|---|---|---|
| **Targeted marketing with response uplift modeling** | *Should we contact the customer or not (active or passive treatment)?* | Positive impact of **direct marketing** campaigns |
| **Customer retention with churn uplift modeling** | *Should we provide the customer a retention offer or not (active or passive treatment)?* | Positive impact of **retention** campaigns |

| Uplift Application | Decision between Treatments | Objective |
|---|---|---|
| **Content selection** | *With which ad, illustration, choice of words, or product should we solicit the customer?* | Response rate of **direct marketing, cross-sell**, and **online and offline ads** |
| **Channel selection** | *Through which channel should we contact the customer (e.g., mail, e-mail, or telephone)?* | Positive impact of **direct marketing** campaigns |
| **Dynamic pricing and discounting** | *Should we offer the customer a higher price or a lower price?* | Revenue of **sales** |
| **Collections** | *Should we offer the debtor a deeper write-off?* | Revenue of **accounts receivable** |
| **Credit risk** | *Should we offer the customer a higher or lower credit limit? A higher or lower APR?* | Revenue from **interest payments** and savings from **fewer defaults** |
| **Electoral politics** | *Should we market to the constituent/in the state (swing voter/swing state)?* | Positive votes resulting from **political election campaigns** *(see this chapter's sidebar for how Obama's 2012 campaign employed uplift modeling)* |
| **Sociology** | *Should we provide benefits to this individual?* | Improved social program outcome: long-term self-sufficiency |
| **Personalized medicine** | *Which medical treatment should the patient receive?* | Favorable patient outcome in **clinical healthcare** |

This chapter covers in detail the first two areas in the table above. Here's a bit more about the rest of them (note that for some of these application areas, no public case studies or proofs of concept yet exist—uplift modeling is an emerging technology).

**Content and channel selection**. Uplift modeling selects for each user the ad, offer, content, product, or channel of contact (phone, e-mail, etc.) most likely to elicit a response. In these cases, there is no passive option and therefore no control set—both data sets test an active treatment.

**Dynamic pricing and collections**. As for any decision, a certain risk is faced for each treatment option when pricing: the higher price may turn a customer away, but the lower price (or deeper discount) unnecessarily sacrifices revenue if the customer would have been willing to pay more.

**Credit risk**. The balance between risk and upside profitability for each debtor is influenced by both the credit limit and the APR offered. Raising one or both may result in higher revenue in the form of interest payments, but may also increase the chance of the debtor defaulting on payments and an ensuing write-off.

**Electoral politics**. When I resided in California, I saw few if any ads for presidential campaigns—the state was a lock; depending on your political affiliation, it could be viewed as either a sure thing or a lost cause. Just as so-called swing clients (influenceables) are potentially persuaded by marketing contact, the same benefit is gained where this term originates: political campaigns that target swing voters. The constituents with the most potential to be influenced by campaign contact are worth the cost of contact. Analogously, only the swing states that could conceivably be persuaded as a whole are worth expending great campaign resources. For more on elections and uplift modeling, see this chapter's sidebar, "Beyond Swing Voters: How Persuasion Modeling Helped Obama Win His Second Term."

**Sociology: targeting social programs**. Speaking of politics, here is a concept that could change everything. Social programs such as educational and occupational support endure scrutiny as possibly more frequently awarded to go-getters who would have succeeded anyway. For certain other beneficiaries, skeptics ask, does support backfire, leaving them more dependent rather than more self-sufficient? Only by predicting how a program will influence the outcome for each individual prospect can programs be targeted in a way that addresses these questions. In so doing, *might such scientifically based, individualized economic policies help resolve the crippling government deadlock that results from the opposing fiscal ideologies currently held by conservative and liberal policymakers?*

**Personalized medicine**. While one medical treatment may deliver better results on average than another, this one-size-fits-all approach commonly implemented by clinical studies means treatment decisions that help many may in fact hurt some. In this way, healthcare decisions backfire on occasion, exerting influence opposite to that intended: they hurt or kill—although they kill fewer than following no clinical studies at all. *Personalized medicine* aims to predict which treatment is best suited for each patient, employing analytical methods to predict treatment impact (i.e., medical influence) similar to the uplift modeling techniques used for marketing treatment decisions. For example, to drive beta-blocker treatment decisions for heart failure, researchers "use two independent data sets to construct a systematic, subject-specific treatment selection procedure." A certain HIV treatment is shown to be more effective for younger children. Treatments for various cancers are targeted by genetic markers—a trend so significant the Food and Drug Administration is increasingly requiring for new pharmaceuticals, as the

*New York Times* puts it, "a companion test that could reliably detect the [genetic] mutation so that the drug could be given to the patients it is intended to help," those "most likely to benefit."

# IMMOBILIZING MOBILE CUSTOMERS

It wasn't long after phone number portability came, raising a hailstorm in the telecommunications industry, that Quadstone spoke with Eva at Telenor about the new uplift modeling technique. It was a revelation. Eva had already confirmed that Telenor's retention efforts triggered some customers to leave rather than persuading them to stay, but she wasn't aware of any established technique to address the issue. The timing was fortuitous, as Quadstone was just starting out, seeking its first few clients to prove uplift modeling's value.

> **PA APPLICATION: CUSTOMER RETENTION WITH *CHURN UPLIFT* *MODELING***
> 1. **What's predicted:** Which customers can be persuaded to stay.
> 2. **What's done about it:** Retention efforts target persuadable customers.

Customers can be as easily scared away as a frightened bunny. Traditional churn models often inadvertently frighten these rabbits, since customers most likely to leave are often those most easy to trigger—sleeping dogs easy to wake up. This includes, for example, the health club member who never gets to the gym and the Netflix subscriber who rarely trades in her rental movie—both just need a reminder before they get around to canceling (it would be more ideal to re-engage them). Someone once told me that, when he received an offer to extend his camera's warranty, it reminded him that coverage was soon ending. He promptly put his camera into the microwave in order for it to break so he could return it. It would inevitably be more cost-effective to avoid triggering such criminal activity than to prosecute for it after the fact.

Prompting a cell phone customer to leave can be especially costly because it may trigger a social domino effect: People tend to stick with the same wireless carrier as their friends. One major North American carrier showed that a customer is seven times more likely to cancel if someone in the person's calling network cancels.

For Telenor, churn uplift modeling delivered an astonishing boost to the return on investment of its retention initiatives: the ROI increased by a factor of 11, in comparison with its existing practice of targeting with standard churn models. This came from decreasing the number of sleeping dog customers the company had been inadvertently waking, and secondarily from reducing the total number of mail pieces sent—like U.S. Bank, Telenor got more for less.

## CASE STUDY: TELENOR, THE WORLD'S SEVENTH LARGEST MOBILE OPERATOR

Business case: Retention campaign for cell phone subscribers.
Approach: Target campaign with an uplift model.
Resulting improvements over conventional analytical retention models:

- Campaign ROI increased by a factor of 11.
- Churn reduced a further 36 percent.
- Campaign costs reduced by 40 percent.

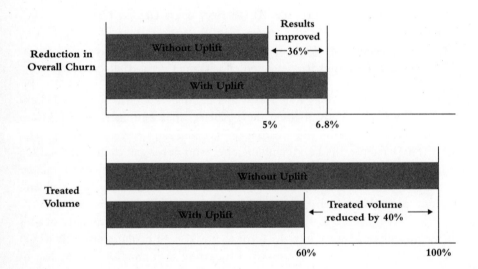

Figure courtesy of Pitney Bowes Software.

For the international mobile carrier, which serves tens of millions of cell phone subscribers across 11 markets, this was a huge win. Beyond addressing the new business challenges that came of phone number portability, it alleviated the systematic "sleeping dog" problem inherent to churn modeling, one Telenor likely had suffered from all along. Even when there's a net benefit from marketing, offers could be triggering some customers to leave who would have otherwise stayed.

For Eva, who has since been promoted to head of customer analytics, and for the rest of the world, this only marks the beginning of the emerging practice of inducing influence and predicting persuasion.

## BEYOND SWING VOTERS

### *How Persuasion Modeling Helped Obama Win His Second Term*

*No other presidential campaign [besides Obama's] has relied so heavily on the science of analytics, using information to predict voting patterns. Election day may have changed the game.*
—Christi Parsons and Kathleen Hennessey, *Los Angeles Times*,
November 13, 2012

Elections hang by a thinner thread than you think.

You may know that Barack Obama's 2012 campaign for a second term *Moneyballed* the election, employing a team of over 50 analytics experts.

You may also know that the tremendous volume of any presidential campaign's activities, frenetically executed into the eleventh hour in pursuit of landing the world's most powerful job, ultimately serves only to sway a thin slice of the electorate: swing voters within swing states.

But what most people do not realize is that presidential campaigns must focus *even more narrowly than that*, taking microtargeting to a whole new level. The Obama campaign got this one right, breaking ground for election cycles to come by applying uplift modeling to drive millions of per-voter campaign decisions, thereby boosting persuasive impact.

However, the buzz in 2012 was about something else. Rather than learning about campaign targeting, when it came to the math behind the election, we heard a great deal about Nate Silver. Silver emerged as the media darling of poll analyzers, soaring past the ranks of guru quant or sexy scientist to become the very face of prediction itself. If mathematical "tomorrowvision" had a name, it was Nate. Even before his forecasts were vindicated by the election results, it was hard to find a talk show host—at least among the left—who hadn't enjoyed a visit from Silver, probing him with evident, slack-jawed fascination.

An election poll does not constitute prognostic technology—it does not endeavor to calculate insights that foresee human behavior. Rather, a poll is plainly the act of voters explicitly telling you what they're going to do. It's a mini-election dry run. There's a craft to aggregating polls, as Silver has mastered so adeptly, but even he admits it's no miracle of clairvoyance. "It's not really that complicated," he told late night talk show host Stephen Colbert the day before the election. "There are many things that are *much* more complicated than looking at the polls and taking an average . . . and counting to 270, right?"

You want power? *True power comes in influencing the future rather than speculating on it.* Nate Silver publicly competed to win election forecasting, while Obama's analytics team quietly competed to win the election itself.

(*continued*)

## BEYOND SWING VOTERS (*CONTINUED*)

This reflects the very difference between forecasting and predictive analytics. Forecasting calculates an aggregate view for each U.S. state, while predictive analytics delivers action-oriented insight: predictions for each individual voter.

### THE RARE BIRD: PERSUADABLE SWING VOTERS

Swing voters are a myth. The concept is ill-defined and subjective. In one approach, the Democratic National Committee (DNC) labels as "not very partisan" those voters who self-reported as independent, or for whom their party is (for any reason) unknown. Despite this information about them, many such voters have indeed made up their minds and are unswingable.

Instead of mythical swing voters—or unicorns, for that matter—what matters to a campaign is concrete and yet quite narrow: *who will be influenced to vote for our candidate by a call, door knock, flyer, or TV ad?*

Presidential campaigns must hold themselves to a higher standard than most marketing campaigns. In this ruthless competition of optimal tweaking, the notion of expending resources—such as a paid mailing or a campaign volunteer's precious time—to contact a constituent who was already going to vote your way is abhorrent. Even worse, it is known that, for some cases, contact will inadvertently change the voter's mind in the wrong direction—it can backfire and cause the person to vote for the other candidate.

In the business world, marketing campaigns often withstand such cases without wincing. They inadvertently hit some "sure thing" and "do-not-disturb" customers, yet carry on happily with high profits. As long as the overall campaign is doing more good than harm, taking on the more sophisticated methods needed to smooth these imperfect edges is often seen as too high an investment relative to the expected payoff (although this determination is often just inertia speaking; *persuasion modeling* is new and not yet widely practiced).

But a presidential campaign comes along only once every four years. Its extraordinarily high stakes demand that all stops be pulled out. It was only a matter of time before campaigns began predicting their potential to influence each voter in order to optimize that influence.

### ANOTHER RARE BIRD: PERSUASION MODELING EXPERTS

Enter Rayid Ghani, chief data scientist of the presidential campaign, Obama for America 2012. He was the man for the job. With a master's degree in machine

## BEYOND SWING VOTERS (*CONTINUED*)

learning from Carnegie Mellon (the first university to have a machine learning department), plus 10 years of research work at the labs of consulting behemoth Accenture, Rayid had rare, sought-after experience in uplift modeling—which the campaign calls *persuasion modeling*. His background included research determining which medical treatment will provide the best outcome for each patient, and which price will provide the best profit from each retail customer. At Obama for America, he helped determine whether campaign contact would provide the right vote from each constituent.

It's a deep analytical challenge. A predictive model that foresees the ability to persuade is not your average predictive model. Beyond identifying voters who will come out for Obama if contacted, Rayid's persuasion models needed to distinguish those voters who would come out for Obama in any case, as well as those who in fact were at risk of being turned off by campaign contact and switching over to vote for the other guy, Mitt Romney. If you think it through, you'll see the idea of "can be positively persuaded" entails all these distinctions.

### PA APPLICATION: POLITICAL CAMPAIGNING WITH VOTER PERSUASION MODELING

1. **What's predicted:** Which voter will be positively persuaded by political campaign contact such as a call, door knock, flyer, or TV ad.
2. **What's done about it:** Persuadable voters are contacted, and voters predicted to be adversely influenced by contact are avoided.

For this project, the campaign needed to collect not donations but data. No matter how smart, the brains on Obama's staff could only tackle the persuasion problem with just the right data sets. To this end, they tested across thousands of swing state voters the very actions they would later decide on for millions. Batches of voters received campaign contact—door knocks, flyers, and phone calls—and, critically, other batches received no contact at all (the control groups). All the batches were then later polled to see whether they would support Obama in the voting booth.

### ACTIVELY CAMPAIGNING ON PERSUASION

*[The Obama campaign job listing for "predictive modeling"] read like politics as done by Martians.*

—Peggy Noonan, *Wall Street Journal*, July 30, 2011

(*continued*)

## BEYOND SWING VOTERS (*CONTINUED*)

*The Martians have landed.*

—Christi Parsons and Kathleen Hennessey, *Los Angeles Times*,
November 13, 2012

If the data proved that campaigning generally helps, it was good news for the team—but then, analysis had only just begun. Rayid's team faced the ultimate campaign imperative: learn to discriminate, voter by voter, whether contact would persuade. This is where persuasion modeling (the technique described in the rest of this chapter as *uplift modeling*) came in and took storm.

"Our modeling team built persuasion models for each swing state," Rayid said. "The models were then employed to predict the potential to persuade for each of millions of individuals in swing states. It told us which were most likely to be won over to Obama's side, and which we should avoid contacting entirely.*

To tweak these models, the team experimented extensively across avant-garde techniques for persuasion modeling. Although they have not disclosed which types of voter data made the difference for detecting persuadability, their related effort predicting a constituent's propensity to vote for Obama (regardless of campaign contact) employed more than 80 fields, including demographics, voting history, and magazine subscriptions. The campaign's most cherished source was the DNC's database, which includes notes regarding each voter's observed response to door knocks—welcoming or door-slamming—during prior presidential election cycles.

The potential persuadability of each voter predicted by these models guided the massive army of campaign volunteers as they pounded the pavement and dialed phone numbers. When knocking on a door, the volunteer wasn't simply canvassing the local neighborhood—this very voter had been predictively targeted as persuadable. As Daniel Wagner, the campaign's chief analytics officer, told the *Los Angeles Times*, "White suburban women? They're not all the same. The Latino community is very diverse with very different interests." This form of microtargeting even brought volunteers to specific houses within the thick of strongly Republican neighborhoods, in this way moving beyond protocols that had become standard during prior election cycles.

---

*Beyond persuasion modeling, the team also employed predictive modeling to predict the propensity to vote for Obama regardless of campaign contact, the probability of voting at all (turnout), and the probability of donating in order to target fund-raising efforts.

## BEYOND SWING VOTERS (*CONTINUED*)

Flyers also targeted the persuadables. As with door knocks, a voter received the flier only if she were predicted to be influenced, if her mind was likely to be changed. Traditional marketing sends direct mail to those expected to buy *in light of* contact, rather than *because of* it. It's a subtle difference, but all the difference in the world. Putting it another way, rather than determining whether contact is *a good idea*, persuasion modeling determines whether contact is *a better idea* than not contacting.

Persuasion modeling worked. This method was shown to convince more voters to choose Obama than traditional campaign targeting. "These models showed significant lift over just targeting voters who were undecided or had registered as nonpartisan," Rayid said.

This relative boost came in part by avoiding those voters for whom contact was predicted to backfire (the "do-not-disturbs"). As one might expect, for certain voters, campaign contact hurt more than helped.[†] So, during the full-scale efforts ultimately guided by the persuasion models, many such voters were predictively identified and shrewdly left uncontacted.

Persuasion modeling also guided the campaign's TV ad buying. A TV spot—such as Fox News in Tampa during evening hours—sells its ad slots by providing a demographic breakdown of its viewers. Team Obama viewed these breakdowns through the filter of their persuasion models in order to decide which spots to hit.

It's advanced, it's analytical, but it's not arcane. Persuasion modeling is the final chapter of this book, and promises to begin a whole new chapter for politics.

---

[†]Even during the analysis of results collected from campaign testing, this is not self-evident from the data, since no individual voter could be both contacted and not contacted to determine which would lead to a better outcome. Detecting the influence of campaign contact, be it positive influence or negative influence, requires modeling, even retrospectively.

# Afterword

## Ten Predictions for the First Hour of 2020

*What's next is what's next. . . . Predictive analytics is where business intelligence is going.*
—Rick Whiting, *InformationWeek*

Good morning. It's January 2, 2020, the first workday of the year. As you drive to the office, the only thing predictive analytics (PA) *doesn't* do for you is steer the car (yet that's coming soon as well).

1. **Antitheft**. As you enter your car, a predictive model establishes your identity based on several biometric readings, rendering it virtually impossible for an imposter to start the engine.
2. **Entertainment**. Pandora plays new music it predicts you will like.
3. **Traffic**. Your navigator pipes up and suggests alternative routing due to pre-dicted traffic delays. Because the new route has hills and your car's battery—its only energy source—is low, your maximum acceleration is decreased.
4. **Breakfast**. An en route drive-through restaurant is suggested by a recom-mendation system that knows its daily food preference predictions must be accurate or you will disable it.
5. **Social**. Your Social Techretary offers to read you select Facebook feeds and Match.com responses it predicts will be of greatest interest. Inappropriate comments are accurately filtered out. CareerBuilder offers to read job postings to which you're predicted to apply. When playing your voice mail, solicita-tions such as robocall messages are screened by predictive models just like e-mail spam.
6. **Deals**. You accept your smartphone's offer to read to you a text message from your wireless carrier. Apparently, they've predicted you're going to switch to a competitor, because they are offering a huge discount on the iPhone 13.

7. **Internet search**. As it's your colleague's kid's birthday, you query for a toy store that's en route. Siri, available through your car's audio, has been greatly improved—better speech recognition and proficiently tailored interaction.

8. **Driver inattention**. Your seat vibrates as internal sensors predict your attention has wavered—perhaps you were distracted by a personalized billboard a bit too long.

9. **Collision avoidance**. A stronger vibration plus a warning sound alert you to a potential imminent collision—possibly with a child running toward the curb or another car threatening to run a red light.

10. **Reliability**. Your car says to you, "Please take me in for service soon, as I have predicted my carburetor will fail within the next three weeks."

PA not only enhances your commute—it was instrumental to making this drive possible in the first place:

**Car loan**. You could afford this car only because a bank correctly scored you as a low credit risk and approved your car loan.

**Insurance**. Sensors you volunteered to have installed in your car transmit driving behavior readings to your auto insurance company, which in turn plugs them into a predictive model in order to continually adjust your premium. Your participation in this program will reduce your payment by $30 this month.

**Wireless reliability**. The wireless carrier that serves to connect to your phone—as well as your car—has planned its robust infrastructure according to demand prediction.

**Cyber-security**. Unbeknownst to you, your car and phone avert crippling virus attacks by way of analytical detection.

**Road safety**. Impending hazards such as large potholes and bridge failures have been efficiently discovered and preempted by government systems that predictively target inspections.

**No reckless drivers**. Dangerous repeat moving violation offenders have been scored as such by a predictive model to help determine how long their licenses should be suspended.

**Your health**. Predictive models determined the medical treatments you have previously received, leaving you healthier today.

## TOMORROW'S JUST A DAY AWAY

All the preceding capabilities are available now or have similar incarnations actively under development. Many are delayed more by the (now imminent) integration of your smartphone with your car than by the development of predictive technology itself. The advent of mobile devices built into your glasses, such as Google Glass, will provide yet another multiplicative effect on the moment-to-moment integration of prediction, as well as further accelerating the accumulation of data with which to develop predictive models.'

Today, PA's all-encompassing scope already reaches the very heart of a functioning society. Organizations—be they companies, governments, law-enforcement, charities, hospitals, or universities—undertake many millions of operational decisions in order to enact services. Prediction is key to guiding these decisions. It is the means with which to improve the efficiency of massive operations.

Several mounting ingredients promise to spread prediction even more pervasively: bigger data, better computers, wider familiarity, and advancing science. A growing majority of interactions between the organization and the individual will be driven by prediction.

## THE FUTURE OF PREDICTION

Of course, the details and timing of these developments are up to conjecture; PA has not conquered itself. But we can confidently predict more prediction. Every few months another big story about PA rolls off the presses. We're sure to see the opportunities continue to grow and surprise. Come what may, only time will tell what we'll tell of time to come.

# APPENDIX A

# Five Effects of Prediction

1. The Prediction Effect: *A little prediction goes a long way.* See the Introduction and Chapter 1.

2. The Data Effect: *Data is always predictive.* See Chapter 3.

3. The Induction Effect: *Art drives machine learning; when followed by computer programs, strategies designed in part by informal human creativity succeed in developing predictive models that perform well on new cases.* See Chapter 4.

4. The Ensemble Effect: *When joined in an ensemble, predictive models compensate for one another's limitations, so the ensemble as a whole is more likely to predict correctly than its component models are.* See Chapter 5.

5. The Persuasion Effect: *Although imperceivable, the persuasion of an individual can be predicted by* uplift modeling, *predictively modeling across two distinct training data sets that record, respectively, the outcomes of two competing treatments.* See Chapter 7.

# APPENDIX B

# Twenty-One Applications of Predictive Analytics

These applications—ways in which predictive analytics is employed—are covered in some detail within the Chapters noted. Others beyond these twenty-one are listed in this book's Central Tables.

### TARGETING DIRECT MARKETING (SEE CHAPTERS 1 AND 7)
1. **What's predicted:** Which customers will respond to marketing contact.
2. **What's done about it:** Contact customers more likely to respond.

### PREDICTIVE ADVERTISEMENT TARGETING (SEE CHAPTER 1)
1. **What's predicted:** Which ad each customer is most likely to click.
2. **What's done about it:** Display the best ad (based on the likelihood of a click as well as the bounty paid by its sponsor).

### BLACK BOX TRADING (SEE CHAPTER 1)
1. **What's predicted:** Whether a stock will go up or down.
2. **What's done about it:** Buy stocks that will go up, and sell those that will go down.

### PREGNANCY PREDICTION (SEE CHAPTER 2)
1. **What's predicted:** Which female customers will have a baby in coming months.
2. **What's done about it:** Market relevant offers for soon-to-be parents of newborns.

### EMPLOYEE RETENTION (SEE CHAPTER 2)
1. **What's predicted:** Which employees will quit.
2. **What's done about it:** Managers take the predictions for those they supervise into consideration, at their discretion. This is an example of decision *support* rather than feeding predictions into an automatic decision process.

## CRIME PREDICTION (SEE CHAPTER 2)
1. **What's predicted:** The location of a future crime.
2. **What's done about it:** Police patrol the area.

## FRAUD DETECTION (SEE CHAPTER 2)
1. **What's predicted:** Which transactions or applications for credit, benefits, reimbursements, refunds, and so on are fraudulent.
2. **What's done about it:** Human auditors screen the transactions and applications predicted most likely to be fraudulent.

## NETWORK INTRUSION DETECTION (SEE CHAPTER 2)
1. **What's predicted:** Which low-level Internet communications originate from imposters.
2. **What's done about it:** Block such interactions.

## SPAM FILTERING (SEE CHAPTER 2)
1. **What's predicted:** Which e-mail is spam.
2. **What's done about it:** Divert suspected e-mails to your spam e-mail folder.

## PLAYING A BOARD GAME (SEE CHAPTER 2)
1. **What's predicted:** Which game board state will lead to a win.
2. **What's done about it:** Make a game move that will lead to a state predicted to lead to a win.

## RECIDIVISM PREDICTION FOR LAW ENFORCEMENT (SEE CHAPTER 2)
1. **What's predicted:** Whether a prosecuted criminal will offend again.
2. **What's done about it:** Judges and parole boards consult model predictions when making decisions about an individual's incarceration.

## BLOG ENTRY ANXIETY DETECTION (SEE CHAPTER 3)
1. **What's predicted:** Which blog entries express anxiety.
2. **What's done about it:** Used to calculate an aggregate measure of mass mood.

## CUSTOMER RETENTION WITH CHURN MODELING (SEE CHAPTER 4)
1. **What's predicted:** Which customers will leave.
2. **What's done about it:** Retention efforts targeting at-risk customers.

## MORTGAGE VALUE ESTIMATION (SEE CHAPTER 4)
1. **What's predicted:** Which mortgage holders will prepay within the next 90 days.
2. **What's done about it:** Mortgages are valued accordingly in order to decide whether to sell them to other banks.

## MOVIE RECOMMENDATIONS (SEE CHAPTER 5)

1. **What's predicted:** What rating a customer would give to a movie.
2. **What's done about it:** Customers are recommended movies that they are predicted to rate highly.

## OPEN QUESTION ANSWERING (SEE CHAPTER 6)

1. **What's predicted:** Given a question and one candidate answer, whether the answer is correct.
2. **What's done about it:** The candidate answer with the highest predictive score is provided by the system as its final answer.

## EDUCATION—GUIDED STUDYING FOR TARGETED LEARNING (SEE CHAPTER 6)

1. **What's predicted:** Which questions a student will get right or wrong.
2. **What's done about it:** Spend more study time on the questions the student will get wrong.

## CUSTOMER RETENTION WITH CHURN MODELING (SEE CHAPTER 7)

1. **What's predicted:** Which customers will leave.
2. **What's done about it:** Retention efforts target at-risk customers.

## TARGETED MARKETING WITH RESPONSE UPLIFT MODELING (SEE CHAPTER 7)

1. **What's predicted:** Which customers will be persuaded to buy.
2. **What's done about it:** Target persuadable customers.

## CUSTOMER RETENTION WITH CHURN UPLIFT MODELING (SEE CHAPTER 7)

1. **What's predicted:** Which customers can be persuaded to stay.
2. **What's done about it:** Retention efforts target persuadable customers.

## POLITICAL CAMPAIGNING WITH VOTER PERSUASION MODELING (SEE CHAPTER 7)

1. **What's predicted:** Which voter will be positively persuaded by political campaign contact such as a call, door knock, flier, or TV ad.
2. **What's done about it:** Persuadable voters are contacted, and voters predicted to be adversely influenced by contact are avoided.

# APPENDIX C

# Prediction People—Cast of "Characters"

**ERIC SIEGEL, PHD—***THIS BOOK'S AUTHOR*
- President of Prediction Impact, Inc. (business-speak for an independent consultant).
- Founder, Predictive Analytics World.
- Executive Editor of the *Predictive Analytics Times*.
- Former computer science professor at Columbia University.

**JOHN ELDER, PHD**
Invested his entire life savings into his own predictive stock market trading system (see Chapter 1).

- CEO and Founder, Elder Research, Inc.
- Founding Chair, Predictive Analytics World for Government.
- Coauthor, *Handbook of Statistical Analysis and Data Mining Applications*.
- Adjunct professor at the University of Virginia.

**GITALI HALDER AND ANINDYA DEY**
Led a staff retention project that earmarks each of Hewlett-Packard's almost 350,000 worldwide employees according to "Flight Risk," the expected chance they will quit their jobs (see Chapter 2).

- Analytics practitioners at Hewlett-Packard.
- Backgrounds in statistics and economics.

**ANDREW POLE**
Led a marketing project at Target that predicts customer pregnancy (see Chapter 2).

- Analytics Manager at Target.
- Previously a lead consumer analyst at Hallmark Cards.
- Master's degrees in statistics and economics.
- View his original newsbreaking presentation on pregnancy prediction: www.pawcon.com/Target.

### ERIC GILBERT, PhD, AND KARRIE KARAHALIOS, PhD

Measured the mass emotions of the public and related them to economic movements (see Chapter 3).

- Scientists at the University of Illinois (Gilbert is now at Georgia Tech).
- Conducted research in *social computing*, the examination of human social behavior within a computer science framework.

### DAN STEINBERG, PhD

Led the prediction of outcome for millions of mortgages at Chase Bank (see Chapter 4).

- President and Founder, Salford Systems.
- Entrepreneur who delivers state-of-the-art predictive modeling from the research lab to commercial deployment.
- PhD in economics from Harvard University.
- Former University of California professor.

### MARTIN CHABBERT AND MARTIN PIOTTE

With no background in analytics, they took Netflix's $1 million predictive contest by storm (see Chapter 5).

- Software engineers in the telecommunications industry.

### DAVID GONDEK, PhD

Led the design of machine learning integration for IBM's *Jeopardy!*-playing computer, Watson (see Chapter 6).

- Research scientist at IBM Research.
- PhD in computer science from Brown University.

### EVA HELLE

At a large telecom, Telenor, she predictively optimized how to best persuade each cell phone customer to stay (see Chapter 7).

- Customer analytics lead at Europe's Telenor, the world's seventh largest mobile operator.
- Master's degree in statistics and marketing.

## RAYID GHANI

Helped Barack Obama's 2012 presidential campaign employ *persuasion modeling* in order to predict which individual swing state voters would be positively influenced by campaign contact (a call, door knock, flier, or TV ad), and which would be driven to vote adversely by contact (See Chapter 7's sidebar).

- Chief Data Scientist, Obama for America 2012 Campaign.
- Master's degree in machine learning from Carnegie Mellon University.
- Ten years of research work at Accenture Technology Labs.

# Notes

## INTRODUCTION

*All case examples in the Introduction appear in this book's Central Tables of examples. See the Notes corresponding to those tables for references.*

**Further information about predictive analytics for business users and prospective practitioners:**

- *Predictive Analytics Times*, a monthly online newsletter. www.predictiveanalyticstimes.com.
- Eric Siegel, PhD, "Seven Reasons You Need Predictive Analytics Today." Prediction Impact, Inc. White Paper, September 2010. www.predictiveanalyticsworld.com/signup-whitepaper.php. This white paper reveals seven strategic objectives that can be attained to their full potential only by employing predictive analytics, namely: Compete, Grow, Enforce, Improve, Satisfy, Learn, and Act.
- Eric Siegel, PhD, "Predictive Analytics with Data Mining: How It Works," published in *DM Review*'s DM Direct, February 2005. www.predictionimpact.com/predictive.analytics.html.
- *Predictive Analytics Guide*: Further reading, articles, and resources. www.predictiveanalytics world.com/guide.

**Leading books for business users of analytics:**

- Thomas H. Davenport and Jeanne G. Harris, *Competing on Analytics: The New Science of Winning* (Harvard Business School Press, 2007).
- James Taylor, *Decision Management Systems: A Practical Guide to Using Business Rules and Predictive Analytics* (IBM Press, 2011).
- Ian Ayres, *Super Crunchers: Why Thinking-by-Numbers Is the New Way to Be Smart* (Bantam, 2007).
- Steven Baker, *The Numerati* (Houghton Mifflin Harcourt, 2008).

**Leading foundational textbooks for practitioners of predictive modeling (technical):**

- Robert Nisbet, John Elder, and Gary Miner, *Handbook of Statistical Analysis and Data Mining Applications* (Academic Press, 2009).
- Tom M. Mitchell, *Machine Learning* (McGraw-Hill Science/Engineering/Math, 1997).

- Trevor Hastie, Robert Tibshirani, and Jerome Friedman, *The Elements of Statistical Learning: Data Mining, Inference, and Prediction*, 2nd ed., corr. 3rd printing, 5th printing (Springer, 2009).

**Training options for business users and prospective practitioners of predictive analytics:**

- Online e-course: *Predictive Analytics Applied*. Instructor: Eric Siegel. Available on demand at any time. www.predictionimpact.com/predictive-analytics-online-training.html.
- Full-day training workshops alongside the conference Predictive Analytics World. Several international events annually. www.predictiveanalyticsworld.com.
- Complete list of degree programs in analytics, data mining, and data science: www.kdnuggets.com/education.

**Conferences for business users and practitioners of analytics:**

- **Predictive Analytics World** (www.predictiveanalyticsworld.com). The leading event for predictive analytics users, managers, and commercial practitioners. This conference, with several international events annually, delivers case studies, expertise, and resources over a range of business applications of predictive analytics. *Readers of this book are eligible for 15 percent off a Predictive Analytics World two-day conference pass. This discount is limited to one use per registrant through the year 2020 and may not be used in combination with any other discount offer. Use discount code "pabook15" when registering.*
- **Text Analytics World** (text analytics is a topic covered in Chapters 3 and 6 of this book). www.textanalyticsworld.com.

# CHAPTER 1

**Most of John Elder's story comes from a direct interview. For a short autobiographical essay by John Elder, see:**

- Mohamed Medhat Gaber, *Journeys to Data Mining: Experiences from 15 Renowned Researchers* (Springer, 2012), 61–76.

**Regarding terrified spouses of astronauts:**

- Mike Mullane, *Riding Rockets: The Outrageous Tales of a Space Shuttle Astronaut* (Scribner, 2006).

**$10 million Grand Challenge:**

- The Defense Advanced Research Projects Agency (DARPA); est. 1958. See: www.darpa.mil/.

**Driverless cars:**

- Daniel Nasaw, "Driverless Cars and How They Would Change Motoring," *BBC News Magazine*, May 10, 2012. www.bbc.co.uk/news/magazine-18012812.

**Quote from Stephen Dubner:**

- Stephen J. Dubner, "Why Can't We Predict Earthquakes?" Freakonomics Radio, March 31, 2011. www.freakonomics.com/2011/03/31/why-cant-we-predict-earthquakes-full-transcript/.

**Quote from Mehmet Oz:**

- Dr. Mehmet Oz, "10 Questions for Dr. Oz," *Time Magazine Online*, Health. www.time
  .com/time/specials/packages/article/0,28804,1912201_1912244_1913478,00.html.

**Advertisement optimization example project:**

- "Case Study: How Predictive Analytics Generates $1 Million Increased Revenue," case study
  provided by Prediction Impact, Inc. (Note that in this project a positive response actually
  entailed an opt-in and click, rather than just a click as with most online advertisements.)
  www.predictiveanalyticsworld.com/casestudy.php.

**To view Malcolm Gladwell's entire speech, "Choice, Happiness and Spaghetti Sauce," visit:**

- Malcolm Gladwell, "Choice, Happiness and Spaghetti Sauce," TEDTalks Online. www
  .ted.com/talks/malcolm_gladwell_on_spaghetti_sauce.html. Video file: www.ted.com/
  talks, February 2006.

**Davenport and Harris quote:**

- Thomas Davenport and Jeanne Harris, *Competing on Analytics: The New Science of Winning*
  (Harvard Business School Press, 2007).

**"Survey results have in fact shown that a tougher competitive environment is by far the strongest reason organizations adopt this technology":**

- David White, "Predictive Analytics: The Right Tool for Tough Times," Aberdeen Group
  White Paper, February 2010. www.aberdeen.com/aberdeen-library/6287/RA-predictive-
  analytics-customer-retention.aspx and www.targusinfo.com/files/PDF/outside_research/
  PredictiveAnalyticsReport.pdf.

**John Elder includes "temporal leak" in his list of top 10 data miner mistakes—see:**

- Robert Nisbit, John Elder, and Gary Miner, *Handbook of Statistical Analysis and Data
  Mining Applications* (Academic Press, 2009), chap. 20.

**John Elder's PhD thesis:**

- John Elder, PhD, "Efficient Optimization through Response Surface Modeling: GROPE
  Algorithm." Dissertation, School of Engineering and Applied Sciences, University of
  Virginia (1993).

**The business case for PA:**

- Patrick Turgeon, "Predictive Analytics—A Case for Early Adoption," Figurs*, February 6,
  2012. www.figurs.ca/pdf/Predictive_Analytics-A_case_for_early_adoption.pdf.

# CHAPTER 2

Some content of this chapter originated from valuable interviews with Gitali Halder, Anindya
Dey, and Alex Beaux of Hewlett-Packard.

**Hewlett-Packard "Flight Risk" score:**

- Gitali Halder, Hewlett-Packard, and Anindya Dey, Hewlett Packard, "Attrition Driver Analysis," Predictive Analytics World London Conference, November 30, 2011, London, UK. www.predictiveanalyticsworld.com/london/2011/agenda.php#day1–5a.

**Regarding Target's use of PA to predict customer pregnancy:**

- "Target Knew Teen Was Pregnant Before Her Dad." www.predictiveanalytics world.com/target-on-fox. Original broadcast, Fox News, February 24, 2012.
- Andrew Pole, Target, "How Target Gets the Most out of Its Guest Data to Improve Marketing ROI," Predictive Analytics World Washington, DC, Conference, October 19, 2010, Washington, DC. www.predictiveanalyticsworld.com/Target.
- Charles Duhigg, "How Companies Learn Your Secrets," *New York Times Magazine*, February 16, 2012. www.nytimes.com/2012/02/19/magazine/shopping-habits.html.
- Rachel Nolan, "Behind the Cover Story: How Much Does Target Know?" *New York Times*, February 21, 2012. http://6thfloor.blogs.nytimes.com/2012/02/21/behind-the-cover-story-how-much-does-target-know/.
- "Will Big Data and Big Money Mean Big Trouble?" *To the Point*, KCRW Los Angeles Public Radio 89.9, Los Angeles, CA. Host Warren Olney, April 2, 2012. www .kcrw.com/news/programs/tp/tp120402will_big_data_and_bi.
- Steven Cherry, "Your Favorite Stores Know You All Too Well." IEEE Spectrum's Techwise Conversations Online, March 30, 2012. http://spectrum.ieee.org/podcast/computing/software/your-favorite-stores-know-you-all-too-well.
- "Target's Deep Customer Data Mining Raises Eyebrows," Martin Moylan, Minnesota Public Radio, MPR News, St. Paul, Minnesota, March 7, 2012. http://minnesota.publicradio.org/display/web/2012/03/07/target-data-mining-privacy/.
- "Targeted Marketing in Your Womb, Digital Product Placement, Pervasive Gaming," *Download This Show*, Australian Broadcasting Corporation's RadioNational, Sydney, Australia, February 26, 2012. www.abc.net.au/radionational/programs/downloadthisshow/ep5/3851666.
- "The Word—Surrender to a Buyer Power," *Colbert Report*, February 22, 2012. www.colbertnation.com/the-colbert-report-videos/408981/february-22–2012/the-word---surrender-to-a-buyer-power.

**The value of a user's data:**

- Alexis Madrigal, "How Much Is Your Data Worth? Mmm, Somewhere Between Half a Cent and $1,200," *The Atlantic*, March 19, 2012. www.theatlantic.com/technology/archive/2012/03/how-much-is-your-data-worth-mmm-somewhere-between-half-a-cent-and-1-200/254730/.

**Quote from David Sobel, privacy advocate:**

- David Sobel, Senior Counsel at Electronic Frontier Foundation, https://www .eff.org/about/staff/david-sobel.

**One in four Facebook users enters false data (i.e., lie):**
- Michael Crider, "1 in 4 Facebook Users Lies over Privacy Concerns," *Slashgear Magazine Online*, May 7, 2012. www.slashgear.com/1-in-4-facebook-users-lies-over-privacy-concerns-07226506/.

**Quote from Alexander Furnas (". . . content is wholly subsidized by targeted . . ."):**
- Alexander Furnas, "It's Not All about You: What Privacy Advocates Don't Get about Data Tracking on the Web." *The Atlantic*, March 15, 2012. www.theatlantic.com/technology/archive/2012/03/its-not-all-about-you-what-privacy-advocates-dont-get-about-data-tracking-on-the-web/254533/.

**Banks and lenders collect your social media activity as information to score your level of creditworthiness:**
- Ken Lin, "What Banks and Lenders Know about You from Social Media," Mashable Social Media, October 7, 2011. http://mashable.com/2011/10/07/social-media-privacy-banks/.

**Quote from Professor Tom M. Mitchell, Carnegie Mellon University:**
- Tom M. Mitchell, "Mining Our Reality." *Science* 326, no. 5960 (December 18, 2009), 1644–1645. www.sciencemag.org/content/326/5960/1644.summary and www.cs.cmu.edu/~tom/pubs/Science2009_perspective.pdf.

**Data mining does not drill down:**
- Letter from the Executive Committee on ACM Special Interest Group on Knowledge, Discover and Data Mining (ACM SIGKDD), "Data Mining Is NOT Against Civil Liberties," June 30, 2003, revised July 28, 2003. www.sigkdd.org/civil-liberties.pdf.

**Civil rights and big data:**
- Alistair Croll, "Big Data Is Our Generation's Civil Rights Issue, and We Don't Know It," O'Reilly Radar Online, August 2, 2012. http://radar.oreilly.com/2012/08/big-data-is-our-generations-civil-rights-issue-and-we-dont-know-it.html.

**HP as one of the largest employers:**
- "Top Companies: Biggest Employers," *CNNMoney*, July 25, 2011. http://money.cnn.com/magazines/fortune/global500/2011/performers/companies/biggest/.

**"I'm surprised" job interview cartoon:**
- The cartoon in Chapter 2 originally appeared in *Computerworld* magazine. Copyright 2003 John Klossner, www.jklossner.com.

**Crime prediction by police:**
- Colleen McCue, PhD, *Data Mining and Predictive Analysis: Intelligence Gathering and Crime Analysis* (Butterworth-Heinemann, 2007).

- Melissae Fellet, "Cops on the Trail of Crimes That Haven't Happened," *New Scientist*, October 12, 2011. www.newscientist.com/article/mg21128333.400-cops-on-the-trail-of-crimes-that-havent-happened.html.
- Lev Grossman, Cleo Brock-Abraham, Nick Carbone, Eric Dodds, Jeffrey Kluger, Alice Park, Nate Rawlings, Claire Suddath, Feifei Sun, Mark Thompson, Bryan Walsh, and Kayla Webley, "The 50 Best Inventions," *Time*, Technology, November 28, 2011. www.time.com/time/magazine/article/0,9171,2099708-1,00.html.
- Jessica M. Pasko, "*Time* Magazine Names Santa Cruz Predictive Policing Program One of the Year's Top Inventions," *Santa Cruz Sentinel*, November 23, 2011. www.santacruzsentinel.com/ci_19400300?source=pkg.
- Erica Goode, "Sending the Police Before There's a Crime." *New York Times on the Web*, August 15, 2011. www.nytimes.com/2011/08/16/us/16police.html.
- Stephen Hollifield, Information Services Manager, Richmond Police Department, "Curbing Crime with Predictive Analytics," Predictive Analytics World for Government, Washington, DC, September 12, 2011. www.predictiveanalyticsworld.com/gov/2011/agenda.php#day1-1115-1145.
- Carrie Kahn, "At LAPD, Predicting Crimes Before They Happen," National Public Radio Online, August 14, 2011. www.npr.org/2011/11/26/142758000/at-lapd-predicting-crimes-before-they-happen.
- Sergeant Christopher Fulcher, Vineland, NJ, Police Department, "To Predict and Serve: Predictive Intelligence Analysis," Part I, July 5, 2011, http://policeledintelligence.com/2011/07/05/to-predict-and-serve-predictive-intelligence-analysis-part-i/. Part II, July 6, 2011, http://policeledintelligence.com/2011/07/06/to-predict-and-serve-predictive-intelligence-analysis-part-ii/.
- G. O. Mohler, M. B. Short, P. J. Brantingham, F. P. Schoenberg, and G. E. Tita, "Self-Exciting Point Process Modeling of Crime," *Journal of the American Statistical Association* 106, issue 493 (2011). www.math.ucla.edu/~mbshort/papers/crime3.pdf.

**Cheating sumo wrestlers:**
- Stephen J. Dubner, "Sumo: More of the Same," Freakonomics Radio, February 2, 2011. www.freakonomics.com/2011/02/02/sumo-more-of-the-same/.

**Students cheating:**
- Stephen J. Dubner, "Fish Gotta Swim, Teachers Gotta Cheat?" Freakonomics Radio, January 26, 2010. www.freakonomics.com/2010/01/26/fish-gotta-swim-teachers-gotta-cheat/.

**Twitter bombs:**
- Eni Mustafaraj and Panagiotis Metaxas, "From Obscurity to Prominence in Minutes: Political Speech and Real-Time Search," in *Proceedings of the WebSci10: Extending the Frontiers of Society On-Line, April 26–27, 2010, Raleigh, NC.* http://journal.webscience.org/317/.

**On the cost of fraud:**
- Progressive Insurance Special Investigative Unit Report from the National Insurance Crime Bureau (NICB). www.progressiveagent.com/claims/special-investigations-unit.aspx.

**Federal Trade Commission on fraud report incidents:**

- Michael B. Sauter, "America's Worst States for Fraud," 24/7 Wall St., April 11, 2012. http://247wallst.com/2012/04/11/americas-worst-states-for-fraud/.

**Estimated that nation's banks experience over $10 billion per year in attempted check fraud:**

- Jay Zhou, Data Miners, LLC, "Building In-Database Predictive Scoring Model: Check Fraud Detection Case Study," Predictive Analytics World Washington, DC, Conference, October 20, 2009, Washington, DC. www.predictiveanalyticsworld.com/dc/2009/agenda .php#day1–19.

**Aggregate fraud loss in the United States sees estimates from $100 billion to $1 trillion:**

- Robert Nisbit, John Elder, and Gary Miner, *Handbook of Statistical Analysis and Data Mining Applications* (Academic Press, 2009), 347.

**PayPal fraud:**

- "The New World of Massive Data Mining," *Diane Rehm Show*, WAMU 88.5, Washington, DC, April 2, 2012. http://thedianerehmshow.org/shows/2012–04–02/ new-world-massive-data-mining.

**1–800-FLOWERS fraud detection:**

- Auren Hoffman, CEO, Rapleaf, "Leveraging Social Media Data to Manage Fraud Risk," Predictive Analytics World San Francisco Conference, February 16, 2010, San Francisco, CA. www.predictiveanalyticsworld.com/sanfrancisco/2010/agenda.php#day1–10.

**Mexican Tax Administration fraud detection:**

- Luis Beltrán Farías, Director, Risk Models Office, Mexican Tax Administration, Ministry of Finance, Mexico, "A Model for Fraud Prevention in VAT Refunds in Mexico," Predictive Analytics World for Government Washington, DC, Conference, September 12, 2011, Washington, DC. www.predictiveanalyticsworld.com/gov/2011/agenda .php#day2–315–335.

**U.S. Defense Finance and Accounting Service fraud detection:**

- Dean Abbott, Abbott Analytics, "Case Study: Defense Finance and Accounting Service— Invoice Fraud Detection." Thanks to Dean Abbott, Abbott Analytics, www .abbottanalytics.com (2004–2012), for this case study. www.abbottanalytics.com/data-mining-case-study-1.php.
- Dean Abbott, Haleh Vafaie, PhD, Mark Hutchins, and David Riney, "Improper Payment Detection in Department of Defense Financial Transactions," Federal Data Mining Symposium, Washington, DC, March 29, 2000. www.abbottanalytics.com/assets/pdf/ Abbott-Analytics-Improper-Payment-Detection-2000.pdf.

**Elder Research fraud modeling project for the IRS (thanks to John Elder for pointing out the fraud scheme as an example detectable only by way of analyzing social data):**

- Mohamed Medhat Gaber, *Journeys to Data Mining: Experiences from 15 Renowned Researchers* (Springer, 2012), 61–76.

**Regarding cyber-security analytics:**

- Seth Robertson, Eric V. Siegel, Matt Miller, and Salvatore J. Stolfo, "Surveillance Detection in High Bandwidth Environments," Third DARPA Information Survivability Conference and Exposition (DISCESSIII), Washington, DC, April 2003. http://secgate-b.hacktory.cs .columbia.edu/sites/default/files/SD-DiscexIII.pdf.

**Spam filter subversion:**

- Blaine Nelson, Marco Barreno, Fuching Jack Chi, Anthony D. Joseph, Benjamin I. P. Rubinstein, Udam Saini, Charles Sutton, J. D. Tygar, and Kai Xia, "Exploiting Machine Learning to Subvert Your Spam Filter," University of California, Berkeley, April 4, 2008. http://static.usenix.org/event/leet08/tech/full_papers/nelson/nelson_html/.

**Computers detect computer-generated text:**

- Allen Lavoie and Mukkai Krishnamoorthy, "Algorithmic Detection of Computer Generated Text," Cornell University Library, August 4, 2010. http://arxiv.org/abs/1008.0706.

**Cheating in online chess tournaments:**

- Garry Kasparov, "The Chess Master and the Computer," *New York Review of Books on the Web*, February 11, 2010. www.nybooks.com/articles/archives/2010/feb/11/the-chess-master-and-the-computer/.

**This chapter's primary source regarding recidivism prediction (including the quotes from Ellen Kurtz):**

- Nadya Labi, "Misfortune Teller," *The Atlantic*, January/February 2012. www.theatlantic .com/magazine/archive/2012/01/misfortune-teller/8846/.

**Oregon's online crime-prediction tool:**

- "The Public Safety Checklist for Oregon," Criminal Justice Commission, last updated August 11, 2012. https://risktool.ocjc.state.or.us/psc/.

**Hungry judges rule negatively:**

- Shai Danziger, Jonathan Levav, and Liora Avnaim-Pesso, "Extraneous Factors in Judicial Decisions," edited by Daniel Kahneman, Princeton University, Princeton, NJ, February 25, 2011. http://lsolum.typepad.com/files/danziger-levav-avnaim-pnas-2011.pdf and www.pnas.org/content/108/17/6889.

**Guilty of a crime you didn't commit (yet):**

- Ben Goldacre, "It's Not So Easy to Predict Murder—The Maths," *The Guardian Online*, December 8, 2006. www.guardian.co.uk/science/2006/dec/09/badscience.uknews.

**Predicting homicide recidivism:**

- Rolf Loeber, Dustin Pardini, D. Lynn Homish, Evelyn H. Wei, Anne M. Crawford, David P. Farrington, Magda Stouthamer-Loeber, Judith Creemers, Steven A. Koehler, and Richard Rosenfeld, "The Prediction of Violence and Homicide in Young Men," *Journal of Consulting and Clinical Psychology* 73, no. 6 (2005): 1074–1088. www.wpic.pitt .edu/research/famhist/PDF_Articles/APA/H%201.pdf.

- Melanie-Angela Neuilly, Kristen M. Zgoba, George E. Tita, and Stephen S. Lee, "Predicting Recidivism in Homicide Offenders Using Classification Tree Analysis," *Sage Journals, Homicide Studies* 15, no. 2 (May 2011): 154–176. http://hsx.sagepub.com/content/15/2/154.abstract.

**Predicting and preventing homicide:**
- Rosanna Louise Buttrick, "Homicide: Prediction and Prevention," University of Nottingham, School of Psychology, June 2009. www.psychology.nottingham.ac.uk/staff/ddc/c8cxpa/further/Dissertation_examples/Buttrick_09.pdf.

**Regarding UK bank search for terrorists:**
- Steven D. Levitt and Stephen J. Dubner, *Superfreakonomics: Global Cooling, Patriotic Prostitutes, and Why Suicide Bombers Should Buy Life Insurance* (William Morrow, 2011).
- Stephen J. Dubner, "SuperFreakonomics Book Club: Ian Horsley Answers Your Questions about the Terrorist Algorithm," September 1, 2010. www.freakonomics.com/2010/09/01/superfreakonomics-book-club-ian-horsley-answers-your-questions-about-the-terrorist-algorithm/.

**For more information on crime-detecting models (e.g., biometric models) to identify terror suspects:**
- Christopher Westphal, *Data Mining for Intelligence, Fraud & Criminal Detection* (CRC Press, 2009).

**Concerns in the United Kingdom regarding the discriminatory effect of predictive models:**
- Christine Evans-Pughe, "Forecasting Human Behavior Carries Big Risks," *The Guardian*, July 18, 2007. www.guardian.co.uk/technology/2007/jul/19/guardianweeklytechnologysection.it.

**Regarding the ethics of criminal prediction:**
- Michael Lotti, "Ethics and the Information Age," *Effect Magazine Online*, Winter 2009/2010. www.larsonallen.com/EFFECT/Ethics_and_the_Information_Age.aspx.

**Quote from Alexander Furnas (" . . . we grant private entities . . . greater powers of persuasion than anyone has ever had . . ."):**
- Alexander Furnas, "It's Not All about You: What Privacy Advocates Don't Get about Data Tracking on the Web," *The Atlantic*, March 15, 2012. www.theatlantic.com/technology/archive/2012/03/its-not-all-about-you-what-privacy-eadvocates-dont-get-about-data-tracking-on-the-web/254533/.

**Regarding the spotlight on Target's pregnancy PA application:**
- KDnuggets poll: "Was Target Wrong in Using Analytics to Find Pregnant Women?" KDnuggets, February 2012 online poll. www.kdnuggets.com/2012/02/new-poll-target-analytics-wrong-to-find-pregnant-women.html.

**Eric Schmidt on face recognition and privacy:**

- Bianca Bosker, "Facial Recognition: The One Technology Google Is Holding Back," *Huffington Post*, June 1, 2011. www.huffingtonpost.com/2011/06/01/facial-recognition-google_n_869583.html.

# CHAPTER 3

Some content of this chapter originated from a valuable interview with Karrie Karahalios.

**The leading story of this chapter is from this research:**

- Eric Gilbert and Karrie Karahalios, Department of Computer Science, University of Illinois at Urbana–Champaign, "Widespread Worry and the Stock Market," Association for the Advancement of Artificial Intelligence (www.aaai.org), March 12, 2010. http://comp .social.gatech.edu/papers/icwsm10.worry.gilbert.pdf.

**Governments such as Bhutan's measure mass mood, e.g., via their *gross national happiness* index, as a means to track prosperity:**

- Jyoti Thottam/Thimphu, "The Pursuit of Happiness," *TIME*, Vol. 180, No. 17, October 22, 2012. www.time.com/time/magazine/article/0,9171,2126639,00.html.

**Can blogs and tweets predict the future?:**

- Jim Giles, "Blogs and Tweets Could Predict the Future," *New Scientist Online*, June 21, 2010. www.newscientist.com/article/mg20627655.800.

**Regarding the oppressiveness of fear/anxiety:**

- Carsten Boers, "Applied Love," Business Buddhism blog, March 28, 2012. http:// carstenboers.com/2012/03/28/applied-love/.

**Source of figure showing Calm and Happy across Election Day and Thanksgiving:**

- J. Bollen, H. Mao, and X. Zeng, "Twitter Mood Predicts the Stock Market," *Journal of Computational Science*, 2, no. 1 (March 2011), 1–8, doi:10.1016/j.jocs.2010.12.007, arxiv: abs/1010.3003.

**Finding a coin in the pay phone (thanks to John Elder, PhD, for pointing out this related study):**

- A. Isen and P. Levin, "Effect of Feeling Good on Helping: Cookie and Kindness," *Journal of Personality and Social Psychology* 21, no. 3 (March 1972), 384–388, doi:10.1037/h0032317. http://psycnet.apa.org/index.cfm?fa=buy.optionToBuy&id=1972-22883-001.

**Alan Greenspan on *The Daily Show with Jon Stewart*:**

- "The Former Federal Reserve Chairman Bums Jon Out with His Thesis on Human Nature," *The Daily Show with Jon Stewart*, Comedy Central, September 18, 2007. www.thedailyshow .com/watch/tue-september-18–2007/alan-greenspan.

**Eric and Karrie were influenced by this Paul Tetlock research paper:**

- Paul C. Tetlock, "Giving Content to Investor Sentiment: The Role of Media in the Stock Market," *Journal of Finance* 62, no. 3 (June 2007). www.gsb.columbia.edu/faculty/ptetlock/ papers/Tetlock_JF_07_Giving_Content_to_Investor_Sentiment.pdf.

**On the author's mom, Lisa Schamberg, and making art of compost:**

- Lisa Schamberg, "Self-Composed," *Seven Days: Vermont's Independent Voice.* www.7dvt .com/lisa-schamberg.
- Lisa Schamberg, "Self-Composed: Photography by Lisa Schamberg." www.lisaschamberg .com.

**On the data of poop:**

- Mark Bowden, "The Measured Man," *The Atlantic*, July/August 2012. www .theatlantic.com/magazine/archive/2012/07/the-measured-man/309018/.

**On the age of big data:**

- Steve Lohr, "The Age of Big Data," *New York Times*, February 11, 2012. www .nytimes.com/2012/02/12/sunday-review/big-datas-impact-in-the-world.html.

**Mandate for U.S. federal agencies to release data sets:**

- Wendy R. Ginsberg, Analyst in Government Organization and Management, "The Obama Administration's Open Government Initiative: Issues for Congress," Congressional Research Service, 7–5700, www.crs.gov, R41361, January 28, 2011. www.scribd.com/ doc/48966713/CRS-The-Obama-Administration%E2%80%99s-Open-Government-Initiative-Issues-for-Congress.

**Regarding the number of blogs:**

- Computing Community Consortium blog, "Big Data," facts and figures posted by IBM, June 28, 2012. www.cccblog.org/wp-content/uploads/2012/06/Big-Data-Final.jpeg.
- Pingdom Team, "Internet 2011 in Numbers," Pingdom blog, January 17, 2012. http:// royal.pingdom.com/2012/01/17/internet-2011-in-numbers/.

**Number of daily tweets:**

- Twitter blog, "200 Million Tweets per Day," Twitter, June 20, 2011. http://blog.twitter .com/2011/06/200-million-tweets-per-day.html.

**Estimation of number of web pages:**

- WorldWideWebSize.com, "The Size of the World Wide Web (the Internet)," updated daily. www.worldwidewebsize.com/.

**Millions of retail transactions per hour:**

- John Naughton, "Why Big Data Is Now Such a Big Deal," *The Guardian*'s *The Observer Online*, March 17, 2012. www.guardian.co.uk/technology/2012/mar/18/big-data-storage-analysis-internet.

**Number of photographs on Facebook:**

- Quora, "How Many Photos Are Uploaded to Facebook Each Day?" January 2011. www .quora.com/How-many-photos-are-uploaded-to-Facebook-each-day.
- Jonathan Good, "How Many Photos Have Ever Been Taken?" 1000memories blog, September 15, 2011. http://blog.1000memories.com/94-number-of-photos-ever-taken-digital-and-analog-in-shoebox.
- Instagram, "Photoset," Instagram blog, September 2, 2012. http://blog.instagram.com/.

**Regarding femto-photography:**

- Ramesh Raskar, Moungi G. Bawendi, Andreas Velten, Everett Lawson, Amy Fritz, Di Wu, Matt O'Toole, Diego Gutierrez, Belen Masia, and Elisa Amoros, "Femto-Photography: Visualizing Photons in Motion at a Trillion Frames per Second," MIT Media Lab, June 14, 2012. http://web.media.mit.edu/~raskar/trillionfps/.
- "Ramesh Raskar: Imaging at a Trillion Frames per Second," YouTube, Web, July 26, 2012. https://www.youtube.com/watch?v=Y_9vd4HWlVA.

**Number of mobile devices:**

- Matt Warman, "50 Billion Devices Online by 2020," *The Telegraph*, January 31, 2012. www.telegraph.co.uk/technology/internet/9051590/50-billion-devices-online-by-2020.html.

**Daily data growth:**

- "The New World of Massive Data Mining," *The Diane Rehm Show*, WAMU 88.5, Washington, DC, April 2, 2012. http://thedianerehmshow.org/shows/2012–04–02/new-world-massive-data-mining.

**Regarding the cost of information storage:**

- Matthew Komorowski, "The History of Storage Cost," MKomo.com. www.mkomo.com/cost-per-gigabyte.

**Covering land masses with data:**

- Marin Hilbert, "That Giant Sifting Sound: A Short History of Big Data," *The Economist*, The Ideas Economy, June 7–8, 2011, Santa Clara, CA. http://fora.tv/2011/06/07/That_Giant_Sifting_Sound_A_Short_History_of_Big_Data#What_Drives_the_Global_Growth_of_Information.
- Martin Hilbert and Priscila Lōpez, "The World's Technological Capacity to Store, Communicate, and Information," *Science* 332, no. 6025 (April 1, 2011), 60–65. doi:10.1126/science.1200970. www.sciencemag.org/content/332/6025/60.

**NSA accumulating Internet traffic:**

- James Bamford, "The NSA Is Building the Country's Biggest Spy Center (Watch What You Say)," *Wired Magazine Online*, March 15, 2012. www.wired.com/threatlevel/2012/03/ff_nsadatacenter/all/1.

**More on the massive accumulation of data:**

- Jeffrey Marlow, "What to Do with 1,000,000,000,000,000,000 Bytes of Astronomical Data per Day," *Wired Magazine Online*, April 2, 2012. www.wired.com/wiredscience/2012/04/what-to-do-with-1000000000000000000-bytes-of-astronomical-data-per-day/.
- Thomas H. Maugh II, "For the First Time, Researchers Track Manta Rays with Satellites," *Los Angeles Times*, May 12, 2012. http://articles.latimes.com/2012/may/12/science/la-sci-sn-manta-satellites-20120512.
- Steven James Snyder, "Inside the Kurzweil SXSW Keynote: On Infinite Mind Power, Robotic Overlords and Immortality," *Time*, Techland, March 14, 2012. http://techland.time.com/2012/03/14/kurzweil-south-by-southwest-keynote-speech-grossman/.

**Eight zettabytes by 2012:**

- Dan Vesset, Benjamin Woo, Henry D. Morris, Richard L. Villars, Gard Little, Jean S. Bozman, Lucinda Borovick, Carl W. Olofson, Susan Feldman, Steve Conway,

Matthew Eastwood, and Natalya Yezhkova, "Worldwide Big Data Technology and Services 2012–2012 Forecast," *ICD Analyze the Future*, March 2012, Doc #233485. www.idc.com/getdoc.jsp?containerId=233485.

**The Prediction Effect: Tom Khabaza says, "There are always patterns."**
- Tom Khabaza, "Nine Laws of Data Mining—Part 2," *Data Mining & Predictive Analytics*, edited by Tom Khabaza, January 14, 2012. http://khabaza.codimension.net/index_files/Page346.htm.

**"Personal data is the new oil of the Internet and the new currency of the digital world":**
- Meglena Kuneva, European Consumer Commissioner, March 2009, "Personal Data: The Emergence of a New Asset Class," An Initiative of the World Economic Forum, January 2011. http://gerdleonhard.typepad.com/files/wef_ittc_personaldatanewasset_report_2011.pdf.

## Table: Bizarre and Surprising Insights—Consumer Behavior (Chapter 3)

**Guys literally drool over sports cars:**
- James Warren, "Just the Thought of New Revenue Makes Mouths Water," *New York Times*, September 29, 2011. www.nytimes.com/2011/09/30/us/just-the-thought-of-new-revenue-makes-mouths-water.html.
- Christopher Shea, "Mouth-Watering Consumer Goods," *Wall Street Journal*, August 24, 2011. http://blogs.wsj.com/ideas-market/2011/08/24/mouth-watering-consumer-goods/.
- David Gal, "A Mouth-Watering Prospect: Salivation to Material Reward," *Journal of Consumer Research* 38, no. 6 (April 2012): 1022–1029. www.jstor.org/discover/10.1086/661766.

**If you buy diapers, you are more likely to also buy beer:**
- Daniel J. Power, "What Is the 'True Story' about Data Mining, Beer and Diapers?" *DSS News* 3, no. 23 (November 10, 2002). www.dssresources.com/newsletters/66.php.
- Ronny Kohavi, "Crossing the Chasm: From Academic Machine Learning to Commercial Data Mining," International Conference on Machine Learning 1998, Slide 21. http://robotics.stanford.edu/~ronnyk/chasm.pdf.

**Dolls and candy bars:**
- Christopher Palmeri, "Believe in Yourself, Believe in the Merchandise," *Forbes Magazine Online*, September 8, 1997. www.forbes.com/forbes/1997/0908/6005118a.html.

**Staplers reveal hires:**
- Based on an example presented by Wayne Eckerson, formerly with TDWI, now founder and principal consultant at BI Leader Consulting. http://tdwi.org/blogs/wayne-eckerson/list/waynes-blog.aspx and www.bileader.com/.

**Mac users book more expensive hotels:**
- Dana Mattioli, "On Orbitz, Mac Users Steered to Pricier Hotels," *Wall Street Journal,* June 26, 2012, and updated August 23, 2012. http://online.wsj.com/article/SB100014240 52702304458604577488822667325882.html.

**Your inclination to buy varies by time of day:**
- Esco Strong, "Search Conversion Rates by Daypart," *Atlas Digital Marketing Insight,* March 2, 2007. http://atlassolutions.com/insights.

**Your e-mail address reveals your level of commitment:**
- From the author's own work.

**Banner ads affect you more than you think:**
- Usama Fayyad, PhD, "Search Marketing and Predictive Analytics: SEM, SEO and On-Line Marketing Case Studies," Predictive Analytics World Washington, DC, Conference, October 20, 2010, Washington, DC. www.predictiveanalyticsworld.com/dc/2010/agenda.php#day2–10.

**Companies win by not promoting customers to think** *(Chapter 7 focuses on this topic)*:
- Jessica Tsai, "Mail Model of the Year: U.S. Bank Accrues Savings by Only Pitching Customers Who Aren't Already Likely to Show Interest," *CRM Magazine,* destinationCRM.com, April 2010. www.destinationcrm.com/Articles/Columns-Departments/REAL-ROI/Mail-Model-of-the-Year-66123.aspx.

**Your web browsing reveals your intentions:**
- Cell phone contract expiration example courtesy of Akin Arikan, "Multichannel Marketing Metrics with Akin." www.multichannelmetrics.com/.

**Friends stick to the same cell phone company (a social effect):**
- Tim Manns, Senior Data Mining Analyst, Optus, "Enhancing Customer Knowledge and Retention at Optus," Taradata Podcast. www.teradata.com/podcasts/enhancing-customer-knowledge-optus/.
- Auren Hoffman, "Birds of a Feather Use the Same Phone Service Provider," Summation blog post, November 4, 2009. http://blog.summation.net/2009/11/birds-of-a-feather-use-the-same-phone-service-provider.html.
- Michael Driscoll, PhD, "The Social Effect: Predicting Telecom Customer Churn with Call Data," Predictive Analytics World San Francisco Conference, February 16, 2010, San Francisco, CA. www.predictiveanalyticsworld.com/sanfrancisco/2010/agenda.php#day1–12.

**Transient web shoppers are less likely to return:**
- Niche retail website customers who make their first purchase after typing in the website URL by hand are twice as likely to return for a second purchase in the future than those who arrived from a Google search (author's internal case study).

## Table: Bizarre and Surprising Insights—Finance and Insurance (Chapter 3)

**Low credit rating, more car accidents:**
- Herb Weisbaum, "Insurance Firms Blasted for Credit Score Rules," ConsumerMan on NBC News, January 27, 2010. www.msnbc.msn.com/id/35103647/ns/business-consumer_news/t/insurance-firms-blasted-credit-score-rules/#.UET1ppbuiSp.
- Dan Collins, "Credit Ratings Drive Car Insurance Costs," CBS News, February 11, 2009. www.cbsnews.com/2100–18563_162–522755.html.
- Federal Trade Commission, "FTC Releases Report on Effects of Credit-based Insurance Scores," FTC News, July 24, 2007. www2.ftc.gov/opa/2007/07/facta.shtm.

**Your shopping habits foretell your reliability as a debtor:**
- Charles Duhigg, "What Does Your Credit-Card Company Know about You?" *New York Times*, May 12, 2009. www.nytimes.com/2009/05/17/magazine/17credit-t.html.

**A small business's credit risk depends on the owner's behavior as a *consumer*:**
- Vernon Gerety, "Credit Scoring in the Leasing Industry," ELA Credit & Collection Management Conference, June 9–11, 2002. www.elfaonline.org/cvweb_elfa/Product_Downloads/Credit_Scoring.pdf.

## Table: Bizarre and Surprising Insights—Healthcare (Chapter 3)

**Genetics foretell cheating wives:**
- Christine E. Garver-Apgar, Steven W. Gangestad, Randy Thornhill, Robert D. Miller, and Jon J. Olp, "Major Histocompatibility Complex Alleles, Sexual Responsivity, and Unfaithfulness in Romantic Couples," *Psychological Science* 2006 17: 830, October 27, 2006. http://psy2.ucsd.edu/~mgorman/garver.pdf.
- Special to *World Science*, "Gene May Help Predict Infidelity, Study Reports," *World Science*, November 30, 2006. www.world-science.net/exclusives/061128_infidelity-genes.htm.

**Retirement is bad for your health:**
- Andreas Kuhn, Jean-Philippe Wuellrich, and Josef Zweimüller, "Fatal Attraction? Access to Early Retirement and Mortality," IZA Discussion Paper, October 2010. www.econ.uzh.ch/faculty/kuhn/wp_499_10_2010.pdf.

**Google search trends predict disease outbreaks:**
- Google Trends, "Flu Trends," www.google.org/flutrends/about/how.html. See also: Jeremy Ginsberg, Matthew H. Mohebbi, Rajan S. Patel, Lynnette Brammer, Mark S. Smolinski, and Larry Brilliant, "Detecting Influenza Epidemics Using Search Engine Query Data," *Nature* 457 (February 19, 2009), 1012–1014. doi:10.1038/nature07634. www.nature.com/nature/journal/v457/n7232/full/nature07634.html.

**Smokers suffer less from repetitive motion disorder:**

- State Compensation Insurance Fund, "Microbreaks," *Ergomatters* 3, no. 4. www .statefundca.com/safety/ErgoMatters/Microbreaks.asp.

**Positive health habits are contagious (a social effect):**

- Alice Park, "Quitting Smoking Is Contagious," *Time*, May 21, 2008. www.time.com/ time/health/article/0%2c8599%2c1808446%2b05.html.
- Nicholas A. Christakis, MD, PhD, MPH, and James H. Fowler, PhD, "The Spread of Obesity in a Large Social Network over 32 Years," *New England Journal of Medicine* 357 (November 1, 2007): 1866–1868. www.nejm.org/doi/full/10.1056/NEJMsa066082#t=letters.

**Happiness is contagious (a social effect):**

- Nicholas A. Christakis and James H. Fowler, "Social Networks and Happiness," *Edge*, December 4, 2008. www.edge.org/3rd_culture/christakis_fowler08/christakis_fowler08_ index.html.
- Allison Aubrey, "Happiness: It Really Is Contagious," NPR News, *All Things Considered*, December 5, 2008. www.npr.org/templates/story/story.php?storyId=97831171.

**Knee surgery choices make a big difference:**

- Lars Ejerhed, MD, Jüri Kartus, MD, PhD, Ninni Sernert, Kristina Köhler, and Jon Karlsson, MD, PhD, "Patellar Tendon or Semitendinosus Tendon Autografts for Anterior Cruciate Ligament Reconstruction," *American Journal of Sports Medicine* 31, no. 1 (January 2003): 19–25. http://ajs.sagepub.com/content/31/1/19.short.

**Music expedites poststroke recovery and improves mood:**

- T. Särkämö, M. Tervaniemi, S. Laitinen, A. Forsblom, S. Soinila, M. Mikkonen, T. Autti, H. M. Silvennoinen, J. Erkkilä, M. Laine, I. Peretz, and M. Hietanen, "Music Listening Enhances Cognitive Recovery and Mood after Middle Cerebral Artery Stroke," *NCBI*, March 2008, 131 (Part 3), 866–876. www.ncbi.nlm.nih.gov/pubmed/18287122.

**Yoga improves your mood:**

- Kazufumi Yoshihara, Tetsuya Hiramoto, Nobuyuki Sudo, and Chiharu Kubo, "Profile of Mood States and Stress-Related Biochemical Indices in Long-Term Yoga Practitioners," *NCBI*, *BioPsychoSocial Medicine* 5, no. 6 (2011). Published online June 3, 2011, doi:10.1186/1751-0759-5-6. www.ncbi.nlm.nih.gov/pmc/articles/PMC3125330/.
- Similar results apply also with other athletic activities: Oxford Food & Fitness Dictionary, www.answers.com/topic/profile-of-mood-states.

## Table: Bizarre and Surprising Insights—Crime and Law Enforcement (Chapter 3)

**Suicide bombers do not buy life insurance:**

- Stephen J. Dubner, "SuperFreakonomics Book Club: Ian Horsley Answers Your Questions about the Terrorist Algorithm," September 1, 2010. www.freakonomics .com/2010/09/01/superfreakonomics-book-club-ian-horsley-answers-your-questions- about-the-terrorist-algorithm/.

**Unlike lightning, crime strikes twice:**

- G. O. Mohler, M. B. Short, P. J. Brantingham, F. P. Schoenberg, and G. E. Tita, "Self-Exciting Point Process Modeling of Crime," *Journal of the American Statistical Association* 106, no. 493 (March 2011), Applications and Case Studies, doi:10.1198/jasa.2011.ap09546. www.math.ucla.edu/~mbshort/papers/crime3.pdf.

**Crime rises with public sporting events:**

- Daniel I. Rees and Kevin T. Schnepel, "College Football Games and Crime," Working Papers Series, Department of Economics, University of Colorado, Denver, January 2008. www.ilr.cornell.edu/cheri/workingPapers/upload/cheri_wp109.pdf.

**Crime rises after elections:**

- Katherine Wells, "Wildfires, Cops and Keggers: A New Marketplace Podcast on Election-Time Mischief," Freakonomics Radio, November 2, 2011. www.freakonomics.com/2011/11/02/wildfires-cops-and-keggers-a-new-marketplace-podcast-on-election-time-mischief/.

**Phone card sales predict Congo massacres:**

- Quentin Hardy, "Bizarre Insights from Big Data," *New York Times*, Bits blog, March 28, 2012. http://bits.blogs.nytimes.com/2012/03/28/bizarre-insights-from-big-data/.

**Hungry judges rule negatively:**

- Shai Danziger, Jonathan Levav, and Liora Avnaim-Pesso, "Extraneous Factors in Judicial Decisions," edited by Daniel Kahneman, Princeton University, Princeton, NJ, February 25, 2011. http://lsolum.typepad.com/files/danziger-levav-avnaim-pnas-2011.pdf and www.pnas.org/content/108/17/6889.

## Table: Bizarre and Surprising Insights—Miscellaneous (Chapter 3)

**Music taste predicts political affiliation:**

- Brian Whitman, "How Well Does Music Predict Your Politics?" Variogr.am blog post, July 12, 2012. http://notes.variogr.am/post/26869688460/how-well-does-music-predict-your-politics.

**Online dating: Be cool and unreligious to succeed:**

- Christian Rudder, "Exactly What to Say in a First Message," OkTrends, OkCupid, September 14, 2009. http://blog.okcupid.com/index.php/online-dating-advice-exactly-what-to-say-in-a-first-message/.

**Hot or not? People consistently considered attractive get *less* attention:**

- Christian Rudder, OkTrends, "Surprising Statistics about Hot People versus Ugly People," Business Insider, January 13, 2011. www.businessinsider.com/surprising-statistics-about-hot-people-versus-ugly-people-2011-1.

**A job promotion can lead to quitting (see Chapter 2 for details on this case study):**

- Gitali Halder, Hewlett-Packard, and Anindya Dey, Hewlett Packard, "Attrition Driver Analysis," Predictive Analytics World London Conference, November 30, 2011, London, UK. www.predictiveanalyticsworld.com/london/2011/agenda.php#day1–5a.

**Vegetarians miss fewer flights:**

- *The Economist* Staff, "A Different Game: Information Is Transforming Traditional Businesses," *The Economist*, February 25, 2010. www.economist.com/node/15557465.
- Quentin Hardy, "Bizarre Insights from Big Data," *New York Times*, Bits blog, March 28, 2012. http://bits.blogs.nytimes.com/2012/03/28/bizarre-insights-from-big-data/.

**A photo's quality is predictable from its caption:**

- Quentin Hardy, "Bizarre Insights from Big Data," *New York Times*, Bits blog, March 28, 2012. http://bits.blogs.nytimes.com/2012/03/28/bizarre-insights-from-big-data/.

**Men on the *Titanic* faced much greater risk than women:**

- Kaggle. "Titanic: Machine Learning from Disaster" Competition, September 28, 2012. www.kaggle.com/c/titanic-gettingStarted.

**Rock Star Mortality:**

- Kim Painter, "Solo Rock Stars at Greater Risk to Die Early," *USA Today, Health and Wellness*, December 19, 2012. www.usatoday.com/story/news/nation/2012/12/19/rock-star-early-death-solo-artists/1780027.
- Mark A. Bellis, Karen Hughes, Olivia Sharples, Tom Hennell, and Katherine A. Hardcastle, "Dying to Be Famous: Retrospective Cohort Study of Rock and Pop Star Mortality and its Association with Adverse Childhood Experiences," *BMJ Open, BMJ Group*, December 19, 2012, Volume 2, Issue 6, 2:e002089 doi:10.1136/bmjopen-2012-002089. http://bmjopen.bmj.com/content/2/6/e002089.full?sid=8f58c788-57df-4d54-a256-e9a6785f831c.

# Chapter 3, Continued (after its Tables):

**Shark attacks increase when ice cream sales increase:**

- Story from BBC News, "Just Because," *BBC News Magazine*, September 3, 2008. http://news.bbc.co.uk/2/hi/uk_news/magazine/7592579.stm.

**Regarding hormone replacement therapy:**

- Debbie A. Lawlor, George Davey Smith, and Shah Ebrahim, "Commentary: The Hormone Replacement–Coronary Heart Disease Conundrum: Is This the Death of Observational Epidemiology?" *International Journal of Epidemiology* 33, no. 3 (2004): 464–467, doi:10.1093/ije/dyh124. First published online: May 27, 2004. http://ije.oxfordjournals.org/content/33/3/464.

**Regarding the growing number of retracted journal publications:**

- G. Naik, "Mistakes in Scientific Studies Surge," *Wall Street Journal*, August 10, 2011. http://online.wsj.com/article/SB10001424052702303627104576411850666582080.html#articleTabs%3Darticle.

**Does smoking cause cancer?:**

- David Salsburg, *The Lady Tasting Tea: How Statistics Revolutionized Science in the Twentieth Century* (W.H. Freeman & Company, 2001), 183.

**Quote from Sigmund Freud:**

- Sigmund Freud, *Group Psychology and the Analysis of the Ego* (W.W. Norton & Company, 1921).

**Eric Gilbert and Karrie Karahalios released the data, code, and models for this research:**

- Eric Gilbert, "Update: Widespread Worry and the Stock Market," Social.CS.UIUC .EDU, March 13, 2010. http://social.cs.uiuc.edu/people/gilbert/38.

**Predicting by social media:**

- Sitaram Asu and Bernardo A. Huberman, "Predicting the Future with Social Media," Cornell University Library, March 29, 2010, arXiv.org, arXiv:1003.5699. http://arxiv.org/abs/1003.5699/.
- Anshul Mittal and Arpit Goel, "Stock Prediction Using Twitter Sentiment Analysis," Stanford University Libraries, December 16, 2011. http://cs229.stanford.edu/proj2011/GoelMittal-StockMarketPredictionUsingTwitterSentimentAnalysis.pdf.
- Allison Aubrey, "Happiness: It Really Is Contagious," NPR News, *All Things Considered*, December 5, 2008. www.npr.org/templates/story/story.php?storyId=97831171.
- Shea Bennett, "Can Twitter Beat the Stock Market? Tweet Sentiment Trading API Bets That It Can," Mediabistro, July 5, 2012. www.mediabistro.com/alltwitter/twitter-trading-api_b24992.
- J. Bollen, H. Mao, and X. Zeng, "Twitter Mood Predicts the Stock Market," *Journal of Computational Science* 2, no. 1 (March 2011): 1–8, doi:10.1016/j.jocs.2010.12.007, arxiv: abs/1010.3003.
- Ciara Byrne, "Social Media Popularity Can Predict Stock Prices," Venture Beat Online, March 17, 2011. http://venturebeat.com/2011/03/17/study-social-media-popularity-can-predict-stock-prices/.
- Nicholas A. Christakis and James H. Fowler, "Happiness Is Contagious," *Edge: The Third Culture*, December 4, 2008. www.edge.org/3rd_culture/christakis_fowler08/christakis_fowler08_index.html.
- Zhi Da, Joseph Engelberg, and Pengjie Gao, "In Search of Attention," University of Notre Dame, June 3, 2010. nd.edu/~pgao/papers/Google_04june2010.pdf.
- Global Pulse, "Unemployment through the Lens of Social Media," Global Pulse Research, in partnership with S.A.S. www.unglobalpulse.org/projects/can-social-media-mining-add-depth-unemployment-statistics.
- Yigitcan Karabulut, "Can Facebook Predict Stock Market Activity?" Miami University, first draft: August 29, 2011, second draft: October 17, 2011. http://bus.miami.edu/umbfc/_common/files/papers/Karabulut.pdf.
- Brian Womack, "Twitter Feeds on Netflix Prompt Stock Service," Bloomberg Online, January 23, 2012. www.bloomberg.com/news/2012-01-23/social-media-predicting-stock-moves-spawn-sentiment-firms-tech.html.

- Charlie White, "Who Will Win a Grammy? Twitter Predicts the Future," Mashable Entertainment, February 11, 2012. http://mashable.com/2012/02/11/grammy-twitter-predictions/.
- Yuan Zhang, Jie Tang, Jimeng Sun, Yiran Chen, and Jinghai Rao, "MoodCast: Emotion Prediction via Dynamic Continuous Factor Graph Model," Tsinghua University, China, October 11, 2010. http://keg.cs.tsinghua.edu.cn/jietang/publications/ICDM10-Zhang-et-al-MoodCast.pdf.
- Xue Zhang, Hauke Fuehres, and Peter A. Gloor, "Predicting Stock Market Indicators through Twitter: 'I Hope It Is Not as Bad as I Fear,'" *Procedia—Social and Behavioral Sciences* 26 (2011): 55–62. www.sciencedirect.com/science/article/pii/S1877042811023895.

**Butter in Bangladesh:**

- David J. Leinweber, *Nerds on Wall Street* (John Wiley & Sons, 2009).

**Regarding stock prediction:**

- Lisa Grossman, "Twitter Can Predict the Stock Market?" *Wired Magazine Online*, October 19, 2010. www.wired.com/wiredscience/2010/10/twitter-crystal-ball/.
- NPR Staff, "Need Stock Tips? Read Your Tweets," NPR News, *All Things Considered*, October 24, 2010. www.npr.org/templates/story/story.php?storyId=130793579.
- "Can Twitter Predict the Future?" *The Economist*, June 2, 2011. www.economist.com/node/18750604.
- Randy Saaf, AlphaGenius, "Using Twitter & the Social Internet to Obtain Above Market Returns," Text Analytics World San Francisco Conference, March 7, 2012, San Francisco, CA. www.textanalyticsworld.com/sanfrancisco/2012/agenda/full-agenda#day1430–450–2.

**Questions about the legitimacy of social media based prediction:**

- Snarky skeptical statistics blog post, "The Junk Science behind the 'Twitter Hedge Fund,'" April 14, 2012. http://sellthenews.tumblr.com/post/21067996377/noitdoesnot.
- Ben Gimpert, "Sour Grapes: Seven Reasons Why 'That' Twitter Prediction Model Is Cooked," Some Ben? blog post, May 13, 2011. http://blog.someben.com/2011/05/sour-grapes-seven-reasons-why-that-twitter-prediction-model-is-cooked/.

# CHAPTER 4

Some content of this chapter originated from valuable interviews with Dan Steinberg, PhD, Chief Executive Officer and President of Salford Systems.

**For further technical details behind this chapter's Chase case study:**

- Ali Moazami and Shaolin Li, "Mortgage Business Transformation Program Using CART-based Joint Risk Modeling," Salford Systems Data Mining Conference, 2005. www.salford-systems.com/doc/MoazamiLi.pdf.

**For Further Technical Reading on Predictive Modeling:**
**For a technical introduction to predictive modeling methods:**

- Robert Nisbit, John Elder, and Gary Miner, *Handbook of Statistical Analysis and Data Mining Applications* (Academic Press, 2009), 347.

**For an academic textbook with the complete probability and math:**

- Tom M. Mitchell, *Machine Learning*, Science/Engineering/Math (McGraw-Hill, 1997).

**For a visual, conceptual breakdown of modeling methods that's clickable:**

- Saed Sayad, PhD, "An Introduction to Data Mining." http://chem-eng.utoronto.ca/~datamining/dmc/data_mining_map.htm.

**Merger that made Chase the largest U.S. bank holding company in 1996:**

- JPMorgan Chase & Co. website, "History of Our Firm." www.jpmorganchase.com/corporate/About-JPMC/jpmorgan-history.htm.

**The history of risk scoring:**

- Vitalie BUMACOV and Arvind ASHTA, "The Conceptual Framework of Credit Scoring from Its Origins to Microfinance (Draft)," Burgundy School of Business, June 2, 2011. http://tinyurl.com/c7fs9cz.
- David Durand, *Risk Elements in Consumer Instalment Financing* (National Bureau of Economic Research, 1941), ISBN: 0-870-14124-4. www.nber.org/books/dura41-1.

**A perspective on micro-risk management:**

- James Taylor, JT on EDM. "Risk by Risk—A Decision-Centric Approach to Risk Management," DecisionManagementSolutions.com blog post, February 15, 2010. http://jtonedm.com/2010/02/15/risk-by-risk-a-decision-centric-approach-to-risk-management/.
- James Taylor with Neil Raden, *Smart (Enough) Systems* (Prentice Hall, 2007).
- James Taylor. *Decision Management Systems* (IBM Press, 2011).

**Insurance companies using predictive modeling:**

- Dr. Thomas Ashley, Dr. Guizhou Hu, and Chris Stehno, "How Does Mortality Modeling Affect Life Insurance Preferred Risk Selection?" ReFocus Conference, Las Vegas, NV, February 27–March 2, 2011. www.soa.org/files/pd/2011-lv-refocus-b3.pdf.

**Predictive modeling and insurance companies:**

- *Insurance Journal* Staff, "How Predictive Modeling Has Revolutionized Insurance," *Insurance Journal*, June 18, 2012. www.insurancejournal.com/news/national/2012/06/18/251957.htm.

**Insurer's use of predictive analytics:**

- Charles Nyce, PhD, CPCU, API, "Predictive Analytics White Paper," AICPACU/IIA, September 28, 2007. www.aicpcu.org/doc/predictivemodelingwhitepaper.pdf.

**Eric Webster quote:**

- Gregory Piatetsky-Shapiro, "Discussion with State Farm's Eric Webster: Insurance and Data Mining," KDnuggets.com, April 15, 2009. www.kdnuggets.com/news/2009/n08/3i.html.

**Stanford's free machine learning course; its Professor Andrew Ng founded Coursera:**

- Terence Chea, "MOOCs from Elite Colleges Transform Online Higher Education," *Huffington Post Online*, August 5, 2012. www.huffingtonpost.com/2012/08/05/mooc-massive-open-online-courses_n_1744430.html.
- Andrew Ng, "The Online Revolution: High-Quality Education for Everyone," ACM San Francisco Bay Area Professional Chapter, Cupertino, CA, May 16, 2012. www.sfbayacm.org/event/online-revolution-high-quality-education-everyone.

**Polls showing decision tree popularity among predictive modeling methods:**

- KDnuggets poll: Algorithms for data analysis/data mining, November 2011. www.kdnuggets.com/polls/2011/algorithms-analytics-data-mining.html.
- Rexer Analytics: Data Miner Survey, August 2012. www.predictiveanalyticsworld.com/survey-signup.php.

**The 30-second rule:**

- Audrey Fukuman and Andy Wright, "You Dropped Food on the Floor—Do You Eat It? The 30-Second Rule: A Decision Tree," SFFoodie, blogs.SFWeekly.com, January 29, 2010. http://blogs.sfweekly.com/foodie/2010/01/you_dropped_food_on_the_floor.php.

**Decision tree trained to predict votes on U.S. Supreme Court rulings by former Justice Sandra Day O'Connor:**

- Andres D. Martin, Kevin M. Quinn, Theodore W. Ruger, and Pauline T. Kim, "Competing Approaches to Predicting Supreme Court Decision Making," *Symposium: Forecasting U.S. Supreme Court Decisions* 2, no. 4 (December 2004), 761–767. http://wusct.wustl.edu/media/man1.pdf.

**Oliver G. Selfridge quote:**

- Marti A. Hearst Haym Hirsh, "AI's Greatest Trends and Controversies," *IEEE Intelligent Systems* 15, issue 1 (January 2000), 8–17, doi:10.1109/5254.820322. http://dl.acm.org/citation.cfm?id=630511.

**For an example of a visual, rich decision tree to play the guessing game:**

- Shana Mlawski and Carlos A. Hann Commander, "Female Character Flowchart," Overthinkingit.com, October 12, 2010. http://big.assets.huffingtonpost.com/flowchart.jpeg.

**Butter in Bangladesh:**

- Jason Zweig, "Data Mining Isn't a Good Bet for Stock-Market Predictions," *Wall Street Journal*, August 8, 2009. http://online.wsj.com/article/SB124967937642715417.html.

- Jason Zweig interviews David Leinweber, author of *Nerds on Wall Street*. Live: The *Wall Street Journal*, August 7, 2009. http://live.wsj.com/video/an-interview-with-nerds-on-wall-street-author/5062DA68-FCF6-42AC-AC62-AE6046BA40AC.html#!5062DA68-FCF6-42AC-AC62-AE6046BA40AC.
- Laura Washington, "What's the Stock Market Got to Do with the Production of Butter in Bangladesh?" *CNNMoney Magazine*, March 1, 1998. http://money.cnn.com/magazines/moneymag/moneymag_archive/1998/03/01/238606/index.htm.

**Buried treasure discoveries predicted the Dow Jones Industrial Average:**
- David Leinweber, "Back into the Data Mine," Nerds on Wall Street blog post, August 2009. http://nerdsonwallstreet.typepad.com/my_weblog/2009/08/back-into-the-data-mine.html.

**Quote by Nassim Nicholas Taleb:**
- Nassim Nicholas Taleb, *Fooled by Randomness: The Hidden Role of Chance in Life and in the Markets*, 2nd ed. (Random House Trade Paperbacks, 2005).

**Another related example of overlearning:**
- Mike Moffatt, "Does the Superbowl Predict Economic Growth?" About.com Economics, April 10, 2012. http://economics.about.com/od/economicindicatorintro/a/superbowl.htm.

**Regarding evolving Tetris players:**
- Eric V. Siegel and Alexander D. Chaffee, "Genetically Optimizing the Speed of Programs Evolved to Play Tetris," in *Advances in Genetic Programming*, ed. Peter J. Angeline and Kenneth E. Kinnear Jr. (MIT Press, 1996), 279–298, ISBN: 0-262-01158-1. http://dl.acm.org/citation.cfm?id=270220.

**Inductive bias:**
- Tom M. Mitchell, "The Need for Biases in Learning Generalizations," CBM-TR 5–110, Rutgers University, New Brunswick, NJ. Converted to electronic version by Roby Joehanes, Kansas State University, November 8, 2007. http://dml.cs.byu.edu/~cgc/docs/mldm_tools/Reading/Need%20for%20Bias.pdf.

**No free lunch theorem:**
- David H. Wolpert, "The Lack of a Priori Distinctions between Learning Algorithms," *Neural Computations* 8, issue 7 (October 1, 1996): 1341–1390. http://dl.acm.org/citation.cfm?id=1362128.

**Early work in decision trees:**
- James N. Morgan and John A Sonquist, "Problems in the Analysis of Survey Data, and a Proposal," *Journal of the American Statistical Association* 58, issue 202 (June 1963): 415–434. www.cs.nyu.edu/~roweis/csc2515-2006/readings/morgan_sonquist63.pdf.

**Decision tree overlearning figures derived from Figure 3.6 of:**
- Tom M. Mitchell, *Machine Learning*, Science/Engineering/Math (McGraw-Hill, 1997).

**Classification and regression trees:**

- Leo Breiman, Jerome Friedman, Charles J. Stone, and R. A. Olshen, *Classification and Regression Trees* (Chapman & Hall/CRC, 1984).

**The history of CART:**

- Ronny Kohavi, "Crossing the Chasm: From Academic Machine Learning to Commercial Data Mining," International Conference on Machine Learning 1998, Slide 21. http://robotics.stanford.edu/~ronnyk/chasm.pdf.

**Chase's acquisition of JPMorgan:**

- Andrew Garfield, "Chase Acquires JPMorgan for $34 bn, but 10,000 Jobs May Go," *The Independent*, September 14, 2000. www.independent.co.uk/news/business/news/chase-acquires-jp-morgan-for-34bn-but-10000-jobs-may-go-699819.html.

**JPMorgan Chase as the largest bank in the United States:**

- Hugh Son, "BofA Loses No. 1 Ranking by Assets to JPMorgan as Chief Moynihan Retreats," Bloomberg, October 18, 2011. www.bloomberg.com/news/2011–10–18/bank-of-america-loses-no-1-ranking-by-assets-to-jpmorgan-chase.html.
- Halah Touryalai, "America's Biggest Banks: Bank of America Fails to Win Back Top Spot," *Forbes*, March 26, 2012. www.forbes.com/sites/halahtouryalai/2012/03/26/americas-biggest-banks-bank-of-america-fails-to-win-back-top-spot/.

**Regarding the macroscopic level and the failures leading to the 2008 recession:**

- Saul Hansell, "How Wall Street Lied to Its Computers," *New York Times*, Bits blog, September 18, 2008. http://bits.blogs.nytimes.com/2008/09/18/how-wall-streets-quants-lied-to-their-computers/.

**Quote from Bart Baesens:**

- Bart Baesens, PhD, "Building Bulletproof Models," *sascom* Magazine, 3rd quarter, 2010. www.sas.com/news/feature/FSmodels.html.

# CHAPTER 5

**Layperson competitors for the Netflix Prize:**

- Eric Siegel, PhD, "Casual Rocket Scientists: An Interview with a Layman Leading the Netflix Prize, Martin Chabbert," September 2009. www.predictiveanalyticsworld.com/layman-netflix-leader.php.

**$1 million Netflix Prize:**

- Netflix Prize, September 21, 2009. www.netflixprize.com/.

**Seventy percent of Netflix movie choices based on recommendations:**

- Jeffrey M. O'Brien, "The Netflix Effect," *Wired Magazine Online*, December 12, 2002. http://www.wired.com/wired/archive/10.12/netflix.html.

- Michael Liedtke, "Netflix Recommendations Are About to Get Better, Say Execs," *Huffington Post Online*, April 9, 2012. www.huffingtonpost.com/2012/04/09/netflix-recommendations_n_1413179.html.

**Netflix Prize team BellKor's Pragmatic Chaos:**
- "BellKor's Pragmatic Chaos Is the Winner of the $1 Million Netflix Prize!!!!" September 17, 2009. www2.research.att.com/ ∼volinsky/netflix/bpc.html.

**Regarding SpaceShipOne and the XPrize:**
- XPrize Foundation, "Ansari X Prize," XPrize Foundation, updated April 25, 2012. http://space.xprize.org/ansari-x-prize.

**Netflix Prize team PragmaticTheory:**
- PragmaticTheory website. https://sites.google.com/site/pragmatictheory/.

**Netflix Prize team BigChaos:**
- Istvan Pilaszy, "Lessons That We Learned from the Netflix Prize," Predictive Analytics World Washington, DC, Conference, October 21, 2009, Washington, DC. www.predictiveanalyticsworld.com/dc/2009/agenda.php#day2–13.
- Clive Thompson, "If You Liked This, You're Sure to Love That," *New York Times*, November 21, 2008. www.nytimes.com/2008/11/23/magazine/23Netflix-t.html.

**Netflix Prize team The Ensemble:**
- Blog post by Aron, "Netflix Prize Conclusion," The Ensemble, September 22, 2009. www.the-ensemble.com/content/netflix-prize-conclusion#comments.

**Recount of the dead heat completion of the Netflix Prize:**
- Gregory Piatetsky-Shapiro, "Netflix Prize Contest Dramatic Finish—and the Winner Is . . . ," *KDnuggets News*, July 28, 2009. www.kdnuggets.com/news/2009/n14/1i.html.
- PragmaticTheory blog post, "By a Nose . . . or Is It a Hair . . ." PragmaticTheory blog, July 28, 2009. http://pragmatictheory.blogspot.com/2009/07/by-nose-or-is-it-hair_28.html.
- Blog post by Aron, "Final Submission Countdown," The Ensemble, July 29, 2009. www.the-ensemble.com/content/final-submission-countdown.

**Netflix Prize Team Just a Guy in a Garage:**
- Gavin, "Supercomputing Made Super Easy," Just a Guy in a Garage blog, July 14, 2011. http://justaguyinagarage.blogspot.com.

**Contest to automatically grade student-written essays:**
- Kaggle, "Develop an Automated Scoring Algorithm for Student-Written Essays," Competition, February 10, 2012. www.kaggle.com/c/asap-aes.
- Mark D. Shermis and Ben Hamner, "Contrasting State-of-the-Art Automated Scoring of Essays: Analysis," Contrasting Essay Scoring, April 12, 2012. http://dl.dropbox.com/u/44416236/NCME%202012%20Paper3_29_12.pdf.

**Contest to predict the distribution of dark matter in the universe:**
- Kaggle, "Mapping Dark Matter," Competition, May 23, 2011. www.kaggle.com/c/mdm.

**Heritage Health Prize ($3,000,000):**
- Kaggle, "Improve Healthcare, Win $3,000,000," Competition, April 4, 2011. www.kaggle.com/host/casestudies/hpn.

**More Kaggle case studies:**
- Anthony Goldbloom, "Machines Learn, but Can They Teach?" Predictive Analytics World Boston Conference, October 2, 2012, Boston, MA. www.predictiveanalyticsworld.com/boston/2012/agenda.php#day2–445a.
- Anthony Goldbloom, "Prediction Competitions: Far More Than Just a Bit of Fun," Predictive Analytics World London Conference, November 16, 2010, London, UK. www.predictiveanalyticsworld.com/london/2010/agenda.php#day2–11.
- Karthik Sethuraman, Kaggle, and Diederik Van Liere, "Solving the Last Mile: Focusing Global Intelligence on Your Data," Predictive Analytics World San Francisco Conference, March 5, 2012, San Francisco, CA. www.predictiveanalyticsworld.com/sanfrancisco/2012/agenda.php#day1–7.
- Mehul Patel, Kaggle, and Giles Pavey, "Predicting Retail Customer Behaviour," Predictive Analytics World London Conference, December 1, 2011, London, UK. www.predictiveanalyticsworld.com/london/2011/agenda.php#day1–16a.

**Crowdsourcing in general, beyond analytics projects:**
- Jeff Howe, *Crowdsourcing: Why the Power of the Crowd Is Driving the Future of Business* (Three Rivers Press, 2008).

**Quote from Anthony Goldbloom about Kaggle's crowdsourcing:**
- Tanya Ha, "Lucrative Algorithms," Catalyst Online, August 18, 2011. www.abc.net.au/catalyst/stories/3296837.htm.

**Regarding the shortage of analytics experts:**
- James Manyika, Michael Chui, Brad Brown, Jacques Bughin, Richard Dobbs, Charles Roxburgh, and Angela Hung Byers, "Big Data: The Next Frontier for Innovation, Competition, and Productivity," McKinsey Global Institute, May 2011. www.mckinsey.com/Insights/MGI/Research/Technology_and_Innovation/Big_data_The_next_frontier_for_innovation.

**More on Kaggle and crowdsourcing predictive analytics:**
- Kaggle, "About Us: Our Team," www.kaggle.com/about.
- Karthik Sethuraman, Kaggle, "Crowdsourcing Predictive Analytics: Why 25,000 Heads Are Better Than One," Predictive Analytics World Chicago Conference, June 25, 2012, Chicago, IL. www.predictiveanalyticsworld.com/chicago/2012/agenda.php#day1–250a.
- Beth Schultz, "Kaggle Makes Sport of Predictive Analytics," All Analytics Online, October 7, 2011. www.allanalytics.com/author.asp?section_id=1411&doc_id=234238.
- Beth Schultz, "Challengers & Competitors Get Their Predictive Analytics Games On," All Analytics Online, October 10, 2011. www.allanalytics.com/author.asp?section_id=1411&doc_id=234275.

- Anna Brown, "Competition Breeds the Best in Analytics," SAS Voices blog, October 21, 2011. http://blogs.sas.com/content/sascom/2011/10/21/competition-breeds-the-best-in-analytics/.
- Quentin Hardy, "Bizarre Insights from Big Data," *New York Times*, Bits blog, March 28, 2012. http://bits.blogs.nytimes.com/2012/03/28/bizarre-insights-from-big-data/.

**For other data mining competitions, see:**

- KDnuggets: Analytics, Data Mining Competitions. www.kdnuggets.com/competitions/index.html.
- Crowdsourcing for Search and Data Mining (CSDM 2011): A workshop of the Fourth ACM International Conference on Web Search and Data Mining (WSDM 2011), Hong Kong, China, February 9, 2011. http://ir.ischool.utexas.edu/csdm2011/.
- CSDM 2011 Crowdsourcing for Search and Data Mining, Hong Kong, China. http://ir.ischool.utexas.edu/csdm2011/.
- CrowdANALYTIX. www.crowdanalytix.com/welcome.
- Netflix Prize, September 21, 2009. www.netflixprize.com/.
- Salford Systems. www.salford-systems.com/en/resources/case-studies/119-teradata-center-for-crm-at-duke-competition.
- Duke University Department of Statistical Science. http://stat.duke.edu/datafest/.
- Data-Mining-Cup, DMC Competition. www.data-mining-cup.de/en/review/dmc-2012/.
- ACM KDD Cup. www.sigkdd.org/kddcup/.
- Nokia Research Center, Nokia Mobile Data Challenge. http://research.nokia.com/page/12000 and Nokia Mobile Data Challenge 2012 Workshop (18–19.6.2012). http://research.nokia.com/page/12340.
- "Predicting Customer Acquisition & Retention Using Structured and Semi-Structured Data." KDnuggets. www.kdnuggets.com/2012/01/wcai-research-opportunity-siriusxm-predicting-customer-acquisition-retention.html.
- EMVIC 2012: "The First Eye Movement Identification and Verification Competition." www.emvic.org/.
- Aspiring Minds Machine Learning Competition. www.aspiringminds.in/mlCompetition/.
- Information Security Amazon Data Security Competition. https://sites.google.com/site/amazonaccessdatacompetition/.

**Approaches to the Netflix Prize:**

- Clive Thompson, "If You Liked This, You're Sure to Love That," *New York Times*, November 21, 2008. www.nytimes.com/2008/11/23/magazine/23Netflix-t.html.

**Regarding collaboration rather than competition on the Netflix Prize:**

- Jordan Ellenberg, "This Psychologist Might Outsmart the Math Brains Competing for the Netflix Prize," *Wired*, February 25, 2008. www.wired.com/techbiz/media/magazine/16-03/mf_netflix.

**Overview of several uses of ensembles by Netflix Prize teams:**

- Todd Holloway, "Ensemble Learning Better Predictions through Diversity," ETech 2008, March 11, 2008. http://abeautifulwww.com/EnsembleLearningETech.pdf.

**Andreas Töscher from Netflix Prize team BigChaos:**

- "Advanced Approaches for Recommender System and the Netflix Prize," Predictive Analytics World San Francisco Conference, February 28, 2009, San Francisco, CA. www .predictiveanalyticsworld.com/sanfrancisco/2009/agenda.php#advancedapproaches.

**Netflix Prize leaderboard:**

- Netflix Prize leaderboard results, September 21, 2009. www.netflixprize.com/leaderboard.

**Winning the Netflix Prize by a matter of 20 minutes:**

- Steve Lohr, "A $1 Million Research Bargain for Netflix, and Maybe a Model for Others," *New York Times*, September 1, 2009. www.nytimes.com/2009/09/22/technology/ internet/22netflix.html.

**Quote from James Surowiecki:**

- James Surowiecki, *The Wisdom of Crowds* (Anchor, reprint ed., 2005).

**A wise crowd guesses the dollars at Predictive Analytics World:**

- Dean Abbott, "Another Wisdom of Crowds Prediction Win at eMetrics/Predictive Analytics World," Data Mining and Predictive Analytics blog, April 26, 2012. http://abbottanalytics .blogspot.com/2012/04/another-wisdom-of-crowds-prediction-win.html.

**InnoCentive website:**

- www.innocentive.com/.

**Foldit:**

- Zoran Popovic, "Massive Multiplayer Games to Solve Complex Scientific Problems," TED2013 @ Vancouver. http://talentsearch.ted.com/video/Zoran-Popovic-Massive- multiplay.
- "Check Out Exactly What Competitive Protein Folding Is All About!" YouTube, May 8, 2008, uploaded by UWfoldit. www.youtube.com/watch?v=lGYJyur4FUA.

**For more crowdsourcing projects, see Wikipedia's list of dozens:**

- Wikipedia, "List of Crowdsourcing Projects." http://en.wikipedia.org/wiki/List_of_ crowdsourcing_projects.

**Ensemble modeling is often considered the most important predictive modeling advancement of this century's first decade:**

- Giovanni Seni and John Elder, *Ensemble Methods in Data Mining Improving Accuracy through Combining Predictions* (Morgan & Claypool Publishers, 2010).

**"The most useful and powerful result of statistical research over the past decade has come to be known as ensemble modeling":**

- Robert Nisbit, John Elder, and Gary Miner, *Handbook of Statistical Analysis and Data Mining Applications* (Academic Press, 2009), 304.

**"Modular Decomposition" musical number:**

- Written and performed by Eric Siegel, PhD, Columbia University, "Modular Decomposition," CS W1007, Introduction to Computer Science, Columbia University. www .cs.columbia.edu/~evs/intro/handouts/songModular.html.

**The ensemble modeling method called bagging:**

- Leo Breiman, "Bagging Predictors," *Machine Learning* 24, no. 2 (1996), 120–140, doi:10.1007/BF00058655. www.springerlink.com/content/l4780124w2874025/.

**The visual of decision boundaries approximating a circle:**

- John Elder and Greg Ridgeway [Combining Estimators to Improve Performance], KDD Tutorial Notes of the Fifth CM SIGKDD International Conference on Knowledge Discovery and Data Mining, 1999. http://datamininglab.com/media/pdfs/kdd99_ elder_ridgeway.pdf.

**The improvement gained by ensemble models:**

- Giovanni Seni and John Elder, *Ensemble Methods in Data Mining Improving Accuracy through Combining Predictions* (Morgan & Claypool Publishers, 2010).
- John Elder and Greg Ridgeway [Combining Estimators to Improve Performance], KDD Tutorial Notes of the Fifth CM SIGKDD International Conference on Knowledge Discovery and Data Mining, 1999. http://datamininglab.com/media/pdfs/kdd99_ elder_ridgeway.pdf.
- Robert Nisbit, John Elder, and Gary Miner, *Handbook of Statistical Analysis and Data Mining Applications* (Academic Press, 2009); see chaps. 13 and 18.

**More regarding ensemble methods:**

- S. S. Lee and John Elder, "Bundling Heterogeneous Classifiers with Advisor Perceptrons," October 14, 1997. http://datamininglab.com/media/pdfs/lee_elder_97.pdf.
- Dean Abbott, Case Study: Air Force Research Laboratory, "Integrated Toxicity Assessment System (ITAS)," AbbottAnalytics.com. www.abbottanalytics.com/data-mining-case-study-0.php.
- Dean Abbott, Data Mining Resources: White Papers, "The Benefits of Creating Ensembles of Classifiers," AbbottAnalytics.com. www.abbottanalytics.com/white-paper-classifiers.php.
- Dean Abbott, "Comparison of Algorithms at PAKDD2007," Data Mining and Predictive Analytics blog, May 1, 2007. http://abbottanalytics.blogspot.com/2007/05/comparison-of-algorithms-at-pakdd2007.html.
- Dean Abbott, "PAKDD-10 Data Mining Competition Winner: Ensembles Again!" Data Mining and Predictive Analytics blog, May 27, 2010. http://abbottanalytics.blogspot .com/2010/05/pakdd-10-data-mining-competition-winner.html.
- Mohamed Medhat Gaber, *Journeys to Data Mining: Experiences from 15 Renowned Researchers* (Springer, 2012), 61–76.
- Dean Abbott, "How to Improve Customer Acquisition Models with Ensembles," Predictive Analytics World San Francisco Conference, February 18, 2009, San Francisco, CA. www.predictiveanalyticsworld.com/sanfrancisco/2009/agenda.php#nra.

- Philip K. Chan and Salvatore J. Stolfo, "On the Accuracy of Meta-Learning for Scalable Data Mining," *Journal of Intelligent Information Systems* 8, issue 1 (January/February 1997): 5–28. http://dl.acm.org/citation.cfm?id=251006.
- Leo Breiman, "Bagging Predictors," *Machine Learning* 24, no. 2 (1996), 123–140, doi:10.1007/BF00058655. www.springerlink.com/content/l4780124w2874025/.
- Michael Murff, PayPal, and Hui Wang, "Ensembles for Online Analytic Scoring Engine," Predictive Analytics World San Francisco Conference, March 14, 2011, San Francisco, CA. www.predictiveanalyticsworld.com/sanfrancisco/2011/agenda.php#day1–11a.
- Mike Kimel, "Revenge of the Clueless: Combining Many Poor Estimates into an Expert Forecast," Predictive Analytics World Toronto Conference, April 26, 2012, Toronto, Canada. www.predictiveanalyticsworld.com/toronto/2012/agenda.php#day2–17a.

**TreeNet has won multiple PA competitions, including:**

- Salford Systems, "Teradata Center for CRM at Duke Competition: Predicting Customer Churn with TreeNet," Challenge. www.salford-systems.com/en/resources/case-studies/119-teradata-center-for-crm-at-duke-competition.

**Both first- and second-place winners of KDD Cup 2010 employed ensemble models:**

- KDD Cup 2012 Educational Data Mining Challenge, "Winners of KDD Cup 2010: Educational Data Mining Challenge," hosted by PSLC DataShop. http://pslcdatashop.web.cmu.edu/KDDCup/results.jsp.

**The generalization paradox:**

- John F. Elder IV, "The Generalization Paradox of Ensembles," *Journal of Computational and Graphical Statistics* 12, no. 4, Statistical Analysis of Massive Data Streams (December 2003): 853–864. http://datamininglab.com/media/pdfs/Paradox_JCGS.pdf.

# CHAPTER 6

Some content of this chapter originated from a valuable interview with David Gondek, PhD, of IBM Research.

**For a historical account of the people behind the development of Watson:**

- Stephen Baker, *Final Jeopardy!: Man vs. Machine and the Quest to Know Everything* (Houghton Mifflin Harcourt, 2011).

**Way back in 2003, researchers developed a system to answer the trivia questions on another TV quiz show, *Who Wants to Be a Millionaire?* The system achieved 75 percent accuracy, in part by ensembling across multiple search engines. However, this show's questions are multiple-choice, so the whittling down of candidate answers is already mostly solved for a question answering system:**

- Shyong (Tony) K. Lam, David M. Pennock, Dan Cosley, and Steve Lawrence, "1 Billion Pages = 1 Million Dollars? Mining the Web to Play 'Who Wants to be a Millionaire?'" UAI '03, Proceedings of the 19th Conference in Uncertainty in Artificial Intelligence, Acapulco, Mexico, August 7–10, 2003, pages 337–345. http://arxiv.org/ftp/arxiv/papers/1212/1212.2477.pdf.

258 NOTES

**Regarding "Time flies like an arrow":**

- Gilbert Burck, *The Computer Age and Its Potential for Management* (Harper & Row, 1965).

**My (the author's) PhD research pertained to the "have a car/baby" example (temporal meaning in verbs):**

- Eric V. Siegel and Kathleen R. McKeown, "Learning Methods to Combine Linguistic Indicators: Improving Aspectual Classification and Revealing Linguistic Insights," *Computational Linguistics* 26, issue 4 (December 2000). doi:10.1162/089120100750105957, http://dl.acm.org/citation.cfm?id=971886.

**Googling only 30 percent of the *Jeopardy!* questions right:**

- Stephen Baker, *Final Jeopardy: Man vs. Machine and the Quest to Know Everything* (Houghton Mifflin Harcourt, 2011), 212–224.

**Quote about Google's book scanning project:**

- George Dyson, *Turing's Cathedral: The Origins of the Digital Universe* (Pantheon Books, 2012).

**Natural language processing:**

- Dursun Delen, Andrew Fast, Thomas Hill, Robert Nisbit, John Elder, and Gary Miner, *Practical Text Mining and Statistical Analysis for Non-Structured Text Data Applications* (Academic Press, 2012).
- James Allen, *Natural Language Understanding*, 2nd ed. (Addison-Wesley, 1994).

**Regarding the translation of "The spirit is willing, but the flesh is weak":**

- John Hutchins, "The Whisky Was Invisible or Persistent Myths of MT," *MT News International* 11 (June 1995), 17–18. www.hutchinsweb.me.uk/MTNI-11-1995.pdf.

**Ruminations on Apple's Siri versus Watson from WolframAlpha's creator:**

- Stephen Wolfram, "Jeopardy, IBM, and WolframAlpha," Stephen Wolfram blog, January 26, 2011. http://blog.stephenwolfram.com/2011/01/jeopardy-ibm-and-wolframalpha/.

**Knowledge Representation Rhapsody:**

- Eric Siegel, PhD, "Knowledge Representation Rhapsody," Columbia University, January 9, 2008. www.cs.columbia.edu/~evs/ai/songKRR.html.

**The leading university classroom textbook on artificial intelligence:**

- Stuart Russell and Peter Norvig, *Artificial Intelligence: A Modern Approach*, 2nd ed. (Prentice Hall, 2002).

**Quote from Douglas Adams:**

- Douglas Adams, *The Hitchhiker's Guide to the Galaxy* (Harmony Books, 1979).

**Theft of the Lion of Nimrud ivory carving:**

- Fiachra Gibbons, "Experts Mourn the Lion of Nimrud, Looted as Troops Stood By," *The Guardian*, April 30, 2003. www.guardian.co.uk/world/2003/apr/30/international educationnews.arts.

**IBM's revenue and size:**
- IBM, "Who We Are." www.ibm.com/ibm/us/en/.

**IBM's rank among top U.S. companies:**
- "The World's Biggest Public Companies," edited by Scott DeCarlo, *Forbes*, April 18, 2012. www.forbes.com/global2000/#p_1_s_d6_All%20industries_United%20States_All%20states_.

**TREC QA system performance:**
- David Ferrucci, Eric Brown, Jennifer Chu-Carroll, James Fan, David Gondek, Aditya A. Kalyanpur, Adam Lally, J. William Murdock, Eric Nyberg, John Prager, Nico Schlaefer, and Chris Welty, "Building Watson: An Overview of the DeepQA Project," *AI Magazine*, Fall 2012. www.aaai.org/Magazine/Watson/watson.php.
- TREC Proceedings. trec.nist.gov/proceedings/proceedings.html.

**Alex Trebek on IBM's investment to build Watson:**
- "Trebek Says IBM Computer Could Answer Wrong on *Jeopardy!*" Bloomberg Television, February 14, 2012. Online video clip, YouTube, accessed March 23, 2012. www.youtube.com/watch?v=tYguL82wk78.

**IBM's estimated spend to develop Watson:**
- Don Tennant, "'Final Jeopardy' Author Stephen Baker on the Impact of IBM's Watson," ITBusinessEdge, February 14, 2011. www.itbusinessedge.com/cm/community/features/interviews/blog/final-jeopardy-author-stephen-baker-on-the-impact-of-ibms-watson/.

**How Watson works:**
- IBM, "IBM Watson: Ushering in a new era of computing," IBM Innovations, April 11, 2012. www-03.ibm.com/innovation/us/watson/.
- IBM, "The DeepQA Project," IBM *Jeopardy!* Challenge, April 22, 2009. www.research.ibm.com/deepqa/deepqa.shtml.
- IBM, "Competing at *Jeopardy!* Is Just the First Step," IBM DeepQA Project, July 1, 2008. www.research.ibm.com/deepqa/index2.shtml.
- IBM, "The Science Behind Watson," *IBM Innovations*, April 11, 2012. www-03.ibm.com/innovation/us/watson/science-behind_watson.shtml.
- David Ferrucci, Eric Brown, Jennifer Chu-Carroll, James Fan, David Gondek, Aditya A. Kalyanpur, Adam Lally, J. William Murdock, Eric Nyberg, John Prager, Nico Schlaefer, and Chris Welty, "Building Watson: An Overview of the DeepQA Project," *AI Magazine* 31, no. 3. www.aaai.org/ojs/index.php/aimagazine/article/view/2303/0.
- D. C. Gondek, A. Lally, A. Kalyanpur, J. W. Murdock, P. A. Duboue, L. Zhang, Y. Pan, Z. M. Qiu, and C. Welty, "A Framework for Merging and Ranking of Answers in DeepQA," *IBM Journal of Research and Development* 56, issue 3.4 (May–June 2012), 14:1–14:12. http://ieeexplore.ieee.org/xpl/login.jsp?reload=true&tp=&arnumber=6177810.
- David C. Gondek, IBM, "Building Watson—An Overview of the DeepQA Project." Predictive Analytics World New York Conference, October 19, 2011, New York, NY. www.predictiveanalyticsworld.com/newyork/2011/agenda.php#keynote-jeopardy.

- Edward Nazarko, IBM, "Putting IBM Watson to Work," Predictive Analytics World Toronto Conference, April 26, 2012, Toronto, Canada. www.predictiveanalyticsworld .com/toronto/2012/agenda.php#day2–1kn.
- Robert Jewell, IBM, "Putting IBM Watson to Work," Predictive Analytics World Boston Conference, October 2, 2012, Boston, MA. www.predictiveanalyticsworld.com/ boston/2012/agenda.php#day2–1kn.
- Clive Thompson, "What Is IBM's Watson?" *New York Times*, June 16, 2010. www .nytimes.com/2010/06/20/magazine/20Computer-t.html.
- "Smartest Machine on Earth," *Nova*, PBS, originally aired May 2, 2012. www.pbs.org/ wgbh/nova/tech/smartest-machine-on-earth.html.

**Roger Craig, the PA practitioner and *Jeopardy!* winner:**

- Roger Craig, "Data Science Meets the Quiz Show *Jeopardy!*" Predictive Analytics World Chicago Conference, June 26, 2012, Chicago, IL. www.predictiveanalyticsworld.com/ chicago/2012/agenda.php#day2–11.
- Chris Jones, "If You Could Master All the Data in the World . . . ," *Esquire*, January 25, 2012. www.esquire.com/features/roger-craig-jeopardy-champ-0212.
- NPR Staff, "How One Man Played 'Moneyball' with *Jeopardy!*," NPR, *All Things Considered*, November 20, 2011. www.npr.org/2011/11/20/142569472/how-one-man-played-moneyball-with-jeopardy.
- Ryan Tate, "How a Geek Cracked the *Jeopardy!* Code," Gawker.com, November 16, 2011. http://gawker.com/5860275/how-a-geek-cracked-the-jeopardy-code.
- Ned Potter, "'Jeopardy!' Champ Wins Jackpot with Web App," ABCNews, Technology Review, November 17, 2011. http://abcnews.go.com/blogs/technology/2011/11/ jeopardy-champ-wins-jackpot-with-web-app/.
- Alexandra Carmichael, "Roger Craig Wins *Jeopardy* Championship with Knowledge Tracking," *Quantified Self*, November 17, 2011. http://quantifiedself.com/2011/11/ roger-craig-on-knowledge-tracking/.

**Ken Jennings used Roger Craig's study system:**

- Ken Jennings, "Map Tourism," Ken-Jennings.com blog post, November 17, 2011. http://ken-jennings.com/blog/archives/3385.

**Ken Jennings quotes:**

- Ken Jennings, "My Puny Human Brain," Slate.com, February 16, 2011. www.slate.com/ articles/arts/culturebox/2011/02/my_puny_human_brain.html.

**View complete Watson *Jeopardy!* match video:**

- YouTube.com, "The Watson *Jeopardy!* Episodes," posted by Kanal Tilhorende Martinm76, February 2011. www.youtube.com/playlist?list=PL30B2E32FF44CB641 (www.bit.ly/ WzXeNa).

**List of questions of the Watson *Jeopardy!* matches:**

- J! Archive, "Show #6086—Monday, February 14, 2011." www.j-archive.com/show-game.php?game_id=3575.

- J! Archive, "Show #6087—Tuesday, February 15, 2011." www.j-archive.com/show-game.php?game_id=3576.
- J! Archive, "Show #6088—Wednesday, February 16, 2011." www.j-archive.com/showgame.php?game_id=3577.

**Applying Watson for healthcare:**
- YouTube, "Progress Report: IBM Watson Utilization Management Pilot at WellPoint, Inc.," posted by IBMWatsonSolutions, May 15, 2012. www.youtube.com/watch?v=7d6c-5kJdGk.

**AI palindrome generation system:**
- Eric V. Siegel, "Iambic IBM AI: The Palindrome Discovery AI Project," White Paper, CiteSeer Online, November 7, 2011. http://citeseerx.ist.psu.edu/viewdoc/summary?doi=10.1.1.34.2132. *Note—here's another pertinent palindrome the system derived—the world's only self-referential, automatically generated, palindromic joke:* Net safety? Byte fasten.

# CHAPTER 7

This chapter benefited greatly from valuable interviews with Patrick Surry, Nicholas Radcliffe, and Neil Skilling.

**For a more applied overview of uplift modeling, see the author's white paper:**
- Eric Siegel, PhD, "Uplift Modeling: Predictive Analytics Can't Optimize Marketing Decisions Without It," Prediction Impact, Inc. White Paper, June 29, 2011. www.predictiveanalyticsworld.com/signup-uplift-whitepaper.php.

**Telenor case study:**
- Suresh Vittal, "Optimal Targeting through Uplift Modeling: Generating Higher Demand and Increasing Customer Retention While Reducing Marketing Costs," Forrester Research White Paper, 2008. www.portraitsoftware.com/resources/white_papers/optimal-targeting-through-uplift-modeling.
- Suresh Vittal, "Optimizing Customer Retention Programs," Forrester Research White Paper, 2008. www.portraitsoftware.com/resources/white-papers/optimizing-customer-retention-programs.

**What to say in an online dating message:**
- Christian Rudder, "Exactly What to Say in a First Message," OkTrends, OkCupid, September 14, 2009. http://blog.okcupid.com/index.php/online-dating-advice-exactly-what-to-say-in-a-first-message/.

**Influencing for ecologically and environmentally sound behaviors:**
- Robert B. Cialdini, "Crafting Normative Messages to Protect the Environment," *Association for Psychological Science*, July 9, 2003. www.psychologicalscience.org/pdf/cialdini.pdf.
- Noah J. Goldstein, Steve J. Martin, and Robert B. Cialdini, *Yes! 50 Scientifically Proven Ways to Be Persuasive* (Free Press; reprint ed., 2009).
- Robert B. Cialdini, PhD, *Influence: The Psychology of Persuasion*, rev. ed. (HarperBusiness, 2006).

- M. Hunecke, S. Haustein, S. Bohler, and S. Grischkat, "Attitude-Based Target Groups to Reduce the Ecological Impact of Daily Mobility Behavior," *Community-Based Social Marketing, Environment and Behavior* 42 (1): 3–43. www.cbsm.com/articles/attitudebased+target+groups+to+reduce+the+ecological+impact+of+daily+mobility+behavior_7771.

**Choice of graft source for ACL-reconstructing knee surgery:**
- Lars Ejerhed, MD, Juri Kartus, MD, PhD, Ninni Sernert, Kristina Kohler, and John Karlsson, MD, PhD, "Patellar Tendon or Semitendinosus Tendon Autografts for Anterior Cruciate Ligament Reconstruction? A Prospective Randomized Study with a Two-Year Follow-Up," *American Journal of Sports Medicine* 31, no. 1 (January 2003): 19–25. http://ajs.sagepub.com/content/31/1/19.short.

**Google comparing 41 shades of blue:**
- Laura M. Holson, "Putting a Bolder Face on Google," *New York Times*, February 28, 2009. www.nytimes.com/2009/03/01/business/01marissa.html.

**Facebook optimizes display rules:**
- Eytan Bakshy, Itamar Rosenn, Cameron Marlow, and Lada Adamic, "Role of Social Networks in Information Diffusion," International World Wide Web Conference Committee (IW3C2), WWW 2012, April 16–20, 2012, Lyon, France. ACM 978-1-4503-1229-5/12/04. arXiv:1201.4145v2 [cs.SI], February 28, 2012. http://cameronmarlow.com/media/bakshy-the_role-2012b.pdf.

**U.S. Bank case study:**
- Thanks to Michael Grundhoefer, Patrick Surry, and Pitney Bowes Software for this example case study.
- Jessica Tsai, "Mail Model of the Year: U.S. Bank Accrues Savings by Only Pitching Customers Who Aren't Already Likely to Show Interest," *CRM Magazine*, destinationCRM.com, April 2010. www.destinationcrm.com/Articles/Columns-Departments/REAL-ROI/Mail-Model-of-the-Year-66123.aspx.

**Uplift decision trees:**
- Nicholas Radcliffe and Patrick Surry, "Real-World Uplift Modelling with Significance-Based Uplift Trees," *Stochastic Solutions Limited*, March 29, 2011. http://stochasticsolutions.com/sbut.html.

**Other approaches to uplift modeling (beyond uplift trees, other analytical approaches to uplift modeling include specialized k–nearest neighbor (k-NN) classifiers, a specialized version of naive Bayes, and other uplift methods):**
- Victor S. Y. Lo, "The True Lift Model—A Novel Data Mining Approach to Response Modeling in Database Marketing," *ACM SIGKDD Explorations Newsletter* 4, issue 3 (2003), 78–86. www.sigkdd.org/explorations/issues/4–2–2002–12/lo.pdf.
- Kim Larsen, "Net Lift Models: Optimizing the Impact of Your Marketing," Workshop at Predictive Analytics World San Francisco Conference, San Francisco, CA, March 9, 2012. www.predictiveanalyticsworld.com/uplift.

**Measuring impact in sociology:**

- James J. Heckman and Richard Robb Jr., "Alternative Methods for Evaluating the Impact of Interventions: An Overview," *Journal of Econometrics* 30, issues 1–2 (October–November 1985): 239–267. http://faculty.smu.edu/millimet/classes/eco7377/papers/heckman%20robb.pdf.

**Personalized medicine:**

- Brian Claggett, Lihui Zhao, Lu Tian, Davide Castagno, and L. J. Wei, "Estimating Subject-Specific Treatment Differences for Risk-Benefit Assessment with Competing Risk Event-Time Data," Harvard University Biostatistics Working Paper Series, Working Paper 125, March 2011. biostats.bepress.com/harvardbiostat/paper125.
- Ross E. McKinney Jr., MD, George M. Johnson, MD, Kenneth Stanley, MD, Florence H. Yong, MS, Amy Keller, Karen J. O'Donnell, PhD, Pim Brouwers, PhD, Wendy G. Mitchell, MD, Ram Yogev, MD, Diane W. Wara, MD, Andrew Wiznia, MD, Lynne Mofenson, MD, James McNamara, MD, and Stephen A. Spector, MD, the Pediatric AIDS Clinical Trials Group Protocol 300 Study Team, "A Randomized Study of Combined Zidovudine-Lamivudine versus Didanosine Monotherapy in Children with Symptomatic Therapy-Naive HIV-1 Infection," *Journal of Pediatrics* 133, issue 4 (October 1998): 500–508. www.sciencedirect.com/science/article/pii/S0022347698700575.
- Ron Winslow, "Major Shift in War on Cancer: Drug Studies Focus on Genes of Individual Patients; Testing Obstacles Loom," *Wall Street Journal*, June 5, 2011. http://online.wsj.com/article/SB10001424052702304432304576367802580935000.html.
- Ilya Lipkovich, Alex Dmitrienko, Jonathan Denne, and Gregory Enas, "Subgroup Identification Based on Differential Effect Search—A Recursive Partitioning Method for Establishing Response to Treatment in Patient Subpopulations," *Statistics in Medicine* 30, issue 21 (September 20, 2011): 2601–2621. onlinelibrary.wiley.com/doi/10.1002/sim.4289/abstract.
- J. C. Foster, J. M. Taylor, and S. J. Ruberg, "Subgroup Identification from Randomized Clinical Trial Data," U.S. National Library of Medicine National Institute of Health, *Statistics in Medicine* 30, no. 24 (October 30, 2011): 2867–2880. doi:10.1002/sim.4322. Epub, August 4, 2011. www.ncbi.nlm.nih.gov/pubmed/21815180.
- Xiaogang Su, Chih-Ling Tsai, Hansheng Wang, David M. Nickerson, and Bogong Li, "Subgroup Analysis via Recursive Partitioning," *Journal of Machine Learning Research* 10 (2009): 141–158. http://jmlr.csail.mit.edu/papers/volume10/su09a/su09a.pdf.
- Andrew Pollack, "A Push to Tie New Drugs to Testing," *New York Times*, December 26, 2011. www.nytimes.com/2011/12/27/health/pressure-to-link-drugs-and50-companion-diagnostics.html.

**Social influence on mobile phone customer cancellations:**

- Auren Hoffman, "Birds of a Feather Use the Same Phone Service Provider," Summation.com blog post, November 4, 2009. http://blog.summation.net/2009/11/birds-of-a-feather-use-the-same-phone-service-provider.html.

**More on uplift modeling:**

- Victor S. Y. Lo, "New Opportunities in Marketing Data Mining," in *Encyclopedia of Data Warehousing and Mining*, 2nd ed. (Idea Group Publishing). doi:10.4018/978-1-60566-010-3.ch218, ISBN13: 9781605660103, ISBN10: 1605660108, EISBN13: 9781605660110. www.irma-international.org/viewtitle/11006/.

- Nicholas Radcliffe, "Generating Incremental Sales: Maximizing the Incremental Impact of Cross-Selling, Up-Selling and Deep-Selling through Uplift Modelling," Stochastic Solutions Limited, February 16, 2008. http://stochasticsolutions.com/cross-sellPaper.html.

- Nicholas Radcliffe, "Nicholas Radcliffe's Uplift Modeling FAQ," Scientific Marketer blog post, September 27, 2007. http://scientificmarketer.com/2007/09/uplift-modelling-faq.html.

- Nicholas Radcliffe, "Hillstrom's MineThatData Email Analytics Challenge: An Approach Using Uplift Modelling," Stochastic Solutions Limited, May 4, 2008. http://stochastic solutions.com/etailPaper.html.

- Nicholas Radcliffe, "Uplift Modelling: You Should Not Only Measure but Model Incremental Response," Predictive Analytics World London Conference 2010, November 15, 2010, London, UK. www.predictiveanalyticsworld.com/london/2010/agenda.php#day1–16.

- Neil Skilling, "Uplift Modelling: You Should Not Only Measure but Model Incremental Response," Predictive Analytics World London Conference 2011, December 1, 2011, London, UK. www.predictiveanalyticsworld.com/london/2011/agenda.php#day2–10.

- Kathleen Kane, Victor S. Y. Lo, Jane Zheng, and Alex Arias-Vargas, "True-Lift Modeling: Mining for the Most Truly Responsive Customers and Prospects," Predictive Analytics World San Francisco Conference March 14, 2011, San Francisco, CA. www.predictiveanalyticsworld.com/sanfrancisco/2011/agenda.php#day1–12b.

- Kim Larsen, "Response Modeling Is the Wrong Modelling: Maximize Impact with Net Lift Modeling," Predictive Analytics World San Francisco Conference 2010, February 17, 2010, San Francisco, CA. www.predictiveanalyticsworld.com/sanfrancisco/2010/agenda.php#day2–2.

- Eric Siegel, PhD, "Persuasion by the Numbers: Optimize Marketing Influence by Predicting It," Predictive Analytics World San Francisco Conference 2012, March 4, 2012, San Francisco, CA. www.predictiveanalyticsworld.com/sanfrancisco/2012/agenda.php#keynote-es.

- Patrick Surry, "Predict Who Is Persuadable Before You Market," Predictive Analytics World Chicago Conference 2012, June 25, 2012, Chicago, IL. www.predictiveanalyticsworld.com/chicago/2012/agenda.php#day1–45.

**Sidebar—How Persuasion Modeling Helped Obama Win:**

- Thanks to Rayid Ghani for valuable interviews that informed this sidebar.

- Christi Parsons and Kathleen Hennessey, "Obama campaign's investment in data crunching paid off." Los Angeles Times, November 13, 2012. http://articles.latimes.com/2012/nov/13/nation/la-na-obama-analytics-20121113.

- Michael Scherer, "Inside the Secret World of the Data Crunchers Who Helped Obama Win." TIME Magazine, November 07, 2012. http://swampland.time.com/2012/11/07/inside-the-secret-world-of-quants-and-data-crunchers-who-helped-obama-win/.

- Colbert Nation, www.colbertnation.com. Stephen Colbert interviews Nate Silver, New York Times blogger about his book, The Signal and the Noise: Why So Many Predictions Fail—but Some Don't. http://www.colbertnation.com/the-colbert-report-videos/420765/november-05-2012/nate-silver.

- Peggy Noonan, "They've Lost That Lovin' Feeling." Wall Street Journal, July 30, 2011. http://online.wsj.com/article/SB10001424053111904800304576474620336602248.html.

- Jack Gillum, "Mitt Romney Uses Secretive Data Mining To Identify Wealthy Donors." *Huffington Post*, August 24, 2012. www.huffingtonpost.com/2012/08/24/mitt-romney-data-mining_n_1827318.html.

# CENTRAL TABLES

## Family and Personal Life—Central Table 1

### Nokia:

- David Talbot, "A Phone That Knows Where You're Going," *Technology Review Online*, July 8, 2012. www.technologyreview.com/news/428441/a-phone-that-knows-where-youre-going/.
- Nokia Data Center, Nokia Mobile Data Challenge. http://research.nokia.com/page/12000.
- KDnuggets, "Nokia Mobile Data Challenge: Your Friends Determine Where You Are Going," July 2012. www.kdnuggets.com/2012/07/nokia-mobile-data-challenge.html.
- Albert-László Barabási, "Human Behavior Is 93 Percent Predictable, Research Shows," PhysOrg.com, February 23, 2010. http://phys.org/news186174216.html.

### Microsoft:

- Adam Sadilek and John Krumm, "Far Out: Predicting Long-Term Human Mobility," Microsoft Research, April 4, 2012. http://research.microsoft.com/en-us/um/people/jckrumm/Publications%202012/Sadilek-Krumm_Far-Out_AAAI-2012.pdf.

### Facebook:

- Kaggle, "Facebook Recruiting Competition," June 5, 2012. www.kaggle.com/c/FacebookRecruiting.

### LinkedIn:

- Manu Sharma, Principal Research Scientist, LinkedIn, "Iterative, Big Data Analytics and You," Predictive Analytics World New York City Conference, October 19, 2011, New York, NY. www.predictiveanalyticsworld.com/newyork/2011/agenda.php#track1-lnk.

### More on predicting who you may know (i.e., predicting edges in social network):

- Kaggle, "IJCNN Social Network Challenge," November 8, 2010. www.kaggle.com/c/socialnetwork.

### Match.com:

- Amarnath Thombre, Vice President of Strategy and Analytics, Match.com, "Intelligent Matching at Match.com," Predictive Analytics World New York City Conference, October 20, 2011, New York, NY. www.predictiveanalyticsworld.com/newyork/2011/agenda.php#track2-9.

### OkCupid.com:

- Christian Rudder, "Exactly What to Say in a First Message," OkTrends from OkCupid.com, September 14, 2009. http://blog.okcupid.com/index.php/online-dating-advice-exactly-what-to-say-in-a-first-message/.

**Target:**

- Andrew Pole, Senior Manager, Media and Database Marketing, Target, "How Target Gets the Most out of Its Guest Data to Improve Marketing ROI," Predictive Analytics World Washington, DC, Conference, October 18, 2010, Washington, DC. www .predictiveanalyticsworld.com/dc/2010/agenda.php#day1–8a.
- Charles Duhigg, "How Companies Learn Your Secrets," *New York Times Magazine*, February 16, 2012. www.nytimes.com/2012/02/19/magazine/shopping-habits.html.

**University researchers (infidelity):**

- Meredith Melnick, "Study: Predicting Whether a Partner Will Cheat Could Be Gender-Specific," *Time Magazine Online*, Healthland, July 29, 2011. http://healthland.time.com/ 2011/07/29/study-predicting-if-a-partner-will-cheat-is-gender-specific/.
- Bonny Albo, "Can You Predict Cheating?" About.com Dating, June 11, 2012. http:// dating.about.com/b/2011/06/01/predicting-infidelity.htm.
- Christine E. Garver-Apgar, Steven W. Gangestad, Randy Thornhill, Robert D. Miller, and Jon J. Olp, "Major Histocompatibility Complex Alleles, Sexual Responsivity, and Unfaithfulness in Romantic Couples," *Psychological Science Research Report*, October 2006. http://psy2.ucsd.edu/~mgorman/garver.pdf.
- World Science Report, "Genes May Help Predict Infidelity, Study Reports," World Science Online, November 30, 2006. www.world-science.net/exclusives/061128_infidelity-genes .htm.

**Clinical researchers (divorce):**

- Ian Ayres, *Super Crunchers: Why Thinking-by-Numbers Is the New Way to Be Smart* (Bantam Dell, 2007). www.amazon.com/Super-Crunchers-Thinking-Numbers-Smart/dp/055380 5401#reader_0553805401.
- Richard E. Heyman and Amy M. Smith Slep, "The Hazards of Predicting Divorce without Crossvalidation," NCBI PubMed Central, *Journal of Marriage and Family*. Author manuscript; available in PMC October 25, 2006; published in final edited form as: *Journal of Marriage and Family* 63, no. 2 (May 2001): 473–479. doi:10.1111/j.1741-3737.2001 .00473.x. www.ncbi.nlm.nih.gov/pmc/articles/PMC1622921/.
- Rose McDermott, James H. Fowler, and Nicholas A. Christakis, "Breaking Up Is Hard to Do, Unless Everyone Else Is Doing It Too: Social Network Effects on Divorce in a Longitudinal Sample Followed for 32 Years," Social Science Research Network Online (SSRN), October 18, 2009. http://papers.ssrn.com/sol3/papers.cfm?abstract_id=1490708.
- Justin Wolfers, "Assessing Your Divorce Risk," Freakonomics.com, December 2, 2008. www.freakonomics.com/2008/12/02/assessing-your-divorce-risk/.
- Divorce360.com, "Marriage Calculator—Calculate Your Chances of Getting Divorced." www.divorce360.com/content/divorcecalculator.aspx.
- Dr. John Gottman, Gottman Relationship Institute, "Research FAQs Online." www .gottman.com/49853/Research-FAQs.html.
- James Bailey, "Driven by Data: Your Bank Can Predict Your Divorce," *Forbes Magazine Online*, November 15, 2011. www.forbes.com/sites/techonomy/2011/11/15/driven-by-data-your-bank-can-predict-your-divorce/ (*this has been denied and is unsubstantiated but is included here as food for thought*).

# Marketing, Advertising, and the Web—Central Table 2

**PREMIER Bankcard:**
- Rex Pruitt, "The Sweet Spot: PREMIER Bankcard Lifts Revenue with SAS Business Analysis," SAS Success Online. www.sas.com/success/premierbankcard.html.
- Rex Pruitt, "Using Base SAS and SAS Enterprise Miner to Develop Customer Retention Modeling," SAS Global Forum 2009. http://support.sas.com/resources/papers/proceedings09/278–2009.pdf.

**First Tennessee Bank:**
- Dan Marks, First Tennessee Bank, "First Tennessee Bank: Analytics Drives Higher ROI from Marketing Programs," IBM.com, March 9, 2011. www.ibm.com/smarterplanet/us/en/leadership/firsttennbank/assets/pdf/IBM-firstTennBank.pdf.

**Target:**
- Andrew Pole, Target, "How Target Gets the Most out of Its Guest Data to Improve Marketing ROI," Predictive Analytics World Washington, DC, Conference, October 19, 2010, Washington, DC. www.predictiveanalyticsworld.com/dc/2010/agenda.php#day1–8a.

**Harbor Sweets:**
- Kate DeBevois, "Harbor Sweets' Billie Phillips on Driving Off-Season Sales," Target Marketing Online, July 2008. www.targetmarketingmag.com/article/harbor-sweets-billie-phillips-driving-off-season-sales-111219/1#.

**Fingerhut:**
- David L. Olson, "Data Mining," University of Nebraska, Lincoln, Korea Telecom: KM1, Slide 7. http://cbafiles.unl.edu/public/cbainternal/facStaffUploads/KM1DM.ppt.
- Michael J. A. Berry and Gordon S. Linoff, *Mastering Data Mining: The Art and Science of Customer Relationship Management* (Wiley Computer Publishing, 2000). www.amazon.com/Mastering-Data-Mining-Relationship-Management/dp/0471331236#reader_0471331236.

**Vermont Country Store:**
- Michael J. A. Berry and Gordon S. Linoff, *Mastering Data Mining: The Art and Science of Customer Relationship Management* (Wiley Computer Publishing, 2000). www.amazon.com/Mastering-Data-Mining-Relationship-Management/dp/0471331236# reader_0471331236.

**Harrah's Las Vegas:**
- Gary Loveman, "Diamonds in the Data Mine," *Harvard Business Review: The Magazine*, May 2003. http://hbr.org/2003/05/diamonds-in-the-data-mine/ar/1.

**Cox Communications:**
- Jim Ericson, "Perfect Pitch," *Information Management*, April 22, 2008. www.information-management.com/specialreports/2008_73/-10001184–1.html.
- Bob Wood, Cox Communications, "Cox Communications: What Happens Next? Automated Smart Demand Forecasting," Predictive Analytics World New York Conference 2011, October 19, 2011, New York, NY. www.predictiveanalyticsworld.com/newyork/2011/agenda.php#track2–2.

**Mutual Fund Investment Management Firm:**

- Thanks to Rexer Analytics (www.rexeranalytics.com) for this case study.

**UK supermarket:**

- Kaggle, "Predicting Grocery Shoppers' Spending Habits," Competition, July 29, 2011. www.kaggle.com/host/casestudies/dunnhumby.

**Elie Tahari:**

- Robert L. Mitchell, "How BI Is Helping to Predict Fashion Trends," *Computer World Online*, September 12, 2011. www.computerworld.com/s/article/357932/The_Art_Science_of_Fashion.

**PREMIER Bankcard:**

- Rex Pruitt, "The Sweet Spot: PREMIER Bankcard Lifts Revenue with SAS Business Analysis," SAS Success Online. www.sas.com/success/premierbankcard.html.
- Rex Pruitt, "Using Base SAS and SAS Enterprise Miner to Develop Customer Retention Modeling," SAS Global Forum 2009. http://support.sas.com/resources/papers/proceedings09/278–2009.pdf.

**FedEx:**

- Rick Whiting, "Businesses Mine Data to Predict What Happens Next," *InformationWeek*, May 29, 2006. www.informationweek.com/businesses-mine-data-to-predict-what-hap/188500520.

**Optus (Australia):**

- Thanks to Tim Manns. For details, see the Predictive Analytics World presentation: Tim Manns, "Know Your Customers by Knowing Who They Know, and Who They Don't: Leveraging the Power of Social Interaction." www.predictiveanalyticsworld.com/TimManns_CaseStudyOptus.pdf.

**Sprint:**

- Junxiang Lu, PhD, Sprint Communications Company, "Predicting Customer Churn in the Telecommunications Industry—An Application of Survival Analysis Modeling Using SAS," SAS Institute Inc., SUGI 27, Data Mining Techniques, Paper 114-27. *Proceedings of the Twenty-Seventh Annual SAS Users Group International Conference* (Cary, NC: SAS Institute Inc., 2002). www2.sas.com/proceedings/sugi27/p114–27.pdf.

**Telenor (Norway):**

- Suresh Vittal, "Optimizing Customer Retention Programs," Forrester Research White Paper, 2008. www.portraitsoftware.com/resources/white-papers/optimizing-customer-retention-programs.
- Suresh Vittal, "Optimal Targeting through Uplift Modeling: Generating Higher Demand and Increasing Customer Retention While Reducing Marketing Costs," Forrester Research White Paper, 2008. www.portraitsoftware.com/resources/white_papers/optimal-targeting-through-uplift-modeling.
- Eric Siegel, PhD, "Uplift Modeling: Predictive Analytics Can't Optimize Marketing Decisions without It," Prediction Impact, Inc. White Paper, June 29, 2011. www.predictiveanalyticsworld.com/signup-uplift-whitepaper.php.

**2degrees (New Zealand):**

- 11Ants Analytics Customer Case Studies, "2degrees Case Study: 1275% Boost in Churn Identification at 2degrees with 11Ants Customer Churn Analyzer." www.11antsanalytics .com/casestudies/2degrees_casestudy.aspx.

**Lloyds TSB:**

- Dr. Patrick Surry, PBS, "Gaining a Competitive Advantage through Improved Customer Experience," Insurance-Canada.ca, sponsored by Pitney Bowes Software, April 26, 2012. www.insurance-canada.ca/social-business/webinars/presentations/PBS-Webinar-Gaining-a-Competitive-Advantage.pdf.
- Nicholas Radcliffe, "Uplift Modelling: You Should Not Only Measure but Model Incremental Response," Predictive Analytics World London Conference, November 15, 2010, London, UK. www.predictiveanalyticsworld.com/london/2010/agenda.php#day1–16.

**Reed Elsevier:**

- John McConnell, "Predicting Renewal Propensities for (and Segmenting) RBI Magazine Subscribers," Analytical People, 2009. Thanks to John McConnell, Analytical People (www.analyticalpeople.com), for this case study. For details, see the Predictive Analytics World presentation: www.predictiveanalyticsworld.com/JohnMcConnell_CaseStudy ReedElsevier.pdf.

**IBM:**

- Tim Daciuk, IBM, and Bob Humphreys, IBM Canada, "IBM: If We Host It, Will They Come? Predictive Modeling for Event Marketing," Predictive Analytics World Toronto Conference 2012, April 26, 2012, Toronto, Canada. www.predictiveanalyticsworld.com/ toronto/2012/agenda.php#day2–17.

**Hewlett-Packard:**

- Govindarajan Krishnaswamy, Aparna Seshadri, and Ronobijay Bhaumik, Hewlett-Packard, "Hewlett-Packard Behavioral Analysis of Account Purchases and Their Predictability," Predictive Analytics World Boston Conference 2012, October 2, 2012, Boston, MA. www.predictiveanalyticsworld.com/boston/2012/agenda.php#day1–255b.

**Bella Pictures:**

- Lauren McKay, "Decisions, Decisions," *CRM Magazine Online* (CRM.com), May 2009. www.destinationcrm.com/Articles/Editorial/Magazine-Features/Decisions-Decisions-53700.aspx.

**Paychex:**

- Frank Fiorille, Paychex, "Paychex Staying One Step Ahead of the Competition—Development of a Predictive 401(k) Marketing and Sales Campaign," Predictive Analytics World Washington, DC, Conference 2010, October 19, 2010, Washington, DC. www.predictiveanalyticsworld.com/dc/2010/agenda.php#day1–12.

**Sun Microsystems:**

- Eric Siegel, PhD, Prediction Impact, Inc., "Six Ways to Lower Costs with Predictive Analytics," B-eye-network.com, January 5, 2010. www.b-eye-network.com/view/12269.

- Jim Porzak and Alex Kriney, Sun Microsystems, "Sun Microsystems Marrying Prediction and Segmentation to Drive Sales Leads," Predictive Analytics World San Francisco Conference 2009, February 19, 2009, San Francisco, CA. www.predictiveanalyticsworld .com/sanfrancisco/2009/agenda.php#sun.

**Amazon.com:**

- Matt Marshall, "Aggregate Knowledge Raises $5M from Kleiner, on a Roll," Venture Beat Online, December 10, 2006. http://venturebeat.com/2006/12/10/aggregate-knowledge-raises-5m-from-kleiner-on-a-roll/.
- Greg Linden, Brent Smith, and Jeremy York, "Amazon.com Recommendations: Item-to-Item Collaborative Filtering," IEEE Computer Society 1089-7801/03, January/February 2003. www.cs.umd.edu/~samir/498/Amazon-Recommendations.pdf.
- USPTO Patent Full-Text and Image Database, "Collaborative Recommendations Using Item-to-Item Similarity Mappings," United States Patent 6,266,649, Linden et al., July 24, 2001. www.google.com/patents/US6266649.

**Netflix:**

- Eric Siegel, PhD, "Casual Rocket Scientists: An Interview with a Layman Leading the Netflix Prize, Martin Chabbert," September 2009. www.predictiveanalyticsworld.com/layman-netflix-leader.php.

**Tesco (UK):**

- Thanks to Giley Pavey, Head of Innovation and Retail Solutions at dunnhumby, for this case study. For more, see www.tescomedia.com/ or www.dunnhumby.com/uk/about-us-what-we-do.

**More cases of predictively couponing at point of sale from Kmart, Kroger, Ralph's, Safeway, Stop & Shop, Target, and Winn-Dixie:**

- Doug Henschen, "Catalina Marketing Aims for the Cutting Edge of 'Big Data,'" *InformationWeek*, September 14, 2011. www.informationweek.com/global-cio/interviews/catalina-marketing-aims-for-the-cutting/231600833.
- SAS Customer Success, "Catalina Marketing Helps Predict Customer Behavior with SAS," SAS Customer Success, modified October 19, 2012. www.sas.com/success/catalina.html.

**Target:**

- Andrew Pole, Target, "How Target Gets the Most out of Its Guest Data to Improve Marketing ROI," Predictive Analytics World Washington, DC, Conference, October 19, 2010, Washington, DC. www.predictiveanalyticsworld.com/dc/2010/agenda .php#day1-8a.

**U.S. Bank:**

- Michael Grundhoefer, U.S. Bank, "US Bank Raising the Bar in Cross-Sell Marketing with Uplift Modeling," Predictive Analytics World Washington, DC, Conference 2009, October 20, 2009, Washington, DC. www.predictiveanalyticsworld.com/dc/2009/agenda.php#day1-14.

**Pandora:**

- Linda Tischler, "Algorhythm and Blues: How Pandora's Matching Service Cuts the Chaos of Digital Music," *FastCompany.com*, December 1, 2005. www.fastcompany.com/54817/algorhythm-and-blues.

**Google:**

- Google is famously tight-lipped about the degree to which machine learning (predictive modeling) is employed to improve search ranking by learning from user feedback and clicks. However, in 2011, Google's "search quality gurus," describing an update (called Panda) to Google search ranking methodology to *Wired* magazine (cf. the citation below), said they designed a method to "look for signals that recreate . . . that same experience [of user satisfaction]". They "came up with a classifier" by working to "find a plane [in hyperspace] which says that most things on this side of the place are red, and most of the things on that side of the plane are the opposite of red." This is descriptive and definitional of machine learning.
- Steven Levy, "TED 2011: The 'Panda' That Hates Farms: A Q&A with Google's Top Search Engineers," Steven Levy interview with Amit Singhal and Matt Cutts of Google, March 3, 2011. www.wired.com/business/2011/03/the-panda-that-hates-farms/all/.
- Aaron Wheeler, "How Google's Panda Update Changed SEO Best Practices Forever—Whiteboard Friday," Daily SEO blog, June 23, 2011. www.seomoz.org/blog/how-googles-panda-update-changed-seo-best-practices-forever-whiteboard-friday.
- Peter van der Graff, "How Search Engines Use Machine Learning for Pattern Detection," Search Engine Watch, December 1, 2011. http://searchenginewatch.com/article/2129359/How-Search-Engines-Use-Machine-Learning-for-Pattern-Detection.

**Education portal:**

- "Case Study: How Predictive Analytics Generates $1 Million Increased Revenue," case study provided by Prediction Impact, Inc. www.predictiveanalyticsworld.com/casestudy.php.

**Google:**

- D. Sculley, Robert Malkin, Sugato Basu, and Roberto J. Bayardo, "Predicting Bounce Rates in Sponsored Search Advertisements," Proceedings of the 15th ACM SIGKDD International Conference on Knowledge Discovery and Data Mining, 2009. www.bayardo.org/ps/kdd2009.pdf.
- Sugato Basu, Ph.D., Google. *"Lessons Learned in Predictive Modeling for Ad Targeting,"* Predictive Analytics World San Francisco 2011 Conference, March 14, 2011, San Francisco, CA. www.predictiveanalyticsworld.com/sanfrancisco/2011/agenda.php#day1-7.

**MTV:**

- "Why Lean and Hungry Entrepreneurs Succeed," *Futurist Update Magazine* 13, no. 5 (May 2012). www.wfs.org/futurist-update/futurist-update-2012-issues/may-2012-vol-13-no-5#1.

**Google:**

- Google.com, "About Gmail: So Much Time, So Little Spam." https://mail.google.com/mail/help/intl/en/fightspam/spamexplained.html.

**Researchers:**

- Sitaram Asur and Bernardo A. Huberman, Social Computing Lab, HP Lab, "Predicting the Future with Social Media," April 8, 2010. www.hpl.hp.com/research/scl/papers/socialmedia/socialmedia.pdf.
- Mark Brown, "Pop Hit Prediction Algorithm Mines 50 Years of Chart-Toppers for Data," *Wired Magazine Online*, December 19, 2011. www.wired.com/underwire/2011/12/hit-potential-equation/.
- Malcolm Gladwell, "The Formula," *New Yorker Magazine Online*, October 16, 2006. www.newyorker.com/archive/2006/10/16/061016fa_fact6.

## Financial Risk and Insurance—Central Table 3

**Allstate:**

- Kaggle, Allstate, "Predicting Liability for Injury from Car Accidents," Competition, April 13, 2012. www.kaggle.com/host/casestudies/allstate. Here is how the $40 million estimate is derived. Allstate's 2010 annual report puts bodily injury claims at roughly $1.6 billion. Industry insiders suggest 20 percent of bodily injury claims actuarially relate to vehicle. If we assume that a 1 percent improvement in error rate impacts claims costs by 0.25 percent, even just doubling the accuracy comes to a $40 million savings. See also www.iihs.org/research/hldi/fact_sheets/BodilyInjury_0911.pdf.

**Accident Fund Insurance:**

- Zubair Shams, Accident Fund Insurance Company of America, "Accident Fund Using Text Analytics to Accurately Segment Workers' Compensation Injuries," Text Analytics World New York City Conference, October 20, 2011, New York, NY. www.textanalyticsworld.com/newyork/2011/agenda/full-agenda#track1–5.

**Leading international commercial lines insurance provider:**

- This was from a case study at a conference presentation; however, the insurance company later rescinded authorization to be named in connection with this example. Here is a reference on the general principle that predictive modeling improves upon standard actuarial methods: Guillaume Briere-Giroux, FSA, MAAA, CFA, "Predictive Modeling Applied to Variable Annuity Lapse Rates," Predictive Modeling for Variable Annuities, Towers Watson neac 11182010. www.claudepenland.com/2011/02/12/predictive-modeling-applied-to-variable-annuity-lapse-rates/.

**Life insurance companies:**

- Dr. Thomas Ashley, Dr. Guizhou Hu, and Chris Stehno, "Does Mortality Modeling Affect Life Insurance Preferred Risk Selection?" ReFocus Conference, Las Vegas, NV, March 14, 2011. www.soa.org/files/pd/2011-lv-refocus-b3.pdf.
- Guizhou Hu, MD, PhD, "Mortality Assessment Technology: A New Tool for Life Insurance Underwriting," May 23, 2002. www.knowyournumber.com/pdf/MAT_Validation_NHANES1.pdf.
- Yuhong (Jason) Xue, FSA, MAAA, "Predictive Modeling as Applied to Life Insurance," Predictive Modelling SOA Annual Meeting 2008, October 21, 2008. www.claudepenland.com/2011/02/12/predictive-modeling-as-applied-to-life-insurance/.

**Chase:**
- See the detailed case study in Chapter 4.
- Ali Moazami and Shaolin Li, "Mortgage Business Transformation Program Using CART-Based Joint Risk Modeling (and Including a Practical Discussion of TreeNet)," Salford Systems Data Mining 2005, New York, May 10, 2005. www.salford-systems .com/doc/MoazamiLi.pdf.

**Citigroup:**
- Stephan Kudyba, *Managing Data Mining: Advice from Experts* (Cybertech Publishing, 2004).

**Canadian Tire:**
- Charles Duhigg, "What Does Your Credit-Card Company Know about You?" *New York Times Online*, May 12, 2009. www.nytimes.com/2009/05/17/magazine/17credit-t.html.

**PREMIER Bankcard:**
- Rex Pruitt, "The Sweet Spot: PREMIER Bankcard Lifts Revenue with SAS Business Analysis," SAS Success Online. www.sas.com/success/premierbankcard.html.
- Rex Pruitt, "Using Base SAS and SAS Enterprise Miner to Develop Customer Retention Modeling," SAS Global Forum 2009. http://support.sas.com/resources/papers/ proceedings09/278–2009.pdf.

**Brasil Telecom (now Oi, which means "hi"):**
- Carlos André R. Pinheiro, Alexandre G. Evsukoff, and Nelson F. F. Ebecken, "Revenue Recovering with Insolvency Prevention on a Brazilian Telecom Operator," SIGKDD Explorations, June 1, 2006. www.sigkdd.org/explorations/issues/8–1–2006–06/9-Pinheiro .pdf.

**DTE Energy:**
- Ozgur Tuzcu, Risk Manager, DTE Energy, as told to Colin Beasty, "Predicting Debt," *CRM Magazine*, December 2007. www.destinationcrm.com/Articles/Columns-Departments/ Secret-of-My-Success/Predicting-Debt-46927.aspx.

**Financial institutions:**
- Don Davey, "Collect More for Less: Strategic Predictive Analytics Is Key to Growing Collections and Reducing Costs," First Data White Paper, April 2009. www.firstdata .com/downloads/thought-leadership/fd_collectmoreforless_whitepaper.pdf.

**London Stock Exchange:**
- "Black Box Traders Are on the March," *The Telegraph*, August 27, 2006. www.telegraph .co.uk/finance/2946240/Black-box-traders-are-on-the-march.html#disqus_thread.
- Kendall Kim, *Electronic and Algorithmic Trading Technology* (Elsevier, 2007) www.elsevier .com/wps/find/bookdescription.cws_home/711644/description#description.

**John Elder:**
- See Chapter 1 for this case study.
- For a short autobiographical essay by John Elder, see: Mohamed Medhat Gaber, *Journeys to Data Mining: Experiences from 15 Renowned Researchers* (Springer, 2012), 61–76.

**Various firms:**
- Dave Andre, PhD, Cerebellum Capital, "Black Box Trading: Analytics in the Land of the Vampire Squid," Predictive Analytics World San Francisco Conference, March 14, 2011, San Francisco, CA. www.predictiveanalyticsworld.com/sanfrancisco/2011/agenda .php#day1–8a.
- Spencer Greenberg, Rebellion Research, "Humans, Rules & Machine Learning: Three Prediction Paradigms," Prediction Analytics World New York City Conference, October 20, 2011, New York, NY. www.predictiveanalyticsworld.com/newyork/2011/agenda .php#track3–9.
- Randy Saaf, AlphaGenius, "Using Twitter & the Social Internet to Obtain Above Market Returns," Text Analytics World San Francisco Conference, March 7, 2012, San Francisco, CA. www.textanalyticsworld.com/sanfrancisco/2012/agenda/full-agenda# day1430–450–2.

# Healthcare—Central Table 4

**A top-five U.S. health insurance company:**
- This was disclosed to the author as a confidential discussion.
- See Chapter 2 for a few more details.

**Riskprediction.org.uk:**
- Jason J. Smith and Paris P. Tekkis, "Risk Prediction in Surgery," updated April 2010. http://riskprediction.org.uk/. This risk-calculation website includes many references— see http://riskprediction.org.uk/refs.php.

**For more recent examples of surgery mortality prediction, see:**
- C. Wu, F. T. Camacho, A. S. Wechsler, S. Lahey, A. T. Culliford, D. Jordan, J. P. Gold, R. S. Higgins, C. R. Smith, and E. L. Hannan, "Risk Score for Predicting Long-Term Mortality after Coronary Artery Bypass Graft Surgery," U.S. National Library of Medicine, National Institutes of Health, May 22, 2012. www.ncbi.nlm.nih.gov/pubmed/ 22547673.
- N. Fukuda, J. Wada, M. Niki, Y. Sugiyama, and H. Mushiake, "Factors Predicting Mortality in Emergency Abdominal Surgery in the Elderly," U.S. National Library of Medicine, National Institutes of Health, May 11, 2012. www.ncbi.nlm.nih.gov/ pubmed/22578159.
- Juan J. Fibla, corresponding author, Division of General Thoracic Surgery, Mayo Clinic; Alessandro Brunelli, Stephen D. Cassivi, and Claude Deschamps, "Aggregate Risk Score for Predicting Mortality after Surgical Biopsy for Interstitial Lung Disease," *Interactive CardioVascular and Thoracic Surgery*, May 17, 2012. http://icvts.oxfordjournals.org/content/ early/2012/05/17/icvts.ivs174.abstract.

**Google Flu Trends:**
- "Google Beats the CDC: Web Tool Predicts Flu-Related Ed Surge," Advisory Board Company, The Daily Briefing, January 13, 2012. www.advisory.com/Daily-Briefing/ 2012/01/13/Google-flu.

**Stanford University:**

- Sebastian Anthony, "Computer More Accurate Than Human Doctor at Breast Cancer Diagnosis," ExtremeTech Online, November 10, 2011. www.extremetech.com/extreme/104407-computer-more-accurate-than-human-doctor-at-breast-cancer-diagnosis.

- Andrew H. Beck, Ankur R. Sangoi, Samuel Leung, Robert J. Marinelli, Torsten O. Nielsen, Marc J. van de Vijver, Robert B. West, Matt van de Rijn, and Daphne Koller, "Systematic Analysis of Breast Cancer Morphology Uncovers Stromal Features Associated with Survival," *Science Magazine Online*; *Science Translational Medicine* 3, issue 108 (November 9, 2011): 108ra113. doi:10.1126/scitranslmed.3002564. http://stm.sciencemag.org/content/3/108/108ra113.

- Andrew Myers, "Stanford Team Trains Computer to Evaluate Breast Cancer," Stanford School of Medicine, November 9, 2011. http://med.stanford.edu/ism/2011/november/computer.html.

**Sisters of Mercy Health Systems:**

- Jeni Fan, "Framework for Detection of Clinical States & Disease Onset Using Electronic Health Record (EHR) Data," Predictive Analytics World San Francisco Conference, March 6, 2012, San Francisco, CA. www.predictiveanalyticsworld.com/sanfrancisco/2012/agenda.php#day2–30a.

**Researchers:**

- Kaggle, "Predict HIV Progression," Competition, April 27, 2010. https://www.kaggle.com/c/hivprogression/details/Background.

**Pfizer:**

- Max Kuhn, Pfizer, "Right Medicine, Right Patient," Predictive Analytics World San Francisco Conference, March 6, 2012, San Francisco, CA. www.predictiveanalyticsworld.com/sanfrancisco/2012/agenda.php#day2-hc4.

- Max Kuhn and Kjell Johnson, *Applied Predictive Modeling* (Springer-Verlag, 2013).

**Brigham Young University and University of Utah:**

- Heidi Toth, "Research Shows Progress in Predicting Premature Births," *Daily Herald*, April 20, 2011. www.heraldextra.com/news/local/central/provo/article_c13c1e9a-ef75–585d-a22f-8a09a3cbb500.html.

- M. Sean Esplin, MD, Karen Merrell, PhD, Robert Goldenberg, MD, Yinglei Lai, PhD, Jay D. Iams, MD, Brian Mercer, MD, Catherine Y. Spong, MD, Menachem Miodovnik, MD, Hygriv N. Simhan, MD, Peter van Dorsten, MD, and Mitchell Dombrowski, MD, Eunice Kennedy Shriver National Institute of Child Health and Human Development Maternal-Fetal Medicine Units Network, "Proteomic Identification of Serum Peptides Predicting Subsequent Spontaneous Preterm Birth," *American Journal of Obstetrics & Gynecology* 204, issue 5 (May 2011): 391.e1–391.e8. www.ajog.org/article/S0002–9378%2810%2901167–1/.

**Pfizer:**

- Pfizer, Inc. Case Study, "Pfizer Enlists CART to Score Male Erectile Dysfunction Diagnostic Test," Salford Systems. www.salford-systems.com/en/resources/case-studies/118-pfizer-inc.

**Heritage Provider Network:**

- Health Prize, "Improve Healthcare, Win $3,000,000," Competition, April 4, 2011. www.heritagehealthprize.com/c/hhp.

**University of Pittsburgh Medical Center:**

- Scott Zasadil, UPMC Health Plan, "A Predictive Model for Hospital Readmissions," Predictive Analytics World Washington, DC, Conference, October 19, 2010, Washington, DC. www.predictiveanalyticsworld.com/dc/2010/agenda.php#day1–17a.

**For more information regarding analytics and hospital admissions:**

- Peter Horner and Atanu Basu, "Analytics & the Future of Healthcare," *Analytics Magazine Online*, January/February 2012. www.analytics-magazine.org/januaryfebruary-2012/503-analytics-a-the-future-of-healthcare.

**FICO:**

- Todd Steffes, "Predictive Analytics: Saving Lives and Lowering Medical Bills," *Analytics Magazine*, Analytics Informs, January/February 2012. www.analytics-magazine.org/januaryfebruary-2012/505-predictive-analytics-saving-lives-and-lowering-medical-bills.

**GlaxoSmithKline (UK):**

- Vladimir Anisimov, GlaxoSmithKline, "Predictive Analytic Patient Recruitment and Drug Supply Modelling in Clinical Trials," Predictive Analytics World London Conference, November 30, 2011, London, UK. www.predictiveanalyticsworld.com/london/2011/agenda.php#day1–16.
- Vladimir V. Anisimov, "Statistical Modelling of Clinical Trials (Recruitment and Randomization)," *Communications in Statistics—Theory and Methods* 40, issue 19–20 (2011): 3684–3699. www.tandfonline.com/toc/lsta20/40/19–20.

**MultiCare Health System (four hospitals in Washington):**

- Karen Minich-Pourshadi for HealthLeaders Media, "Hospital Data Mining Hits Paydirt," HealthLeaders Media Online, November 29, 2010. www.healthleadersmedia.com/page-1/FIN-259479/Hospital-Data-Mining-Hits-Paydirt.

**Medical centers and healthcare providers:**

- Customer Potential Management Marketing Group, "Predictive Market Segmentation in Healthcare: Increasing the Effectiveness of Disease Prevention and Early Intervention," CMP White Paper, CiteSeer$^x_B$ Online, January 14, 2002. http://citeseerx.ist.psu.edu/viewdoc/summary?doi=10.1.1.134.756.

**Blue Cross Blue Shield of Tennessee:**

- Rick Whiting, "Businesses Mine Data to Predict What Happens Next," *InformationWeek*, May 29, 2006. www.informationweek.com/businesses-mine-data-to-predict-what-hap/188500520.

# Crime Fighting and Fraud Detection—Central Table 5

**Internal Revenue Service:**

- Case study described by John Elder and Cheryl Howard in Mohamed Medhat Gaber's *Journeys to Data Mining: Experiences from 15 Renowned Researchers* (Springer, 2012), 61.

**U.S. Department of Defense's Defense Finance and Accounting Service:**

- Thanks to Dean Abbott, Abbott Analytics (www.abbottanalytics.com), for this case study: "Case Study: Defense Finance and Accounting Service; Project Title: Invoice Fraud Detection." www.abbottanalytics.com/data-mining-case-study-1.php.
- Dean Abbott, Haleh Vafaie, PhD, Mark Hutchins, and David Riney, "Improper Payment Detection in Department of Defense Financial Transactions," Data Mining Symposium, Washington, DC, March 28–29, 2000. www.abbottanalytics.com/assets/pdf/Abbott-Analytics-Improper-Payment-Detection-2000.pdf.

**U.S. Postal Service:**

- Antonia de Medinaceli, "Fraud Detection: Fraught with Frightful Modeling Hurdles," Predictive Analytics World Chicago Conference, June 25, 2012, Chicago, IL. www.predictiveanalyticsworld.com/chicago/2012/agenda.php#day1–1040b.
- Shawn Hessinger, "Data Mining for Fraud at the US Postal Service," All Analytics Online, October 21, 2011. www.allanalytics.com/author.asp?section_id=1412&doc_id=234817.

**Citizens Bank:**

- Jay Zhou, "Building In-Database Predictive Scoring Model: Check Fraud Detection Case Study," Predictive Analytics World Washington, DC, Conference, October 20, 2009, Washington, DC. www.predictiveanalyticsworld.com/dc/2009/agenda.php#day1–19.

**$40+ billion U.S. insurance company:**

- Case study at a conference presentation; the insurance company later rescinded authorization to be named in connection with this example.

**Aviva Insurance (UK):**

- Thanks to Chekuri Swarochish of Capillary Technologies (www.capillary.sg) for this case study example (which was conducted with WNS for knowledge process outsourcing).

**Hewlett-Packard:**

- Joe Fallon, Investigations Manager, Hewlett-Packard, "Hewlett-Packard Warranty Fraud: Using Data Mining to Identify Fraud," presentation at Data Mining to Identify Fraud, an Association of Certified Fraud Examiners Boston Chapter Seminar, May 2010. http://rexeranalytics.com/ACFE-decks/ACFE_Presentation_Dist.pdf.

**U.S. Postal Service:**

- Antonia de Medinaceli, Director of Business Analytics and Fraud Detection, Elder Research, and Bryan Jones, Director, Data Mining Group, USPS OIG, Office of Investigations, "Fighting the Good Fraud Fight: USPS OIG Contract Fraud Detection." Predictive Analytics World for Government, Washington, DC Conference, September 13, 2011. www.predictiveanalyticsworld.com/gov/2011/agenda.php#day2-1020-1105.

**Maryland:**

- Nadya Labi, "Misfortune Teller," *The Atlantic*, January/February 2012. www.theatlantic.com/magazine/archive/2012/01/misfortune-teller/8846/.

**Chicago, Los Angeles, Memphis (TN), Richmond (VA), Santa Cruz (CA), and Vineland (NJ):**

- Melissae Fellet, "Cops on the Trail of Crimes That Haven't Happened," *New Scientist*, October 12, 2011. www.newscientist.com/article/mg21128333.400-cops-on-the-trail-of-crimes-that-havent-happened.html.
- Erica Goode, "Sending the Police Before There's a Crime," *New York Times on the Web*, August 15, 2011. www.nytimes.com/2011/08/16/us/16police.html.
- Stephen Hollifield, Information Services Manager, Richmond Police Department, "Curbing Crime with Predictive Analytics," Predictive Analytics World for Government Washington, DC, Conference, September 12, 2011, Washington, DC. www.predictiveanalyticsworld.com/gov/2011/agenda.php#day1–1115–1145.
- Carrie Kahn, "At LAPD, Predicting Crimes Before They Happen," National Public Radio Online, August 14, 2011. www.npr.org/2011/11/26/142758000/at-lapd-predicting-crimes-before-they-happen.
- Sergeant Christopher Fulcher, Vineland, NJ, Police Department, "To Predict and Serve: Predictive Intelligence Analysis." Part I, July 5, 2011, http://policeledintelligence.com/2011/07/05/to-predict-and-serve-predictive-intelligence-analysis-part-i/. Part II, July 6, 2011, http://policeledintelligence.com/2011/07/06/to-predict-and-serve-predictive-intelligence-analysis-part-ii/.
- Emily Badger, "How to Catch a Criminal with Data," Atlantic Cities Online, March 14, 2012. www.theatlanticcities.com/technology/2012/03/how-catch-criminal-data/1477/.
- Samuel Greengard, "Policing the Future," *Communications of the ACM* 55, no. 3 (March 2012), 19–21. http://cacm.acm.org/magazines/2012/3/146249-policing-the-future/abstract#comments.
- Nadya Labi, "Misfortune Teller," *The Atlantic*, January/February 2012. www.theatlantic.com/magazine/archive/2012/01/misfortune-teller/8846/.

**U.S. Armed Forces:**

- Neal Ungerleider, "A Computer Program That Predicts Terrorist Attacks," Co.EXIST. www.fastcoexist.com/1680540/a-computer-program-that-predicts-terrorist-attacks.
- A. Mannes, J. Shakarian, A. Sliva, and V. S. Subrahmanian, "A Computationally-Enabled Analysis of Lashkar-e-Taiba Attacks in Jammu & Kashmir," Laboratory for Computational Cultural Dynamics, July 1, 2011. https://lccd-content.umiacs.umd.edu/main/papers/let_eisic_camera.pdf.
- Ryan Jacobs, "Afghan War Games: Computer Scientists Accurately Predict Attacks," *Mother Jones Online*, July 30, 2012. www.motherjones.com/mojo/2012/07/afghan-war-games-researchers-predict-conflicts.
- *The Economist* Staff, "What Makes Heroic Strife: Computer Models That Can Predict the Outbreak and Spread of Civil Conflict Are Being Developed," *The Economist*, April 21, 2012. www.economist.com/node/21553006.
- Paulo Shakarian, Margo K. Nagel, Brittany E. Schuetzle, and V. S. Subrahmanian, "Abductive Inference for Combat: Using SCARE-S2 to Find High-Value Targets in

Afghanistan," Association for the Advancement of Artificial Intelligence, last modified August 4, 2011. www.aaai.org/ocs/index.php/IAAI/IAAI-11/paper/view/2740.

- Andrew Zammit-Mangion, Michael Dewar, Visakan Kadirkamanathan, and Guido Sanguinetti, "Point Process Modeling of the Afghan War Diary," *Proceedings of the National Academy of Sciences of the United States of America*, edited by Stephen E. Fienberg, Carnegie Mellon University, Pittsburgh, PA, and approved June 8, 2012 (received for review February 25, 2012). www.pnas.org/content/early/2012/07/11/1203177109.abstract.

**New York City:**
- Alex, Howard, "Predictive data analytics is saving lives and taxpayer dollars in New York City," O'Reilly, June 26, 2012. http://strata.oreilly.com/2012/06/predictive-data-analytics-big-data-nyc.html.

**Oregon and Pennsylvania:**
- Public Safety Checklist Website in Oregon, "The Public Safety Checklist for Oregon," Criminal Justice Commission, last updated August 11, 2012. https://risktool.ocjc.state.or.us/psc/.
- Nadya Labi, "Misfortune Teller," *The Atlantic*, January/February 2012. www.theatlantic.com/magazine/archive/2012/01/misfortune-teller/8846/.

**Chicago Police Department:**
- Megan A. Alderden and Timothy A. Lavery, "Predicting Homicide Clearances in Chicago: Investigating Disparities in Predictors across Different Types of Homicide," *Sage Journals Homicide Studies*, May 5, 2007. http://hsx.sagepub.com/content/11/2/115.abstract.

**Amazon.com:**
- Amazon Information Security Data Science Competition. http://sites.google.com/site/amazonaccessdatacompetition.

**Researchers (hacker and virus detection):**
- Chih-Fong Tsai, Yu-Feng Hsu, Chia-Ying Lin, and Wei-Yang Lin, "Intrusion Detection by Machine Learning: A Review." ScienceDirect Online, May 29, 2009. www.sciencedirect.com/science/article/pii/S0957417409004801.

**Reverse engineering spam filters:**
- Blaine Nelson, Marco Barreno, Fuching Jack Chi, Anthony D. Joseph, Benjamin I. P. Rubinstein, Udam Saini, Charles Sutton, J. D. Tygar, and Kai Xia, University of California, Berkeley, "Exploiting Machine Learning to Subvert Your Spam Filter," April 8, 2008. http://static.usenix.org/event/leet08/tech/full_papers/nelson/nelson_html/.

**Computers detect computer-generated text (for search engine spamming):**
- A. Lavoie and M. Krishnamoorthy, "Algorithmic Detection of Computer Generated Text," 2010. http://arxiv.org/abs/1008.0706v1.

# Fault Detection for Safety and Efficiency—Central Table 6

**Large commercial satellite company:**

- Thanks to Matthew Strampe at Elder Research, Inc. (www.datamininglab.com) for this case study. "Reliability Analytics: Predicting Equipment Failure," Predictive Analytics World San Francisco Conference, February 7, 2010, San Francisco, CA. www.predictiveanalyticsworld .com/sanfrancisco/2010/agenda.php#day2–12.

**Argonne National Laboratory:**

- S. Mohanty, S. Majumdar, and K. Natesan, "A Review of Stress Corrosion Cracking/ Fatigue Modeling for Light Water Reactor Cooling System Components," Argonne National Laboratory, June 2012. https://inlportal.inl.gov/portal/server.pt/document/ 106726/environmental_fatigue_pdf.
- Also see a related case study described in John Elder's chapter in Mohamed Medhat Gaber, *Journeys to Data Mining: Experiences from 15 Renowned Researchers* (Springer, 2012), 61–76.

**Con Edison:**

- Philip Gross, Albert Boulauger, Marta Arias, David Waltz, Philip M. Long, Charles Lawson, Roger Anders (Columbia University), Matthew Koenig, Mark Mastrocinque, William Fairechio, John A. Johnson, Serena Lee, Frank Doherty, and Arthur Kressner (Consolidated Edison Company of New York), "Predicting Electricity Distribution Feeder Failures Using Machine Learning Susceptibility Analysis," March 31, 2006. www .phillong.info/publications/GBAetal06_susc.pdf. This work has been partly supported by a research contract from Consolidated Edison.

**BNSF Railway:**

- C. Tyler Dick, Christopher P. L. Barkan, Edward R. Chapman, and Mark P. Stehly, "Multivariate Statistical Model for Predicting Occurrence and Location of Broken Rails," Transportation Research Board of the National Academies, January 26, 2007. http://trb .metapress.com/content/v2j6022171r41478/. See also: http://ict.uiuc.edu/railroad/cee/ pdf/Dick_et_al_2003.pdf.

**TTX:**

- Thanks to Mahesh Kumar at Tiger Analytics for this case study, "Predicting Wheel Failure Rate for Railcars."

**Fortune 500 global technology company:**

- Thanks to Dean Abbott, Abbot Analytics (http://abbottanalytics.com/index.php) for information about this case study. "Inductive Business-Rule Discovery in Text Mining." Text Analytics World San Francisco Conference, March 7, 2012, San Francisco, CA. www.textanalyticsworld.com/sanfrancisco/2012/agenda/full-agenda#day11040–11–2.

**Leading payments processor:**

- Thanks to Robert Grossman, Open Data Group (http://opendatagroup.com), for this case study. "Scaling Health and Status Models to Large, Complex Systems," Predictive Analytics World San Francisco Conference, February 16, 2010, San Francisco, CA. www .predictiveanalyticsworld.com/sanfrancisco/2010/agenda.php#day1–17.

**Universities in Iran:**

- Vahid K. Alilou and Mahammad Teshnehlab, "Prediction of 28-Day Compressive Strength of Concrete on the Third Day Using Artificial Neural Networks," *International Journal of Engineering (IJE)* 3, issue 6, February 2, 2010. www.cscjournals.org/csc/manuscript/Journals/IJE/volume3/Issue6/IJE-126.pdf.

**Poll: 18 percent of IT departments:**

- Esther Shein, "Predictive Analytics Key to Unlocking Big Data's Value, Reducing Cloud Complexity," Network Computing Online, March 8, 2012. www.networkcomputing.com/storage-networking-management/predictive-analytics-key-to-unlocking-bi/232602217.

**Washing machine manufacturer:**

- G. Dounias, G. Tselentis, and V. S. Moustakis, "Machine Learning Based Feature Extraction for Quality Control in a Production Line," *Integrated Computer Aided Engineering* 8, no. 4 (2001), 325–336. http://iospress.metapress.com/content/b2546qy4aqb8akty/.

**National Iranian South Oil Company:**

- A. Mirzaei-Paiaman and S. Salavati, "The Application of Artificial Neural Networks for the Prediction of Oil Production Flow Rate," *Taylor & Francis Online* 34, issue 19 (2012), 1834–1843. www.tandfonline.com/doi/abs/10.1080/15567036.2010.492386.

**Canadian Automobile Association:**

- Thanks to Richard Boire, BoireFillerGroup (www.boirefillergroup.com), for this case study. "The Diminishing Marginal Returns of Variable Creation in Predictive Analytics Solutions," Predictive Analytics World London Conference, November 15, 2010, London, UK. www.predictiveanalyticsworld.com/london/2010/agenda.php#day1–16a. For more, see: www.campana.com/axis/products/SSERS0308.pdf.

**Analytics leaders:**

- G. Miner, D. Delen, J. Elder, A. Fast, T. Hill, and B. Nisbet, *Practical Text Mining and Statistical Analysis for Non-Structured Data Text Applications* (Academic Press, 2012), Part II, Tutorial B, p. 181, by Jennifer Thompson and Thomas Hill.

**Continental Airlines:**

- Tim Grovac, PASSUR Aerospace, "Predicting the Health of Air Traffic Systems," Predictive Analytics World San Francisco Conference, February 17, 2010, San Francisco, CA. www.predictiveanalyticsworld.com/sanfrancisco/2010/agenda.php#day2–8.

**New South Wales, Australia:**

- Kaggle, "RTA Freeway Travel Time Prediction," Competition, November 23, 2010. www.kaggle.com/c/RTA.

**Nokia Siemens Networks:**

- Shirish Nagaraj and Kashyap Kamdar, Nokia Siemens Networks, "Understanding Mobile User Outages: Predictive Analytics in Wireless Broadband Networks," Predictive Analytics

World Chicago Conference, June 25, 2012, Chicago, IL. www.predictiveanalyticsworld
.com/chicago/2012/agenda.php#day2–1045b.

## Government, Politics, Nonprofit, and Education—Central Table 7

**Obama for America 2012 Campaign:**
- See the sidebar at the end of Chapter 7.

**Charlotte Rescue Mission:**
- JMP Statistical Discovery Customer Brief, "A Smarter Approach to Fundraising," August 9, 2011. www.jmp.com/software/success/pdf/102799_charlotte_rescue.pdf.

**The Nature Conservancy:**
- John Blackwell and Tracy DeCanio, The Nature Conservancy, "Successfully Implementing Predictive Analytics in Direct Marketing," NESUG 2009. www.nesug.org/Proceedings/nesug09/sa/sa09.pdf.

**JustGiving:**
- Mike Bugembe, JustGiving, "Analytics at JustGiving—Using Data to Unlock and Increase Individual Generosity," Predictive Analytics World London Conference, November 30, 2011, London, UK. www.predictiveanalyticsworld.com/london/2011/agenda.php#day1–8b.

**University of Utah's School of Business:**
- Rick Whiting, "Businesses Mine Data to Predict What Happens Next," *Information Week*, May 29, 2006. www.informationweek.com/businesses-mine-data-to-predict-what-hap/188500520.

**University of Melbourne:**
- Kaggle, University of Melbourne, "Predict Grant Applications," Competition, December 13, 2010. www.kaggle.com/c/unimelb.

**Energex (Australia):**
- Jared McKee, Energex, "Spatially Simulating Electricity Demand Growth," Predictive Analytics World London Conference, November 30, 2011, London, UK. www.predictiveanalyticsworld.com/london/2011/agenda.php#day1–9a.

**Kiva:**
- Danielle Muoio, "Students Compete in First Annual Duke DataFest," *Duke Chronicle*, April 16, 2012. www.dukechronicle.com/article/students-compete-first-annual-duke-datafest. For final results, see http://stat.duke.edu/datafest/results.
- G. Miner, D. Delen, J. Elder, A. Fast, T. Hill, and B. Nisbet, *Practical Text Mining and Statistical Analysis for Non-Structured Data Text Applications* (Academic Press, 2012), Part II, Tutorial K, p. 417, by Richard Foley of SAS.
- Tap directly into Kiva's loan database with the Kiva API: http://build.kiva.org.

**U.S. Social Security Administration:**

- Thanks to John Elder, PhD, Elder Research, Inc. (www.datamininglab.com), for this case study. John Elder, PhD, "Text Mining to Fast-Track Deserving Disability Applicants," Elder Research, Inc., August 7, 2010. http://videolectures.net/site/normal_dl/tag=73772/kdd2010_elder_tmft_01.pdf.
- John Elder, PhD, "Text Mining: Lessons Learned," Text Analytics World San Francisco Conference, March 7, 2012, San Francisco, CA. www.textanalyticsworld.com/sanfrancisco/2012/agenda/full-agenda#day1520–605.

**Infinity Insurance:**

- James Taylor, JT on EDM, "Putting Predictive Analytics to Work at Infinity Insurance," DecisionManagementSolutions.com, September 15, 2009. http://jtonedm.com/2009/09/15/putting-predictive-analytics-to-work-at-infinity-insurance/. Thanks to James Taylor, Decision Management Solutions (www.decisionmanagementsolutions.com), for this case study.
- James Taylor, "Putting Predictive Analytics to Work," Predictive Analytics World Washington, DC, Conference, October 19, 2009, Washington, DC. www.predictiveanalyticsworld.com/dc/2009/agenda.php#day1–5.

**British Broadcasting Corporation:**

- John McConnell, "Identifying and Helping the Most Vulnerable," Predictive Analytics World San Francisco Conference, February 16, 2010, San Francisco, CA. www.predictiveanalyticsworld.com/sanfrancisco/2010/agenda.php#day1–16.

**The American Public University System, Arizona State University, Iowa State University, Netherlands' Eindhoven University, Oklahoma State University, and University of Alabama:**

- Tim Daciuk, "Taking the 'Risk' out of 'At-Risk'—Identifying Students Before They Drop Out," Predictive Analytics World Washington, DC, Conference, October 20, 2010, Washington, DC. www.predictiveanalyticsworld.com/dc/2010/agenda.php#day2–7–2.
- Gerben W. Dekker, Mykola Pechenizkiy, and Jan M. Vleeshouwers, "Predicting Students Drop Out: A Case Study," Educational Data Mining 2009. www.educationaldatamining.org/EDM2009/uploads/proceedings/dekker.pdf.
- Dursun Delen, "Predicting Student Attrition with Data Mining Methods," *Journal of College Student Retention: Research, Theory and Practice* 13, no. 1 (2011–2012). http://baywood.metapress.com/app/home/contribution.asp?referrer=parent&backto=issue,2,7;journal,5,51;linkingpublicationresults,1:300319,1.
- Chong Ho Yu, Samuel DiGangi, Angel Jannasch-Pennell, and Charles Kaprolet, University of Arizona, "A Data Mining Approach for Identifying Predictors of Student Retention from Sophomore to Junior Year," *Journal of Data Science* 8 (2010): 307–325. www.jds-online.com/file_download/242/JDS-574.pdf.
- Hanover Research, "How Data Mining Helped 11 Universities Improve Student Retention Strategies," Higher Education blog, January 18, 2012. www.hanoverresearch.com/2012/01/how-11-universities-will-improve-student-retention/.

- SAS Customer Success, "Alabama Posts Gains with Recruiting, Retention," SAS Customer Story, July 27, 2007. www.sas.com/success/uofalabama.html.

**Hewlett Foundation:**
- Kaggle, The Hewlett Foundation: Automated Essay Scoring, "Develop and Automated Scoring Algorithm for Student-Written Essays," Competition, February 10, 2012. www.kaggle.com/c/asap-aes.
- Mark D. Shermis and Ben Hammer, "Contrasting State-of-the-Art Automated Scoring of Essays: Analysis," National Council on Measurement in Education (NCME), March 29, 2012. http://dl.dropbox.com/u/44416236/NCME%202012%20Paper3_29_12.pdf.
- Randal Stross, "The Algorithm Didn't Like My Essay," *New York Times*, June 9, 2012. www.nytimes.com/2012/06/10/business/essay-grading-software-as-teachers-aide-digital-domain.html.
- Kaggle, The Hewlett Foundation: Short Answer Scoring, "Develop a Scoring Algorithm for Student Responses," Competition, June 25, 2012. www.kaggle.com/c/asap-sas.

**University of Phoenix:**
- Rebecca Barber and Mike Sharkey, Apollo Group, "Course Correction: Using Analytics to Predict Course Success," *Learning Analytics and Knowledge*, May 2012, 259–262. http://dl.acm.org/citation.cfm?id=2330664&dl=ACM&coll=DL.

**Rio Salado Community College:**
- Marc Parry, "Big Data on Campus," *New York Times*, July 28, 2012. www.nytimes.com/2012/07/22/education/edlife/colleges-awakening-to-the-opportunities-of-data-mining.html.

***Jeopardy!* winner:**
- See Chapter 6 for more details.
- Roger Craig, "Data Science Meets the Quiz Show *Jeopardy!*," Predictive Analytics World Chicago Conference, June 26, 2012, Chicago, IL. www.predictiveanalyticsworld.com/chicago/2012/agenda.php#day2–11.
- NPR Staff, "How One Man Played 'Moneyball' with 'Jeopardy!,'" National Public Radio Online, November 20, 2011. www.npr.org/2011/11/20/142569472/how-one-man-played-moneyball-with-jeopardy.

**Facebook, Elsevier, IBM, Pittsburgh Science of Learning Center:**
- ACM KDD Cup 2010 Annual Data Mining "Student Performance Evaluation" Challenge. www.sigkdd.org/kddcup/index.php?section=2010&method=info.

**Grockit:**
- Kaggle, "Improve the State of the Art in Student Evaluation by Predicting Whether a Student Will Answer the Next Test Question Correctly," Competition, November 18, 2011. www.kaggle.com/c/WhatDoYouKnow.

- Grockit, "Machine Learning for Student Achievement," Competition, May 9, 2012. http://grockit.com/blog/main/2012/05/09/kaggle-results/.

**For more overviews of education applications of data mining:**
- International Educational Data Mining Society. www.educationaldatamining.org/.
- Ryan S. J. D. Baker and Kalina Yacef, "The State of Educational Data Mining in 2009: A Review and Future Visions," *International Educational Data Mining Society* 1, issue 1 (October 28, 2009). www.educationaldatamining.org/JEDM/images/articles/vol1/issue1/JEDMVol1Issue1_BakerYacef.pdf.
- C. Romero and S. Ventura, "Educational Data Mining: A Review of the State of the Art," *IEEE Transactions* 40, issue 6 (November 2010). http://ieeexplore.ieee.org/xpl/login.jsp?reload=true&tp=&arnumber=5524021. For more information on the author: (www.uco.es/~in1romoc/).

# Human Language Understanding, Thought, and Psychology—Central Table 8

**IBM:**
- See Chapter 6, which focuses entirely on this story.
- "The AI Behind Watson—The Technical Article," *AI Magazine*, Fall 2010. www.aaai.org/Magazine/Watson/watson.php.

**University at Buffalo:**
- N. Bhaskaran, I. Nwogu, M. G. Frank, and V. Govindaraju, "Lie to Me: Deceit Detection via Online Behavioral Learning," Automatic Face & Gesture Recognition and Workshops, 2011 IEEE International Conference, March 21–25, 2011. http://ieeexplore.ieee.org/xpl/freeabs_all.jsp?reload=true&arnumber=5771407.

**Researchers (lie detection):**
- G. Miner, D. Delen, J. Elder, A. Fast, T. Hill, and B. Nisbet, *Practical Text Mining and Statistical Analysis for Non-Structured Data Text Applications* (Academic Press, 2012), Part II, Tutorial N, p. 509.
- Christie M. Fuller, David P. Biros, and Rick L. Wilson, "Decision Support for Determining Veracity via Linguistic-Based Cues," *Decision Support Systems* 46, issue 3 (February 2009), 695–703. www.sciencedirect.com/science/article/pii/S0167923608001991.

**Imperium:**
- Kaggle, "Predict Whether a Comment Posted during a Public Discussion Is Considered Insulting to One of the Participants," Competition, August 7, 2012. www.kaggle.com/c/detecting-insults-in-social-commentary.

**British Broadcasting Company:**
- Mark Tabladillo, "Data Mining for Social Moderation," Predictive Analytics World Chicago Conference, June 25, 2012, Chicago, IL. www.predictiveanalyticsworld.com/chicago/2012/agenda.php#day1–315b.

**The Hebrew University:**

- Oren Tsur, Dmitry Davidov, and Ari Rappoport, "ICWSM—A Great Catchy Name: Semi-Supervised Recognition of Sarcastic Sentences in Online Product Reviews," Association for the Advancement of Artificial Intelligence (www.aaai.org), 2010. http://staff.science.uva.nl/~otsur/papers/sarcasmAmazonICWSM10.pdf.

**PayPal:**

- Han Sheong Lai, PayPal, "Identifying Customers Who Expressed Intend-to-Churn or Defect from Large Number of Surveyed Verbatim," Text Analytics World New York Conference, October 18, 2011, New York, NY. www.textanalyticsworld.com/newyork/2011/agenda/full-agenda#day1-gold.

**Citibank:**

- Ramendra Sahoo, Citibank, and Hui Xiong, "Analyzing and Scoring Customer Problem Descriptions through Multi-Focal Learning," Text Analytics World New York Conference, October 20, 2011, New York, NY. www.textanalyticsworld.com/newyork/2011/agenda/full-agenda#track1-tba4.

**Ford Motor Company:**

- Kaggle, "Stay Alert! The Ford Challenge," Competition, January 29, 2011. www.kaggle.com/c/stayalert.

**Averitt:**

- Qualcomm.com, "C.R. England and Averitt Express Expand Adoption of FleetRisk Advisors' Predictive Analytics and Remediation Services," press release, April 11, 2012. www.qualcomm.com/media/releases/2012/04/11/c-r-england-and-averitt-express-expand-adoption-fleetrisk-advisors-predict.

**Air Force:**

- Qiang Ji, Zhiwei Zhu, and Peilin Lan, "Real-Time Nonintrusive Monitoring and Prediction of Driver Fatigue," *IEEE Transactions on Vehicular Technology* 53, no. 4 (July 2004). www.ecse.rpiscrews.us/homepages/qji/Papers/IEEE_vt.pdf.

**Online Privacy Foundation:**

- Kaggle, "Identify People Who Have a High Degree of Psychopathy Based on Twitter Usage," Competition, May 14, 2012. www.kaggle.com/c/twitter-psychopathy-prediction.
- Kashmir Hill, "Using Twitter to Identify Psychopaths," *Forbes Magazine Online*, July 20, 2012. www.forbes.com/sites/kashmirhill/2012/07/20/using-twitter-to-help-expose-psychopaths/.
- Lauren Dugan, "Psychopaths Might Give Themselves Away in Their Tweets," *Media-Bistro Online*, October 13, 2011. www.mediabistro.com/alltwitter/psychopaths-might-give-themselves-away-in-their-tweets_b14805.

**Analytics leaders and a psychiatry professor:**

- G. Miner, D. Delen, J. Elder, A. Fast, T. Hill, and B. Nisbet, *Practical Text Mining and Statistical Analysis for Non-Structured Data Text Applications* (Academic Press, 2012), Part II, Tutorial I, p. 395.

**University of California, Berkeley:**

- These researchers write, "This [research] is a critical step toward the creation of brain reading devices that can reconstruct dynamic perceptual experiences." The researchers speculate on applying this technology to reveal what you see in dreams. Practical applications include assisting those unable to communicate verbally (e.g., stroke victims and coma patients). Watch this YouTube clip: www.youtube.com/watch?v=6FsH7RK1S2E.
- Shinji Nishimoto, An T. Vu, Thomas Naselaris, Yuval Benjamini, Bin Yu, and Jack L. Gallant, "Reconstructing Visual Experiences from Brain Activity Evoked by Natural Movies," *Current Biology*, 2011, doi:10.1016/j.cub.2011.08.031. www.sciencedirect .com/science/article/pii/S0960982211009377.
- Laura Shin, "Video: Mind-Reading Tech Reconstructs Moving Images Others See," *SmartPlanet Online*, September 22, 2011. www.smartplanet.com/blog/science-scope/ video-mind-reading-tech-reconstructs-moving-images-others-see/10507.
- Yasmin Anwar, "Scientists Use Brain Imaging to Reveal the Movies in Our Mind," *UCBerkeley News Center*, September 22, 2011. http://newscenter.berkeley.edu/2011/09/ 22/brain-movies/.

**Researchers (thought detection):**

- Francisco Pereira, Greg Detre, and Matthew Botvinick, "Generating Text from Functional Brain Images," *Frontiers Journals Online*, August 23, 2011. www.frontiersin.org/ human_neuroscience/10.3389/fnhum.2011.00072/abstract.
- In 2011, IBM predicted that mind-reading technology would be mainstream within five years. Steve Harrim, "The IBM 5 in 5: Our Forecast of Five Innovations That Will Alter the Tech Landscape within Five Years," December 19, 2011. http://asmarterplanet .com/blog/2011/12/the-next-5-in-5-our-forecast-of-five-innovations-that-will-alter- the-landscape-within-five-years.html.

**Radical games:**

- Classic 20Q games. http://20Q.net.
- Karen Schrock, "Twenty Questions, Ten Million Synapses," Scienceline, July 28, 2006. http://scienceline.org/2006/07/tech-schrock-20q/.

# Staff and Employees—Human Resources—Central Table 9

**Hewlett-Packard:**

- See Chapter 2 for this case study.
- Anindya Dey, Hewlett-Packard, and Gitali Halder, Hewlett-Packard, "Attrition Driver Analysis," Predictive Analytics World London Conference, November 30, 2011, London, UK. www.predictiveanalyticsworld.com/london/2011/agenda.php#day1–5a.

- Jyotirmay Nag, Hewlett-Packard, "An Innovative Approach to Analyze Employee Satisfaction Response in Light of Customer Satisfaction Response," Predictive Analytics World Chicago Conference, June 26, 2012, Chicago, IL. www.predictiveanalyticsworld .com/chicago/2012/agenda.php#day2–235a.

**Wikipedia:**
- Kaggle, "This Competition challenges data-mining experts to build a predictive model that predicts the number of edits that an editor will make five months from the end date of the training dataset," Competition, June 28, 2011. www.kaggle.com/c/wikichallenge.
- Karthik Sethuraman, "Crowdsourcing Predictive Analytics: Why 25,000 Heads Are Better Than One," Predictive Analytics World Chicago Conference, June 25, 2012, Chicago, IL. www.predictiveanalyticsworld.com/chicago/2012/agenda.php#day1–250a.
- Wendy Zukerman, "Kaggle Contest Aims to Boost Wikipedia Editors," *New Scientist Online*, July 4, 2011. www.newscientist.com/blogs/onepercent/2011/07/kaggle-competition-aims-to-giv.html.
- Dell Zhang, "Wikipedia Edit Number Prediction Based on Temporal Dynamics Only," Cornell University Library, arXiv:1110.5051v1[cs.LG], October 23, 2011. http://arxiv .org/abs/1110.5051v1.

**University researchers:**
- Donald H. Kluemper, Peter A. Rosen, and Kevin W. Mossholder, "Social Networking Websites, Personality Ratings, and the Organizational Context: More Than Meets the Eye?" *Journal of Applied Social Psychology* 42, issue 5 (May 2012): 1143–1172. Wiley Online Library, 2012. http://onlinelibrary.wiley.com/doi/10.1111/j.1559–1816.2011.00881.x/full.
- Todd Wasserman, "Facebook Profiles Accurately Predict Job Performance [Study]," Mashable Business Online, February 21, 2012. http://mashable.com/2012/02/21/facebook-profiles-job-performance/.

**U.S. Special Forces:**
- Dean Abbott, "Hiring and Selecting Key Personnel Using Predictive Analytics," Predictive Analytics World San Francisco Conference, March 4, 2012, San Francisco, CA. www.predictiveanalyticsworld.com/sanfrancisco/2012/agenda.php#day1–1040a.

**LinkedIn:**
- Manu Sharma, LinkedIn, "Data Science at LinkedIn: Iterative, Big Data Analytics and You," Predictive Analytics World New York Conference, October 19, 2011, New York, NY. www.predictiveanalyticsworld.com/newyork/2011/agenda.php#track1-lnk.
- Scott Nicholson, LinkedIn, "Beyond Big Data: Better Living through Data Science," Predictive Analytics World Boston Conference, October 1, 2012, Boston, MA. www .predictiveanalyticsworld.com/boston/2012/agenda.php#keynote-900.
- Scott Nicholson, LinkedIn, "Econometric Applications & Extracting Economic Insights from the LinkedIn Dataset," Predictive Analytics World San Francisco Conference, March 5, 2012, San Francisco, CA. www.predictiveanalyticsworld.com/sanfrancisco/ 2012/agenda.php#day1–20a.

**Careerbuilder:**

- Kaggle, "Predict Which Jobs Users Will Apply To," Competition, August 3, 2012. www.kaggle.com/c/job-recommendation.
- Careerbuilder.com, "Make Your Job Search Easier: Get Job Recommendations from Careerbuilder." www.careerbuilder.com/JobSeeker/Resumes/JobRecommendations NoDID.aspx.

**For more on HR analytics, as applied internally by IBM:**

- Stephen Baker with Bremen Leak, "Math Will Rock Your World," *Bloomberg BusinessWeek Magazine Online*, January 22, 2006. www.businessweek.com/stories/2006–01–22/math-will-rock-your-world.

# Acknowledgments

I could not have written this book without the love, guidance, and encouragement of my family: Lisa Schamberg (mother), Andrew Siegel (father), Maria de Fatima Callou (wife), Rachel Siegel (sister), Ene Piirak (stepmother), Patrick Robins (stepfather), and Anita King (grandmother).

A few cherished advisers provided extensive guidance and feedback on my writing. More than a mother to me—if such a thing is possible—Lisa Schamberg is also a natural scholar and brilliant former English teacher who took the time to provide insightful input for every single page. John Elder, a top industry leader (and the subject of Chapter 1), has patiently enhanced my knowledge and writing in astounding ways, and placed his company's resources at my disposal to support the development of this book. Jim Sterne's patience and dedication assisting with my writing is matched only by his profound talent; he is also the godfather of Predictive Analytics World, which would not exist without him.

Shannon Vargo, my editor at John Wiley & Sons, Inc., provided for me resources, flexibility, and encouragement to nurture this project to life. The dynamic publishing duo Lee Thompson (throughout) and Myles Thompson (early in the process) gave me the extensive feedback and worldly context needed to bring this topic into the realm of the relevant.

Several people went above and beyond with extensive feedback and guidance: my father Andrew Siegel, David Waltzer, Adam Cohen, Gary Miner, Dean Abbott, Paul Hofmann, and David Dimas.

I would like to thank the subjects of my writing—all pioneers of prediction—most of whom endured extensive interviews filled with many probing questions: John Elder, Rayid Ghani, Gitali Halder, Anindya Dey, Andrew Pole, Eric Gilbert, Karrie Karahalios, Dan Steinberg, Martin Chabbert, Martin Piotte, David Gondek, and Eva Helle. See this book's Cast of "Characters" on the previous pages for more information about these practitioners and where they fit into the book.

Thanks to Eleazar Eskin and Ben Bullard for generous technical guidance on some hairy topics.

These proficient reviewers provided critical feedback on my writing, keeping it up to snuff: Laura Bahr, Femi Banjo, Carsten Boers, Richard Boire, Alexander Chaffee, Erin Cowan, Roger Craig, Kenny Darrell, Udi Dotan, Anthony Goldbloom, Mikhail Golovnya, Michael Grundhoefer, Paul Hofmann, Jason Howard, Tracy Jiang, Elise Johnson, Kathleen Kane, Karrie Karahalios, Joseph Kaszynski, Max Kuhn, Kim Larsen, Victor Lo, Anne Milley, Jesse Parelius, James Plotkin, Nicholas Radcliffe, Karl Rexer, Jacques Robin, Anne Schamberg, Jay Schamberg, Neil Skilling, Daniel Sokolov, Patrick Surry, Astro Teller, Dana vanderHeyden, Marc vanderHeyden, Geert Verstraeten, Matthew Wagner, Phil Wagner, Maria Wang, Ezra Werb, and Margit Zwemer.

I gained access to this book's extensive case study examples primarily through the productive and vibrant industry community that is Predictive Analytics World. I'd like to thank all the speakers and attendees of this conference, as well as my primary business partner in its production, Matthew Finlay of Rising Media, who knows how to make events excite and unite. This conference has helped catalyze and solidify the field, following predictive analytics from a nascent industry to a commercial movement.

Thanks to my assistant, Barbara Cook, for her endless efforts setting up this book's extensive Notes, and to the supremely gifted designer Matt Kornhaas for the figures throughout these chapters.

Here's a shout-out to the extra-special educators, of whom I had more than my fair share: Thomas McKean (kindergarten), Chip Porter (grades 4–6), Margaret O'Brien (Burlington High School, Vermont), Harry Mairson (Brandeis University), Richard Alterman (Brandeis University), James Pustejovsky (Brandeis University), and Kathleen McKeown (Columbia University).

The aforementioned have molded me and bolstered this book. Nevertheless, I alone take responsibility for errors or failings of any kind in its contents.

# About the Author

Eric Siegel, PhD, founder of Predictive Analytics World and Text Analytics World, and Executive Editor of the *Predictive Analytics Times*, makes the how and why of predictive analytics understandable and captivating. Eric is a former Columbia University professor—who used to sing educational songs to his students—and a renowned speaker, educator, and leader in the field.

*Eric Siegel is available for select lectures. To inquire, see* www.ThePredictionBook.com.

*Interested in employing predictive analytics at your organization? Get started with the Predictive Analytics Guide:* www.pawcon.com/guide.

# Index

**Notes:**
- *PA* stands for *predictive analytics*.
- Page numbers in *italics* followed by "i" refer to pages within the Central Tables insert.
- The "n" after a page number refers to an entry that appears in a footnote on that page.